The Motley Fool's

INVESTMENT TAX GUIDE 2000

Smart Tax Strategies for Investors

Selena Maranjian and Roy A. Lewis, E.A.

Published by The Motley Fool, Inc., 123 North Pitt Street, Alexandria, Virginia, 22314, USA

First Printing, November 1999

10 9 8 7 6 5 4 3 2 1

ISBN 1-892547-05-8

Printed in the United States of America

Set in GillSans and Plantin

Distributed by Publishers Group West

Cover design by Johnson Design

Design and layout by Sharp & Company

Printed by United Book Press, Inc.

Roy A. Lewis, E.A., has his tax practice in Tempe, Arizona, serving clients throughout the United States. He received his undergraduate degree in 1974 from California State University-Fullerton and did his graduate work at CSU-Long Beach. Roy has been in public practice since 1978 and has been associated with The Motley Fool since 1995.

Selena Maranjian is a senior writer at The Motley Fool. She lives in New Hampshire with her two dogs. (Whoops! Scratch that—that's every other writer.) Armed with a Wharton MBA and a Masters in Teaching from Brown University, one of Selena's missions in life is to render the incomprehensible comprehensible.

ACKNOWLEDGMENTS

It's time for a confession. We didn't create this book by ourselves. There are many unsung heroes who contributed to this project and we'd like to tip our belled caps to them right now.

For starters, there's our business development team of Alissa Territo and Craig Fowler. They attended to little details, like making sure that the book had a cover. Heading up editing was Robyn Gearey, who read every page several times (yikes!). Generously contributing some content to our retirement and dividend reinvestment plan sections were, respectively, Dave Braze and Jeff Fischer. Contributing some laughs were Fool wits Keith Pelczarski and David Wolpe. Bolstering our efforts with some vital research was Mona Sharma. And finally, reviewing the book for accuracy were Kaye Thomas and Eugene D. Helbig, Jr., CPA, CFP. Thanks a lot, folks!

CONTENTS

INTRODUCTION

I have something my tax doctor calls "narcotaxis." Within 20 seconds of hearing someone launch into an explanation of tax laws, my eyes become glassy, my body loses all feeling, and I go into a shallow coma.
—Russell Baker

You're holding in your hands the second edition of The Motley Fool's tax guide for investors. We decided to come out with a second edition primarily because the first edition was such a smash hit. We were hounded by Hollywood types eager to snap up movie rights. There was talk of Tom Hanks playing EveryFool and James Woods or Christopher Walken playing the friendly neighborhood IRS agent. One high-profile talk-show hostess was so moved by how the book helped so many with its money-saving tax tips that she entered the movie-rights bidding war interested in playing EveryFool herself. (We remain confounded, though, as to why this modest little book was never selected for her book club.)

Okay, perhaps we exaggerate a little. There was no talk of movie rights. No chorus of "For Roy and Selena are jolly good fellows" sung in Congress. No Nobel Prize for Tax Demystification. But our little book *was* well received. People appreciated that it focused on tax issues relevant to investors. It didn't come with pages and pages on obscure topics irrelevant to most people, such as the Carpetweaver Tax Credit or the Deduction for Show Turtles. Instead, it explained how to account for shares of stock that you buy and sell throughout the year, how to decide whether to open a Roth IRA, what to do with worthless stock, how to avoid and deal with audits, and so on.

In this edition, we've stuck with the same premise—how to help investors understand tax rules and minimize their tax burden—and we've expanded on it. We've broadened the topics covered to include more topics relevant to the *life* of a Fool. The topics now addressed include:

• Your investments
• Your home
• Your spouse and family
• Education
• Your home office
• Retirement instruments

Obviously, a book this size can't be everything to everyone. So here's a short summary of what you can expect it to do and not to do.

It *won't:*

- Cover absolutely every tax topic in existence.
- Take you line by line through every tax form.
- Tell you what to do in every tax situation.
- Give your toddler a significant boost at the dinner table.

It *will:*

- Demystify just about every major tax topic of interest to investors.
- Explain what you need to know about each topic in order to make smart decisions.
- Suggest many money-saving strategies that you might consider, depending on your personal situation.
- Give you many examples to help you understand concepts that aren't always easy to grasp.
- Keep you from getting bored by interjecting a little humor here and there. (We tested many of the jokes on animals and they were rolling on the floor laughing. No animals were hurt in the writing process. Well, one rabbit sprained an ear, but that's it.)

People often think that taxes are simply a chore, something to attend to once a year. Anyone with that attitude is likely leaving money on the table, though. This is particularly true for investors, because investing is much more than just deciding which stocks to buy or sell.

There are many tax-related matters that investors should learn about and consider in order to strategize effectively. How long you hold a stock or security makes a difference. Your cost basis for various securities may have to be adjusted on various occasions. If you're giving a gift to a child or a charitable donation to a cause, you should consider giving stock instead, as you could come out ahead. If you're generating sizable capital gains this year, you might be expected by the IRS to file estimated taxes each quarter. If you use your computer for investment purposes, you might have some deductions available to you. If you sell a stock for a loss, you should think twice before repurchasing it within 30 days. Got employee stock options? You can minimize your taxes by exercising and holding them for certain time periods. Heck—even your home is an investment, and a big one at that. Learn about the massive tax benefits available to you if you plan your home sale properly.

You'll see a lot of references to (free) IRS publications in this book. That's because even when we restrict our discussion to investor-related tax issues, there remains an enormous amount of information to cover. We explain the basics and then some for most topics, including some strategies that you might employ. When appropriate, we include a pointer to where you can get more details and the final word on your particular situation. We also point out topics that we discuss in more detail online at the Fool. If you haven't done so already, you should see what we have to offer online. If you don't have your own computer, you can probably use one at your local public library. Or visit a "wired" friend and let him or her show you around cyberspace a little. It can be an amazing resource for you.

We expect that when you turn the last page, you'll be brimming with confidence and raring to make decisions that will minimize your tax liability. Come February, March, or April, whether you decide to prepare your own tax return or to pass the work on to a professional, you'll be doing so as a much more informed Fool.

By now you're probably trembling with excitement at the prospect of learning about taxes. (Well, perhaps dreading it a little less?) We won't tarry much longer. We close with a little verse from one of our favorite doggerel mongers, Ogden Nash:

Indoors or out, no one relaxes
In March, that month of wind and taxes,
The wind will presently disappear,
The taxes last us all the year.

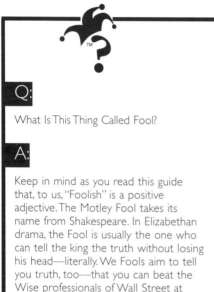

Q:

What Is This Thing Called Fool?

A:

Keep in mind as you read this guide that, to us, "Foolish" is a positive adjective. The Motley Fool takes its name from Shakespeare. In Elizabethan drama, the Fool is usually the one who can tell the king the truth without losing his head—literally. We Fools aim to tell you truth, too—that you can beat the Wise professionals of Wall Street at their own game. To learn more about The Motley Fool, drop by our website at http://www.fool.com or visit us on America Online at keyword: Fool.

Nash meant these words as a frivolous joke, but they're really quite true. If you take a Foolish approach to taxes, you'll tend to them all year long, a little at a time. Wherever you are, at any hour of the day or night, you can visit The Motley Fool online for the latest in tax advice. There you can post questions and receive answers on our message boards. You can build on what you learned in this modest tome, and come tax season you won't be left to deal with the aftermath of regrettable decisions you made during the year. More power to you, Fool!

FIRST THINGS FIRST

*It's income tax time again, Americans:
time to gather up those receipts, get out
those tax forms, sharpen up that pencil,
and stab yourself in the aorta.*

—Dave Barry

What you'll find in this chapter:
- Your Tax Return
- What's My Rate?
- How Deductions Work
- How Credits Work
- 1040 Good Buddy: A Cacophony of Forms
- Filling Out Your Return
- Records to Keep
- Putting Your Computer to Work

YOUR TAX RETURN

We'll be delving into tax issues in some detail soon, but before we do, it's useful to review exactly what's involved in preparing a tax return. This is obviously important for those new to proper tax return preparation (that means you, Leona Helmsley). It's also good for those who are experienced in filling out the forms but don't have a good handle on the general concepts involved. This section will give you a framework on which to hang all the information contained in the following chapters. In other words, we'll introduce you to the forest here before we examine the trees.

So perhaps you've never prepared your own tax return before. You look over the handy instruction book that accompanies Form 1040. Goodness—it's about 40 pages long! Alarmed, you rush back to your local public library and grab a copy of the 1040EZ form. Jeepers—its instructions are nearly 30 pages long! What's an intimidated Fool to do? Well, first, relax. Despite the fact that many tax guides on sale at your friendly bookstore look like phone books for Manhattan, the concepts behind preparing a tax return are really not that complicated.

"Above/Below the Line"

Have you ever heard anybody talk about "above-the-line" or "below-the-line" deductions? They're common phrases in tax speak. It doesn't mean the line that you can't cross before you get an IRS audit. Instead, simply think of "the line" as nothing more than your adjusted gross income, or AGI.

Above-the-line deductions are deductions and expenses that allow you to arrive at AGI. They include Schedule C or F business deductions, rental deductions, or even adjustments to your AGI such as moving expenses and student loan interest paid. Below-the-line deductions are deductions that you take *from* AGI— deductions that you claim *after* you arrive at your AGI. They typically include itemized deductions such as medical, tax, interest, charity, casualty, and miscellaneous expenses.

Above-the-line deductions are generally more beneficial than below-the-line deductions because they not only reduce your taxable income, but also reduce your AGI, which may favorably affect many of your subsequent computations. Below-the-line deductions simply reduce your taxable income. So keep this in mind. And when dealing with tax issues, make sure to walk the line.

The Tax Return Process, in a Theoretical Nutshell

It all begins with income. This part of the equation is fairly straightforward because for most of us, it's automatically reported to the IRS. Our employers report what was paid to us as salary. Our banks report interest we earned. Our brokerages report dividends paid to us and stocks that we sold (for which we'll need to calculate our gains or losses). There's little decision-making or finagling to be done here. Sometimes there are additional income sources that you need to remember to include, though, such as tips, gambling winnings, business income, rental income, alimony income, or the 7.6 million Swedish kroner you received when you were awarded that Nobel Peace Prize (whoops— that's tax-free—congrats!).

Total all your income for the year and you'll be looking at what's called your "gross income." To this, you'll now make "adjustments." You'll subtract whatever amount you contributed to qualifying IRAs or other retirement accounts. You'll subtract any alimony payments you made and any moving expenses that qualify. If you're self-employed, you'll subtract half of the self-employment tax. You'll also subtract any qualified student loan interest paid, and any medical savings account deduction. Once you've made all your adjustments, you'll be left with a very important sum: your "adjusted gross income," or "AGI."

The AGI is used throughout your tax return—expect it to pop up all over the place like the little critter in carnival "Whack-a-Mole" games. It's used when determining limitations on a number of tax issues, including exemptions, IRA contributions, and itemized deductions.

From your AGI, you now claim your exemptions and make your deductions. (Deduction: voted one of the top-10 nicest-sounding words or phrases in the English language, after "refund" and "free parking.") You can take either an itemized deduction or the standard deduction—whichever is greater. The standard deduction ranges from about $3,500 to $7,000, depending on your filing status.

You're entitled to one exemption for yourself plus one each for your spouse and/or dependents, if you have them. The exemption is a set amount that you're permitted to deduct from your income, reducing the sum on which you're taxed. Exemption levels are tied to inflation and change from year to year, usually increasing. Once you've taken your exemptions and deductions, you're left with your "taxable income." It's this number that determines your tax. (You just flip to tax charts, which tell you, for example, that if your taxable income is at least $35,300 but less than $35,350 and you're single, your tax is $6,596.)

Sound simple enough? It is. Except that we're not done yet. Although you may think this is the total amount of tax that Uncle Sam would like you to cough up, there are still a few steps left.

You now take the tax due on your taxable income and subtract any credits. Then you add any other taxes. Credits are usually for children, the elderly, the disabled, adoptions, or foreign taxes paid. Other taxes include self-employment taxes and taxes on qualified retirement plans. The end result is your total tax. This is the sum that you must fork over to the government.

You're not going to sit down and write a check for this amount, though, because there's one step left. Remember all that money withheld from your paycheck every payday? Or the estimated tax payments you've already made? Items like these are subtracted from your total tax, leaving you with either a positive or negative number. If the number is positive, it's what you have to make a check out for. If it's negative, you can expect a tax refund in that amount.

You know what? You're done. That's it. Finito. It does take a while to do (it's estimated that upwards of 30 hours are required to complete Form 1040 and Schedules A, B, C, and D), but it isn't brain surgery. You can do it. (Well, you can *probably* do it. If your situation is reasonably straightforward, you may find that the preparation of your taxes is not that much of a problem. But if your situation is more complex, it might be necessary or advantageous to use the services of a qualified tax professional.)

Let's review the preceding section quickly:

    Gross Income
    - Adjustments
    = Adjusted Gross Income (AGI)

    Adjusted Gross Income (AGI)
    - Exemptions
    - Deductions
    = Taxable Income

Taxable Income: With this number, look up your "tax on taxable income" using the chart at the end of the IRS's tax preparation booklet.

    Tax on taxable income
    - Credits
    + Other taxes
    = Total Tax

    Total tax
    - Withheld taxes
    - Estimated tax payments
    = Refund or Payment Due

The general strategy when planning and preparing your tax return is to minimize your taxable income and maximize your deductions—thereby minimizing your tax. This doesn't mean, of course, that you should be hiding income under shrubs and bushes in your backyard or manufacturing specious deductions. Not at all. There are perfectly legal things you can do. For example, in a year when you have significant capital gains, you might sell some stocks that have done poorly and offset the gains with the losses. Alternatively, you can read up on deductions and discover that there are some that you qualify for. We'll offer a lot of tax planning advice in the pages ahead.

WHAT'S MY RATE?

Throughout this book, we'll make reference to your individual tax rate. Certain tax strategies and issues will have a direct impact on your tax rate, so it's something that you should know how to compute.

When people speak about their tax rate, they're generally referring to their "marginal" tax rate. It's the rate of tax that you pay on your last dollar of taxable income. You may commonly hear a friend say that she is in the 28% bracket, which means that she paid 28% federal tax on her last dollar of income. But all her income wasn't taxed at 28%. Tax rates are "graduated," which means that the lower your taxable income, the lower your marginal tax bracket. Conversely, the higher your taxable income, the higher your marginal bracket.

It may be easier if you look at the actual tax schedules, so we include them below. But note: If your taxable income is below $100,000, then you shouldn't use these schedules when you prepare your return. Instead, refer to the tax tables in the instructions that accompany the 1040 form. The tax tables show you at a glance what your tax is (for incomes up to $100,000), but they don't offer any clue as to how that amount of tax was determined. That's why the schedules are valuable. They can help you understand how our tax system is set up and works—for all sorts of income levels.

So in summary, if your taxable income tops $100,000, you'll need to use these schedules to calculate your tax. If your income is below $100,000, then just look them over and learn from them. A clear understanding of how brackets work and where you are in relation to them can be important to your future tax planning and strategizing.

Tax Rate Schedules for 1999 Income

For single filers:

If your taxable income (line 38 on Form 1040) is over	But not over	Then your tax is	Plus	Of the amount over
$0	$25,750	—	15%	$0
25,750	62,450	$3,862.50	28%	25,750
62,450	130,250	14,138.50	31%	62,450
130,250	283,150	35,156.50	36%	130,250
283,150		90,200.50	39.6%	283,150

For those who are married and filing jointly, or qualifying widow(er)s:

If your taxable income (line 38 on Form 1040) is over	But not over	Then your tax is	Plus	Of the amount over
$0	$43,050	—	15%	$0
43,050	104,050	$6,457.50	28%	43,050
104,050	158,550	23,537.50	31%	104,050
158,550	283,150	40,432.50	36%	158,550
283,150		85,288.50	39.6%	283,150

For those who are married and filing separately:

If your taxable income (line 38 on Form 1040) is over	But not over	Then your tax is	Plus	Of the amount over
$0	$21,525	—	15%	$0
21,525	52,025	$3,228.75	28%	21,525
52,025	79,275	11,768.75	31%	52,025
79,275	141,575	20,126.25	36%	79,275
141,575		42,644.25	39.6%	141,575

For Heads of Households:

If your taxable income (line 38 on Form 1040) is over	But not over	Then your tax is	Plus	Of the amount over
$0	$34,550	—	15%	$0
34,550	89,150	$5,182.50	28%	34,550
89.150	144,400	20,470.50	31%	89,150
144,400	283,150	37,598.00	36%	144,400
283,150		87,548.00	39.6%	283,150

Let's look at an example. Clothing inspector #13, Susan Phillips, is a single person. If she has taxable income of $25,750 or less, her marginal tax rate is 15%. But when her taxable income climbs to between $25,751 and $62,450, her marginal tax rate is 28%. So if Susan has taxable income of $26,400, the first $25,750 of her taxable income would be taxed at 15% (that's $3,863), and the remaining $650 would be taxed at 28% (yielding an additional $182). Add those sums together and you get Susan's total tax liability, $4,045.

Why do you care about your marginal tax rate? Because this is the rate of tax on your *next* dollar of taxable income. It's very important for future tax planning. You've probably heard people say, "That income will throw me into the next tax bracket." These are exactly the brackets that they talk about. (Note that sometimes these folks are operating under the misconception that as soon as they enter a higher bracket, *all* their income will be taxed at the new rate. Not true at all. Just the amount by which they've crossed the higher bracket's threshold is what gets taxed at that rate.)

But if you're only a little bit into the next tax bracket, should you really consider that bracket as your very own? Sure... when looking forward. But when looking at your current big picture you should compute your "effective" tax rate. This is simply your total tax liability divided by your taxable income. In the example above, while Susan's marginal tax bracket is 28%, her effective tax bracket is only 15.32%. ($4,045 divided by $26,400 equals 0.1532.) The effective bracket tells Susan that most of her income is being taxed at the lower 15% bracket, and only a small portion is being taxed at the next (28%) bracket.

In summary:

Susan's marginal tax rate: 28%
Susan's effective tax rate: 15.32%
Most of her dollars were taxed at 15%
Her next dollars will be taxed at 28%

TAX TIP

Marginal vs. Effective Tax Rates

Your marginal tax rate is the rate at which your last and your next dollar of taxable income are taxed. It's not the rate at which all your dollars are taxed. It's the maximum rate you're paying on any of your dollars of taxable income. If you're single, for example, your marginal tax rate will be 15%, 28%, 31%, 36%, or 39.6%.

But remember that your marginal tax rate only deals with the specific tax on your income. As you know, there are other taxes that you may have to pay—such as self-employment taxes, Alternative Minimum Tax, and even penalty taxes on retirement plan distributions. There are also credits that you may benefit from, such as the child tax credit, the dependent care credit, or the education credits. So after the jumble of other taxes and credits, your marginal tax rate may lose a bit of its importance. Which is why you'll want to take a peek at your effective tax rate.

To find out the average rate of taxation for all your dollars, you need to compute your effective tax rate. This is simply your total tax obligation (including your income tax and any other additional taxes and/or credits) divided by your total taxable income.

After all is said and done, it is very possible that your effective tax rate could be much higher than your marginal rate. Why? Because you may be self-employed and get hit with the SE tax as an addition to your normal income tax.

For many people who have a number of credits (such as the child tax credit) and additional taxes (such as the self-employment tax), the effective rate can be a very meaningful number.

HOW DEDUCTIONS WORK

When you hear the word "deduction," you probably think of an "itemized" deduction. But deductions come in many shapes and sizes. For now, let's focus on the itemized type of deduction, though.

As noted earlier, after you determine your AGI, you calculate your "taxable income" by subtracting from AGI: (1) your personal exemption(s) and (2) either the "standard deduction" or an "itemized deduction." The amount of tax owed the federal government is then calculated based on what's left—your "taxable income."

If you don't elect to itemize, you're allowed the standard deduction. The standard deduction is a simplification device that lets you avoid having to account for modest amounts of itemized deductions.

As an alternative to the standard deduction, taxpayers may elect to itemize their deductions. Some examples of itemized deductions include: unreimbursed employee business expenses, expenses in connection with investment activities, charitable contributions, medical expenses, state and local taxes, real estate taxes, home mortgage interest, and casualty losses.

Many of the deduction rules are complex and require informed judgment before entering into a transaction. For example, medical expenses and "miscellaneous itemized deductions" such as education expenses and unreimbursed employment-related expenses must exceed a certain percentage of AGI before they can be deducted. We'll talk about those percentages later on.

TAX TIP

Prove It!

As a fundamental rule, taxpayers are entitled to take deductions only where specifically authorized by the Internal Revenue Code. Since deductions are a matter of "legislative grace," when disputes arise, courts closely scrutinize taxpayer claims and reject those that do not clearly satisfy the letter of the law. Each taxpayer bears the burden of proving his or her entitlement to a deduction, and ambiguities are often resolved in favor of the government. An expense is not deductible until proven deductible. Sorry.

The most important thing to understand about itemized deductions is that you do not receive "dollar-for-dollar" tax relief for a deduction dollar spent. This is a common misconception and one we'd like to put to rest right here and now. As you've seen, your tax rate is a percentage of your taxable income. So for any part of your income in the 28% bracket, $100 of taxable income would be subject to $28 in tax. Likewise, a $100 itemized deduction would only relieve you of $28 in taxes. A $100 itemized deduction will never offer tax relief of $100. At least not until our tax rates hit 100%, and we don't expect that any time in the near future.

HOW CREDITS WORK

Credits, unlike deductions, do reduce your tax liability on a dollar-for-dollar basis. They directly offset your actual income tax liability.

So are credits more valuable than deductions? They sure are. If you have the chance to make a financial transaction that gives you a $100 deduction *or* a $100 credit,

always take the credit. If you're in the 28% tax bracket, a $100 deduction will save you $28 in taxes. But a $100 credit will knock $100 directly off of your income tax liability, and will save you the whole $100. Dollar-for-dollar tax savings. This is why credits are so valuable, and why you want to make sure that you know enough to take advantage of all the ones available to you. We'll talk about a number of these credits later on, but right now we offer an overview of credits and a little peek at how they work.

Although a number of income tax credits are available, they may be broken down into five basic groups:

• Nonrefundable personal credits
• Miscellaneous nonrefundable credits
• Refundable credits
• The general business credit
• The credit for the prior year minimum tax liability

Nonrefundable personal credits include the household and dependent care credit, the credit for the elderly and disabled, the adoption expenses credit, the Hope and Lifetime Learning education credits, and the home mortgage interest credit. As their names suggest, these credits are for personal expenses and are applied to reduce your income tax—but generally not below zero. If you have more credits than tax liability, Uncle Sam isn't eager to write you a check for the excess. (That's why they're called "non-refundable"—they aren't likely to create a tax refund for you.) If there is an excess credit, only the adoption expenses credit and home mortgage interest credit may be carried forward to another tax year. The other excess credits are lost forever. (Sniff.)

Miscellaneous nonrefundable credits include the foreign tax credit, the nonconventional source fuels credit, the qualified electric vehicle credit, and the Puerto Rico economic activity credit. A silver lining is that any unused foreign tax credit may be carried back as much as two years and forward as far as five years.

Refundable credits include: the credit for taxes withheld on wages and other amounts; the earned income credit and the child tax credit, which are designed to aid low-income taxpayers; the credit for tax withheld on payments to nonresidents and foreign corporations; and the gasoline and special fuels credit. As the name implies, if your refundable credits exceed your total tax liability, Uncle Sam *will* normally write you a check for the excess credits. This is done in the form of an "income tax refund"—possibly the most beautiful words in the English language.

The general business credit encompasses a number of credits designed to encourage certain business activities. They include (take a *big,* big breath now if you're reading this aloud to your children): the investment tax credit (composed of the rehabilitation credit, the energy credit, and the reforestation credit), the work opportunity credit, the alcohol fuels credit, the research credit, the low-income housing credit, the enhanced oil recovery credit, the disabled access credit, the renewable electricity production credit, the empowerment zone employment credit, the Indian employment credit, the employer Social Security credit, the orphan drug credit, the trans-Alaska pipeline liability fund credit, the community development credit, and the welfare-to-work credit.

The prior year minimum tax credit is designed to reimburse taxpayers for Alternative Minimum Tax paid in earlier years as a result of certain "deferral" items. Deferral items are preference items such as accelerated depreciation, which do not result in a permanent reduction in regular tax liability. The credit is available to individuals, corporations, trusts, and estates. As with any AMT item, the rules for calculating and applying it are complex.

Since we're on the subject, let's take a few minutes to talk about the AMT. (We'll discuss it in more detail later on.) Many of the credits noted above will reduce your "regular" tax, but may not reduce your AMT. So when you're reviewing your credit transactions, you really need to know which are which. You may think that a certain credit will really slash your tax liability, only to find out later that the AMT reached out and grabbed you by the throat. If you aren't familiar with what kind of impact the AMT will have on each and every credit, make sure that you pick up this knowledge. AMT surprises can be very ugly. We'll be discussing many of these credits in upcoming chapters, and we'll alert you to the AMT impact of various credits. But remember that the laws change—almost on a daily basis. Make sure that you don't run into a tax credit/AMT problem.

1040, GOOD BUDDY: A CACOPHONY OF FORMS

It might be less intimidating if the IRS required you to file Forms 1, 2, and 3 (and perhaps Forms 4 and 5, if your situation were complicated). But life is rarely that simple, right? Here's a list of the main tax forms that you might need to be familiar with. Realize, though, that most folks will only need to use a few of these.

- **Form 1040:** This is the mother of all forms. For those who want (and qualify for) something easier, there's the 1040A. Of course, this quickly proved itself not that easy after all, and so the 1040EZ was born. For a complete overview of Form 1040 and all of the other forms noted here, check out IRS Publication 17. (Yes, the IRS seems to have as many publications as forms.) Note that any investors with capital gains or losses to report on Schedule D can't use Form 1040A or 1040EZ and will have to fill out Form 1040.

- **Schedule A:** This is for all of your itemized deductions, including medical, taxes, interest, charity, and miscellaneous. Publication 17 provides an overview of Schedule A and its related components.

- **Schedule B:** Report your interest and dividend income here. Publications 17 and 550 deal with this schedule.

- **Schedule C:** This is for reporting your business income and expenses. If you have a business profit, you'll also need to become acquainted with Schedule C's first cousin, Schedule SE. You'll use Schedule SE to report and pay your Self-Employment Tax (otherwise known as FICA and Medicare). IRS Publication 334 deals with Schedule C. Schedule SE is discussed in IRS Publication 533.

- **Schedule D:** This is a biggie for investors. It's where you'll report the sale of capital assets, including stocks, bonds, mutual funds, and the sale

TAX TIP

Your Friend the W-4

You've most likely been handed a Form W-4 to fill out at least several times in your life. The W-4 is the form that employers use to determine how much in taxes should be withheld from your paychecks. You usually get it when you start a new job. Between trying to figure out the W-4, looking for the required items from column A or B on the I-9 form, and determining whom to list as your next of kin on your new employer's emergency contact form, you're bound to be a little frazzled. Well, we can't help you figure out who should be contacted in an emergency, but here are a few things to keep in mind regarding W-4 forms:

- Strive to be accurate. You may face a $500 penalty if you end up (for no good reason) having too little tax withheld.

- On the form, you claim exemptions for yourself, your spouse, and any dependents. (The more you claim, the less is withheld.) You can also claim allowances for certain deductions or credits, such as earned income credit, IRA contribution deductions, alimony deductions, the dependent care credit, and the credit for the elderly or totally disabled. If you don't file this form with your employer, the employer will have to withhold taxes at the highest rate.

- You should fill out a new W-4 form whenever the number of your exemptions changes or whenever your withholding allowances increase or decrease. In other words, don't forget your W-4 at times such as the following: when your marital status changes, when you have or adopt a child, when a child spreads his or her wings and is no longer a dependent, or when your deductible expenses change (such as when you buy a house). In some cases, you need to file a new W-4 within 10 days.

- If you're getting married, pay particularly close attention to your withholding. You may be assuming that when you get married, you'll pay less in taxes. If you and your spouse both work, that's likely not the case. Read up on the marriage penalty later in this book.

- You don't have to (and might not want to) claim all the exemptions available to you. The more you claim, the less will be withheld. But depending on your situation, this might leave you at the end of the year with too little having been withheld and therefore facing a penalty of some sort. If you're a careful tax planner, you'll estimate how much you expect to owe in taxes for the year and will ensure that at least 90% of that is being withheld. As a margin of safety, you might shoot for 100%, but if you notice that 140% of your anticipated tax liability is being withheld, consider tweaking your W-4.

- You should be able to resubmit a new W-4 form to your employer at any time during the year. It's not something that can only be submitted once or only changed after a major life event.

- Use the W-4 as a tool. For example, if you expect to sell some significantly appreciated stock during the year and think your total tax due this year will be substantial, consider having more money withheld from your paychecks. This can help you avoid having to pay estimated taxes throughout the year. (Read more on this in the "Estimating Taxes" section of this book.)

For more information on the W-4 form, get a copy of it from your employer (or from the IRS) and read its instructions. Some employers will just give you the lower part of the form that has to be turned in—don't accept just that. Ask for the entire two-page form, so that you can read all about what you're doing. For more information on withholding and estimated taxes, you might want to look at IRS Publication 505.

of your personal residence. IRS Publications 544 and 550 will provide you with additional information.

- **Schedule E:** A multipurpose form on which you should report your rental income and expenses on page 1, and your income/losses from Partnerships, S-Corporations, LLCs, and Trusts on page 2. IRS Publication 17 provides an overview of Schedule E.

- **Schedule F:** If your business is a farm, then this schedule is for you. IRS Publication 225 will give you more help with farm income and expenses.

- **Schedule SE:** Did you have a profit from your Schedule C or F business? Then you might have even more taxes to pay in the form of "self employment" taxes. Bummer. Read more about SE taxes in IRS Publication 533.

- **Form 2106:** This is the form that the IRS doesn't want you to know about. Report your nonreimbursed employee business expenses here so that you can deduct them. IRS Publications 463 and 529 will provide greater insight.

- **Form 2210:** Did you have to send Uncle Sam a check for more than $1,000? Then Form 2210 may be in your future. You'll use it to compute the tax underpayment penalty that might be due. It may also give you clues regarding a loophole that you can use to avoid the underpayment penalty. IRS Publication 505 will provide the additional details.

- **Form 2441:** Here's where you compute your Dependent Care Credit. IRS Publication 503 offers instructions and examples.

- **Form 3903:** Did you have a business-related move in which you incurred expenses? Then this is the form for you. IRS Publication 521 is what you'll want to review to learn more about deducting your moving expenses.

- **Form 4562:** This is your depreciation schedule. If you have assets that were purchased for business or rental use, you'll report 'em here. IRS Publication 946 will give you additional information.

- **Form 4797:** This form is for reporting the sale of business assets, including rental property and personal property used in your trade or business. It also reports a bunch of other stuff not reported on any other form or schedule.

- **Form 4952:** Have you paid margin interest? Have you paid interest on a piece of investment property? Then Form 4952 is the form that you'll use to compute your appropriate interest deduction. IRS Publication 550 will give you the guidelines for the investment interest deduction.

- **Form 5329:** This is where you compute your "penalty" taxes on the early distribution from an IRA, SEP, or other qualified pension/profit sharing/deferred compensation plan. IRS Publication 590 will explain in detail.

- **Form 6251**: Horrors! The dreaded form for the Alternative Minimum Tax computation. We would *love* to provide you with an IRS Publication reference for the AMT and this specific form, but it seems that the IRS may not really understand it either, since they don't have a publication that addresses the AMT. Your best bet is to check the instructions for Form 6251 and Form 8801.

- **Form 8283**: Are your non-cash charitable contributions more than $500? Then this form must be completed and attached to your tax return. IRS Publication 561 will help you understand this form and how to value the property that you are contributing.

TAX TIP

Where to Get IRS Publications

You'll see that throughout this book, we point you to various IRS publications for further information. You can get these forms for free from our friends at the IRS either by calling them up (800-TAX-FORM or 800-829-3676), or by downloading them at the IRS website (www.irs.gov).

If you don't have a computer and want to receive the forms fast (albeit smudged) you can order them by fax by calling 703-368-9694. (If you select option #2, you'll go directly to the index of forms.)

- **Form 8606**: Did you make a nondeductible contribution to a traditional IRA? How about a conversion from a traditional IRA to a Roth IRA? Or perhaps even a distribution from a traditional or Roth IRA? Maybe a distribution from an Education IRA? If any of these things happened to you, then Form 8606 will be something that you'll want to get your hands on. The instructions for Form 8606 (about eight pages worth) will help you (maybe) with the completion of the form.

- **Form 8615:** Use this form to compute the tax for a child who was under age 14 and who had more than $1,400 of investment income. IRS Publication 929 will help you decide whether you want to report the child's tax on your return or file a separate return for the child.

- **Form 8812:** If you have only one or two children who qualify for the child tax credit, you can get away with a worksheet to figure your credit. But if you have three or more qualifying children, you may also benefit from an additional child tax credit. Form 8812 helps you compute the credit. There is no specific publication for this credit, but the form includes helpful instructions.

- **Form 8863:** The Hope Scholarship Credit and Lifetime Learning Credit are reported on this form. These can be a big boon to you if you're going to school and have education-related expenses. IRS Publication 970 will walk you down the right path.

- **Form 9991-6B:** This form is for left-handed wicker furniture makers to use to report their earnings. A sample wicker loveseat must be attached to the form. (Okay, okay, we're just kidding. There is no Form 9991-6B. We just wanted to make sure you were paying attention.)

All of these forms and publications and many others are available at the IRS website at http://www.irs.gov.

TAX TIP

Where's the White-Out?

Whoops! You mailed off your tax return a few weeks (or years!) ago and now you realize that you made a mistake. Is all lost? Are the authorities coming with handcuffs to cart you away? Fear not.

The tax form you prepare and mail in isn't the only one you're ever allowed to file for that year. After you've filed the regular return, if you need to, you can file an amended return, via Form 1040X. In fact, you can even amend an amended return! You're permitted to amend your return until three years after the date the original return was filed (or its due date), or until two years after the date the tax was paid—whichever is later. Also, know that if you change your federal tax return, it's likely that you will be required to amend your state return, as well. Contact your state tax department for the appropriate forms. (See the appendix for a list of state tax offices.)

FILLING OUT YOUR RETURN

You may have read everything in this book twice. You may have spent five hours having your spouse grill you with questions about taxes. You may have even trained the denizens of your ant farm to assemble into a formation that spells "Taxes!" Despite all this, if you've never prepared your own tax return, you're likely to find yourself flummoxed when you get right down to it, wondering where to start and how to proceed.

Don't assume that you'll simply fill out form 1040 first and then fill out your various required forms and schedules. Or that you'll fill out the forms and schedules first and then tackle the 1040. Unfortunately, it's not that simple.

The path of least resistance when preparing your tax return is to start with your 1040 form and begin filling it out. At a certain point, it will likely require information from line X of a particular schedule. At that moment, shift gears and switch to the schedule. Fill it out as much as you can, at least to line X. Take the required number back to the 1040 form and continue with the 1040, until you're again interrupted by a required number from another schedule or form. Keep up this pattern—slogging through (or merrily skipping through, depending on the degree of pleasure you're getting out of the process) the 1040 and pausing intermittently to fill out the required forms or schedules.

RECORDS TO KEEP

"The woods are lovely, dark and deep.
But I have records to keep,
And taxes to file before I sleep."

—Anonymous

Preparing your tax return doesn't have to be as painful as watching all 24 hours of a "Cop Rock" marathon on TV. If you've kept the appropriate records, you should have a relatively hassle-free time of it.

Here's a list of some of the investment-related records that you should put aside for tax time. (Don't forget where you put them, though!)

• Keep confirmation reports of stock purchases and sales, including the execution prices and trade dates.

• Keep all statements and reports sent to you by your brokerage, mutual fund company, or other investment services company, and from other sources. Perhaps most important are 1099 forms, which show your proceeds from sales of securities (1099-B) and other capital assets, as well as interest income (1099-INT), state tax refunds and other government payments (1099-G), dividend income (1099-DIV), Social Security earnings (1099-SSA), and distributions from IRAs, pensions, and annuities (1099-R).

- Keep records of how you acquired any securities (such as through purchase, inheritance, etc.) and your cost basis.

- If you participate in a dividend reinvestment plan (for stocks and/or mutual funds), keep track of the dividends you receive and how many shares they purchase at what price. This information is necessary to help you calculate the new cost basis for your shares. You might set up a chart for each separate plan/stock where you keep track of these details. A three-ring binder can be effective, as it will allow you to add sheets of paper wherever you need to.

- Keep records of contributions to IRAs and other retirement plans. If you make nondeductible contributions to an IRA, make sure you declare these on IRS Form 8606 so that you don't end up paying a second tax on them down the line. You should have year-end account statement as well as receipts for your contributions.

- If one of your securities becomes worthless, keep any documentation relating to that, especially something that includes the date on which it became worthless.

- Keep records relating to interest expense and how you used the loaned funds. This is an advanced topic, but it's an important one. For more information, consult IRS Publications 535 and 550.

- If you plan to deduct travel or meal expenses relating to investment-related travel, keep records of exactly what the trip involved. Know, though, that many investment-related trips are not deductible, such as travel to attend a shareholder meeting or an investment seminar. IRS Publications 463 and 550 will give you more details.

- Keep records of improvements made to your home. These can be added to your basis price, decreasing your taxable gain when you sell the home.

- Keep records of expenses related to selling your home. They can also be deducted from your capital gains.

- If you donate stock, keep records of what you donated, the day of the donation, your cost basis for the shares, and their fair market value. Keep track of cash donations, too.

- If you give stock away, also keep records of what you gave, the day of the gift, your cost basis for the shares, and their fair market value.

- Keep records of expenses for professional help, such as tax preparers and advisors, legal counsel, etc.

- Keep all locks of your hair after haircuts and all fingernail clippings. (Whoops! Scratch that. That's only for eccentric millionaires, not ordinary taxpayers.)

The list above is long, but it isn't comprehensive. You basically should keep a record of any and every investment-related expense and anything that will relate to your tax return.

What to Save *After* You Prepare Your Return

So you've completed your tax return. And you find that you have enough records to fill a large dump truck and a small wheelbarrow. Now what? How long do you have to hang on to all this stuff? Well, the answer is a bit complicated.

Unless fraud, evasion, or a substantial understatement of income is involved in your tax return, Uncle Sam generally has only three years in which to tap you on the shoulder and ask for the underlying documents necessary to support information reported in your tax return. Remember, unlike the common "innocent until proven guilty" principle, where the IRS is concerned, you must prove the validity of your tax return. You have to sweat out three years before you can rest easy that your return hasn't been selected for audit. Usually that countdown period begins on the date that the tax return is required to be filed (April 15). If you file after your normal filing date, then the three-year clock begins to tick on the date that the IRS actually receives your return. This three-year period is commonly called the "statute of limitations." (Don't confuse it with the *statue* of limitations—that's under a few pigeons somewhere in New Jersey and has nothing to do with taxes.) In some cases, the statute of limitations can extend for a longer period of time. But normally, you're looking at three years.

As an example, your 1999 individual income tax return will be due on April 17, 2000 (because April 15 falls on a Saturday). Even if you file your tax return on January 25, 2000 (or any other date prior to April 17), your three-year extension will begin to run on April 17. This means that your statute period for the 1999 return will expire on April 17, 2003. If you decided to "extend" the due date of your tax return by submitting an automatic extension form, you have also extended your statute of limitations. So if you file your return on June 20, 2000, your statute will not expire until June 20, 2003.

Much of what you need to keep in the form of records depends directly on the statute of limitations. Here are some guidelines:

- **Your copy of the tax return:** Keep it forever. That's right. You never want to dispose of your copy of the tax return. You never know when this document will come in handy. Remember that in many cases, the IRS destroys the original returns after four or five years. It's always best to have *your* copy to fall back on.

- **Cancelled checks, deposit statements, and receipts:** Generally, keeping these for three years is enough. Because of various combinations of the statute of limitations and technical carryback and carryforward provisions in the code, though, keeping them for longer than three years is preferred. (Five years is better, and seven years is best.) But make sure that these cancelled checks and receipts are only for transactions that have an impact on this single year only... such as receipts for your itemized deductions or interest income. In other words, if a receipt is for something that won't appear on your tax return for several years (such as home improvements), then you'll want to hang on to it for at least three to seven years beyond when it appears on your return.

- **Stock trade confirmation receipts/statements:** Keep these statements for at least three years after both ends of the transaction (both buy and sell) have closed. Again, five or seven years is even better. For example, say that you bought 200 shares of Gap stock in 1981 and sold them in 1999. You'll want to hold on to both the buy and sell confirmations until at least April 2003. In effect, you will have held on to the 1981 purchase statement for about 23 years—but that's what's required in order to prove both ends of a stock transaction.

- **Improvements to property:** Keep proof of those improvements until at least three years after the sale of the property in order to prove your basis in the property when it is sold. This is true for rental property, investment property, and even your own personal residence. Remember when you put that new roof on your rental property in 1987? Well, you'd better still have that receipt—and keep it with receipts for the other improvements to that property for at least three years after you sell it. In cases like this, it is very possible that you'll have records 10, 20, 25 years old, or older. It's not uncommon—if you're retaining your records appropriately. And again, five or seven years beyond the sale date is even better.

- **Escrow closing documents:** Keep these a minimum of three years after the property is sold. You'll want to retain both the purchase escrow and sales escrow statements. Much like your stock confirmation statements, you'll need to show both sides of the transaction *and* be able to prove your improvements. And, as always, keeping the records for five or seven years past the sale is an even better bet.

The key is to *think* before you throw anything out.

PUTTING YOUR COMPUTER TO WORK

We spend a lot of time at The Motley Fool helping people make the most of their computers and the Internet in order to invest effectively. We've become convinced that there are few areas in life where computers and cyberspace can't make a positive difference. Indeed, online with your computer you can now buy books and compact discs, manage your portfolio, choose names for your baby, read your favorite magazines and newspapers, and even order your groceries.

Tax planning and tax return preparation are no exception. On the World Wide Web, you'll find many great reference sites—chief among them the IRS's own site at http://www.irs.gov. There, for example, you can download and print any form and any publication. (That's right—every form or publication that we've mentioned in this book should be available there.)

In the appendix, we list several sites of interest, including our own Foolish tax resource area at http://www.fool.com/school/taxes. There you can post tax questions and get answers—or just read through other people's questions and answers. Our tax expert, and co-author of this guide, Roy Lewis, regularly provides articles on important tax subjects. It's a good place to get the latest word on tax law developments.

Tax Preparation Software

Perhaps when you've been preparing your taxes in the past, you've thought to yourself, "Gee... I'm not sure I'm doing all this correctly. I wish someone who understood taxes would just ask me for all the required information and then fill out the forms for me." Just a few years ago, your dream could come true—for up to several hundred dollars. You'd have to hire a tax professional. Today, however, you can use inexpensive software to prepare your returns. In fact, you can even bypass the software and prepare them on the Web for a modest fee. With these applications, you end up printing filled-out tax forms, which you sign and then mail in, perhaps with a check attached.

The main contenders when it comes to tax preparation software are Intuit's TurboTax and MacinTax and Kiplinger TaxCut. If you're the type who loves filling out questionnaires and answering questions, you might actually enjoy (gasp!) preparing your taxes this way. They have many advantages:

• You don't have to gather any forms; they're all in the program already.

• You can revise and revise and revise, without making a mess with White-Out or an eraser. Enter your information, see what your tax liability is, and then you can make adjustments, playing out different scenarios to see which is most cost-effective. (You might see that it's smart to realize some capital gains this year, for example.)

• The software can assist you with decisions. It will ask you questions and either make decisions for you (regarding which forms to use, for example) or offer you some information and ask you to make a choice.

• You can pay less attention to details. Once the program has certain information, it will make sure that it's carried over to all required places. You don't have to worry about that.

• Carryovers from year to year get taken care of automatically—if you used the same program to prepare your return last year.

There are, of course, some disadvantages to electronic tax return preparation. The main one is that you have to trust the software, even though you're still the one responsible for filing your return. There's always a small chance that the software caused an error—or that you provided an incorrect number and generated the error yourself. (Of course, even manually prepared returns may contain errors.)

Our best piece of advice regarding tax preparation software is that you try it—at least once. Consider using it as a cross-check for yourself the first year. In other words, fill out your return the old-fashioned way and then do it electronically. Compare the results and you'll get a much better feeling for how accurate and/or helpful the software is. You can choose whether you want to file your original return or the computer-generated one, and you'll probably have an idea of which approach to use the following year.

Perhaps the most powerful advantage of tax preparation software is that it lets you play "what if" games. Once you've entered the necessary information, change one variable and see how the bottom line is affected. See what will happen if you get a big raise at work or if you sell some stocks for a sizable capital gain. This can be enormously valuable if you think you might have to pay estimated taxes.

When buying tax preparation software, make sure that the package includes state tax forms for your state if you'd like it to prepare those forms, as well. Verify that it is indeed compatible with your computer system. Make sure that it contains all the forms you'll need. If you buy the software early in the year, make sure you get an updated final version later in the year, so that you're preparing your return incorporating the latest information and tax code revisions. You can read more about available software at the software company websites—and in many cases, you can get demo versions there as well. Keep in mind that you can often prepare your return online without even buying the software—by paying a fee online instead.

Filing Electronically

Besides preparing your return electronically, you can also *file* electronically. The advantage to this is that it speeds up your refund and you get an acknowledgment of receipt. Your refund can even be electronically deposited directly into your bank account. You can file early but not send payment until April 15. Know, though, that you'll still have to mail papers in, such the ones you'd normally staple to your return. One of the papers that you'll have to mail in, ironically enough, is Form 8453, which basically tells the IRS that you're filing electronically.

You can file electronically via your home computer and modem, via your friendly local (wired) tax professional, and in some cases, via telephone.

Other Electronic Aids

Tele-Tax is the IRS's automated information-by-phone service. You can get answers to many common tax questions 24 hours a day at 800-829-4477. You can also get status reports on your refund during working hours. The list of available topics is printed in your tax return instruction booklet, so you might want to select and highlight them before you call.

Federal Tax Payments by Credit Card

As you may know, the 1997 Tax Act allowed the IRS to accept payment for federal taxes by any "commercially acceptable means" it deems appropriate under the conditions provided in the regulations. This means that payment by credit card is now acceptable.

Late in 1998, the IRS issued temporary regulations for paying taxes by credit or debit card. Those regulations indicated that credit cards could be used for payments made on or after January 1, 1999. However, there were just a few small problems. The IRS didn't announce which cards it would accept. The IRS didn't tell us how to make the credit card payments. And finally, the IRS didn't disclose the types of tax liabilities allowed to be paid via credit or debit card. Whoops.

In effect, Uncle Sam said, "You can pay your taxes by credit card, but we don't know exactly how you can do it. But you can rest easy knowing that you *can* do it."

All that has been resolved now. The IRS recently announced that under a new pilot program, you may pay your federal income taxes via credit card in one of two ways:

- **By phone:** Once you determine the amount you owe, you can call 888-2PAY-TAX (toll-free) and pay your 1999 income taxes with a MasterCard, a Discover Card, or an American Express card. (As of this writing, Visa has decided not to participate in this program... so Visa cards are not accepted.)

- **By computer:** E-filers (those filing tax returns electronically) who use Intuit's TurboTax software may, under an arrangement between Intuit and Discover Card, charge their balance due to a Discover Card. The

TAX RELIEF

Pre-Tax-Return Warm-Up Exercises

Here are some handy exercises to get your number-crunching juices flowing.

1) Byron Hufnagle has just finished a two-week grapefruit-and-licorice diet. (He lost three pounds.) He zips to the supermarket and loads up his cart. That night, he downs: two ice cream sandwiches (169 calories each), a bag of potato chips (1,500 calories), two hamburgers (450 calories each), two fistfuls of chocolate chip cookies (total calories: 980), and a low-fat cheesecake (2,300 calories). As the paramedics are rushing him to the emergency room, he wonders how many calories he consumed. Can you help him?

2) Weezie is an avid reader. She goes to her local library and starts collecting books to borrow. First she grabs The Pig Oinks at Midnight and A Dastardly Villain's Embrace. Then she picks up Car Wash Dreams and Murder at the Office Park. She puts two of the books back. Next she adds Last Train to Uzbekistan, Pyramid Schemes for Fun and Profit, and The Secret Life of the Moth. Before checking her books out, she puts back one book. How many books does Weezie check out?

3) Argot-7 is an alien life form living on Jupiter. He has 12 arms and no legs. (And moves about with some difficulty.) For his spawnday, his life-giver gives him a dozen gloves. A quarter of the gloves are red, a third are blue, 16.7% are black, and 25% are invisible. How many of each type are there?

Answers: (1) 6,018 calories (2) Four books (3) Three red, four blue, two black, and three invisible.

payment information will be part of the electronic file sent to the IRS should you decide to use this feature.

Under either method, private-sector companies process the credit card transactions and report payment amounts to the IRS. But private-sector companies do not provide the IRS with your credit card numbers (thankfully).

You should also know that under either method you will be required to pay any convenience fee (generally, the percentage fee that the merchant is required to pay on your purchase). And you should know that the IRS is not involved in setting or collecting these convenience fees. In fact, the IRS is prohibited from paying fees to credit card companies. This was one of the hurdles that had to be overcome before the IRS could begin to accept credit card payments.

Also, understand that the pay-by-phone system isn't linked to how you file. Therefore, even if you file a normal paper tax return, you can still use the pay-by-phone system. If you've filed your return but haven't yet paid your tax, this is an option for you. It can also apply if you filed an extension and find you have tax balances due when you actually prepare your tax return.

By March of 2000 you should be able to pay your estimated taxes using the pay-by-phone system.

Perhaps the biggest question on the minds of people intrigued by the pay-by-credit-card option is "What about 'freebies' such as the airline miles or cash-back rewards I receive with many cards? Will these still apply?" Perhaps not. The credit card companies are likely to treat these tax payments as "cash advances" and will not attach any of your associated freebies to them. So before you leap, contact your credit card company and see how they specifically will handle the payment, and if you'll receive your airline miles and/or cash rebates on the transaction.

One final note: The pay-by-phone system is also in effect in several states, such as California and New Jersey.

If only Uncle Sam could make computing your tax balance due as easy as paying it!

TWO

INVESTOR TAX BASICS

Logic and taxation are not always the best of friends.

—James C. McReynolds

What you'll find in this chapter:

- Tax Law Changes
- Capital Gains and Losses
- Selling Stock
- Mutual Funds
- Direct Investing Plans
- Holding Periods
- Interest and Dividend Income
- Worthless Securities
- Dividends Paid on Shorts
- Wash Sales
- Stock Splits
- Stock Spin-Offs, Split-Ups, and Buyouts
- Hedging and the Constructive Sale Rules
- The Alternative Minimum Tax
- Stock Options
- Investment-Related Deductions and Credits
- Estimating Taxes
- Traders and Taxes
- Investment Club Taxes
- Finding a Good Financial Advisor

TAX LAW CHANGES

Ch-ch-ch-ch-Changes
(Turn and face the stranger)
Ch-ch-Changes
Don't want to be a richer man
Ch-ch-ch-ch-Changes
(Turn and face the stranger)
Ch-ch-Changes
Just gonna have to be a different man

—David Bowie

Mr. Bowie might well have been lamenting the state of the U.S. tax code when he wrote "Changes." (Maybe not, though. We don't know—we weren't there. And don't ask us who the stranger is, either.)

You should feel free to skip this section, as most of the relevant information presented here also appears elsewhere in the book, in appropriate chapters. But if you're a bit of a historian, or if you've simply been asleep

- Even lower capital gains rates are on the way. After 2000, the top tax rate for long-term capital gains will be 18% (8% for taxpayers in the 15% bracket) if a five-year holding period is met. The 18% rate (but not the 8% rate) will apply only if the holding period for the assets begins after 2000.

- The reduced capital gains rate applies for purposes of *both* the regular tax and the Alternative Minimum Tax.

- Up to $250,000 of the profit on the sale of your principal residence is now tax-free if the sale takes place after May 6, 1997, and other restrictions are met. The exclusion is doubled to $500,000 for married persons filing jointly. The new break replaces the home-sale rollover rules and the "once in a lifetime" $125,000 exclusion rules for home-sellers age 55 and over. (This one is a very big deal!)

- Certain sales of assets entered into after June 8, 1997, are treated as taxable sales even though you could previously defer reporting gain on those sales as income. This law is targeting the practice of "shorting against the box." But it can also apply to options and other hedging transactions.

- A number of new tax incentives for higher education were introduced: the Hope Scholarship Credit, the Lifetime Learning Credit, and the Education IRA.

- More of a person's assets can be passed on or given to family members (or anyone else, for that matter) free of estate or gift taxes. The amount exempted from estate or gift tax rises from $600,000 to $1,000,000 over a number of years.

- For individuals who die after 1997, executors who choose the installment method of paying estate taxes arising from closely held businesses will qualify for a lower interest rate (2% instead of 4%). And the lower rate will apply to a larger amount of deferred estate tax.

- Taxpayers will no longer be penalized for taking large withdrawals from IRAs, qualified plans, and tax-sheltered annuities, or leaving large retirement plan accumulations to their heirs.

There were quite a few business provisions in the new tax law. The major ones include:

- For tax years beginning after 1997, the Alternative Minimum Tax is repealed for small corporations. Briefly, the exemption from the AMT for the past few years, you might want a brief run-down on major changes that have occurred in recent years.

Note also that we're never quite done with changes. In fact, despite our best efforts, something in this book might be out of date as soon as it hits the printer. That's the nature of the ever-changing tax laws. At the end of this section we'll offer a glimpse into some changes that may be around the corner. We'll also email you an update on major recent tax changes in early 2000 if you visit www.fool.com/taxguide2000 and enter your email address. (Finally, rest assured that you can always get the latest in tax information and advice online at www.fool.com.)

The Taxpayer Relief Act of 1997

The Taxpayer Relief Act of 1997 brought with it a wide variety of important tax changes affecting individuals, families, investors, and businesses. One of the most complex tax laws enacted in recent memory, it offered many new tax breaks and a few crackdowns.

Here's a quick overview of the major new tax breaks for individuals and families. Note that the information in this section is extremely abbreviated. Don't act on any of it until you read more. (There's more in the rest of the book.)

• Starting in 1998, parents get a new tax credit equal to $400 ($500 in 1999 and future years) for each qualifying dependent child under age 17.

• Beginning in 1998, more people are able to make deductible IRA contributions. The new law increased the adjusted gross income levels at which the IRA deduction begins to phase out for individuals who participate in an employer retirement plan. And a spouse who isn't a retirement plan participant is able to make a deductible IRA contribution even if the other spouse is a retirement plan participant, within certain AGI limitations.

• The 1997 act introduced the Roth IRA, which doesn't yield deductions when you put money in, but offers tax-free distributions for withdrawals made after five years if you are at least 59½, or because of death, disability, or the need to pay for certain first-time homebuyer expenses.

• The top tax rate on long-term capital gains was reduced from 28% to 20% (and to 10% for taxpayers in the 15% bracket).

applies to a corporation that has under $5 million of three-year-average annual gross receipts, and continues to apply as long as it has under $7.5 million of average gross receipts.

- The AMT adjustment requiring use of a generally longer depreciation write-off period than applies for regular tax purposes is repealed, effective for property placed in service after 1998.

- Retroactively effective to tax years beginning in 1987, qualified farmers are eligible to use the installment method of accounting for AMT and regular tax purposes.

- A self-employed individual's above-the-line deduction for health insurance costs (60% of eligible expenses for 1999) will increase at a quicker pace than it would have under prior law.

- Beginning in 1999, more people will be able to claim home-office deductions.

Some other provisions of general interest include:

- The annual exclusion for up to $5,250 of employer-provided educational assistance has been extended and will apply to expenses paid for courses beginning before June 1, 2000 (it had expired for courses beginning after June 30, 1997).

- The estimated tax rules are overhauled for individuals with adjusted gross income over $150,000 in the tax year preceding the current year.

- The estimated tax penalty safe harbor rules for higher-income taxpayers will change again for tax years beginning in 1999 through 2003.

- For tax years beginning after 1997, the estimated tax penalty is not imposed if the shortfall for the year is less than $1,000 (up from $500).

- The standard mileage rate deduction for charitable use of a car is increased from 12 cents a mile to 14 cents a mile.

- Charitable givers can continue to deduct the fair market value of qualified appreciated stock (publicly traded stock that is capital gains property) donated to private foundations.

Some business-related crackdowns in the new law:

- A number of relatively specialized corporate provisions are subject to tougher rules (e.g., gain recognition on certain distributions of controlled corporate stock, tougher holding period rules for the corporate dividends received deduction, registration of certain confidential corporate tax shelters).

- There are several changes in the partnership area. For example, contributing partners recognize gain on the property distributed to another partner or on distribution of other property to the contributing partner within seven years of the original contribution (the old law had been five years). In addition, effective generally for sales, exchanges, and distributions after August 5, 1997, gain on the sale or exchange of a partnership interest generally is taxed as ordinary income to the extent it is attributable to inventory. This had previously applied only to the extent attributable to substantially appreciated inventory.

- Gross proceeds reporting will be required on all post-1997 payments to attorneys made in the course of a trade or business (except those now reported on Form 1099-MISC or Form W-2).

- The net operating loss (NOL) carryback period is decreased from three to two years, but the carryforward period is increased from 15 to 20 years, effective for NOLs arising in tax years beginning after August 5, 1997. But the three-year carryback is retained for losses in disaster areas by farmers or a small business, and for an individual's casualty losses.

So there you have it. And remember that these are only the *major* provisions in the Taxpayer Relief Act of 1997. There were additional, more specialized provisions, to boot.

1998 Tax Changes

The Internal Revenue Service Restructuring and Reform Act of 1998 contains a wide variety of tax provisions that may affect you, including various technical corrections that clarify—and in some cases, change—key provisions of the 1997 Taxpayer Relief Act.

We'll briefly look at some of the key provisions in the pages that follow. Note, as before, that we're presenting a very cursory look at each. For the full scoop, read more in each item's section later in the book, or in IRS publications.

Capital Gains Break

Obviously, the biggest tax-saving change for noncorporate taxpayers is a retroactive reduction in the holding period to qualify for the lowest capital gains tax rate (20% for most people, but 10% if the gain otherwise would be taxed at a 15% rate). Effective for all sales that took place on or after January 1, 1998, the gain on the sale of most capital assets (including stock) held more than one year will qualify for the lowest rates. As you may remember, before this change, in order to receive the lowest rates, you had to hold the assets for more than 18 months. In addition, the 25% rate that applies to certain real property gains will be available for property held for more than one year, rather than more than 18 months. The new law also makes clear (if that is possible) how gains and losses are netted against one another in computing your capital gains.

Roth IRA Changes

As we had all anticipated, the 1998 Act retroactively closed a loophole that would have allowed taxpayers to spread out the tax on regular-to-Roth IRA conversions while pulling funds out of the Roth IRA without paying the 10% premature distribution penalty.

Additionally, the new act permitted, effective retroactively to January 1, 1998, those converting their regular IRA to a Roth IRA in 1998 to pay the resulting tax in only *one* year instead of requiring the income to be spread out over a four-year period. In some situations, this would result in a lower overall tax.

As we were also anticipating, there is a "gracious exit" provision in the new act. This provision provides relief for a taxpayer who makes a contribution or a conversion to a Roth IRA and then later finds he was not eligible to make all or part of that contribution because his income exceeded the allowable adjusted gross income limitation. The 1998 Act allows him to transfer the excess contribution to a regular IRA without penalty if the transfer is made before the filing due date for his tax return for the contribution year.

Another anticipated change that came to pass in the new act was the repeal of the "restart" of the five-tax-year period for Roth IRA conversions. Taxpayers no longer will have to segregate Roth IRA rollover accounts, as the five-tax-year holding period no longer applies separately to each individual rollover.

Finally, the 1998 Act will eventually allow more older taxpayers to convert regular IRAs to Roth IRAs than currently can do so. This is because starting in 2005, required minimum distributions in IRAs *do not* count toward the $100,000 AGI limit for conversions or rollovers. As a result, more taxpayers will have to decide whether or not it is in their best interest to convert to a Roth IRA.

Home Sale Gain Exclusion

The 1998 Act clarifies the amount of the reduced exclusion allowed if a taxpayer was unable to meet the two-year ownership and use requirements. The new law specifically states that the reduced exclusion is based on the total exclusion limitation, and not the actual gain on the sale. For example, John owned and used his personal residence for only one year (out of the required two-year period). He sells his home and realizes a $50,000 gain on the sale. Since John is a single person, his maximum exclusion is $250,000. Under the old law, it was unclear if the excluded amount would be half of the $50,000 gain, or half of the $250,000 exclusion amount. The new law is perfectly clear: The exclusion is half of the total exclusion amount ($125,000 in this example), so none of John's $50,000 would be subject to tax. (But remember that there are restrictions on the two-year requirement that we'll discuss in detail later in the book.)

Additionally, there was some confusion as to the exclusion for married persons filing jointly. Under the old rules, the tax issues were unclear if one spouse (or both spouses) did not meet the required ownership and use requirements. But the new law says that if the spouses don't meet the requirements for the $500,000 exclusion, the amount of gain eligible for the exclusion is the sum of the amounts to which each spouse would be entitled if they had not been married. This means that if a married couple filing a joint return doesn't qualify for the maximum $500,000 exclusion, the amount of the maximum exclusion that may be claimed by the couple is the sum of each spouse's maximum exclusion determined on a separate basis. This allows the taxpayer to specifically nail down the maximum exclusion when there is a question on the use and ownership requirements.

Finally, for those of you who sold your principal residence *on* August 5, 1997, the 1998 Act clarifies that you have the option to treat that sale either under the new rules ($250,000/$500,000 gain exclusion) or under the old "rollover" rules. Before this clarification, the requirements were uncertain for a property that sold and closed directly on August 5.

The Burden of Proof

Much has been made about the "burden of proof" issues found in the new law. Many think that this means that they will not have to provide any information if they are audited in the future because the burden of proof is on the IRS to prove taxpayer errors. Nothing could be further from the truth. First, the burden of proof issue applies only to court proceedings, which take place *long* after the initial audit has taken place. Not only does the burden of proof shift very late in the process, and only in court cases, it will *only* shift if the taxpayer:

• Complies with statutory and regulatory requirements for substantiation of any item (which means that you must comply with the law and cooperate with the IRS during the examination of your return);

• Maintains records (meaning you can't just throw your paper bag full of scraps of paper on the IRS auditor's desk and say, "You find it!!!"); and

• Cooperates with reasonable requests by the IRS for meetings, interviews, witnesses, information, and documents.

So for the vast majority of us, the burden of proof issue is more sizzle than steak. If you *do* find yourself face to face with the IRS in the courtroom, the burden of proof issues may play to your advantage, but for the majority of us who never move past the audit or appeals level, these changes will mean virtually nothing.

Innocent Spouse Rules

The new law makes innocent spouse relief easier to get. Before the passage of the act, if spouses filed a joint return, each spouse would be jointly and "severally" liable for the full amount of the tax, penalties, and interest arising out of that tax return, regardless of the amount of the spouse's separate income. (If you're "severally" liable, the IRS can collect from either spouse.) But the new law provides for new elections that can be filed by spouses who previously filed jointly, but who are now divorced or separated, that may provide total relief for underpayments of tax that the "innocent" spouse knew nothing about. Those who don't qualify for total relief may at least be able to get partial relief from liability.

Accountant-Client Privilege

You're probably aware of the "attorney-client" privilege to withhold confidential information, but you might not know that privilege did *not* cover an accountant-client relationship prior to the passage of the 1998 Act. That's all changed now. (Phew!) The new law extends the attorney-client privilege of confidentiality to tax advice furnished to a client by any individual authorized to practice before the IRS (CPAs, Enrolled Agents, and Enrolled Actuaries). And while this privilege is only limited to tax advice (and not necessary documents and work product), the taxpayer has been provided at least some additional protection. (Note that this privilege only applies to taxes. If you confess to your accountant about your recent adventures in shoplifting, there's nothing stopping him from mentioning this to his friendly neighborhood law enforcement official.)

IRS Restructuring

The new law revamps the governance and structure of the IRS in a number of ways designed to make it more responsive to taxpayers' needs. The IRS's current geographic structure will give way to operating units serving particular groups of taxpayers, such as individuals or small business. In addition, the Taxpayer Advocate's office will be more independent and will have the authority to provide assistance to taxpayers in a wider array of circumstances. The IRS has also been mandated to do more to promote paperless filing and to provide incentives for use of electronic filing of returns.

Collections

There have been a number of *major* changes relative to collections, liens, levies, and seizures, as well as to the offer-in-compromise and statute of limitation issues. Many tax professionals, especially those who deal with IRS collection issues on an ongoing basis, believe that these changes are the backbone of the new law. The changes are many and technical, and certainly can't be satisfactorily addressed here. But be aware that if you find yourself in a problem with the IRS collection people, you now have many new rights and options.

Education IRAs

As you'll remember, the 1997 Tax Act allowed an individual to make a nondeductible contribution of up to $500 per year to an Education IRA to pay for qualified higher education expenses of a qualified person (such as yourself, a child, or spouse). Earnings on the Education IRA are not subject to tax until distributed, and even on distribution won't be taxed if used to pay qualified higher education expenses. Distributed earnings that are *not* used to pay higher education expenses can be included in income and are subject to a 10% penalty. But there have been a few changes and clarifications to the Education IRAs.

First and foremost, the 1998 Act provides that any balance remaining in an Education IRA is treated as distributed within 30 days after the date that the beneficiary reaches age 30 or dies, whichever occurs first. At that time, the earnings in the account will be subject to tax and a 10% penalty.

In addition, the new law waives the 10% penalty tax for distributions from an Education IRA not used to pay qualified higher education expenses if:

- The beneficiary waives the tax-free treatment of a distribution from an Education IRA; and

- The distribution is made on or before the beneficiary's income tax return due date (including extensions) for the year.

This provision was placed into law because there are certain other education benefits that are *not* available to an individual who receives a tax-free distribution from an Education IRA (such as the Hope credit or the Lifetime Learning credit). In a year when you will benefit more from using those credits than from having a tax-free distribution from an Education IRA, you may now waive the tax-free treatment of the Education IRA distribution without being subject to the 10% penalty tax. (Obviously, you should always try to avoid having distributions from an Education IRA in the same year that you expect to have other education tax breaks available that can't be used in conjunction with the Education IRA.)

Finally, the new law makes clear that the Education IRA beneficiary must be "a life in being." That is, a living person, and not an unborn child or grandchild. And not the "inner child" of a 65-year-old, either, for that matter.

Deduction for Student Loan Interest

The 1997 Tax Act provided for certain individuals who have paid interest on qualified education loans after December 31, 1997, to claim an above-the-line deduction for such interest expenses up to a maximum specified amount ($1,000 of interest paid in 1998, $1,500 in 1999, $2,000 in 2000, and $2,500 in 2001 and following years).

The 1998 Act makes it clear that the student loan interest deduction may be claimed only for loans incurred solely to pay qualified higher education expenses. This being the case, revolving lines of credit generally would not constitute qualified education loans unless the borrower agreed to use the line of credit to pay only qualifying education expenses.

The 1998 Act also provides that the 60 months during which the deduction is allowed will be determined in the manner prescribed by the IRS in the case of multiple loans that are refinanced by, or serviced as, a single loan. As noted above, these are only some of the highlights of the 1998 Act.

We have tried to very briefly cover some of the major components of the new law in this section, but please remember that there are a number of changes that we have not discussed. If you are curious about the additional changes, or would like some additional information on any of the issues that have been discussed here, keep reading. We cover many of them in this book. More information is also always available from the horse's mouth, the IRS.

Pending Tax Changes

Although both the House and Senate recently approved H.R. 2488 (The Taxpayer Refund and Relief Act of 1999), the chances of this nearly $800 billion tax cut actually becoming law are slim. President Clinton has said that he will veto it, and there doesn't appear to be any incentive for him to change his mind. However, Washington politics being what they are, the promised veto will likely be nothing more than the beginning of a process that may drag on well into the fall of 1999.

It's virtually certain that not all of the tax reduction provisions found in this legislation will be signed into law. But the President has said that he would be interested in a tax cut bill in the $250 billion range. So it's very possible that some of the changes would remain, at least in some form.

Since this process is fluid at the time we go to press, we'll not spend a lot of time on what we think might happen. Instead, here are some of the highlights of the proposed Taxpayer Refund and Relief Act of 1999.

- **Reduction of Individual Tax Brackets:** The 15% bracket would drop to 14%, phased in over a three-year period beginning in 2001. In addition, there would be a one-percentage-point reduction in all other rates (including the AMT) beginning in 2005.

- **Reduction in Capital Gains Rates:** For tax years beginning in 1999, the maximum tax rate on long-term capital gains would be reduced from 20% (or 10%) to 18% (or 8%).

- **Marriage Penalty Issues:** The standard deduction on a joint return would be increased to twice that of an unmarried taxpayer. This provision would be phased in over a five-year period beginning in 2001. In addition, the 14% bracket for a joint return would be increased to twice that of unmarried taxpayers. This provision would be phased in over four years beginning in 2005.

- **IRA Contributions:** Beginning in 2001, the contribution limit would increase to $3,000 and would eventually reach $5,000 by 2006. In addition, individuals age 50 and above would be able to make "catch-up" contributions of 10% to 50% of the normal contribution limit.

- **Roth IRAs:** Effective for tax years beginning in 2003, the phase-out range for contributions to a Roth IRA would be $200,000 to $210,000 for joint filers, and $100,000 to $110,000 for all other filers. At the same time, the income limit for conversions from a traditional IRA to a Roth IRA would be increased to $200,000.

- **IRA Distributions:** Beginning in 2003, taxpayers who are over age 70½ would be able to have their IRA trustee make a distribution directly to a qualified charity without having to pay tax on the distribution.

- **Education IRAs:** They would be renamed "Education Savings Accounts" and the annual contribution limits would be raised to $2,000 per year. Additionally, qualified education expenses would be expanded to include expenses related to elementary and secondary school and, in some cases, home schooling. These provisions would generally be effective for tax years beginning in 2001.

- **Elective Deferral Pension Plans:** Beginning in 2001 the annual contribution limit for 401(k) plans, section 403(b) annuities, and grandfathered SARSEPs would increase by $1,000 per year until it reached $15,000. At the same time, the SIMPLE plan contribution limit would also increase at the rate of $1,000 per year until it reached $10,000. In addition, individuals age 50 and up would be able to make "catch-up" contributions of from 10% to 50% of the normal contribution limits.

- **Alternative Minimum Tax:** Individual taxpayers' ability to use personal credits (such as the $500 child tax credit, Hope credit, Lifetime Learning Credit, etc.) against the AMT would be made permanent beginning in 1999. Additionally, the AMT would be phased out altogether for individuals beginning in 2005.

These are only a few of the major provisions that have the broadest impact. As this legislation progresses, we'll keep our eyes and ears open. The emailed update that we'll make available to you in early 2000 will cover any changes that transpire. In the meantime, if you want to watch how these issues progress, you can always visit us online in the Fool's Tax Strategies message board (see the "Resources" section in the appendix).

CAPITAL GAINS AND LOSSES

Many people are used to thinking about capital gains as something that only the rich have to worry about. That might have been the case many years ago, but according to the Tax Foundation's Senior Economist Arthur P. Hall, between 1942 and 1992 some 38% of capital gains were reported by those earning $100,000 or less per year in constant 1992 dollars. Nearly 20% were reported by those earning $50,000 or less. This is good news, in a sense, because it means that many average Americans are investing.

In 1997, as part of the 1997 Taxpayer Relief Act, the IRS unveiled a shiny new capital gains tax schedule, with some rates considerably lower than before. (These rules were tweaked further in 1998.) What rate applies to you specifically? Well, it all depends on:

- The type of asset you sold
- Your cost basis
- The length of time you held the asset before selling it
- Your income level

Qualifying for the lowest new rates are stocks, bonds, mutual funds, and many other capital assets. Taxed at a slightly higher rate are business or rental real estate, collectibles, depreciation, and some other things. For the rest of this chapter, we'll be referring to the rates and rules pertaining to securities investments.

Your cost basis is important to understand and calculate correctly. If you buy 100 shares of a stock at $30, the value of that bundle of equity is $3,000. But that's not the number that should figure into your taxes. For that, you need to calculate your cost basis, incorporating any expenses

Don't Get Creative With Commissions

Many people would like to treat commissions paid as "investment expenses." They imagine a commission as an itemized deduction, or some other type of investment expense. While that might seem like a nifty idea, Uncle Sam doesn't quite agree. The *only* place you can mess around with brokerage commissions is on the purchase or sale of the specific stock, using them to decrease your gain or increase your loss. The law does not allow you to treat these expenses in any other way. Brokerage commissions are treated as an addition to the cost of the shares purchased. Period. So when you pay a commission to purchase shares, that commission must remain with those shares, and can't be used by you as any other type or kind of deduction. When you add the commission to the actual purchase price of the stock, you receive your tax benefit for this expense when the stock is sold. But not before.

incurred in carrying out the transaction. If you paid a $25 commission to your broker, that means your cost basis is now $3,025. If you sell the 100 shares when they hit $45, your proceeds for the sale will be $4,500, less the commission. If it was also $25, your net proceeds would be $4,475.

Is calculating your cost basis a pain? Yes. But it's worthwhile. Look at what it has done to your gain. Instead of reporting a $1,500 gain ($4,500 less $3,000), you'll report a $1,450 one ($4,475 less $3,025). If you would have paid 20% tax on the $50 difference, you've just saved 10 bucks. This might not seem like much, but it adds up. For those Fools who haven't yet switched to a discount broker and who pay commissions in the neighborhood of $100 and up per pop, this makes a big difference.

Also, know that commissions paid when you sell a stock may be treated in either of two ways on Form 1099-B, which reports your proceeds from the sale of assets: They can be deducted from proceeds or not deducted. If they're deducted from proceeds (which seems to be the way most brokers handle it), you report the net as sale proceeds. If they're not deducted from proceeds, add them to the basis you report on Schedule D. There's a checkbox on Form 1099-B where the brokerage indicates which way it's reporting. The reason this is important is because 1099-B information is reported automatically to the IRS and the IRS will be reconciling that information with what's on your Schedule D. So you want to be consistent with the way that your brokerage is reporting your proceeds.

There are two holding periods for capital assets sold on or after January 1, 1998. Assets held for a year or less are considered short term. Those held for more than one year are considered long term. Here's the bottom line.

If you're in the 15% tax bracket:
Assets held for a year or less: Taxed at ordinary income tax rate
Assets held for more than a year: 10% tax

If your tax bracket is greater than 15%:
Assets held for a year or less: Taxed at ordinary income tax rate
Assets held for more than a year: 20% tax

Note that when you place an order to buy or sell a security with your broker, there will be a "trade date" and "settlement date" recorded for the order. Which one counts for tax purposes? The trade date, which is the date that the order was executed. (The settlement date is the date when the cash or securities from the transaction are plunked into your account.)

Coming Soon: New Super-Foolish Tax Rates

Here's something you should keep in mind as you plan your investing. In addition to the recently reduced capital gains tax rates, an even lower rate will soon be available to you.

Beginning January 1, 2001, the maximum capital gains rates for assets held more than five years are 8% and 18% (rather than 10% and 20%). If you're normally in the 28% (or higher) tax bracket, if you qualify, your capital gains rate could be reduced from 20% to 18%. Likewise, if you're in the 15% tax bracket, your long-term capital gains rate could fall as low as 8%. (Keep reading, though. As with most tax-related topics, this isn't as simple as it might appear. Sigh.)

Those in the 15% and higher-than-15% tax brackets are treated a little differently, regarding when they can start taking advantage of the new rates.

The 18% rate only applies to assets with holding periods that begin on or after January 1, 2001—no sooner. Using simple math, you can see that your long-term benefit will not kick in until 2006 at the earliest—when you actually sell the qualifying asset and meet your more-than-five-year holding period requirement.

For taxpayers in the 15% tax bracket, the five-year holding period begins on the date of actual purchase—and you are *not* required to wait and make your purchases in 2001 or later. It is very possible, if you're in the 15% bracket, that a stock you bought in 1996 will be subject to the lower capital gains rates if you hold it for more than five years and sell it after January 1, 2001.

But what about those in the normal 28% (or higher) bracket? What if you already have a long-term holding that you bought before 2001, and don't want to add to your position? How can you participate in the new capital gains rates?

In effect, you would have to "sell" and then "repurchase" those shares. The law says that if you have shares that you hold on January 1, 2001, you may elect to treat the shares as having been sold on January 1, 2001, for an amount equal to their fair market value. Then you get to turn right around and treat those same shares as if they were originally purchased on January 1, 2001, for an amount equal to the fair market value. (You read that right. You're pretending that you sold and then repurchased the shares on the same day, at fair market value.) Note that according to current law (which may change in the future, as always), the imaginary transfer *must* take place on January 1, 2001. It appears, though, that this election will not have to be made until the 2001 tax return is filed—sometime in 2002.

Be warned, though: If you elect to sell and repurchase, any gain is recognized (and taxable). And any loss would not be allowed. It's really all a big game of "let's pretend" since no money actually changes hands and nothing is really bought or sold. (Your broker is also not involved, and no commissions figure into the picture.) The IRS simply allows you to wave a magic wand over your stock and pretend that it has been sold. Confused? Let's look closer.

Example: Jeb Bishop bought 100 shares of medical supply company Smooth Operations (ticker: SMOOP) on October 11, 1996, for $15 per share. January 1, 2001, rolls around, and he still owns those shares. (Way to buy and hold, Jeb!) He wants to participate in the new, lower capital gains rates, but is in the 28% bracket in 2001. The fair market value of the shares on January 1, 2001, is $65 per stub, and Jeb elects to treat those shares as sold on January 1, 2001. His gain will amount to $50 per share, or a total gain of $5,000. That gain will be taxable to him on his 2001 tax return. As the law is currently written, Jeb will pay 20% long-term capital gains tax (or $1,000) on that gain. He will be treated as if he were buying the same 100 shares on January 1, 2001, for a total basis of $65 per share—exactly what he "sold" it for. Jeb's holding period will begin all over again on January 1, 2001.

Note that transferring your holdings to take advantage of the extra low rate isn't necessarily always worth it. You get the opportunity for gains going forward to be taxed at 18% instead of 20%. But you also have to suddenly pay taxes now on your current gains. For anyone with significant gains in a holding, it might make very little sense. For those with a small gain or a loss, it's a more attractive prospect. It's certainly not for everybody.

Another example: Let's begin with the same facts as above, except that we'll put Jeb in the normal 15% bracket when he sells his shares in 2001. If he waits until at least October 12, 2001, to make the sale, Jeb can receive the benefit of an 8% capital gains rate. Why? Because he is in the 15% bracket when the shares are sold, which allows him to begin his holding period for the shares sold on the actual date of purchase—and not on January 1, 2001.

Be Careful With Brackets!

There's one very important point that you must understand with respect to capital gains income. In effect, your capital gains income is added to your regular income—and it is on that *total* income that you compute your "normal" tax bracket. Then you're able to use Schedule D to compute your tax using a preferred tax rate on your long-term capital gains. Please don't think that if you have $100 in other income and $1 million in long-term capital gains that you're in the 15% bracket, and that all of your $1 million in long-term gains will be taxed at the preferred 8% (or 10%) rate. It's just not true. You have to add your $1 million to your $100 and *then* look at your tax bracket. That would be considered "normal" for your income for that year—and you'll see that that amount would put you considerably beyond the 15% bracket. So while some of your gain would be taxed at the lower, preferred rates, the vast majority of the income would be taxed at the 20% long-term capital gains rates.

Buying and Holding Can Save Taxes

That's the lowdown on the new capital gains tax rates. What does it all mean for you as a Foolish investor? Well, a quick glance at the numbers above reveals the most important implication: The longer you hold your stocks, the less tax you're probably going to pay.

One bone of contention between Fools and the Wise is the value of holding stocks for the long term. A Foolish investor usually tries to find great companies in which to invest, aiming to hold the stock for years (or decades) as long as the reasons for buying the stock remain unchanged. The Wise, though, will frequently assert that it can be more profitable to jump in and out of the right stocks at the right time, holding them until you reap the expected gain or until something better comes along.

Let's look at the tax implications of both strategies.

Consider an Italian-Irish-American Fool named Foolio O'Fool. His ordinary tax bracket is 31%, but by investing for the long haul, he can enjoy capital gains tax rates of only 20%—and eventually, even just 18% or 8%. On a gain of $5,000, Foolio will be taxed at 20%, paying $1,000. The difference between his regular income tax rate of 31% and the lower long-term capital gains rate of 20% amounts to $550, a rather significant sum.

Next, consider the Anglo-German-American Wise guy, Wiseworth Wisenheimer, whose income has him in the 28% ordinary tax bracket. He's a relatively active trader, buying a little of this, then selling a little of that, jumping into this, leaping out of that... you get the idea. If he also racks up gains of $5,000 and they're all short-term, they'll be taxed at Weisenheimer's 28% rate. He'll be forking over $1,400 in taxes, fully $400 more than Foolio.

Now forget these two. Look at your own situation and tax bracket. For example, if you hold on to a security for longer than a year, you're likely to be paying 20% of your gain in taxes. If your holding period is a year or less, the gain could be taxed as much as 39.6%. With a mere $1,000 gain, that's a difference of $190, or 19%. Are your short-term trading earnings going to be substantial enough to compensate for the fact that you'll be paying nearly twice as much in taxes? It's not terribly likely.

Of course, why believe a coupla Fools when we recommend buying and holding over frequent trading? Consider instead the research of business school professors Brad M. Barber and Terrance Odean of the graduate school of management at the University of California at Davis. They studied the trading activity of some 78,000 households that used a large discount brokerage. They divided the group into subgroups according to trading frequency and found that between February 1991 and December 1996, the most frequent traders earned an annual average return of 10%, versus 17.5% for the least-frequently trading group. This is a whopping difference, and doesn't even include taxes, which make the difference starker still. (During this period, their proxy for "the market" advanced about 17.1%.) As Barber and Odean conclude, "Trading is hazardous to your wealth."

For more information, visit our online tax area and review IRS Publications 544 (Sales and Other Dispositions of Assets) and 550 (Investment Income and Expenses).

Offsetting Gains With Losses

Even very savvy Fools make some blunders when picking stocks. Warren Buffett himself has admitted to several very regrettable investments. When it happens to you, try to look on the bright side and you'll see a few modest benefits to investments gone awry. If you spend a little time thinking about what went wrong, you might learn some valuable lessons. For example, perhaps you lost money investing in a Swiss chain of ocean resorts, based on the enthusiasm of a colleague at your health club... only to learn later that Switzerland is landlocked and has no beachfront. The moral: Do your own research. Lessons learned best are sometimes learned the hard way.

Another benefit of losses is that you can apply them against gains, thereby reducing your income and taxes. This is not insignificant. If your gains were $10,000 and your losses $4,000, you would effectively reduce your gains by $4,000 and would only be taxed on a $6,000 gain. If the gains were to be taxed at the 20% rate, the $4,000 loss has saved you $800 (20% times $4,000 equals $800). It's a lot better than nothing!

While the example above seems to show you an $800 gain, don't be misled. True, you managed to save $800. But only because you lost $4,000 in real dollars in the first place. That $4,000 invested in the stock market for 30 years, earning 11% per year, would turn into $91,569. Occasional losses are pretty much inevitable for all investors—just don't let yourself think of them as desirable tax advantages.

Capital Loss Carryovers

If you're unfortunate enough to have racked up so much in capital losses that they exceed your capital gains, you can still get some mileage out of the excess losses. Go ahead and offset every dollar of capital gains with your capital losses. With what's left, you can deduct up to $3,000 from your income via Schedule D. (Note: For married people filing separately, the limit is $1,500 each.)

Some Offsetting Words

When offsetting gains with losses, remember one important thing: Long-term gains are preferable to short-term gains. Why? Because of the preferred tax rate that's applied to long-term gains. So be careful when taking losses against your gains. You'll generally want to keep your long-term gains intact, offsetting any losses against short-term gains whenever possible. And remember that you can't simply take your losses randomly against any gain that you might have—there are specific rules you must follow.

You must first offset all of your short-term losses against your short-term gains. Then you must offset all of your long-term losses against your long-term gains. And then you must offset (or net out) these two results. So if you have large short-term losses and small short-term gains, some of those "excess" short-term losses may then be forced against your long-term gains. This may not be something that you want to do, as you may want to wait for a future tax year when you anticipate some large short-term gains that can eat up those short-term losses. This can be confusing, so let's look at an example.

For 1999, Frank has the following stock transactions:

$1,000 in short-term capital gains
$5,000 in short-term capital losses
$15,000 in long-term capital gains
$3,000 in long-term capital losses

In order for Frank to compute his "net" capital gain or loss, he must first offset his short-term gains and losses. Doing the math, you see that Frank has $4,000 in net short-term capital losses ($5,000 less $1,000 equals $4,000). Then Frank must offset his long-term gains and losses. Subtracting $3,000 from $15,000 amounts to a net long-term gain of $12,000. Now Frank must "net" his short and long term transactions. Doing so will give Frank a net long-term capital gain of $8,000. (A $12,000 gain less $4,000 in losses yields $8,000.) So Frank has lost some of the benefit of the preferred tax rates on his long-term capital gains because he was forced to offset those gains with short-term losses.

If this seems confusing, it can be. But Schedule D will walk you through the entire process. We just wanted you to know that your short- and long-term gains and losses do intermingle, and poor planning could cost you significant tax dollars.

Whatever excess losses surpass $3,000 (or $1,500 as described above) can be carried forward and applied against capital gains in the following year. Anything remaining beyond your gains can be applied against income—up to (again) $3,000.

For example, if your gains in year one were $5,000, but your losses were $12,000, you could apply $5,000 in losses to offset all your gains. You could also apply $3,000 against your income, reducing it. Then you could carry forward the remaining $4,000 in losses to the next year. You could apply up to all of it against capital gains. If after applying it against capital gains there is anything left, you can deduct up to $3,000 of that from your income that year and carry forward any remainder to the following year.

One final thought with respect to capital loss carryovers: Stay away from them if you feel sickly. While capital losses may be carried over "forever," it's only *your* forever. You can't bequeath or otherwise pass capital losses to your family or friends after your death. (Your stamp collection, yes. Your investment loss on that miracle hair growth company, no.) The losses will go with you to the grave. If the losses are joint, your spouse may be able to participate in some of them after you're gone—but those computations can get pretty tricky and the law is complex. So if you do have large capital loss carryovers, make sure to see your doctor at least once a year for an annual checkup. And you might want to rethink your decision to become a professional bungee jumper.

For additional tax information on capital losses and capital loss carryovers, see IRS Publications 544, 550, and 551.

Gains and Your AGI

Finally, remember that while the new tax rates are indeed reason for celebration, these silver linings are not without clouds. The rates may entice you to sell a bunch of stocks you've held for a few years or more and realize the gains now. Recognize, though, that the gains continue to be included in adjusted gross income. Thus, they will still have an impact on any related tax area that's dependent on AGI. These include (but are not limited to) itemized deductions for medical expenses, casualty losses, and miscellaneous itemized deductions, as well as the phase-out of itemized deductions and personal exemptions and the inclusion in gross income of Social Security benefits.

Capital Gains Distributions on 1099-DIV Forms

Sometimes capital gains can appear where you least expect them, like on a dividend statement related to a stock or mutual fund that you own. It's good to look closely at the 1099-DIV forms you receive to see if they say anything like "Capital Gains Distribution" on them.

Most stock dividends are treated as normal, or ordinary, dividends and don't count as capital gains—and should be reported directly on Schedule B. If

An Opportunity for Parents

Remember that 10% capital gains rate? The one you almost regretted not being able to take advantage of because you're far from the 15% tax bracket? Believe it or not, you might still be able to use it. If you have teenagers, that is.

If you have appreciated stock or other capital assets that you are thinking of selling, you might transfer those assets to children over age 13. To the extent that their other taxable income is below the 28% tax bracket amount ($25,750 for 1999), they can take advantage of the 10% rate for net capital gains. (For children 13 or under, the "kiddie tax" rules can cause the child's income to be taxed at the parent's (higher) tax rates.)

Be careful, though. For capital gains attributable to collectibles, the tax rate remains at the old maximum rate of 28%. And part of the capital gains from the sale of depreciable real property may be subject to a 25% tax rate where the depreciation recapture rules apply.

Finally, don't forget that this "income shifting" technique may also be applicable if you have parents who are retired and in a lower tax bracket. It's also worth noting that to use this strategy, you must truly be giving the assets away, without intending to keep them.

Read more about gift issues and income shifting later in this book.

your portfolio is pretty much all stocks and no mutual fund shares, this section is unlikely to apply to you. But let's review it, just in case.

If you see a "Capital Gains Distribution" mentioned on a 1099-DIV statement that you receive, report those distributions directly on Schedule D. Just a few years ago, those distributions were required to first be reported on Schedule B (Interest and Dividends). But no longer. Take your capital gains distributions directly to Schedule D (Capital Gains and Losses).

SELLING STOCK

Selling stock and accounting for your gain or loss can be easy or slightly less easy. The simplest situation is when you sell all the shares of a stock that you own.

The less-simple scenario is when you only sell some of them and keep the rest. In this case, you have to decide exactly which shares you're selling. This can make a difference in your gains or losses. For example, if you've been adding to a pile of shares over the years and then you sell some, have you sold ones you bought long ago or the last ones you bought? The difference matters because the tax rate varies according to holding period, and your choice can save you much moolah. In addition, you might have paid much less for the earliest shares, so your gains would be bigger if you sell them.

Let's look at your options. Note that in this section, we're dealing only with individual securities (and not mutual funds, which have their own rules). With individual securities like stock, you have only two options when determining the basis (or cost, for tax purposes) of shares. They are:

• Specific Identification Method
• First In-First Out Method (FIFO)

First, the specific identification method:

Let's say that you made the following purchases:
June 1, 1998:   100 shares @ $10 each
June 5, 1998:   200 shares @ $11 each
June 10, 1998:   300 shares @ $13 each

The stock is now trading at $15 a stub. You decide you want to sell 300 shares. You also know that you want to sell the shares you originally bought on June 10, 1998. You very emphatically tell your broker that those are the shares that you want to sell, and not the 100 shares bought on June 1 or the 200 bought on June 5.

Why would you want to do this? Because of the tax implications. If you sell the first 300 shares that you bought, your capital gains will be $1,300 (not including commission adjustments). But by selling the later shares, your capital gains only amount to $600. That could be a significant tax saving—just by making a simple decision and specifically identifying the shares that you want to sell.

It's important to think about your current tax and income situation and what you expect your situation to be in the next few years. If you're getting out of school soon and expect that you'll soon be in a higher tax bracket, you might want to sell the earliest shares and take a bigger tax hit now. This might make sense if you plan to have a much heftier salary next year and perhaps expect that the stock will have appreciated considerably, as well. On the other hand, if the last shares you bought have not yet been held long enough to qualify for the lowest capital gains tax rate, it might be worth it to sell the ones you've held longer. Look at your options from many different perspectives and see which one saves you the most money—both now and in the long run.

If you decide to use the FIFO method, you specify that the first securities you bought are the first ones sold. The basis of the stock for capital gains purposes is the cost of the first securities you purchased. In the example above, using the FIFO method could very well have cost you an additional $280 in tax dollars.

Using specific identification requires a certain amount of preparation and that you follow regulations precisely. Generally, you'll make an adequate identification if you show that your broker received certificates representing shares of stock that you bought on a certain date or for a certain price. As long as the broker has the stock certificates, an adequate identification is made if you:

- Tell your broker the particular stock to be sold at the time of the sale; and

- You receive a written confirmation of this from your broker within a reasonable time.

Although IRS regulations require that you follow the above procedures in order to secure specific identification, the Tax Court has stated that these regulations are really a safe harbor, and not the "exclusive" means of adequately identifying stock sold to avoid the FIFO accounting method. In one case, for example, a stockbroker held a taxpayer's stock in "street name" and had a standing oral instruction to sell the highest cost basis shares first in any sales transaction. While the monthly brokerage statements didn't indicate whether or not the highest cost basis stock was sold, the taxpayer maintained cost records of each lot of stock that was purchased, the date of purchase, and the price per share. This information was used to prepare the tax returns to compute gain or loss. The court ruled that the taxpayer had sufficiently identified the stock sold to avoid the FIFO method of reporting.

So while the rules and regulations are clear regarding the broker "confirmation" process, the courts have muddied the waters a bit. Many brokers will not provide a written confirmation in their normal course of business, and this is especially true of deep discount online brokers. But that doesn't automatically mean that your shares can't be identified. In general, though, whenever possible, try to do whatever needs to be done to keep your shares "identifiable." This will allow you to control your gains and losses to a much greater extent.

Here are some ways that you might identify the shares you're selling:

- You can identify them by the date that you bought them ("the shares I bought on April 1, 1992"), or by the price that you paid for them ("the shares I bought at $33½"), or even in a vaguer way, perhaps by saying "the shares I bought most recently." You simply want to avoid any possible confusion. If you bought at two different prices on the same date, then the date alone isn't sufficient. If you bought on several different dates, but always at the same price, then the price alone won't do.

- If you're placing your order by phone, you could identify the shares over the phone to your broker. Just make sure that you get a written confirmation of your specification from the broker.

- If you're placing your order online and there's nowhere in the order process to specify shares, send an email to the brokerage when you place the order. In the email, specify the order number and which shares you're selling (most likely by the date you bought them). Ask for a written confirmation that you specified the shares at the time of the sale.

It may not even matter whether the broker's confirmation mentions which shares you specified—the main point is that the broker needs to confirm that you did indeed specify the shares at the time of sale. Note also that the confirmation from the broker should come soon after the sale. If it's sent much later, the IRS might have reason to wonder whether you are trying to make it look like you specified shares when you didn't.

MUTUAL FUNDS

The rules and procedures we've outlined for securities like stocks and bonds also apply to mutual funds. You might be thinking to yourself now, "Goodness—mutual funds buy and sell shares of stock each day... do I have to account for each such transaction?" The answer is no, you don't. But you do have to account for the shares of the mutual fund that you sold during the year. And if you're like many people, regularly buying shares of various funds each month, perhaps even having your dividends reinvested in additional shares, the accounting can quickly begin to seem insurmountably complicated. It isn't, though—as long as you've kept good records of when and how you got each share.

Gains and Losses

The first thing to calculate for the shares sold is their cost basis. It will depend on how you got them. If you purchased them, your cost basis is the purchase price plus any commission costs. If you got the shares as part of a dividend reinvestment plan, the cost basis is their price at the time of purchase. If you inherited the shares from someone like Great Aunt Norma, the cost basis is usually their fair market value (the "net asset value") on the day when Norma went to that great bingo hall in the sky.

If the shares were given to you as a gift, things get a bit more complicated. For details on determining the cost basis of such shares, read the material regarding gifts of stock and property later in this book.

Once you have the initial cost basis for the shares, you'll need to continue to add the cost of additional shares purchased to your basis. If you received a dividend that was reinvested back into additional shares in the fund, you should increase your basis by the amount of the dividend, thereby incorporating the value of the dividend in your basis.

You can read much more about the taxation of mutual funds in IRS Publications 564 and 550.

Specifying Mutual Fund Shares

When accounting for mutual fund shares sold, you have more choices than with individual securities. You can use either of the two methods outlined above, or you can average the cost of the shares.

With the Specific Identification Method, you've kept clear records of when you acquired each share of a mutual fund and you clearly specify which ones you're selling when placing the order, just as with stock.

The First In-First Out (FIFO) method, also described above, simply means that you specify that the shares sold were the first ones you owned. So if you accumulated 337 shares over many years and then sell 50 shares, you'll be subtracting the adjusted basis for the first 50 shares you owned from the sale price in order to determine your gain or loss. The disadvantage is that this method can maximize your gain, as your earliest shares are likely to have the lowest basis, but the upside is that since you've held them the longest, these shares are most likely to qualify for the lower long-term tax rate.

Your third option is averaging the cost of all your shares. It might sound simple, but there are actually two ways it can be done: the Single Category Method and the Multiple Category Method.

With the Single Category Method, you add up the purchase prices of all the shares you have, and then divide by the total number of shares. For example, let's say that you started out with 100 shares of the Hogs-of-the-Dow Fund, purchased for $50 each. Later, you bought 100 more shares, at $60 each. In the meantime, your dividends have been reinvested and you get a notice that you received 5 shares, purchased at $52 each. With the Single Category Method, you average them as follows:

100 shares @ $50 = $5,000
100 shares @ $60 = $6,000
  5 shares @ $52 = $ 260
205 shares totaling $11,260

$11,260 divided by 205 equals a cost basis of $54.93 per share.

So if at some point you sell 50 shares for $65 each, you calculate your gain using a cost basis of $54.93 (note: to simplify, we haven't incorporated commission costs here). You record your gains or losses on Schedule D, where you must also explain the method you used to calculate any average bases. The basis you calculated stays in effect until you acquire more shares. Then you'll have to recalculate. Note also that you still have to pay attention to holding periods. Whenever you sell any share, you'll have to figure out its holding period and its appropriate tax rate. But no matter what the holding period and tax rate, with the Single Category Method, the cost basis is the same.

Most reputable mutual fund companies will provide cost basis information for you when you sell your shares—averaged according to the Single Category Method.

Next up, the Multiple Category Method. This is pretty much the same as the Single Category Method, but you average the shares in subsets, according to holding period. It is further complicated when you sell off shares over time—you'll have to recalculate, incorporating new shares acquired in the interim and recategorizing all the shares as their holding periods change.

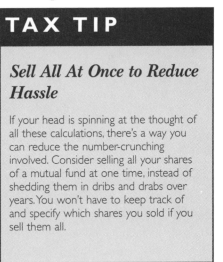

TAX TIP

Sell All At Once to Reduce Hassle

If your head is spinning at the thought of all these calculations, there's a way you can reduce the number-crunching involved. Consider selling all your shares of a mutual fund at one time, instead of shedding them in dribs and drabs over years. You won't have to keep track of and specify which shares you sold if you sell them all.

The Multiple Category Method is a little more work, but it often decreases the taxes you pay. To use this method, you should make all the calculations whenever you sell any shares. Here's an example of what your results might look like:

Short-term shares (held for a year or less):
200 shares @ $40 = $8,000 (Bought this April)
100 shares @ $30 = $3,000 (Bought this May)
  5 shares @ $32 = $ 160 (Bought this June)
305 shares totaling $11,160 = average cost basis of $36.59 per share

Long-term shares (held for more than a year):
200 shares @ $28 = $5,600 (Bought last April)
200 shares totaling $5,600 = average cost basis of $28 per share

With this method, when selling shares, you simply use the cost basis that corresponds to the holding period of the shares you're selling. So if you were selling shares you'd held for 14 months, your cost basis would be $28 per share.

As time marches on, shares in your short-term category will eventually become long-term holdings as long as they remain in your portfolio.

You should choose the method that serves you best, but know that with some methods, you'll have to stick with them for as long as you hold shares in that particular fund.

And while we're touching briefly on the subject of mutual funds here... something not every Fool realizes is that even tax-exempt mutual funds leave you with taxable gains or losses. Most of the income produced from the fund might be tax exempt, but the fund can produce some taxable income (perhaps if it sells bonds at a taxable gain) and the shares themselves remain taxable assets upon sale.

Again, remember that you can read much more about mutual fund taxation issues in IRS Publications 564 and 550. Many of the tax issues can be a bit complicated and difficult to understand, but you should be familiar with them if you decide to invest in mutual funds.

DIRECT INVESTING PLANS

Before we go any further, for those in the dark, a word of explanation about "direct investing plans." Specifically, we're talking about two similar kinds of plans that more and more companies are offering. (More than 1,000 do already.) One kind is the dividend reinvestment plan (sometimes called a "Drip"), which permits you, once you own at least one share of a company, to buy additional shares through the company. You bypass brokers and save on commission costs. The other kind of plan is the direct stock purchase plan, which operates much like a Drip, but permits you to buy even your first share through the plan. (You can read more about these plans in our book, *The Motley Fool's Investing Without a Silver Spoon: How Anyone Can Build Wealth Through Direct Investing.*)

We'd like to plunge right into how to deal with taxes related to direct investing plans. But it's hard to do that without first discussing how you should account for the many shares that you'll accumulate through the plan(s). Share price accounting can be a little intimidating until you get the hang of it. And you really should get the hang of it, as you need accurate cost basis numbers with which to figure your capital gains or losses whenever you sell shares.

Perhaps the first thing you should know is that once you begin direct investment plans, it's vital to keep good records. Your records will help you track portfolio returns and the cost basis of your individual company shares. Keep all of your investment plan statements organized. They provide the price of each share or fractional share you buy and they'll get you through tax season. Some investors track their stocks on paper record sheets. Others, to make things easier, track share costs and dividends in a computer spreadsheet. Recording your investments in a spreadsheet also makes it easier for you to track your performance.

Tracking Your Performance With Share Price Accounting

When you add money to your portfolio every month, measuring your results isn't simple. (But it won't make your head explode, either.) The process involves an accounting method that mutual funds use and that you would use if you were investing monthly in a mutual fund—such as in an S&P 500 fund through your 401(k).

Starting now, think of your portfolio as your own personal mutual fund. (With you as the portfolio manager. That's right—from now on you might want to start strolling around in a suit and wingtips.) Just as mutual funds and companies have "shares," your direct portfolio will, as well. You'll need to set up a separate special portfolio for each Drip plan you join.

First, you need to decide how many shares to begin your direct portfolio with as you begin to buy stocks. (Pick a number, any number.) Then, in the future, every time you add money, you're simply buying new shares in your portfolio at that day's cost basis (which is determined by your portfolio's total performance up to that point). This is called "share price accounting." We'll explain it in more detail soon.

When you're investing money on a regular basis, it's inaccurate to assess performance by counting the new money as if it had been invested for the entire life of your portfolio. If you start with $500 and invest $100 more per month for 12 months, you'll have $1,700 invested. But some of that money will have been invested for just a few months, meaning that it would've been difficult to earn much of a return on it. On the other hand, your initial $500 will have been invested for a year and it might have appreciated or depreciated a more significant amount.

If you judge your performance based only on your portfolio's total value, ignoring the fact that much of the money was invested only recently, you'll weigh the money you invested recently more than you will the older money. This means that if you have done poorly, your performance will look better, but if you have done well, your performance will look less impressive than it actually was. The share price accounting method smoothes this out by weighting each dollar *equally* as you convert them into shares.

Consider an example. You begin your portfolio with $500 plunked into the stock of Scrunchie Manufacturing (ticker: SCRNCH). On that day, you decide that your direct investing portfolio has 20 shares. This means that, before you spent a single dollar, your 20 shares were each worth $25.

Total Port Value: $500
# of Shares: 20
Per Share Value: $25

Now imagine that you buy your first shares of stock (congratulations!), incurring some expenses in the process. At the end of one month, your portfolio is now worth $459.50 rather than $500. (You paid some fees and maybe the stock price slumped a mite, too.) Beginning a new month, you want to add $100 in savings to the portfolio and buy more stock. Let's first calculate the current price per share. That's what you're going to "pay" for more shares of your portfolio when you add money.

Total Value: $459.50
# of Shares: 20
Per Share Value: $22.975

The current price per share is $22.975. Now you're ready to add money to the portfolio. Divide the amount you're investing by the price per share and you'll see how many new shares you'll be getting:

Money Added: $100
Price Per Share: $22.975
New Shares: 4.35

The answer: 4.35 new shares. Add these to your original 20 and you now have 24.35 shares of your portfolio, worth $22.975 apiece, for a total portfolio value of $559.50. The portfolio's performance—rightly so—has not changed at all in the course of adding money. However, you've added $100 and the appropriate amount of new shares, and this permits you to continue to accurately measure your performance. To see the portfolio's performance to date, compare the current value per share against the previous value. As you can see, the portfolio is down 8.1% to date, with the price per share now being $22.975 vs. $25 when you began—that's $22.975 - $25 divided by 25 = -0.081, or -8.1%. It could be this way in the beginning due to expenses alone. (With Drips you sometimes have to wait a few years for the effect of fees to become insignificant.)

To find the value of your portfolio's shares at any point, you need to know how many shares you have and the total cash and stock value of your portfolio. Divide the total porfolio value by the share count to arrive at the current value per share. Compare that to your $25 per share starting point. Each time that you add cash you need to know what your portfolio is worth, so you can add the new shares at the correct price per share. And you only add shares to your portfolio's share count when you add cash or buy more shares with reinvested dividends.

Remember—the shares we're talking about here are not shares of company stock, but shares of your portfolio. For the purposes of calculating your performance, you're treating your portfolio like a mutual fund and are creating theoretical "shares" of it. It may be confusing, but in this example, although the price per share is in the $20s, the price per share of the actual stock that's trading on the market might be in the $60s or $100s. You started with an arbitrary number of shares in your direct portfolio, but as long as you remain consistent and accurately add shares, your records will be correct.

Here's another way of thinking about it. Yes, maybe the actual stock price is $60. But that's today. Next month you might buy a few more shares at $65, and some the next month at $70. After that, if the price falls, you might pick up additional shares at $63. See how it's suddenly become hard to determine your return? You've now held various shares for different lengths of time, and from different starting prices. That's why the process of accounting for a theoretical "direct portfolio" is so helpful (especially for taxes). If you know that your initial price per theoretical share was $25 and it's now $28, a little simple math will show you a return of 12% ($28 minus $25 is $3. $3 divided by $25 is 0.12, or 12%).

You may not want to use share price accounting at all. Instead, you might merely "eyeball" your performance over the years—sensing whether or not you're doing well based on the total value of your holdings. Although a Foolish investor should want to beat the S&P 500 and should know if she's doing so, the world won't end if your objective is less quantifiable. You might simply want to reach a certain dollar amount before retirement, for instance, and so you won't fret about your performance against the S&P as long as you meet your goal. Whatever

TAX TIP

Viva Automation!

Even if you understand this accounting system completely, the paperwork can be a hassle. At the Fool we use our Portfolio Tracker software to do all of the dirty work for our real-money Drip Portfolio online. It's available for a reasonable price from FoolMart at www.foolmart.com. There are also other computer programs that do the job, such as Quicken from Intuit (at www.intuit.com).

If you'd rather track your investments by hand, that's perfectly acceptable and—allow us to say—even quite fanciful (maybe turn off the power and light candles while working, too). Many people track their direct investments in a ledger, much like an accountant would in the good old days. One downside is that it'll be difficult to track your actual performance because share price accounting isn't automatic when using paper and pencil. The choice is yours, however.

you do, keep good records and keep all of your investment statements organized. You need to know the cost basis for every full and fractional share you've ever bought when it comes to taxes.

Taxes and Direct Investing

It's time to plunge into direct investment plan tax issues. For each plan you begin, you should keep a folder to store all of your statements in. Most important are the cumulative year-end statements you'll receive (keep these on file *forever*—or at least three to seven years after you sell all of the shares in question) and the 1099-DIV forms sent to you once each year.

Direct investment-related tax reporting can sometimes get a little complicated, but in most cases your experience will be straightforward. Assuming that you're not going to sell your shares for a number of years, the first taxable income that you'll have are the dividends you receive, even if they're all reinvested in stock. Mutual fund investors deal with this same issue.

Dividends

The annual 1099-DIV form that your company will send you shows how much you received in dividend payments, even if it all went to buy more stock. Report all dividends as income on your annual tax return. Pretty simple. It's much like reporting interest from a savings account—a one-line entry. As of 1998, you report the dividends you receive on Schedule B, which is an interest and dividend income form, but only if you receive more than $400 worth in one year. Otherwise, you simply report dividend income on your main 1040 tax form. (This may change for 1999, but we don't expect that it will.)

Be aware that some companies don't send you Form 1099-DIV when the dividend payments that you received for the year amounted to less than $10. The dividends are still taxable, however. Your year-end account statement will show the total amount of dividends that you received. You should report that number as income, just as if you'd received a 1099-DIV.

Shares Purchased With Dividends

One of the best aspects of dividend reinvestment or direct purchase plans is that they'll take your dividend payments and buy additional shares (often fractions of shares) with them. You probably have to check a box on the enrollment form requesting this. Having the dividend sent to you as cash may just buy you a hamburger every now and then. But having them reinvested into additional stock can add up to thousands of dollars in the future.

Shares purchased with dividends are accounted for exactly as if you had bought them with money sitting in your bank account. So you must keep the statements showing your cost basis on dividend reinvestment-acquired shares just as you do when you make optional cash payments to buy shares. When it comes time to sell, you need to know the cost basis for all of your shares—those bought with reinvested dividends and those bought separately with your hard-earned money.

Commissions Paid *for* You

Although most direct investment plans are commission-free, somebody is paying a brokerage commission for you, and that somebody is usually the company. Coca-Cola, Intel, Johnson & Johnson—through their direct investing plans, these big guys are eating the cost for you. In return, they hope you'll be a loyal shareholder. But something even bigger than these companies (the government) requires that they report any commissions paid for you to the IRS. In turn, you're required to report the commissions, also—as income. The argument is that you'd normally have to pay a commission, but since somebody paid it for you, it's similar to *income* for you.

The commission paid for you is included on the same annual 1099-DIV form that holds your dividend information and that you'll receive in the mail come January or February. The commission is usually minor. If you had bought some shares of Coca-Cola almost every month in 1997, the total commission on your year-end 1099-DIV was $0.45. Yup, 45 cents total. It's incredibly cheap because your company buys every shareholder's shares at once and then divides the commission among the thousands (or hundreds of thousands, in Coca-Cola's case) of direct investment participants. That 45 cents of "income" will hardly change your taxes, but if you don't report it you might find yourself on a midnight plane to Brazil (no cheap plane ticket, that one).

So, to stay in your home country, be aware that when companies pay commissions for you, you *usually* report it as income. Check your individual year-end direct investment plan statement for specifics, because in many cases, this minor commission "income" is lumped with your total dividend income and it's all reported together. That makes it much simpler for you—it's just one number to report. Look at your year-end statement to see how it's being reported and then proceed accordingly.

Commissions Paid *by* You

If there are commission fees that you pay when you buy or sell stock in your direct investment plan, these should, respectively, be added to the cost of shares bought and deducted from the proceeds when you sell shares. This is the same process you apply to your usual gains and losses in non-Drip stock transactions. Incorporating commissions decreases your taxes because it lowers your overall amount of income, increasing your cost basis whenever you purchase, and decreasing your income when selling. Almost every direct investment plan has slight fees for selling stock, so remember to deduct the fee from your proceeds.

Also worth noting: When you begin your portfolio, you might have additional fees to start. If it costs $20 to buy your first share of Coca-Cola, you *can't* add this, for tax cost-basis purposes, to the share price that you paid for the first share. This is because as the IRS sees it, it's a one-time expense for the production of income, not a direct commission paid to buy the stock. It doesn't become part of your cost basis. You can only deduct this fee if it is itemized on Schedule A, subject to the 2% of adjusted gross income limitation. Unless you already itemize deductions, it's probably not worth the trouble to record these small start-up costs.

Selling Shares

A Drip plan's most significant tax event occurs when you sell shares. At this point, you need to know all of the prices that you paid for any shares that you sell, as well as the length of time you've held the shares. This is why good recordkeeping is vitally important.

In the end, the taxation method is basically the same as with a regular stock sale. You pay a capital gains tax, often 20%, on any profit from shares held for more than a year ("long-term" gains). On profits that were achieved over a period of a year or less ("short-term" gains), you pay a higher rate, typically 28%. If you sustained losses, you can use them to offset any capital gains, as well as other income (up to $3,000 annually when offsetting other income).

What's different with direct investment plans is that you'll have several different purchase dates and prices paid per stock—you'll even have fractional shares bought at varying prices. It sounds daunting, but it isn't too horrible. In fact, you'd probably rather do this than hear "Stairway to Heaven" played on the radio again.

So how do you do it?

Although you'd probably like to lump all of your shares together, figure the total amount that you invested, and then divide that by the total shares you sold to determine your average price paid per share, you can't do that. Mutual fund investors can, but direct investors must use one of two IRS-approved methods of accounting to figure their cost basis when selling shares. We discussed these earlier in the book, but to review, they're:

The First In-First Out (FIFO) method. This is a relatively self-explanatory system. The first shares that you sell are deemed to be the first shares that you purchased. First in, first out.

Assume you're selling 100 shares of a 230-share position in Exxon. You've been investing in Exxon's Drip regularly for five years. The 100 shares you sell could theoretically be the first 100 shares you bought, the last 100, or 100 randomly chosen shares. With this reporting system, however, in order to figure the price you paid per share, the 100 shares that you sell must be the *first* 100 shares you bought through both cash investments and dividend reinvestments. (This can work in your favor, because often you'd rather sell the oldest shares first and pay the lower long-term capital gains tax rate.) Notice how important recordkeeping is. If you don't sell for 20 years after your first purchase, you'll need your very first direct investment plan statement (or the first year-end statement) to show the prices you paid for your earliest shares. (Reminder: You'll need to know how many times the stock has split, too, if it has. You can track this from the start, call the company and ask, or find the information online.)

If you sell only some of your shares at some point, as with this Exxon example, make a note of which early shares you sold in your records. Note the specific shares as "sold" and mark your complete records "sold up to this date." This way, the next time you sell shares you'll know the date to begin counting from and you won't incorrectly record the same shares as being sold twice.

If you sell all of your shares at once, you still need to determine your income on a "when bought" basis. If you sell shares that you bought within the last 12 months, you pay a higher, short-term tax rate on those shares (if you made money). Your older shares should qualify for the (lower) long-term tax rate, assuming you owned them for more than one year. You simply must know all of your dates of purchase and the prices you paid. If all of your purchases occurred more than one year before selling, or all of them occurred within the last year, that makes things easier—all the shares will qualify for the same tax rate.

Specific Identification of Shares. The FIFO method determines which shares you're selling according to a set formula, but the second option, the "specific identification" method, allows you to specify the shares any way you wish. You could, for example, specify that the 100 shares you're selling include the first 27 shares you bought, the 44th share you bought, shares 109, 150, 201, and 212, and the last 68 shares you bought. Sound too good to be true? Well, it is.

The specific identification method of accounting doesn't always work well with direct investment plans.

Some Drip experts advise against it, arguing that fractional shares and reinvested dividends tend to become commingled in direct investment plans. Also, investment dates for optional cash investments and dividend reinvestments are usually the same every three months. As you pay cash to buy new shares in your plan, the dividend that you're paid is buying you more shares, too, that same day and at the same cost. This can get pretty confusing.

Other experts see no reason you can't identify shares even if they're commingled in a Drip. They point out that identification doesn't require the broker to actually sell the specific shares you identify. If you choose to specify in a Drip, you might specify something like this: "Sell the 3.45 shares bought on 5/5/98, the 2.87 shares bought on 8/5/98, and 1.63 of the shares bought on 11/5/98." Of course, you might run into difficulty getting the Drip administrator to provide the written acknowledgment you need for a valid identification. Look into how cooperative the administrator will be.

So what can you do?

One laborious way to avoid this "commingling" problem is to have your stock certificates mailed to you by your transfer agent or plan administrator. If you have the actual certificates for each of your stock purchases, you can use the specific share method of accounting when you sell. One downside to this, however, is that the direct investment program will almost always send you stock certificates representing the highest amount of shares possible, not one certificate for every individual purchase made. Plus, if you request individual certificates, the fees get expensive.

So, unless you don't mind fees and piles of stock certificates, you must use the FIFO method or else not sell anything until you can afford to dump all of the work on an accountant. (Good recordkeeping will keep the accountant's fees lower.) Using FIFO, the tax issue is easy enough, however, as long as your records are in order.

Reporting on Schedule D

When selling and using FIFO or *any* tax accounting method, having different cost bases for all of your shares would make reporting each share, and fractional share, individually on your Schedule D tax form (Capital Gains and Losses) a nightmare. You might need 20 pages to list your various purchase dates and prices over the years. Fortunately, the government cuts us some slack here. (Conveniently, they're cutting *themselves* some slack, too.)

Schedule D is where you report gains and losses on the sale of stock. If you read the instructions to Schedule D, you'll find that you don't need to disclose each and every share of stock. What you must do instead is separate the "blocks" of shares sold by holding period, with short-term currently being one year or less and long-term more than a year—so there are only two different kinds of holding periods. With direct investing, in the "date purchased" section of Schedule D you can simply state "various." Be ready to support this one-line entry by producing purchase records (run and get your folders!) if the IRS ever wants details.

If you're selling all of your shares, break them into their respective holding periods (if they're all long-term, great). Write "various dates," enter the total costs for each time period, and finally, state the money made or lost on the entire "time block" of shares. If you're selling only some of your shares, do the same, but remember, if you're using the FIFO system the first shares that you bought need to be the first shares you sell. Use the earliest prices paid to determine the gains or losses to report.

HOLDING PERIODS

Concepts that seem obvious to the experienced tax-return preparer can confound the newcomer. The holding period is one such concept. If you can't believe that we're devoting a few pages to this, just move on to the next section. If you're secretly delighted, good. Read on.

Let's take a brief look at what "holding period" actually means, and how it is applied in various situations.

In general, a property's "holding period" is the length of time that you have held it or the period that it is treated as having been held. Well, that certainly makes sense, doesn't it? The calculation of a property's holding period is a fundamental component of the tax treatment of capital gains and losses. This is because the capital gains and losses provisions of the Internal Revenue Code distinguish between short-term and long-term gains and losses. The correct classification of gains and losses is essential to the correct calculation of your net capital gains or losses and the determination of the limit on your capital losses. That is why the holding period is so important.

As you've learned, long-term capital gains are now taxed at lower rates than ordinary income. As the law is currently written, an asset has a long-term holding period if it has been held, or is deemed to have been held, for more than one year.

To compute the holding period of property, you begin counting on the date after the day you acquired the property and stop counting on the day that you dispose of it. But you don't merely count out 365 days. Nope. Instead, you use that first day as a benchmark for each succeeding month. You then use that benchmark to determine your sale date, and your ultimate holding period. If you've held the property for more than one year, your gain or loss is a "long-term" capital gain or loss. If, on the other hand, you've held the property one year or less, your capital gain or loss is "short-term."

Example: With money she saved from her job as a wading pool lifeguard, Christina King bought 100 shares of Scruffy's Chicken Shack (ticker: BUKBUK) on January 1, 1999. For purposes of determining her holding period, she should start counting on January 2. The second day of each month thereafter counts as the beginning of a new month, regardless of how many days that month contains. If she sells the property on January 1, 2000, her holding period will be one year or less and she will realize a "short-term" capital gain or loss. If, on the other hand, she sells the property on January 2, 2000, her holding period will have been one year and a day, and she will realize a "long-term" capital gain or loss. See how it works?

Here are some examples of investment property and the specific rules regarding the calculation of holding periods that apply to each:

- Securities traded on an established market: For these, the holding period begins the day after the trading date on which you buy the securities and ends on the trading date on which you sell them. You ignore the settlement date for holding period purposes. The *trade* date controls. (The trade date is the date on which the transaction occurred. Settlement dates, usually a few days after the trade date, represent when payment must be made for a purchase or when assets must be delivered for a sale.)

- Nontaxable trades: If you acquire new investment property in exchange for old investment property (such as in a tax-deferred exchange), the holding period begins on the day after the date the original (or old) property was acquired. So if you exchange or trade a beachfront lot that you bought in May of 1995 and use the proceeds to buy a cabin in the mountains in 1999, your holding period for the mountain cabin begins on the day after the day you bought the beachfront lot.

- Real estate property: If you purchase real property under an unconditional contract, you begin counting on the earlier of the day you received title to the property or the day after you took possession and assumed the incidents of ownership. Taking delivery or possession of real property under an option to purchase, however, is not enough to start the holding period. The holding period cannot start until there is an actual contract of sale. Likewise, the holding period of the seller cannot end before that time.

- Gifts: If you receive a gift of property and your basis in the gift is figured by using the donor's basis (such as in the gift of appreciated stock), then your holding period includes the donor's holding period. This is known as "tacking on" the holding period. Why? Because your holding period "tacks on" to the original donor's holding period. If, however, your basis in the gift is determined by the fair market value of the gift (such as with a gift of stock that has decreased in value), your holding period starts on the day after the date of the gift.

- Inheritance: If you inherit investment property, your gain or loss on any later disposition of such property is generally treated as a long-term gain or loss regardless of how long *you* may have actually held the property. This being the case, you are considered to have held the inherited property for more than one year even if you dispose of the property within one year of the decedent's death.

INTEREST AND DIVIDEND INCOME

Two of the most common forms of income for investors are interest and dividend income. Interest income is exactly what it seems to be—moolah forked over to you as interest payments from your bank, credit union, or other financial institution. Bonds will often pay you interest, as well. At the end of the year, you'll receive 1099-INT forms reporting the interest income you received. This income should be reported on Schedule B of your tax return.

Note that for interest earned that's less than $10, many institutions won't issue a 1099 form. This doesn't excuse you from including the interest on your tax return— the IRS expects those few dollars to be reported. The IRS also expects you to report any interest a friend is paying you on a personal loan.

Dividend income can be generated by dividend-paying stocks or mutual funds that you hold. The income is reported to you on 1099-DIV forms and needs to be included on Schedule B of your tax return.

Mutual funds often generate "capital gains distributions," which are a special kind of dividend income. You can read more about them under the "Capital Gains Distributions on 1099-DIV Forms" heading near the end of the "Capital Gains and Losses" section.

A final word: If neither your interest income nor dividend income exceeds $400, you don't have to fill out Schedule B. You still do have to report the income on your 1040 form, though.

WORTHLESS SECURITIES

You thought those 5,000 shares of Stained Glass Windshield Co. (ticker: STAIN) were a bargain at $0.25 per share, but now, six months later, the stock seems to have disappeared from all listings. When you asked someone about it, she said the shares were worthless. Are we looking at a capital loss here? It's very likely. Let's just clear up a few things.

Sell Worthless Securities to Your Mother-in-Law

Since dealing with rules regarding worthless securities can be a bit of a hassle, consider selling the junk for pennies to a friend or relative. (In-laws qualify, as does anyone other than your spouse, siblings [either whole or half-blood], ancestors, or lineal descendants.) You then have a closed transaction, and the loss is certain. If the stock ever comes back and is worth something, at least the money is kept in the family. Here's how you might do it:

1. Get the actual stock certificates from your broker.

2. Formally sell the shares to the purchaser, with a check for payment and a bill of sale.

3. Sign over the stock certificate (on its back) to the purchaser. Have the signatures verified by your banker and/or a local stockbroker.

4. Send the certificate to the stock transfer agent. Explain that the shares have been sold, and ask them to cancel the old shares and issue a new certificate to the new owner.

Some brokerages will offer you a quicker alternative, buying all your shares of the stock for a penny. They do it to help out their customers and because over time, some of the shares may actually be worth more than the penny they paid for them.

If the company was literally liquidated, you'll receive a 1099-DIV form at the end of the year that shows a liquidating distribution to you, the shareholder. Treat this liquidating distribution as if you sold the stock for the amount of the distribution. The date of "sale" is the date that the distribution actually took place. With this information, using your original cost basis in the shares, you can compute your gain or loss.

If the company has not actually been liquidated but is just deemed worthless, the rules are a little bit different. You *can* deduct a loss from worthless stock or other securities (i.e., a bond, debenture, note, certificate, or other evidence of indebtedness, etc.). But keep in mind that total worthlessness of the security is required for the loss deduction to be claimed. No loss deduction is allowed for partial worthlessness, or for a mere decline in the value of the security.

Make sure that the stock is worthless. Many stocks that have taken major hits may still be alive, even though they are trading for mere pennies per share. Your broker should be able to tell you if the security is still trading. Some brokers even have divisions that will buy back your remaining shares (for pennies), allowing you to close out your position.

By selling the shares, you have a closed transaction with the stock and can declare a tax loss. For a pittance, your friend, relative, or broker has just bought a placemat or birdcage liner.

For more information on worthless securities, check out IRS Publication 550. Even Publication 550 doesn't address the complex issue of exactly *when* a stock becomes worthless in the eyes of the IRS, though. For additional discussions on this issue, visit our online tax discussion area.

DIVIDENDS PAID ON SHORTS

If you're a more advanced Foolish investor, you may have shorted stock. Essentially, this involves buying low and selling high, but in the reverse order. You (legally) "borrow" shares via a broker and then sell them, hoping and expecting that the price will decline in the near future. Once the share price drops, you buy back shares on the open market at the new lower price, replace the ones you borrowed, and pocket the difference. You risk losing money if the stock price climbs. This all might sound bizarre, but it's commonly done.

In general, accounting for shorted stocks is much the same as with stocks on which you're "long." (You're long on a stock if you bought it in the usual manner, expecting it to increase in value.) You incorporate commission fees into the cost basis for the shares and itemize gains or losses on Schedule D. Things can get a little more complicated, though, if the stock you've shorted pays a dividend.

Here's how it happens. You shorted a stock that pays dividends—perhaps the Planet Paparazzi Café eater-tainment chain. You discover that while you held your short position, a dividend was paid on the stock. Your broker notified you of that fact, and reduced the cash position in your account by the amount of the dividend. You're now going through your records in order to prepare your Schedule D for gains and losses, and you run across this little gem. Where do you report this payment? Is it an adjustment to the basis of the stock in the short sale? Or is it a current expense that can be deducted immediately, even if the short position was not closed in the tax year?

Here's the rule: If you borrow stock to make a short sale, you may have to remit to the lender payments in lieu of the dividends distributed while you maintain your short position. You can deduct these payments only if you hold the short sale open at least 46 days and you itemize your deductions.

If you close the short sale by the 45th day after the date of the short sale, you can't deduct the payment in lieu of the dividend that you made to the lender. Instead, you must increase the basis of the stock used to close the short sale by that amount.

What's Substantially Similar?

Occasionally the IRS uses terms like "substantially similar" and "basically identical." What do these really mean, though, when we're talking about stocks? Is stock in Dell Computer substantially similar to stock in Compaq Computer? Nope. Is Ford stock basically identical to General Motors stock? Not at all.

The IRS simply doesn't want you to find and use some way of essentially buying the same stock. For example, Warren Buffett's company, Berkshire Hathaway, has two classes of stock: BRK.A and BRK.B. Are these substantially similar? Probably. Their voting rights and prices are very different, but, proportionately, they each have the same claim on the company's net assets and profits. They're both chunks of the same company.

Stock warrants and options to purchase or sell the underlying stock may also be considered substantially identical to that underlying stock.

To determine how long a short sale is kept open, don't include any period during which you hold, have an option to buy, or are under a contractual obligation to buy substantially identical stock or securities. In addition, don't include any period during which you are considered to have diminished your risk of loss from the short sale by reason of holding one or more other positions in substantially similar or related properties.

To deduct these expenses, treat them as investment interest expenses, subject to all of the rules and regulations involving investment interest expense. Report these expenses on Schedule A.

Example: You short 100 shares of the Free-Range Onion Company (ticker: BULBZ) on February 1, 1999, for $10 per share. On February 15, 1999, your broker notifies you that your account will be reduced by $50 for the dividend paid by Free-Range to its shareholders. On March 10, 1999, you close your short position by buying 100 shares of Free-Range at $8 per share. Since the short position was not open for at least 46 days, you cannot use the $50 dividend "in lieu payment" as a current expense. Rather, this $50 is added to the price of the stock that you purchased in order to close the position. In the example above, your net gain on your short position would be $150 (here's the math: $1,000 - ($800 + $50) = $150).

Let's use the same example with different dates. Suppose that you don't close the short position until May 15, 1999. In this case, the in lieu payment of $50 would be treated as "investment interest," deductible on Schedule A, and your "regular" gain on the closing of the short position would be $200.

Now, this might not make much difference during the year, but at year-end, it might make the difference between a current period deduction (affecting the tax return you're preparing this year) and an adjustment to your basis (which figures only when you cover and close your short position, perhaps a few years later).

IRS Publication 550 will provide you with additional information on short sales and dividends paid on them.

WASH SALES

Due to a recent market (insert event here… crash, blip, downturn, correction, buying opportunity, etc.), you might find yourself sitting on stocks that you really like from a fundamental standpoint, but that are now worth less than what you initially paid for them. What to do?

All of a sudden your brain crosses a red and black wire, and a flash appears. You say to yourself: "I'll just sell these shares, take the loss on my tax return, and then immediately buy those shares back. I'll then be able to keep the stock that I really like, and take a tax loss all at the same time. Sweet."

Our advice: Don't do it unless you know the rules. You might end up with a wash sale on your hands. You may say, "What? I'm not beating my shirts against a rock here—I'm just selling stock." True, but Uncle Sam doesn't see the beauty of your retaining an economic position in your stock while having bought yourself a tax deduction, with no risk to you in the future. Therefore, in order to close this glaring loophole, the Feds long ago called this transaction a "wash sale," and deemed that any loss on a wash sale could not be currently recognized.

Under the wash sale rules, if you sell stock for a loss and buy it back within the 30-day period after *or before* the loss sale date, the loss cannot be claimed for tax purposes. Note that the rule applies to a 30-day period before or after the sale date to prevent buying the stock back before it's even sold.

This might sound outrageously unfair to you. After all, if it was *your* money that you plunked into shares of the film editing company Splice Girls Inc. (ticker: SPLIC), and *your* dollars that were lost, how can it be that you're not allowed to claim the loss? Well hold on for a second. Don't call *60 Minutes* just yet. You *do* get to claim the loss—just not now. Although the loss can't be claimed on a wash sale, the disallowed amount is added to the cost of the repurchased stock. This being the case, the loss can be claimed when it is finally disposed of other than in a wash sale.

An example will help shed some light. Let's visit Jeff Fischer, who manages a circus act called the Amazing Typing Monkeys.

Jeff buys 500 shares of the new extreme sport chain, Ultimate Bowling Inc. (ticker: ALLYUP) for $10,000 and sells them on June 5 for $3,000. On June 30, he buys 500 shares of Ultimate Bowling again, this time for $3,200. Since the stock was bought back within 30 days of sale, the wash sale rules apply. Jeff can't claim his $7,000 loss. Instead, he must adjust his basis in the repurchased shares. His basis in the "new" 500 shares is $10,200: the actual cost of $3,200 plus the $7,000 disallowed loss. (Per share, the basis would be $20.40. Note that to simplify the example, we're not including the cost of commissions.)

Jeff would also be in violation of the wash sale rules if he had tried to be clever with a "double-up" strategy. This would happen, for example, if he bought 100 shares of Ultimate Bowling in February for $50 a share, bought another 100 shares in April when the stock dropped to $30 per share, and then turned around a few days later and sold 100 shares. He might think that he can specify that it was the *first* 100 shares that he was selling for a loss, ones he'd held for some two months, but that's not allowed. It's a wash sale. Remember—the rule is that you can't buy (back) shares within 30 days *before or after* the date of the loss sale. In this instance, Jeff bought the same stock within 30 days of selling it. While the normal chain of events is buy... sell... buy, Jeff flipped the order and doubled-up with a buy... buy... sell sequence.

How about if you repurchase fewer shares than you originally sold for a loss? Is all of the loss disallowed? Nope. Only that portion of the loss attributable to the "washed" shares will be subject to disallowance. In short: If only a portion of the stock sold is bought back, then only that portion of the loss is disallowed. Thus, in the first Jeff example, if he had only bought back 300 of the 500 shares (60%), he would be able to claim 40% of the loss on the sale ($2,800 under the facts above). The remaining $4,200 of loss disallowed under the wash sale rules would be added to Jeff's cost of the 300 shares, and Jeff's basis in the new shares would be $7,400.

As you can see, if you're doing a lot of trading in a specific stock (not very Foolish, by the way), the wash sale rules can really jump up and complicate your life. Buying and selling, different numbers of shares, different prices, gains and losses, basis adjustments, yada, yada, yada. Whew—that's way too much work for many people.

But, and this is a very big but, if you play your cards right, the wash sale rules can become moot! You simply need to close out your entire position in the stock prior to the end of the year, and then stay out of the stock for the required 30-day period before or after the date of the loss sale. Let's look at Jeff again. (Wow—that typing monkey on the left is doing 65 words per minute!)

Jeff certainly had a wash sale in the previous example—but it might be a moot one. Let's say that he tires of his position in Ultimate Bowling (it's just not catching on as he expected), and sells his 500 shares on December 20 for $4,000. His adjusted basis in the shares is $10,200 based upon his wash sale computations, so his overall loss would amount to $6,200. But if you break down the two separate buy and sell transactions, you see that Jeff generated a loss of $7,000 on the first transaction, and a gain of $800 on the second transaction—which amounts to a net loss of $6,200. So you see that the cost basis readjustment for the wash sale hasn't changed his net loss. Since Jeff closed out his entire position in the shares prior to the end of the year (and stayed out of the stock for the required period), the wash sale transactions actually become meaningless, and Jeff can compute his gains and losses as he normally would.

One final point: while the wash sale provisions work on shares that you sell for a loss, there are no corresponding provisions for stock that you sell at a gain and turn around and immediately repurchase. So while wash sale losses can't be claimed, gains can't be avoided. That is, if you sell stock for a gain and buy it right back, you must still report the gain—no special rule applies.

If you're eager to read more about the wash sale rules, check out IRS Publication 550. (Don't worry—it was typed by people, not monkeys.)

STOCK SPLITS

In "tax speak," stock splits are called stock dividends. As a general rule, when a corporation distributes its own stock (or a right to acquire its stock) to its shareholders, the shareholders are not required to include the fair market value of the stock (or stock right) in their gross income. For most stock splits, this is the case. There are a few exceptions, though.

The following five categories of stock "dividends" are taxable to the shareholders:

- Distributions in which a shareholder has the option to receive cash or other property instead of stock or stock rights.

- Disproportionate distributions—in which some shareholders receive cash or other property and other shareholders receive stock or stock rights.

- Distributions of common stock to some common stock shareholders and preferred stock to other common stock shareholders.

- Certain distributions on preferred stock.

- Distributions of convertible preferred stock that result in a disproportionate distribution.

It's unlikely that you'll run across these types of transactions in your investing life. Just understand that they *are* out there and that not *all* stock dividends are tax-free. If you find yourself with a taxable stock dividend that falls into one of these special categories and you need additional assistance with the tax issues surrounding the taxable distribution, please ask your question in our tax area online.

All that being said, the vast majority of stock dividend transactions you encounter will be of the tax-free variety. So let's take a closer look at how they work from a tax standpoint.

A distribution of stock that does not fall within any of the exceptions discussed above is *not* included in your gross income. In general, your adjusted basis in the stock is determined by spreading the old cost basis amount evenly over both the old and new shares. The holding period of the "new" stock received in a nontaxable distribution includes the period during which the old stock was held.

A Simple Example

On February 10, 1997, you bought 100 shares of XYZ Corp. for $30 per share. Your cost basis is $30 x 100 shares, or $3,000, plus any broker commission paid.

On January 5, 1999, the Board of Directors of XYZ Corp. voted to issue a stock dividend to the shareholders. The board authorized a stock dividend in the amount of one "new" share for each "old" share held. In your case, you will receive 100 "new" shares. This type of transaction is commonly know as a "two-for-one" stock split, and you soon have 200 shares of XYZ Corp.

You decide that you now want to sell 50 shares of this stock. (Let's say it's trading around $25 per share.) But, you scratch your head and wonder. Which shares are you selling—the "old" shares or the "new" shares? And what is your cost basis in those shares for tax purposes? Would it be zero, since you paid nothing for your "new" stock? How do you figure the gain?

While this seems like a complicated matter, it really isn't. Remember that your adjusted cost basis in the stock is determined by spreading the old cost basis amount evenly over both the old and new shares. Let's return to our example.

We computed your total basis in the "old" shares as $3,000 (100 shares at $30 per share). Let's also say that you paid a $20 broker commission. This would make your tax basis in the old shares $3,020. Now that you have 200 shares, you are required to spread the cost basis over *all* of your shares. This means that your new "per-share" cost basis would be $3,020 divided by 200, or $15.10 per share. This basis is for each and every share that you own. That's it! (See how easy it was?)

Note that spreading the basis over all of the shares is *not* an election or an option. It is something that *must* be done. You can't simply decide to treat the new shares as having a zero-dollar basis and the old shares as having *all* of the basis. It just doesn't work like that.

Remember also that your holding period for the new shares includes the period for which the old shares were held. This simply means that the holding period for *all* of your shares would begin February 10, 1997. With this knowledge, let's complete the example.

Let's say you sold 50 of your shares at a price of $25 per share on March 5, 1999. As noted earlier, your "per-share" cost basis in these shares would be $15.10. So your total basis would be 50 times $15.10, or $755.

You sell the shares for $25 each, and pay a $20 broker commission, for net proceeds of $1,230 (50 times $25 is $1,250, less the commission). Simple subtraction ($1,230 - $755) tells you that your gain on the sale of these 50 shares is $475.

Your holding period for these shares is from February 10, 1997, to March 5, 1999, which means that you receive long-term capital gains tax treatment for these shares—and the preferred tax rate that goes along with it.

Pretty easy, eh? But, what if you had "odd lot" shares and your "split" didn't turn out even—and you were forced to sell fractional shares? How does that all work? The theory is the same, but the math is a bit more complicated.

Splits With Fractional Shares

Stock splits don't always happen in easy-to-deal-with round numbers. Splits often produce fractional shares that are automatically sold by the company.

Example #1: Warren Gump, a bowling pin refinisher, owns 55 shares of stock in the Sisyphus Transport Co. (ticker: UPDWN). He bought these shares in May 1997 for $125 per share. He also paid $20 in commission for the purchase, making his total cost basis in these shares $6,895 (55 shares times $125 per share equals $6,875, plus $20).

In January 1999, the Board of Directors of Sisyphus Transport declared a stock dividend. Each shareholder would receive three new shares of Sisyphus Transport stock for every two shares currently owned.

What does this mean for shareholders like Warren who have an odd number of shares? The math works like this: Take the 55 shares and divide by two, since the number of shares he'll get is based on how many sets of two shares he already has. That gives you 27.5. Multiply this result by three (the number of shares he will receive for every two shares he owns), yielding a new result of 82.5 shares. This amount represents the number of new shares that he'll receive. Add his new shares to his old shares and you'll see that he will have a grand total of 137.5 shares.

To arrive at Warren's new "per-share" cost basis, we simply take his original cost basis and divide it by the total number of shares he now has (both new and old). But wait—we have a fractional share (one-half share, in this case). This will complicate matters somewhat.

Remember that companies will not issue fractions of shares. (Dividend reinvestment plans and direct investment plans are the exceptions to this rule.) Instead, a company will *purchase* that fractional share from the shareholder at the fair value of the stock on the date the new shares are issued.

If you ended up with a fractional share after a split, you can expect the company to purchase it and to send you IRS Form 1099B at the end of the year, which will report the sale to the IRS and to you. Remember, this is a real, live sale that must be reported on Schedule D on your tax return. So be prepared to adjust your cost basis for the stock dividend, to compute your basis for this fractional share, and to report the sale on Schedule D at tax time.

Let's see how the computations work.

Using the same facts as in the earlier example, let's now assume that the Sisyphus Transport Co. issued Warren an additional 82 whole shares, sold off his fractional share at a fair market value of $80 per share, and sent him a check for $40 (proceeds from selling the half share).

TAX TIP

Don't Ignore Sales of Fractional Shares

If you receive a Form 1099B after a company purchases a fractional share from you following a stock split, don't ignore it. It's not likely to involve too many dollars, but the IRS still expects you to report that income on Schedule D.

Furthermore, you'll need to adjust the cost basis of the remaining shares by the amount of the sale proceeds. If your total cost basis was $2,000 and the cost basis of the fractional sale amounted to $35, your new cost basis will be $1,965. Divide that result by the number of remaining shares to get the per-share basis.

Many people believe that they can ignore their basis allocation computations, reporting the fractional share sale as a dividend on Schedule B. Other taxpayers simply report the sale of the fractional shares on Schedule D, but with no basis allocated to the shares. In either case, you'll be paying more taxes on this sale than you're legally required to. And, if you ignore the basis computations when dealing with these fractional shares, it will only make your calculations that much more difficult when you finally *do* undertake the basis computations.

He now has the "sale" end of the transaction accounted for, but what is his cost basis in this half share? The theory is the same as we discussed earlier—simply spread the entire original cost basis over all of the shares. And that means all of them... even the fractional shares. Since Warren's original cost basis was $6,895, and after the split he had a total of 137.5 shares, his new cost basis per share is $50.15 (total cost basis of $6,895 divided by 137.5 shares).

Simple division shows Warren that his half share's cost basis is $25.08. When he receives his check from Sisyphus Transport for $40, representing the sale of the fractional share, his cost basis for that half share would be $25.08 and his gain on the sale would be $14.92 ($40 minus $25.08). This information is required to be reported on Schedule D. Also, remember that the holding period for this share reaches all the way back to his original purchase date—May 1997, in this example—which qualifies it as a long-term capital gain on this fractional share sale.

This may seem like a lot of work for such little consequence, but this is what is required by the Internal Revenue Code. Many people will recommend simply reporting the fractional share sale on Schedule D with a cost basis of zero—in other words, claiming the entire sale proceeds ($40 in this case) as your gain—and then calculating your new per-share cost basis using just the number of full shares you have. While this is not the technically correct (or legal or recommended) procedure, it is done often.

Regardless of how you handle the fractional share sale, you must still allocate your basis correctly over both the old and new shares.

Adjusting Your Cost Basis After the Sale of a Fractional Share

Let's double-check our math and see where Warren stands with his remaining shares. He now has a total of 137 shares. The cost basis for those shares is $6,869.92. We get that amount by taking the original cost basis of $6,895 and subtracting the cost basis for the fractional share that was sold ($25.08). Just like before, we calculate the per-share cost by dividing his total cost basis (now $6,869.92) by his total number of shares (137), arriving at a per-share basis of $50.15. Since this is exactly the same amount we arrived at when we completed the first computation (which is exactly the way it should be), it confirms that the math was done correctly.

That's how you deal with fractional shares in a stock split. As you can imagine, the numbers can get a little more complicated, but the theory and process will still remain the same. You spread your basis over all of your shares. The holding period is the same for the new shares as the old ones. If you remember these things and are careful with your computations, you should never go wrong when computing the cost basis on fractional shares sold.

A last note: Fractional shares sold because of a stock split are not exactly the same as fractional shares sold when a company goes through some type of reorganization, stock swap, stock split-up, or stock buyout. Those rules are completely different, and are completely separate and apart from the rules noted above.

STOCK SPIN-OFFS, SPLIT-UPS, AND BUYOUTS

There will probably be many times in your investing life when a company you own a chunk of spins off part of itself, splits itself up, or is involved in a buyout (either acquiring or being acquired for cash, stock, or a combination of the two). When this happens, you're likely to begin scratching your head and wondering how to figure out your cost basis, now that things have changed.

What you need to do is follow the directions. Only in this case, the directions will be coming not from an IRS publication (or a Fool book), but from the company itself. When these events happen, many shareholders are affected and the companies involved offer formulas for the required calculations. The horse's mouth is the *only* place that you'll find those directions.

When these transactions take place, the companies' legal and accounting folks get together and create a formula that you must follow in order to recalculate your basis in the old and new shares. These computations can be fairly easy or quite complex.

You'll typically receive the announcement of the formula in a notice from your broker. (You can also usually look up the information on the company's website.) If you're like many people, you'll open it, glance at it, recoil at what seems like a bunch of legal jargon, and then toss it out. You figure that you already know about the spin-off or buyout, and you don't really want to read any more about it. This would be a mistake, though.

Face the Formula Immediately

Wade through the paperwork and you'll find the formula. Don't assume that it's not very important to you now since you're not planning to sell the stock just yet. Dealing with it now will allow you to track the performance of your new shares and, when you're thinking of selling, it will help you determine your potential gain or loss. Dealing with it now will also mean that there will be one less thing to deal with at tax time after you do sell the shares. (Because at that time, you *must* correctly account for your cost basis in figuring your gain or loss.) The last thing you'll want to do when you're fighting the April 15 deadline is to try and find the appro-

A Real-Life Example: AT&T Spins Off Lucent Technologies

Here's the formula that AT&T shareholders received upon the company's spin-off of Lucent Technologies. For every share of AT&T you owned, you'd receive 0.324084 shares of Lucent.

If you owned 200 shares of AT&T, you'd end up with 200 shares of AT&T *plus* 64.8168 shares of Lucent (200 times 0.324084 equals 64.8168). Note that you'll really end up with just 64 shares of Lucent, as companies usually pay out cash for fractional shares. (See the previous section on stock splits.)

Now let's see what your new cost basis will be. Note that as a shareholder you'd also have been informed that 72.01% of your original investment (your total initial cost basis) is now attributable to AT&T. The remaining 27.99% should be attributed to your Lucent shares. Let's see how this applies to your 200 shares of AT&T and your 64.8168 shares of Lucent.

If you bought your AT&T shares at $25 each, you paid a total of $5,000. Let's tack on a $20 commission, to make it even more realistic. Your initial cost basis is $5,020. To find the new cost basis for your AT&T shares, multiply the original cost ($5,020) times 0.7201. This gives you a new cost basis for those 200 shares of $3,614.90. The new cost per share, then, is $18.07.

The remaining $1,405.10 (your original investment of $5,020 less the new AT&T cost basis of $3,614.90) is the cost basis for your 64.8168 new shares of Lucent. Divide $1,405.10 by 64.8168 and you'll get a cost basis per share of $21.68.

Remember that you will be paid in cash for your 0.8168 of a share of Lucent. Let's see how this works. You know that your cost basis per *whole* share is $21.68. Multiply that by 0.8168 and you'll get a cost basis for your fractional share of $17.71. The only step left is to see how much you get in payment for the fractional share. Compare that amount with your cost basis to determine your gain or loss, and then make sure to account for it in your tax return. Also, subtract the cost basis for the 0.8168 share from the 64.8168 shares to get the basis for your remaining 64 shares ($1,405.10 less $17.71 equals $1,387.39).

priate formula, apply it to your basis, and determine your taxable gain or loss. In some cases, what you thought was a large gain may be only a marginal gain. This could really screw up your tax planning. So the very *best* time to obtain the formula and allocate your basis is as soon as possible after the stock transaction has taken place.

In many cases, the formula will produce fractional shares that the company will purchase from you. Understand that this is a real, live stock sale, which must be reported on Schedule D in the year that the fractional shares are sold. And, again, the only way to compute your basis and your taxable gain or loss on those fractional shares is to correctly refigure your basis from the formula provided by the company.

So what do you do if you find April 15 looming, and you've not yet computed your basis on a spin-off, split-up, or buyout transaction that may have taken place a few months (or years) ago? You get the formula from the company—or from another resource, such as the company website, the company's investor relations department, or your broker. The Motley Fool message boards are a great place to discuss these computations and to obtain formulas. On the PepsiCo message board, for example, you can compare computation results with fellow shareholders regarding the spin-off of Tricon Global restaurants.

What you can't do is find the exact formula in some IRS publication, tax form, or tax guide. It just won't exist there. There's only one specific, unique formula that applies to *your* stock transaction. Get it. Grab your calculator, a pencil, a few sheets of paper, and perhaps a cup of coffee. Then do your computations and get your new tax basis. You'll be glad you did.

HEDGING AND THE CONSTRUCTIVE SALE RULES

The Taxpayer Relief Act of 1997 added a few twists into the law regarding "hedging" your stock positions. If you're a Foolish investor through and through, who simply holds stock for the long term without a thought to hedging or things like options or "shorting against the box," then we've got some good news for you. You can skip this section! (And believe us, that's worth celebrating, as this is a very complicated issue.)

If you *are* an investor prone to hedging, then you should definitely read this section, as well as the additional reading we recommend.

First off, it's helpful to review the background that caused the new law to be written. So let's see what all the hubbub is about.

History

In general, a gain or loss is taken into account for tax purposes when it's realized. With capital assets (such as stocks), this generally happens at the time the asset is sold, exchanged, or otherwise disposed of. You compute your gain or loss by comparing your net sales price on the sale with the cost (or basis) of the asset sold. Pretty simple stuff, eh?

Prior to the Taxpayer Relief Act of 1997, investors could engage in some transactions designed to reduce or eliminate risk of loss on stock or financial assets—and these transactions generally did not cause income realization. For example, you could lock in a gain on a security by "shorting against the box" (when you own securities that are the same as, or substantially similar to, securities borrowed and sold short). You could also make use of "straddles." Let's discuss these strategies now.

Shorting Against the Box

Example #1: Keith Pelczarski, a certified shoe fitter, owns 1,000 shares of Lord-of-the-Trance Hypnotics (ticker: GLAZE), with a cost basis of $20 per share. The shares are now trading for $90 a stub. Keith would like to lock in his gains on this stock, but doesn't really want to sell the shares and face a large tax liability. So instead of selling, Keith "shorts" 1,000 shares. Since Keith has not sold the original stock, there are no taxes to pay since the gain is not "recognized." He has taken virtually all of his cash out of the stock (via the short sale), but is now protected against any future losses on the shares.

This is a difficult concept to grasp—so don't fret if you're having trouble wrapping your brain around it. Thinking of it this way might help: Keith has now placed bets that the stock will both rise in value *and* fall in value. (And these offset each other.) If the stock goes up, his "long" position increases, but his "short" position decreases. If the stock goes down, his "short" position increases, but his "long" position decreases. So he has, in effect, locked in his gain and received his cash without selling any of the shares or creating a taxable transaction.

Of course, Keith will have his day of reckoning sometime in the future, but he may be able to manipulate his finances in such a way that the future gain will have a smaller tax impact (such as being used to offset a substantial capital loss in the future). This is an example of a "short sale against the box."

Shorting against the box in this manner was, in the recent past, allowed for income tax purposes, and gain on the substantially identical property was not recognized at the time of the short sale. According to rules that allowed investors to identify which specific shares of a stock were sold, Keith could identify the borrowed (shorted) shares as the ones he sold, thereby keeping his original (long) position in the stock intact and open. Since it was still technically open, he had technically realized no gain.

When he chose to close out his short position and buy back shares to replace the borrowed ones, he could choose to deliver either his original shares (the ones he held before he shorted) or his newly purchased shares (the ones he bought to replace the borrowed ones). The tax code's rules only prevented him from using short sales against the box to accelerate a loss or to convert a short-term capital gain into a long-term capital gain or a long-term capital loss into a short-term capital loss.

Straddling

Another method that in the past allowed investors to lock in a gain on a financial position without actually selling the position was straddling. This strategy offered you another way to lock in a gain on certain property by entering into offsetting positions in the same or similar property.

Under the straddle rules, when you realize a loss on one offsetting position in actively traded personal property, you generally can deduct this loss only to the extent that the loss exceeds the unrecognized gain in the other positions in the straddle. In addition, rules similar to the short sale rules prevent you from changing the tax character of gains and losses recognized on the offsetting positions in a straddle. (Read more on this in IRS Publication 550.)

But all of this changed recently. According to the changes made by the Taxpayer Relief Act of 1997, you must now recognize gain (but not loss) upon a "constructive sale" of any appreciated financial position in stock, a partnership interest, or certain debt instruments. A constructive sale occurs when you:

- Enter into a short sale of the same or substantially identical property.

- Enter into an offsetting notional principal contract relating to the same or substantially identical property.

- Enter into a futures or forward contract to deliver the same or substantially identical property (including a forward contract that provides for cash settlement).

- Acquire the same or substantially identical property (if the appreciated financial position is a short sale, an offsetting notional principal contract, or a futures or forward contract).

If you have such a constructive sale, you must recognize gain (but *not* loss) as if your holdings in question were disposed of at their fair market value on the date of the constructive sale. This gives you a new holding period for the new position that begins on the date of the constructive sale. Then, when you close the new transaction, you reduce your gain (or increase your loss) by the gain recognized on the constructive sale.

But what exactly is an "appreciated financial position"? It's really pretty simple. It's any interest you have in stock, a partnership, or a debt instrument (including a futures or forward contract, a short sale, or an option) that, if you sold or otherwise disposed of, would result in a gain.

TAX TIP

The New Constructive Sale Rules in a Nutshell

The new rules apply to those who are interested in temporarily protecting gains by using various traditional "hedging" strategies. Think of it this way. Instead of having just two events in the history of the position—when you bought and when you sold the security—the hedging techniques inserted two more events, such as the opening and closing of a short sale position in the same security. Whereas before, the position's history involved just points A and B, it would now include A, B, X, and Y (in this order: A, X, Y, and B).

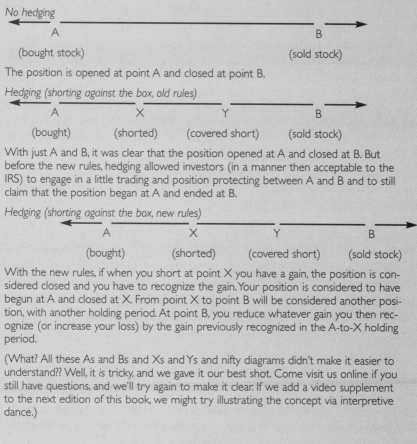

No hedging

    A   B
(bought stock)   (sold stock)

The position is opened at point A and closed at point B.

Hedging (shorting against the box, old rules)

    A   X   Y   B
(bought)   (shorted) (covered short) (sold stock)

With just A and B, it was clear that the position opened at A and closed at B. But before the new rules, hedging allowed investors (in a manner then acceptable to the IRS) to engage in a little trading and position protecting between A and B and to still claim that the position began at A and ended at B.

Hedging (shorting against the box, new rules)

    A   X   Y   B
(bought)   (shorted) (covered short) (sold stock)

With the new rules, if when you short at point X you have a gain, the position is considered closed and you have to recognize the gain. Your position is considered to have begun at A and closed at X. From point X to point B will be considered another position, with another holding period. At point B, you reduce whatever gain you then recognize (or increase your loss) by the gain previously recognized in the A-to-X holding period.

(What? All these As and Bs and Xs and Ys and nifty diagrams didn't make it easier to understand?? Well, it *is* tricky, and we gave it our best shot. Come visit us online if you still have questions, and we'll try again to make it clear. If we add a video supplement to the next edition of this book, we might try illustrating the concept via interpretive dance.)

Related Interlopers Beware

You're also treated as having made a constructive sale of an appreciated financial position if a person related to you enters into a transaction described above with a view toward avoiding the constructive sale treatment. For this purpose, a related person is:

- A member of your family. This includes your brothers and sisters, half-brothers and half-sisters, spouse, ancestors (parents, grandparents, etc.), and lineal descendants (children, grandchildren, etc.).

- A partnership in which you directly or indirectly own more than 50% of the capital interest or the profits interest.

- A corporation in which you directly or indirectly own more than 50% in value of the outstanding stock.

There are other parties who are also considered "related," so this list is not inclusive at all. It just includes the most common related persons. (For more detail on related party transactions, check out IRS Publication 550.) Let's move on to an example of how the constructive sale rules actually work.

Some Examples

Example #1: On May 1, 1999, you bought 100 shares of Legal Beagles Inc. (ticker: WOOFF), a new company providing legal advice for house pets. The total cost for the stock was $1,000. On September 3, 1999, you sold short 100 shares of Legal Beagles for $1,600 (the classic "short against the box"). You engaged in no other transactions involving this stock for the rest of 1999 and the first 30 days of 2000 (we'll discuss the importance of the timing a bit later).

Your short sale is treated as a constructive sale of an appreciated financial position because a sale of your Legal Beagles stock on the date of the short sale would have resulted in a gain. Therefore, in 1999, you're required to recognize $600 in short-term capital gains from the constructive sale. In addition, you're required to begin a new holding period in your Legal Beagles stock that starts on September 3, 1999, and your cost basis in these shares would be increased to $1,600.

Example #2: On January 10, 1999, you "short" 200 shares of Dodgeball Supply Co. (ticker: WHAPP) stock for $5,000. On August 15, 1999, you "go long" 200 shares similar Dodgeball Supply stock for $3,500. You made no other transactions in Dodgeball Supply stock for the rest of 1999 and the first 30 days of 2000. Your "long" position will now be treated as a constructive sale, and you will be required to recognize a short-term gain in the amount of $1,500 for 1999. The new basis for your short position will be $3,500.

The importance of Example #2 is to show you that the rules work either way. An appreciated financial position could be a "long" position *or* a "short" position.

"Jeepers," you may be thinking to yourself. You may have gotten yourself into a constructive sale position without even knowing it. And now you may have to recognize a gain that you were never intending to recognize. Are you completely sunk? Not necessarily.

The Exceptions

You are *not* required to treat a transaction as a constructive sale if all of the following are true:

- You closed the transaction before the end of the 30th day after the end of your tax year (generally January 30 for most people); and

- You held the appreciated financial position throughout the 60-day period beginning on the date you closed the transaction; and

- Your risk of loss was not reduced at any time during that 60-day period by holding certain other positions.

In other words, you're *required* to ignore the constructive sale rules if you close the offsetting position prior to January 30 of the following tax year, and if you retain your original position for at least 60 days after closing the offsetting position. In addition, you're prohibited from entering into any other type of offsetting position for that same 60-day period. If you re-read examples 1 and 2 above, you'll see the statement "you made no other transactions in the stock for the rest of 1999 and the first 30 days of 2000," and you should now see the importance of this statement. With a little planning, you can overcome the constructive sale rules.

Some More Examples

Example #1: On May 1, 1999, Kurt Foster bought 100 shares of McDonald Farm, Inc. (ticker: EIEIO) stock for $1,000. On September 3, 1999, he sold short 100 shares of McDonald stock for $1,600. He held both of these positions until January 10, 2000. On that date, he closed his offsetting short position for $1,800 and kept his "long" position open until at least March 11 (at least 60 days). During that time, he did not enter into any other offsetting positions that would have reduced his risk of loss on his original position. Since Kurt has met all of the exceptions to the constructive sale rules, he has *no* constructive sale for 1999. When he closes his short position on January 10, he'll recognize a short-term capital loss in 2000 of $200. His basis in his long position will remain at $1,000, but his holding period will move to January 10, 2000.

Example #2: Imagine now Joe Zitz, whose transactions differ slightly. On May 1, 1999, Joe bought 100 shares of McDonald Farm for $1,000. On September 3, 1999, he sold short 100 shares of similar McDonald stock for $1,600. He held both of these positions until January 10, 2000. On that date, he closed his offsetting short position for $1,800. But because of the fluctuations in the stock, he sold his long position on March 1 (well before his required holding date of March 11) for $1,500. He has now violated the exceptions to the constructive sale rules, and he must now recognize the constructive sale of the original position back in 1999 (when the constructive sale actually took place), and *not* in 2000, when he actually sold the stock.

In 1999 Joe will recognize a short-term gain of $600 because of the constructive sale, and his basis in the stock will be $1,600. When he actually sells his original position on March 11 for $1,500, he'll recognize a $100 short-term loss (since his basis in the original shares was $1,600 and he

TAX TIP

Avoiding the Rules

In order to avoid the constructive sale rules, make sure that you:

• Close the "short" end of the transaction on or before January 30 of the following year. You can certainly close the position any time *before* this date and comply with the exceptions. But remember that the January 30 date is your drop-dead deadline. If the position is not closed by that time, you have realized a constructive sale.

• Whatever date that you close the "short" end of the transaction, you must hold the "long" end of the deal for at least 60 days beginning on the date that you actually closed the original short position. If you wait until the last minute (January 30), you need to hold your long position open until at least March 31 for normal years and March 30 for leap years. Whenever you close your short position, make sure to keep your long position open for a period of 60 days.

• During that same 60-day period, make sure that you don't enter into another short position and/or any other hedging position in respect to the same or similar stock. If you do, you'll be in violation of the constructive sale rules, and you'll have a constructive sale on your hands.

ASK ROY

Digging Deeper

Q:

How do the new constructive sales rules affect strategies like collars, straddles, etc.?

A:

I'm personally waiting for the regulations from IRS on these very issues, which should provide specific examples for various financial transactions. But as of this writing, those regulations are still not published. Nevertheless, we'll briefly address some of these strategies as well as we can in the sections that follow.

Your best source of additional information would be the *General Explanation of Tax Legislation* (commonly referred to as the "Blue Book"), prepared by congressional staff. If you're really interested in this subject, read the entire text at http://www.house .gov/ways_means/publica.htm. (Look for "1997 Joint Committee on Taxation Blue Book—General Explanation of Tax Legislation Enacted in 1997, JCS-23-97, December 17, 1997.") It's not a quick read, but you should be able to find the appropriate section (Part II, Title X, under the heading "Revenue Increase Provisions").

made the sale for $1,500). In addition, he'll also be required to recognize a short-term loss of $200 in 2000 on the short position that he closed in that year.

Here's one very important thing you should remember: Once you meet the constructive sale rules exceptions, you are then allowed (should you desire) to enter into *another* offsetting position. But you'll have to be sure that you meet the exceptions for the *new* offsetting position.

Let's go back to Kurt in example #1. Since he met the exception for 1999, at anytime after March 11, 2000, he can again "short against the box" on his long position. But in order to avoid constructive sale recognition for 2000, all of the usual requirements must be met. And he must make sure that he waits until after the 60-day "waiting period" has passed before entering into another offsetting position. Exception #3 requires the waiting period.

We've still got a little ground to cover. While we've focused mainly on the "shorting against the box" strategy so far, there are other ways that a "long" position can be hedged. And the constructive sale rules affect some of these, depending on the situation.

One-Sided Hedging

Remember that the constructive sale rules were implemented to affect transactions that eliminated substantially all of your risk of loss *and opportunity for income and gain* with respect to the appreciated financial position. That's the standard and it's very clear. Applying this reasoning, Congress intended that transactions that reduce *only* risk of loss or *only* opportunity for gain would *not* be covered under the constructive sale rules.

Example: You hold an appreciated financial position in stock. You then buy a "put" option with an exercise price equal to the current market price (an "at the money" option). Because such an option reduces *only* your risk of loss, and *not* your opportunity for gain, the above standard would not be met, and this would *not* be considered a constructive sale.

When you hedge only one end of a transaction, the constructive sale rules don't apply.

Collars

Another financial position that may be affected is what is commonly called a "collar." In a collar, you commit to an option that requires you to sell a financial position at a fixed price (the "call strike price") and you have the right to have your position purchased at a lower fixed price (the "put strike price").

Example: Sumner owns stock in the Titanic Iceberg Lettuce Co. (ticker:

ASK ROY

Calls and Puts

What are calls and puts?

They're the two main types of options. (We're not talking about employee stock options here—that's another beast.) Buying a call option gives you the right to buy a set amount of shares at a set price within a certain period of time. For this right, you pay a price premium. It's the same with puts, except with them, you buy the right to sell shares.

Let's look at an example. If Downsizers Diet Centers Inc. (ticker: SLIMM) is selling for $50 per share and you expect it to rise, you could buy October $55 calls on it. If, just before your option expires in October, Downsizers is selling for $75 per share, you can exercise your option and buy shares for $55. Then you can keep them or sell them for $75.

If you sell, you make $20, right? Not exactly. That option wasn't free. Let's say the premium you paid was $6 per share. That means your profit is down to $14.

We're not big fans of options, though, as with them, you're generally just buying time, not ownership in a business. Most options expire unexercised.

BRRRR). He then enters into a collar for the stock (currently trading at $100) with a put strike price of $95 and a call strike price of $110. The effect of the transaction is that he has transferred the rights to all gain above the $110 call strike price and all loss below the $95 put strike price. But—he has retained all risk of loss and opportunity for gain in the price range between $95 and $110. A collar can be a single contract or a combination of put and call options. So while Sumner's gain *and* loss is eliminated above $110 and below $95, his gain *or* loss is alive and well between those two prices.

So is this an example of a constructive sale? Based upon what we know so far, it's difficult to say whether a collar will be treated as a constructive sale. The IRS regulations will provide specific standards that take into account various factors with respect to appreciated financial positions, including their volatility. You can certainly expect that the regulations will review several aspects of the collar transaction, such as the spread between the put and call prices, the period of the transaction, and the extent to which the taxpayer retains the right to periodic payments on the appreciated financial position (such as the dividends on collared stock). So is *your* collar (which may be substantially different than mine) a constructive sale? That's up to you, your God, and the IRS (and likely your tax pro)—and your collective interpretation of the IRS code.

"In-the-Money" Options

Another common transaction for which regulations would be helpful is a so-called "in-the-money" option. That would be a put option where the strike price is significantly above the current market price or a call option where the strike price is significantly below the current market price.

Example: Ethan Kiczek owns stock in Global Telepathic Messaging (ticker: ESPME). He then purchases a put option with a strike price of $120 for it. (It's currently trading at $100 per share.) He's eliminated all risk of loss on the position for the option period. He may have also effectively transferred substantially all of the potential gain on the stock—because only if its value rises above $120 can there be any gain to him.

Is this a constructive sale? We'll have to wait for the regulations. They will probably provide a specific standard that takes into account many of the factors described above with respect to collars, including the yield and volatility of the stock and the time period and other terms of the option.

Other Transactions

For collars, options, and some other transactions, one approach that the IRS might take in issuing regulations is to rely on option prices and option pricing models. The price of an option represents the payment the market requires to eliminate risk of loss (for a put option) or to purchase the right to receive yield and gain (for a call option). Thus, option pricing offers one way that the IRS and investors can quantify both the total risk of loss and opportunity for gain with respect to an appreciated financial position, as well as the proportions of these total amounts that the taxpayer has retained.

In addition to setting specific standards for treatment of these and other transactions, it may be appropriate for Treasury regulations to establish "safe harbor" rules for common financial transactions that do not result in constructive sale treatment. An example might be a collar with a sufficient spread between the put and call prices, a sufficiently limited period, and other relevant terms such that, regardless of the particular characteristics of the stock, the collar probably would not transfer substantially all risk of loss and opportunity for gain. But only time will tell what the Treasury will place in the regulations. Again, that is why these regulations (and the guidance they'll provide) are desperately needed.

The good news: It appears that whatever regulations are written, they will be prospective and *not* retroactive. So if you (or your tax pro) determines that one of your transactions is not a constructive sale, but the regulations (when finally issued) say that it is, you may very well be off the hook. It may not require a restatement of your transaction, or an amended return (if the transaction took place in a prior year). We would anticipate that the only regulations that would be applied retroactively would be those necessary to prevent abuse.

In Summary

The entire constructive sale issue is very complicated. If you are non-Foolish, and use a bunch of financial transactions in order to hedge your various stock positions, you'd better become very well-versed in the constructive sale rules. They'll be complicating your life. And while you're waiting for the regulations, you'd better at least read IRS Publication 550 and the section in it on the constructive sale rules.

But for Fools—simple buy and hold investors who don't try to guess or time the market and hedge transactions—these compli-

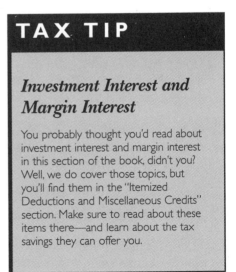

TAX TIP

Investment Interest and Margin Interest

You probably thought you'd read about investment interest and margin interest in this section of the book, didn't you? Well, we do cover those topics, but you'll find them in the "Itemized Deductions and Miscellaneous Credits" section. Make sure to read about these items there—and learn about the tax savings they can offer you.

cated tax issues have no meaning whatsoever. They simply won't apply to you... and you can ignore them. That should give you much more time to spend with your family and friends—rather than with brokerage statements and tax codes and regulations. And isn't that what Foolishness is really all about?

THE ALTERNATIVE MINIMUM TAX

Fools flush with funds have an extra tax twist to worry about. If your income, adjusted in a certain way, exceeds a certain amount, you might have to pay a little more in tax than you expected. We're talking about the Alternative Minimum Tax, or the AMT.

The AMT was designed to increase the tax bill of taxpayers who too often take advantage of certain types of deductions and other tax benefits known as "preferences." It starts with your regular taxable income and, in general, makes you give back certain deductions and benefits until you arrive at "alternative minimum taxable income" (AMTI). Then, after subtracting an exemption amount, a tax rate of 26% applies to the first $175,000 of this income and 28% applies to amounts above $175,000. (For married taxpayers who file separately, the rate changes at $87,500.)

If your tax liability under the AMT system is higher than your regular tax liability, you must pay the higher amount. (Not much of an alternative, eh?) If the AMT liability is less than your regular tax liability, then the AMT has no tax impact on you and you simply pay your regular tax liability. You compute the AMT on Form 6251, which you attach to your Form 1040.

The AMT is a very complicated tax—much too complicated to deal with here in any great detail. But here are some of the more common adjustments or preferences required to arrive at AMT taxable income:

• Tax-exempt interest. Tax-exempt interest from certain private activity bonds isn't exempt for AMT purposes. Thus, although you exclude this interest from your regular taxable income, you must include it for AMTI.

• Interest deduction. For AMT purposes, you can only deduct mortgage or home equity loan interest on funds you borrowed to buy, build, or substantially improve your home or a second residence (or on the refinancing of that debt). So if you claimed a regular tax deduction for interest on a home equity loan that you didn't devote to the home, you would have to add it back when determining AMTI. Also, an adjustment may have to be made to your investment interest deduction, in some cases, for AMT purposes.

• State and local tax deduction. For AMT purposes, you get no deduction for state and local income taxes or real estate or other property taxes.

• Medical expenses. For regular tax purposes, medical expenses are deductible to the extent they exceed 7.5% of adjusted gross income. For AMT purposes, however, they are only deductible to the extent they exceed 10% of AGI. Thus, you would compute your reduced deduction amount and add the difference back to your taxable income in determining AMTI. (For example, if your "regular" medical deduction was $8,000 and your AMT medical deduction is $6,000, you would add back $2,000 to taxable income.)

• Miscellaneous itemized deductions. If you are entitled to a regular tax deduction for any miscellaneous itemized expenses (these are deductions that are limited, even for regular tax purposes, to the excess over 2% of your AGI), you would not get any deduction for them for AMT purposes, regardless of what they comprise.

• Personal and dependency exemptions. These aren't allowed. You must add them back to your regular taxable income in determining AMTI.

• Depreciation deductions. For certain depreciable property, you are placed on slower depreciation schedules for AMT purposes. Therefore, some adjustments may have to be made in your depreciation deductions and gain or loss on the sale of this property.

• Stock options. The favorable tax treatment allowed for incentive stock options isn't allowed for AMT purposes.

If any of these adjustments or preferences apply to you, it could be that you are subject to the AMT. If that's the case, read IRS Publication... umm... ahh... oh boy. It looks like the IRS doesn't understand the AMT either. There is no current IRS Publication that specifically addresses the AMT. The best that you can do is to review IRS Form 6251 and the related instructions. Hop to it, Fool!

STOCK OPTIONS

Employee Stock Options

Employee stock option plans generally fall into one of two categories: Incentive Stock Options (ISOs) or Nonqualified Stock Options (NQs).

ISOs are not necessarily open to everybody in the company. They are generally reserved only for executives and other key employees, although in recent years, many companies are issuing them to broader groups of workers. NQs can be granted to both employees and non-employees alike (such as vendors and/or customers), and they're granted on a discretionary basis. When held to maturity, ISOs are generally more favorable, tax-wise. If you participate in an option plan with your company, it's important that you know exactly which type of plan that you have. Why? Because the tax issues are completely separate for each type of option.

In a nutshell, with ISOs you typically do not recognize any taxable income until you sell the stock that you acquired when you exercised your option. (Although the act of exercising the option does result in income that must be counted when figuring out if you qualify for the Alternative Minimum Tax—and how much of it you'll pay.)

What are the holding period requirements for ISOs? Well, an employee who has acquired stock through the exercise of an ISO cannot dispose of the stock within two years after the option is granted, and he must hold the stock itself for at least one year to qualify for the favorable tax treatment for ISO stock (i.e., no tax consequences on option exercise or capital gains on post-exercise appreciation in value of stock).

If you've held your ISO shares for more than 12 months after exercising and more than two years since the options were granted, you get to apply the long-term capital gains tax rate to the difference between the exercise price and sale price. (If you haven't held it that long, the tax rate is higher.)

With NQs, when you exercise the option and buy the shares, you generally do recognize as ordinary income the difference between the option price and fair market value of the shares. (In fact, this income will probably appear on your pay stub, with taxes and Social Security withheld on it.) This tax bill can be substantial, as your ordinary tax rate could be quite steep. Once you're taxed on this amount, in order to avoid being taxed on it again later, you add the ordinary income to the basis of the stock purchased. Any subsequent gains from the sale of the stock are capital gains.

Here are a few other things to keep in mind:

• With both kinds of options, the granting of them is usually not a taxable event. The specter of taxes is only raised if and when you exercise them and/or sell the shares.

• With ISOs, the difference between the option price and the fair market value of the shares when the option is exercised is sometimes called the "bargain element." It's a tax preference item for the Alternative Minimum Tax, which means that it must be added to your ordinary income when calculating your AMT tax basis and the tax itself, if you qualify.

Aren't tax laws fun? Let's try some simplification in the form of an example: On January 1, 1997, as part of a qualified ISO, your employer, the Fingernail-on-Chalkboard Car Alarm Company (ticker: AIEEEE), grants you an option to buy up to 100 shares of its stock at $5 per share. On September 1, 1997, when the fair market value of the stock is $8 per share, you exercise the option and purchase all 100 shares for $500. On February 1, 1999, you sell all 100 shares for $10 per share, or a grand total of $1,000, realizing a gain of $500.

Since the holding requirements have been met, the entire $500 gain is treated as long-term capital gains. In 1997 (the date of the exercise), you would have reported $300 (the difference between the option price and the fair market value of the shares at purchase) as a tax preference for Alternative Minimum Tax. If you had sold the shares before the end of the holding period, $300 of the gain (the difference between the option price and the fair market value of the shares at purchase) would be taxed as ordinary income, and the remaining $200 would be taxed as capital gains.

Under a nonqualified stock option plan, using the same facts as in the example above, you would be taxed on the $300 (bargain element) in 1997 at the time the option was exercised. Your basis in the stock would then be $8 per share ($5 actually paid *plus* the $3 difference between the option price and the fair market value of the shares at purchase, on which you were already taxed). The remaining gain of $200 would be long-term capital gains.

Strategizing

There's no universal best strategy to offer you, as everyone's situation is different. But we'll offer some food for thought regarding when and how to exercise options.

First, know that there are several factors to consider, and not all of them are in your control. For example, much depends on when you exercise the option, the exercise price, the fair market price when you exercise the option, how long you hold the stock, and how much it appreciates before and after you exercise the option.

Here's one way to think through the how-to-exercise-them decision process. You can exercise your ISOs and then sell the stock on the same day. Or you can exercise them and then sell the stock at least a year and a day later.

If you exercise your ISOs and then immediately sell, you'll be taxed on the gain at your ordinary income tax rate. If this is considerably higher than the long-term capital gains rate, then this is an issue to consider. An advantage of this approach, though, is that you end up with money—it creates some immediate wealth for you.

If you choose to hang on to the shares for more than a year, you can benefit from long-term capital gains rates (which can be a big deal, if your marginal rate is rather high). But you're parking some of your valuable cash in the stock instead of investing it elsewhere. The trade-off might or might not be worth it. Be aware that whereas the selling-immediately method spits out cash, this approach consumes it.

But also remember that while your income tax may not be affected when holding ISOs, your Alternative Minimum Tax will be tested in the year that you exercise the options. Remember that the difference between the fair market value of the stock and the price that you pay for the options is a tax preference for AMT purposes. So it's very possible that although you hold the shares, you'll have tax to pay (in the form of AMT) in the year that the options are exercised. And these are real dollars that we're talking about. When you sell the shares, some of your gain for regular tax purposes may be reduced because of the AMT taxes that you paid in prior years. So it's not like you'll get taxed twice on the same gains. But the AMT is a very real issue if you deal with ISOs. If you're not comfortable with the AMT concept and how it applies to ISOs, make sure to seek out a qualified tax pro to help you with your tax planning.

Once you have some possible option-exercising scenarios in mind, try running the numbers. Plot your actions in this year, next year, and following years. See what will happen if you exercise and sell now and if you exercise and sell later. See what happens if the stock price rises rapidly over time or if it grows slowly. Estimate how much cash will be generated in each year, and apply the appropriate tax rate to it.

With NQ options, many of the considerations are the same. Remember, though, that merely exercising them usually will generate income taxable at your ordinary rate. (The tax would be on the fair market value of the stock when you exercise it, less the exercise price.)

If you would like to read more about employee stock options, read IRS Publication 525. In addition, you might want to check out the book *Stock Options: An Authoritative Guide to Incentive and Nonqualified Stock Options* by Robert R. Pastore. It may seem a little pricey at $39.95, but if you're sitting on potentially very valuable options, the expense can be well worth it.

The *Other* Options

Besides the stock options that your employer may grant you, there are other options that can appear in a Fool's portfolio. These include calls and puts and their many variations and combinations. As we discussed earlier, we're not fans of these kinds of options. With them, you're typically making a bet that a certain security will move in a certain direction within a certain (usually brief) time frame. It's often the case that what you expect to happen doesn't happen—until it's too late. We'd rather invest directly in stocks, where we can patiently wait for long-term growth, and not have to worry about short-term moves.

Nevertheless, if you've got some options in your pocket and are wondering how to deal with them on your tax return, check out IRS Publication 550. If you have yet to jump into options, you'd do well to read more about them and their many tax implications before committing yourself to dealing with the extra rules and paperwork.

INVESTMENT-RELATED DEDUCTIONS AND CREDITS

A later section of this book deals with various deductions and credits in more detail. But here we'll touch on some of those that relate to investing.

Investment expenses, by definition, are those expenses directly connected with the production of investment income. They're another form of Miscellaneous Itemized Deductions, are reported on Schedule A, and are subject to a 2% "floor."

Some investment expenses that may be deducted as miscellaneous itemized deductions on Schedule A include:

The 2% Floor

The 2% floor is an important concept. It means that once you total your miscellaneous itemized deductions, they'll need to exceed 2% of your adjusted gross income in order to be of any value. If they do exceed it, the only amount you'll be able to deduct is the amount by which the deductions exceed the 2%. For example, if your AGI is $100,000, your floor will be $2,000. If your miscellaneous itemized deductions total $1,455, you can't do anything with them—sorry. But if they total $2,455, you can deduct $455.

Note that the 2% limit is applied *after* other deduction limits are applied. Imagine that your deductions include a $100 meal (only 50% of which is allowable) and a $100 home office computer depreciation expense (only 75% of which might be allowable, if you use it 25% of the time for personal purposes). If so, you would only count the $50 and $75 deductions toward your 2% floor. (Got that? You would apply $125 to your running total of deductions, not $200.)

- Investment-related legal and professional fees

- Fees for investment advice

- Fees for tax preparation/advice

- Investment and/or tax books

- Magazines and subscriptions

- Safe deposit box fees

- IRA custodial fees

- Certain investment travel expenses

- Certain investment entertainment expenses

Deducting Online Service Expenses

If you subscribe to America Online or some other online service to access investing resources in cyberspace, you may be looking at another investment expense deduction. Online service subscription fees are a new kind of expense that can qualify as a deduction.

The Motley Fool's sites, at http://www.fool.com and on America Online at keyword: Fool, can arguably be considered an "investment publication." One can certainly learn substantially more in the Fool's area than in many so-called investment publications. You can obtain general investment information, specific industry information, information on specific issues, and much more. We used the word "arguably" above because this is a new kind of deduction and many tax specialists might not yet understand it well enough to concur with our conclusion. (Especially if they're likely to mistake a CD-ROM drive for a cup holder and a mouse for a foot pedal.)

All online service expenses aren't automatically deductible, though. You need to determine how much of the bill reflects personal use. Remember that you can't deduct noninvestment-related online activities like looking for love in chat rooms, making airline reservations, or reading the latest issue of *Salon*. Only the investment portion of the bill can be considered an investment expense.

How do you determine the correct portion? Well, you could log every hour of online time for the entire year, compute your percentage of investment time versus other personal time, and deduct the appropriate investment amount. (Perhaps you're thinking, "Yeah, and I could poke toothpicks into my eyes, too." Keep reading—there are other alternatives.)

Another suggestion is that you use different screen names or online accounts, one for investing purposes and one for pleasure, and simply log the time spent with each name. America Online makes this relatively easy. If you have several screen names, just go to keyword: Billing, select "display your detailed bill," and you can view your minutes online for all your screen names for the current month and the last month. Now, you might sigh and mumble, "That's still too much trouble." Well, remember that deductions are not birthrights but legislative allowances that must be proved. If you want to take advantage of them, you've got to follow the rules.

Another issue is that of what is "reasonable." If you're spending $2,500 per year on investment publications (regardless of whether they are paper or online) to manage a portfolio of $5,000, in which you make only one or two trades per year, you may be looking at rather unreasonable expenses. Perhaps the IRS is even doing you a favor by helping you notice exactly how much you're spending on such things! Unreasonable deductions may be reviewed and disallowed for not being "ordinary and necessary."

Done properly and under certain circumstances, at least a part of your online service bill could be an allowable deduction. For more information on all kinds of investment-related deductions, check out IRS Publication 550 (Investment Income and Expenses).

Deducting Home Computer Expenses

While deducting online expenses is a relatively new phenomenon, deducting home computer expenses is a more established practice. As usual, though, there are rules and issues to consider. The first thing to think about is what equipment is involved. It's likely that in addition to your computer, you have one or more of the following: a monitor, modem, Zip drive, scanner, or printer. To the extent that you use them for investment (or business) purposes, these items might represent deductions for you.

Not surprisingly, the deductibility of computers and related equipment will depend on how you use them. Each type of use has different tax rules. It may well be that you use your computer for a combination of the uses listed below. If so, you'll apply the appropriate treatment in corresponding percentages. Let's take a quick look at the various uses.

Strictly personal use: As you might have guessed, you will receive no tax deduction whatsoever if you use the computer for entertainment, education, avocation, hobbies, or other personal purposes.

Strictly for your employer's work: You can deduct the operating expenses and depreciation for a home computer that you buy for your employer's business if the computer is required as a condition of your employment and it is used for the convenience of your employer. A home computer, even if required by your employer and used exclusively for your employer's work, is still subject to so-called "listed property" deduction limitation rules (unless you qualify for the "office at home" rules discussed below).

Home office business use: If you use the computer in an office at your home that qualifies as your "regular business establishment," you get the maximum deduction. You get the same deduction as the employee (as discussed above), but the 2% "miscellaneous itemized deduction" rules do not apply. In addition, the listed property rules also don't apply.

TAX TIP

A Letter From Your Boss

If you're ever audited and the deduction of an employment-related expense is questioned, you'll need to back it up with a letter from your employer. This is especially true when you are dealing with computers used for business purposes. The letter will have to explain that the expense is: A) required as a condition of your employment, B) for the convenience of your employer, and C) not reimbursed by your employer.

Investment or income-producing use: You can deduct operating expenses plus depreciation if you use your computer to:

- Produce or collect income (for example, to keep track of your investments and to visit The Motley Fool) even though this activity doesn't qualify as a trade or business for you.

- Manage, conserve, or maintain property held for producing income.

- Determine, contest, pay, or claim a refund of any tax.

If you do use your computer for investment or income producing purposes, these are the deductions that apply:

• You can take accelerated depreciation over six tax years if the computer is used more than 50% for investment-related purposes; or

• If you use the computer 50% or less for qualified investment-related purposes, you are required to use a straight-line method of depreciation, also over six years.

Example: Fernando uses his home computer 30% of the time to track and record his investments, 20% of the time for stock and investment research, and 10% of the time for tax planning and tax preparation purposes. Since Fernando is using his computer more than 50% of the time for investment purposes, he can depreciate 60% of the computer and related components and will be able to claim that plus 60% of the operating costs as investment expenses in the form of a miscellaneous itemized deduction. The remaining 40% personal use is considered completely nondeductible.

One last expense to consider is software. Software and hardware expenses are treated differently. If

TAX TIP

Section 179 Depreciation

Depreciation can be a very complex issue, depending on an asset's type and how it is used (business purpose, investment purpose, etc.). You may have heard about a depreciation technique that will allow you to write off (or "expense") the entire purchase price of a business asset in the year of purchase. It's true, and this election is called the Section 179 Deduction.

Rather than depreciating the cost of business property over several years, Section 179 allows you to expense up to $19,000 in 1999 of tangible depreciable property used in the active conduct of a trade or business. (The limit will increase annually, reaching $25,000 in 2003.) The Section 179 election is made on an item-by-item basis for qualifying property, and must be made in the year the property is first purchased and placed in service. Once made, the election can not be revoked (such as on a subsequent amended tax return) without IRS consent.

For the Section 179 election to be allowed, the property must be used 50% or more for business purposes. Also, the property must be used in an active trade or business. So any property purchased for investment purposes (such as your home computer to track your portfolio and visit The Motley Fool website) does not qualify. Sorry.

For more information on depreciation in general and the Section 179 election specifically, make sure to read IRS Publication 534.

the software is specifically business or investment-related, it is 100% deductible, even if the computer is only 75% deductible due to 25% personal use. Conversely, 0% of personal software would be deductible, even if you use the computer 15% of the time for investment.

Please remember that the above is simply an overview of general guidelines that you can use to help determine the deductibility of your home computer and its accessories. As you can imagine, the rules get even more complex when you get down to the nuts and bolts of things. For additional information regarding the deductibility of home computer equipment, see IRS Publication 529. To find out more about "listed property" rules and depreciation tables, check out IRS Publication 946.

ESTIMATING TAXES

Are you tempted to just skip this section, thinking that you're not self-employed, so you don't need to worry about paying quarterly estimated taxes? Well, sorry, but we've included this section for a reason. Investing offers you many benefits and advantages in life. It can be not only a fun avocation, but also a highly profitable one, funding your kid's college education, a trip to Africa, and a comfortable retirement. Unfortunately, there's a dark side of investing, too: occasional losses, capital gains taxes, filling out Schedule D, and now... paying estimated taxes.

The same principle dictating that the self-employed must pay quarterly estimated taxes is at work dictating that many investors should do the same. The reason: *Taxes are meant to be paid throughout the year, not just on April 15.* We may not think about it this way, but it's really a pay-as-you-go system. That's why we're blessed with tax withholding; it ensures that Uncle Sam is collecting revenue all year 'round. When this is not happening, as with the self-employed or Foolish investors with sizable dividend income or capital gains, the IRS expects taxes on this income to be coughed up during the year. To be precise, the IRS requires you to file quarterly estimated taxes if your withheld taxes won't represent at least 90% of the taxes you'll owe for the current year.

You might be thinking, "Gee... I never heard of this and never worried about it and nothing has ever happened... so I'm probably okay." If this is so, it merely means that you've been lucky—so far. Neglecting this means you may be hit with a penalty, and a sizable one, at that.

If you fall into the must-pay-estimated-taxes group, here are the things you need to keep in mind. And it really is up to you to attend to these things. The IRS won't be reminding you, except in the form of a penalty if you goof.

The taxes are due in April, June, September, and January of each year. (The astute Fool will notice that these are not evenly spaced out three months apart. Don't ask us why.) The total tax bill that you'll need to estimate and pay in quarterly chunks is figured by taking all the taxes you owe and subtracting all the credits you have. The taxes are filed with 1040-ES forms, available from the IRS and sometimes at your local library or post office, as well.

For the tax year 1999, the due dates are:

- First Quarter: April 15, 1999
- Second Quarter: June 15, 1999
- Third Quarter: September 15, 1999
- Fourth Quarter: January 17, 2000

For the tax year 2000, the due dates are:

- First Quarter: April 17, 2000
- Second Quarter: June 15, 2000
- Third Quarter: September 15, 2000
- Fourth Quarter: January 15, 2001

You might be willing to risk the penalty, though. The penalty varies each quarter depending on current Treasury Bill rates, but in 1999 it was around 8%. If you plan to be earning more than 8% on the money that you would otherwise fork over as estimated taxes, the penalty might look attractive. Just keep in mind that it isn't quite this clear-cut. Get a copy of IRS Form 2210 and use it to figure out exactly what your penalty would be so that you can make a Foolishly informed decision. You can also use software like Kiplinger's TaxCut or Intuit's TurboTax to figure out your options. If you're too lazy (er... busy?) to complete Form 2210, the IRS will be more than happy to complete it for you. Of course, they'll complete it in the manner that benefits them most, which may not be in your best interest.

Keep in mind that if your income spike occurs early in the year, you can't put off paying estimated taxes until a later quarter. Each quarter is treated independently.

If you experience a major unexpected loss during the year and have already paid some estimated taxes, you're not entitled to a refund until the time when you file your return. This could be nearly a year away, so if your financial situation is shaky, you might consider not paying estimated taxes and risking the penalty in order to keep your cash flow under control.

If this is the first year that your income has spiked or otherwise increased substantially, you still might not have to pay estimated taxes and might be able to pay the entire balance due on April 15 without penalty by using the so-called "exception #1." Essentially, if your current year's withholding is at least as much as your previous year's total tax (assuming that your AGI for the prior year is $150,000 or less), you can ignore any increases in 1999 income and pay any balance due with the tax return on April 15 without penalty.

If you're getting discouraged thinking about this extra work, know that you have one last possible way out of it. There's a threshold for the underpayment penalty of $1,000. This means that if your total tax liability for the year, reduced by any withholding or credits, is less than $1,000, no estimated tax penalty will be imposed. This is a significant boon for many taxpayers.

If you can't get out of paying estimated taxes, there's a convenience you need to know about: the "safe harbor." For the average Fool, this means that as long as you pay 100% of your previous year's total tax liability in estimated taxes, you'll be free from any penalty for underpayment of estimated tax, no matter what the current year's taxes actually end up being. So if your tax liability was $12,000 last year, but this year you expect to sell some stock and have substantially higher taxes to pay, you'll probably have to pay estimated taxes. But you can use the safe harbor and just make sure that you pay at least $12,000 in estimated (or withheld) taxes.

Note that the above-100% safe harbor is not for every one. If you're a high-income Fool with AGI of more than $150,000 in the prior year, your safe harbor is different. According to the 1997 Tax Relief Act, the safe harbors that apply to you are:

• For tax year 1999, if you pay 105% of your 1998 tax liability, you'll be safe.
• For tax year 2000, if you pay 106% of your 1999 tax liability, you'll be safe.

Prepayment of Estimated State Income Taxes

One of the most overlooked tax "loopholes" concerns the prepayment of fourth quarter state estimated taxes. (If you live in a state that doesn't impose a state income tax, you may want to skip this section.)

The fourth quarter estimated payment for federal taxes is due by January 15 of the following tax year (January 17 for 2000, because of weekend interference). Generally, the corresponding state estimated tax payment is also due at that time. But remember that if you itemize your deductions, one of those deductions is for state taxes *paid*. So why wait until January of year two to make those final state estimated tax payments (and wait 15 months to get any federal benefit for them), when you can make them in December of year one and generate a federal tax deduction in the same tax year? This also works if you don't normally make any state estimated tax payments, but have had a good year and estimate that you *will* have a hefty state tax balance due on April 15. Why wait to make the payment? Make an estimated tax payment in December of year one instead and claim the deduction on your federal tax return.

For example, consider Kevin DeWalt, a tricycle repairman in the 28% tax bracket, who has a $500 state estimated tax payment to make by January 17, 2000. If Kevin, who itemizes his deductions, makes this final state estimated tax payment on December 30, 1999, he will generate an additional $500 federal tax deduction. And that deduction will save him $140 in federal taxes for the 1999 tax year.

It's true that Kevin would still get that $140 benefit if he made the payment in January 2000. And if he makes the state payment in December rather than January, he'll be losing the use of that $500 payment for about 16 days. But—he'll be gaining the use of the $140 refund for almost 16 months.

Note that state taxes are a preference item for Alternative Minimum Tax purposes. So if you are in the situation where the AMT may kick in, the early prepayment of these state taxes may not be of any real benefit to you.

• For tax year 2001, if you pay 106% of your 2000 tax liability, you'll be safe.
• For tax year 2002, if you pay 112% of your 2001 tax liability, you'll be safe.
• For tax year 2003 and beyond, if you pay 110% of your last year's tax liability, you'll be safe.

Let's consider a high-income scenario now. Imagine that in 1998, your total tax liability was $51,000. In 1999, you know that you'll be selling some major stock holdings and will be realizing some hefty capital gains. It's clear that your total tax liability for 1999 will be considerably higher than that for 1998. Just to be sure, you check to see how much tax will be withheld for you, and it's well under 90% of what you expect to owe. Thus, you definitely will have to pay estimated taxes (unless you opt to crank up your W-2 withholding at work). How much do you fork over, then? Well, according to the table above, for 1999, you can actually get away with simply paying 105% of what you paid in 1998, or $53,550. So you might not even need to bother tinkering with your W-2 withholding, if it will suffice.

The entire amount of $53,550 will have to be withheld and/or paid via estimated taxes. If you have no W-2 withholding, the entire $53,550 amount will have to be paid via estimated taxes equally over all of the installments. This amounts to $13,387.50 per quarter and gets you under the safe harbor umbrella. If it is a combination of W-2 withholding and estimated tax payments, the estimated tax payments must still be made equally over the year, regardless of the amount. Remember that the W-2 withholding can still be "backloaded." As long as the total of the two equals or exceeds the $53,550 amount, things will be just fine.

If we jump in our trusty time machine and scoot forward a year, you'll be obligated to fork over in estimated taxes 106% of your previous year's tax liability.

The safe harbor is mighty handy when your tax liability is spiking upward. But not when your taxes are dropping.

When You Have to Estimate

When your income drops (such as after a year with extraordinarily large gains), you may have a bit of a problem. If your normal withholding will cover your total tax liability for the year, then you're in phat city—and have no worries. But what if your withholding still won't cover your total tax liability, and there's nothing you can do to get enough withholding? Or what if you're retired and don't have any withholding from wages? If that's your situation, you don't have any safety net. You'll be required to pay in, at least quarterly, a minimum of 90% of your taxes for that period. You'd basically be running a little "mini" tax return each quarter, and basing your estimated tax payments on the results of your computations. It's a pain, but it may have to be done if you do want to avoid the penalty.

You might say to yourself, "Heck... I'll just pay in 100% of my last year's taxes and not deal with these stupid quarterly computations." That sounds good in theory, but think about it. If your 1999 total tax liability was $75,000, and you expect your 2000 total tax liability to only amount to $15,000, do you *really* want to overpay your taxes by $60,000 simply to avoid some computations? Probably not. That's just way too much money for Uncle Sam to be holding (interest free) for you. It's probably best to just struggle and complete the computations on a quarterly basis.

On the other hand, if you have a pretty good handle on what your total tax liability will be for 2000, you can simply divide that amount by four and send those payments in for your quarterly tax payments. It's not the best way to do it—you're still making some overpayments that you really don't need to make—but it's quick and easy. All you'll have to do is to make sure that your estimate remains valid as the year goes on. If your total tax liability is greater than you originally thought, you'll have to make some changes in your quarterly estimated taxes down the road in order to stay penalty free—which will require some computations.

It's a fine line. You don't want to pay too much, but you don't want to pay too little and get hit with the penalty. So you'll have to make sure to keep an eye on your estimates all year 'round—and not just once or twice a year.

To summarize, you avoid paying estimated taxes if:

- Your total tax liability (less withholdings and credits) is less than $1,000.
- Your withheld taxes for the current year are at least 90% of your total tax liability for the year.
- For those with prior-year AGI of $150,000 or less, your current year's total taxes withheld are at least as much as your prior-year's total tax liability.
- For those with prior-year AGI of more than $150,000, your 1999 withholdings amount to at least 105% of your total 1998 tax liability.

You've probably got the gist of this now. If you want to learn more about estimated taxes, head over to our online tax area or call the IRS and request Publication 505, "Tax Withholding and Estimated Tax." High-income Fools should definitely read up on this topic in order to fully understand the safe harbor computations and percentages and the special rules that apply to you as noted above.

TRADERS AND TAXES

We hope that you don't need to read this section. If you've been a Fool for long, you've probably learned that there's a difference between investors and traders. Investors, especially Foolish ones, carefully buy stock in companies they believe in, holding on for the long term. They think of themselves as part-owners of businesses, and follow the companies' progress over years—sometimes decades. Traders, meanwhile, flit in and out of various stocks, holding them for weeks, days, hours, or even just minutes. They try to time the market and look for short-term gains. This isn't investing; it's speculating, or gambling.

For those who are traders and those who are simply curious about trading, in this section we'll discuss briefly how taxes differ for traders. The upside to trader status is that you'll likely be able to take advantage of some tax breaks, such as deductions for all your investing expenses. The downside is that it's hard to define a trader.

Who's a Trader?

It's probably clear to you that there's a continuum here. On one end, traders. On the other, nontraders, or investors. At what point along the continuum does a trader become an investor? How much trading is the IRS looking for? Well, these are the right questions to ask, but unfortunately, there's no clear answer. At the end of this section, we won't be able to recommend that you read IRS Publication number such-and-such—because there is no IRS publication about traders.

Ask yourself these questions and you'll probably get a sense of whether you're a trader.

• Is trading my vocation or avocation?
• Is trading my primary income-generating occupation, my main line of business?
• Is most of my investing income in the form of long-term capital gains and dividends or short-term capital gains?
• Do I trade significantly every day? Do I have a regular, continual investing pattern? Do I spend much of every day that the market is open trading?
• Am I the one doing all this short-term trading, or is my broker doing it for me? (To be a trader, *you* must be the one calling the shots.)
• Do I engage in the kinds of transactions that traders engage in (such as futures, options, etc.)?

Here are some examples: Tiffany, a tree surgeon, is an active investor/trader. She spends about two hours per day following the stock market and buying and selling stocks. She engages in four or five transactions per day, on average. She hangs on to each stock she buys for no more than a week, in general. Is Tiffany a "trader" in the eyes of the IRS? Probably not.

Buck, meanwhile, is a much more active investor/trader than Tiffany. He quit his job whittling sticks at a Popsicle factory in order to trade more. Averaging about five or more hours of trading per day (25+ hours per week), he places roughly 30 to 60 buy or sell orders per day. Is Buck a "trader" in the eyes of the IRS? Probably so.

Trader Tax Rules

Now that you have an idea of what a "trader" is, let's see why anyone might want that designation. It's mainly because traders enjoy some tax advantages. For starters, they can often deduct more expenses. Mere investors are usually limited to a 2%-of-AGI floor for deducting investing expenses, whereas since traders' "investing" expenses are considered business expenses, they can deduct all of them on Schedule C, as self-employed taxpayers. Schedule C deductions have the added benefit of reducing your adjusted gross income, too, which will make it easier for you to take other personal deductions. In addition, your trading profits won't be subject to the self-employment tax, as capital gains are exempt. Deductions on Schedule C for investment interest expense (such as margin interest paid) are also unlimited for traders. Finally, you can deduct thousands of dollars per year for your trading-related equipment, providing that you use it more than 50% of the time for trading. This includes computer equipment, telecommunications equipment, furniture, etc. (Unfortunately, Tums and anti-stress medications are *not* deductible.)

Of course, there are disadvantages for day traders, as well (in addition to facial twitches and ulcers). Note that they're not called 12-month traders. The fact that these folks typically have such fleeting holding periods means that their capital gains are virtually all short-term ones, taxed at ordinary income rates. Ouch. How about capital losses? Well, remember the rule that you can only deduct up to $3,000 of your losses per year against your income, once you've offset your gains? It's true even for traders. Those with persistent significant losses are out of luck. Ouch again.

Another disadvantage is the paperwork and recordkeeping. Just as with any investor, the IRS wants to know about every single trade—the security bought or sold, the gain or loss, the dates of purchase or sale, the cost, and the proceeds. If you trade 50 times a day, that's more than 12,000 trades per year. You'll go through a lot of pens or pencils writing all that down. One option is to simply report your net short-term and long-term gains and losses on Schedule D (in other words, a total of four line items), and to attach a copy of the trade details to the tax return. Another alternative is to use a software program, like Intuit's Quicken, that can automatically incorporate records from many online brokers. This data can then be transferred to

TurboTax software, sparing you even more labor. Also useful is The Motley Fool's PortTrak software, which will help you keep track of stock purchases, sales, and adjusted bases. It's meant for Foolish long-term investors, of course, but anyone can benefit from it, and in some ways, active traders can benefit more. (For more information on PortTrak, head to FoolMart at http://www.foolmart.com or call 888-665-3665.)

The tax returns of traders look a little different from the returns of regular investors. Both have Schedule D forms detailing gains and losses. But the trader will have a Schedule C form, with mostly just expenses on it. (The income that most Schedule C filers have is listed on Schedule D for traders.) Some pros advise traders to attach a note to their return, explaining their status and situation. This may keep your return from raising anyone's eyebrows at the IRS.

Note that you can be *both* a trader and an investor—if you separate your holdings into long-term investments and short-term trader investments. To do this right, on the day that you buy any particular investment, you should record which category you're placing it in. You'll need these records, should the IRS ever come knocking.

Mark-to-Market Rules

Traders can take advantage of another beneficial tax treatment—the "mark-to-market" rules. If you elect to be a mark-to-market trader, you follow these rules:

On the last trading day of the year, you go to the land of Let's Pretend and record all your holdings as having been sold at the current market price. (Thus, they're "marked to market.") You still actually hold them, of course, but you record the gains and losses that would result *if* you sold them on that day. Next, you pretend to buy them all back on the same day. So your new cost basis in them is their current price on that day.

As a mark-to-market trader, wash sale rules won't apply to you. You can sell and then buy back a security within fewer than 30 days. A potentially bigger advantage is that unlike other investors, you're not limited to deducting only $3,000 in capital losses each year. Your allowable capital loss deductions are now unlimited.

Here's a big disadvantage, though. Note that you'll *never* have anything but short-term gains and losses as a mark-to-market trader. This is because long-term holding periods are those longer than a year, and you're forced to "sell" every year at the end of the year. (Yes, the selling takes place in your mind—but it occurs in the IRS's mind, as well!) Also, instead of short-term capital gains or losses, you'll have *ordinary* income or losses. And note that mark-to-market traders don't have self-employment income even though they do have ordinary income and are essentially self-employed.

If you're intrigued by mark-to-market trading, read more about whether and how you can elect to be a mark-to-market trader in IRS Revenue Procedure 99-17, in IRS Bulletin 99-7. It's required reading for anybody thinking about making the election. (Note that it deals just with mark-to-market traders, and not with other issues regarding traders.)

In Summary

The one main point we'd like to make about active trading is that for many, if not most people, it's likely to prove a very regrettable venture. Academic studies have demonstrated the superiority of infrequent trading over frequent trading. Warren Buffett, the second-richest American, has also demonstrated it. Starting with modest means, he's increased his worth to many billions of dollars, largely by carefully choosing companies in which to invest, and then hanging on for decades. (When asked when the best time to sell is, he's responded "never.")

Back to trading issues. The important thing to know about taxes for traders is that the rules are very complicated and can be difficult to figure out. Remember, this tax realm is so cryptic that there isn't even an IRS publication on it! That's right—the IRS, which seems to have a publication available on everything, doesn't even seem to want to explain it. If you insist on trading, read up on it more. Much more.

Also, know that the rules with respect to trading are a bit arcane in the IRS code. Many tax scholars differ on the tax treatment of "traders." Heck, the courts have even contradicted themselves as to who is a "trader" and who is an "investor." Our advice to you: If you believe that you may be a trader, first visit your local chapter of Traders Anonymous. ("Hi, my name is Buck, and I'm a day trader.") Next, pay a visit to a qualified tax pro with experience in this issue. The tax pro can review your situation and help you with your actual status and may be able to provide you with the procedures (and possible pitfalls) relative to the trader status.

In the meantime, you can check out the section on trader status at http://www.fairmark.com and read sections of *The Trader's Tax Survival Guide,* written by Ted Tesser, for more information on this issue. In addition, tax expert Kaye Thomas of Fairmark Press recommends the book

Trading for a Living, by Dr. Alexander Elder. If there were ever an issue where you need to look closely before you leap, this is it.

INVESTMENT CLUB TAXES

You can reap a heck of a lot of benefit from membership in an investment club. You get to learn about investing in the company of others, instead of going it alone. You get to make joint decisions on stock purchases and sales, hearing many opinions instead of just the sound of your own (perhaps uncertain) voice. Many people can research many more stocks than just one person, so this leverage permits the group to pick the cream of a bigger crop. You can end up with many stock ideas to act on for your own personal portfolio. Plus, on top of all this, you usually get to enjoy some socializing and snacks. It's practically a perfect arrangement!

Into this rosy scene pops the (uninvited) tax collector. You didn't think you'd escape taxes in an investment club, did you? Even if you were just thinking that individual members would simply report their share of the club's income on their personal returns, you'd be wrong.

Investment clubs are advised to establish themselves as legal partnerships. If they don't, it means that somebody in the group will have his or her Social Security number attached to the master brokerage statement. And transferring all the trades, gains, losses, and distributions from his or her name and Social Security number to the other individual investors would be a complete train wreck. An e-freaking-normous nightmare.

When organizing yourselves into a partnership, you need to apply for and receive a "tax identification number." This is what will be used for your club's brokerage account instead of a single member's Social Security number.

In a partnership, the partnership itself doesn't pay any taxes. Instead, each member does, individually. The partnership's income is reported to the IRS by the club treasurer, who files Form 1065 in April. Attached to it is a K-1 form for each member, which details the member's allocation of income and expenses according to the partnership arrangement. In other words, if the partnership agreement is that each member will have an equal share, then club income and expenses will be divided equally among members. If the partnership has allowed some members to contribute more and hold bigger stakes, then the K-1 form should reflect their shares accurately.

Each club member gets a copy of the K-1 to file with his or her own personal tax return. This, along with Schedule D, will show the member's gains or losses.

Your club might want to have an accountant or other tax professional prepare (or at least review) your paperwork. This is fine, but realize that just as with personal tax forms, the filer (and not the professional) is still responsible for the content of the returns. Regardless of who prepares the paperwork, it's probably smart to have someone double-check the information. Or better yet, perhaps a second person can prepare the forms independently. They can then be compared.

To fill out these forms, you'll need records of exactly when each stock was purchased and/or sold, the price at which the transactions occurred, and the holding's current value.

Although the tax form preparation might seem daunting, you don't have to do it alone. You can tap the experience of older clubs or post questions online at the Fool's Investment Club message folder. Also helpful is the club accounting software offered by the National Association of Investors Corp. (NAIC). (The NAIC is a terrific organization that has been championing and supporting investment clubs for half a century. For more information, call 800-ASK-NAIC or visit www.better-investing.org.)

For more information on starting and running investment clubs, visit our online area for clubs. Just point your browser to: http://www.fool.com/investmentclub.

FINDING A GOOD TAX ADVISOR

We Fools tend to be do-it-yourselfers. When it comes to investing, we're particularly likely to make our own decisions. This is because we've found that we're capable of studying companies on our own, of evaluating their investment merit, and of building wealth without much guidance from the professionals on Wall Street.

Taxes can be a different matter, though. In *some* cases, the smart thing to do is to hire a professional to tend to your tax return. If your situation is straightforward enough that you're comfortable preparing your own return, by all means do so. If it's rather complicated, but you enjoy scrutinizing the intricacies of the tax code and feel confident you can do a good job, then go for it.

Just know that it's okay to consult a tax advisor along the way. It can save you a lot of time—and money. The only problem is... how can you make sure you've found a good one?

Here are some suggestions to help you find and evaluate a tax accountant/tax preparer:

- Ask around. Ask others in your profession. Any professional can pay for advertising, but a satisfied client is always the best referral. Just make sure that you ask people whom you respect and who have at least a little business and tax savvy.

- Find somebody who is familiar with your business or industry. Don't expect someone who specializes in service businesses to also be an expert in manufacturing. Avoid the people who try to convey that they know everything about everything. Everyone has areas of expertise. Look for a person who knows your business.

- Ask for an interview. In most cases, he or she will be glad to give you an hour (at no charge) to discuss your situation and assess your specific needs and desires. At that time, you'll want to ask some questions. We've prepared a list of some of these questions for you in this section. You might want to make a copy of it to take with you when you meet a candidate for your business.

- Once you are done with your questions, see if the professional has any questions for you. If they're established and successful, they don't have to take any Tom, Dick, or Sherry who walks in the door. They may have some very pointed questions for you. In fact, the more questions they ask, the better. At least it shows some interest.

How big is the firm?

(You want to determine whether you'll be a little frog in a big pond and just how important your business would be to this person.)

Who exactly will be doing my work—you or somebody else? If I have problems or questions, do I speak with you or am I shuffled off to another person?

(Make sure that you're comfortable with the answers here. Ideally, you should be speaking with the person who will actually be doing your work.)

Why do you want me for a client?

(This one always throws 'em for a loop. If they stutter and stammer, you can bet that it's just for the money. But if they tell you that your business would be a good mix for the firm, or that they specialize in your business and are anxious to expand, or offer some other reasonable explanation of how you fit well with them, you at least have a fighting chance.)

What is your experience and educational background?

(People always like to talk about themselves. See if you get the information in a matter-of-fact fashion, or if you're being treated to a dog and pony show.)

How many continuing professional education (CPE) hours are you required to take, and how many do you normally take on an annual basis?

(If you're not comfortable with the answer, ask to see his/her written CPE report, which is required to be filed with his/her professional organizations. You don't have to be rude about it. You can just say, "I'm just curious about your areas of CPE interest. Would you mind showing me your written CPE report?")

What research material do you use or subscribe to? CCH? Research Institute? BNA?

(If you find that the only research material is a current copy of the Federal Tax Handbook, run—don't walk—to the nearest exit. Taxes evolve from regulations and court cases. Sometimes complicated problems arise that require deep research. You don't want your tax geek to give it his or her "best shot." Being correct is always best when dealing with the IRS.)

If my return is audited, will you represent me before the IRS in examination on my behalf? Not with me, but instead of me? And what will be the fee for any audit work?

(If the accountant sources out the audit work, think twice. If you are asked to be present in an audit, think a third time. Potentially, the worst situation in the world is when both the accountant and client are present at audit time. Then the IRS will be able to ask just about any question it wants and expect an answer. If you're not there, when asked some questions, the accountant may be able to say that he'll have to ask you and submit an answer later—perhaps by mail. When you're present, experienced auditors also may be able to get a lot of extra information out of you. They might in a friendly manner, for example, strike up a conversation about cars and car repairs or about nice vacation spots—hoping that you'll mention a Mercedes or fancy vacation in Bali that you don't seem able to afford. Don't let yourself get in the hot seat in an audit!)

Speaking of fees, how do you set them? Can I get an estimate of what my fees would be? What are your billing policies?

(Make sure that the answers here are reasonable to you.)

- Last but not least, select someone you're comfortable with. The person you finally select might be the very best tax technician, but if you're not comfortable with him or her, you'll hesitate to call for further information, and you might not provide the information that he or she needs to do a good job for you. If you like needlepoint, find out if he also likes it. If you're a golf aficionado, see if she is, as well. Find as much common ground as possible. Once you've verified (at least to the best of your ability) technical competence, evaluate the comfort factor.

Don't be afraid to ask questions and challenge his or her position. When challenged, if the best answer you receive is "trust me" or "that's just the way it's done," be careful. Be very careful. The professional should be able to put your mind at ease with logical explanations—backed up by the law and regulations. (Some logical explanations, unfortunately, are not legal!)

Be aware that this is an unusual routine for someone seeking a tax advisor. Advisors are not accustomed to getting many questions from potential clients. Most people don't know what to ask or look for in an accountant, so they make hasty decisions that either turn out well or badly.

Just as with investing, the deeper you dig and the more questions you ask, the more you reduce your risk. Why not take some time to maximize your chances of finding a terrific professional who'll do good work for you, perhaps for a long time?

A Fool Lib

(Play this with a friend. Without revealing the story, ask your friend to think of and give you the required missing words. Fill them in as you get them. Then read the story aloud.)

A Taxing Transformation

_____ never really had a handle on taxes.
[Name of a person]

Part of_____'s problem was that his/her situation was so unique, making tax
[initial person named]
preparation extra complex. For example, he/she raised_____s and_____s for
[kind of animal]   [kind of animal]
a living. A sideline business was renting _____s to _____people for_____parties.
[noun]   [adjective]   [event]
His/her family situation was also nontraditional, as in addition to a_____spouse, there
[adjective]
were_____children and_____foster children. Even the commute to the animal
[number]   [number]
grounds was complicated, involving a _____ trip by _____ .
[a distance]   [vehicle]

_____ also owned a bunch of stocks, such as: _____ _____
[initial person]   [nationality]   [product]
Manufacturing Inc., Consolidated _____ _____ Corp.,
[adjective]   [noun]
International_____ Machines, and Global _____Transport Co. Some of
[noun]   [noun]
these had been held for_____, while others had been held for_____.
[period of time]   [period of time]

Fortunately, _____ stumbled into Fooldom. He/she soon discovered many
[initial person]
ways to save money, such as the Deduction for_____s, the Dependent _____
[noun]   [adjective]
_____ Credit, the _____Treatment Credit, and the_____Allergy Deduction.
[a relative]   [a vice]   [a food]

When_____ finished preparing the return, amazingly enough, the government
[initial person]
owed him/her_____!
[dollar amount]

THREE

MARRIAGE AND FAMILY

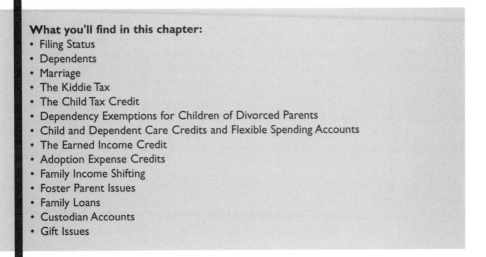

One fool at least in every married couple.
—Henry Fielding

FILING STATUS

Depending on the situation you find yourself in, you're usually viewed by others as having a particular status. At a PTA meeting, for example, you're likely to be either a P or a T. Your alma mater's development office may think of you as a "major donation candidate," "reliable modest contributor," or "someone not to bother hitting up again."

The IRS is no exception; it also has classifications for you. And you often have some choice in which category ("filing status") you use. Each filing status is attached to a specific series of tax rates. In addition, your filing status will determine your standard deduction. So you've got to get your filing status correct in order to use the correct tax tables and standard deduction.

Here are the five filing statuses:

• Single

• Married filing jointly

• Married filing separately

• Head of Household

• Qualifying widow(er)

Filing status is determined as of the last day of the year. To use the Single status, for example, you must be unmarried or separated from your spouse either by divorce or by a written separate maintenance decree on the last day of the year. So even if you were married for 95% of the year and finalized your divorce in the middle of December, you can't file as a married person. It's your status on December 31 that matters.

You may file jointly if on the last day of the year you are:

• married and living together as husband and wife; *or*

• married and living apart, but not legally separated under a decree of divorce or separate maintenance agreement; *or*

• separated under an interlocutory (i.e., not final) decree of divorce.

There are a lot of issues involved in deciding which married status you can or should file under. For more on this, refer to our "Marriage" section.

Head of Household Filing Status

Some taxpayers get to file their returns as a "Head of Household." This status gives its bearer some special treatment and tax breaks. But not everyone understands who qualifies as a head of a household.

TAX TIP

Common Law Marriages

When it comes to common law marriages, Federal law defers to state law. You will be able to file married-joint if you and your significant other live together in a common law marriage that is recognized in the state where you currently reside. So you really need to check your individual state law. Some states recognize common law marriages and some don't. Note that if you have relocated from a state that recognized your common law marriage, you can file married-joint in your new state—even if your new state doesn't recognize it!

Misconceptions and misunderstandings are prevalent. For example, if you're recognized by your spouse and children as the one who calls the shots and perhaps you're also the family's chief breadwinner, that does *not* make you a Head of Household in the eyes of our friends at the IRS.

So let's run down the requirements. In order to qualify for Head of Household filing status, the following five tests *must all* be met:

- The taxpayer should not be married at the end of the year. (There's an exception to this rule, which we'll tackle after this list.)

- The taxpayer must maintain a household for his or her child, dependent parent, or other dependent relative. (See notes below for additional discussion of dependents.)

- The household must be the taxpayer's home, and the household must also be the main home of a qualifying relative (as defined above) for more than half of the year. There is an exception to this rule: A dependent parent need not live with the taxpayer; however, the taxpayer must provide more than 50% of the cost of maintaining the dependent parent's separate household that was the parent's main home for the entire year. (See the notes below for additional discussion of a qualifying individual.)

- The taxpayer must provide more than 50% of the cost of maintaining the household.

- The taxpayer must be a U.S. citizen or a resident alien during the entire tax year.

Notes on Dependents and Qualifying Individuals

These relate to the second and third items above.

- Cousins do not qualify as dependent relatives.

- The taxpayer's unmarried child, stepchild, adopted child, or grandchild does not have to be a dependent.

- A foster child must be a dependent.

- With respect to the taxpayer's married child, stepchild, adopted child, or grandchild, the taxpayer must be entitled to claim that child as a dependent. (The taxpayer needn't actually claim the dependent, but must be eligible to do so.)

- Make sure to check the other dependent rules to ensure that any individual in question does, in fact, qualify. (We cover these in our "Dependents" section.)

Exceptions That Allow Married Taxpayers to Claim Head of Household Status

A married taxpayer living apart from a spouse may qualify as "unmarried" and use the Head of Household rates if all of the following tests are met:

- Taxpayer and spouse file separate tax returns.

- Taxpayer's spouse did not live in the household during the last six months of the year.

- Taxpayer maintains his/her home as a household that was the main home for a child, stepchild, or adopted child for more than half of the year. However, a foster child must be a member of the household for the entire year.

- Taxpayer is entitled to claim that child as a dependent.

- Taxpayer provides more than 50% of the cost of maintaining that household.

- Taxpayer is a U.S. citizen or a resident alien during the entire tax year.

These are the basics of the Head of Household filing status. As you can see, it can get a little complicated. If you have any follow up questions, or a real-life example that you have questions about, visit us online and ask away!

DEPENDENTS

Whether or not you have dependents to claim will probably make a big difference on your tax return. For the tax year 1999, you can reduce your taxable income by $2,750 for each dependent you claim, regardless of whether or not you itemize deductions.

That's a significant reduction, so make sure you're taking maximum advantage of the opportunity. In case you have any doubt as to who qualifies as a dependent, here's an explanation.

Who's a Dependent?

For someone to be claimed as a dependent, they must meet all five of the following tests:

• Support Test

• Gross Income Test

• Citizenship Test

• Joint Return Test

• Member of Household or Relationship Test

The Support Test

The support test requires you to: 1) provide more than 50% of the person's total financial support, or 2) provide more than 10% of the person's total financial support if you share that responsibility with others. The total shared support must be more than 50% of the person's total financial support.

Support includes things such as food, lodging, clothing, education, medical and dental expenses, recreation, transportation, and other necessities. You can't include your own mortgage payments, though. The fair rental value of the lodging, not the mortgage payment, is classified as support. The fair rental value is the amount the dependent would have been required to pay on the open market for comparable lodging.

Also considered to be support are student loan proceeds used for education and living expenses provided by the individual responsible for repayment of the loan. Scholarships received by a dependent who is a full-time student for at least five months during the year are not considered support. But if a parent takes out a student loan and the money is spent on the dependent's education, then the money is considered support. (After all, the parent will be paying it back later.) If a parent cosigns a student loan with a child, with the expectation that the student will be paying the money back, then that shouldn't be considered support.

When the support test is fuzzy: Most people can easily meet the support test, but for some, the support question is very difficult to answer. Many parents whose children have substantial other income (such as college students), for example, need to pay close attention to the rules.

ASK ROY

Which Sister Should Claim?

My two sisters and I support our mother who lives alone on a small pension. Who can claim the dependent exemption?

A:

As long as you and your sisters together provide more than 50% of your mother's total financial support and each sister provides at least 10% of her total financial support, and all of the other tests are met, you can decide among yourselves who will claim the dependent. Use IRS Form 2210, "Multiple Support Declaration," signed by each of you, and attach it to the return of the one who will claim the dependent. In such cases, the dependent exemption usually floats from person to person annually. But depending on your tax status and the tax status of your sisters, there are some tax planning opportunities available. For example, if the exemption will drop one of you into a lower tax bracket, or will permit one of you who's in a higher bracket to save more money, then that might be taken into account.

Another concern is the child who may have a substantial custodial account or trust account. Don't blow your dependent exemption by letting the child receive too much income from these financial vehicles in the early years.

With careful planning, you can postpone losing the dependency exemption.

The Gross Income Test

For 1999, the rules state that a person must have less than $2,750 of gross income to be claimed as a dependent—with a few exceptions.

• The gross income test does not apply to children under 19 as of the end of the tax year.

• It also doesn't apply to children under 24 who were full-time students during at least five months of the tax year.

The Citizenship Test

Don't worry—the citizenship test doesn't mean that your dependents need to be able to recite the Declaration of Independence. Instead, it requires that the dependent must be either a U.S. citizen, resident, or national—or a resident of either Canada or Mexico.

Joint Return Test

This test states that no exemption may be claimed for a dependent who files a joint return. But there is an exception. If the joint return is filed: (a) only to claim a refund of tax withheld; *and* (b) if neither spouse is required to file; and (c) no tax liability would exist for either spouse if separate returns were filed, then a joint return can be filed and the dependent exemption can still be claimed. The exception is very narrow, but it can sometimes apply.

Member of Household (or Relationship) Test

To meet this test, the dependent must:

• Live in your household for the entire year *or*

• Be "closely" related to you.

Persons closely related to you do not have to live in your household to meet the test. Who do our friends at the IRS consider to be closely related? Here's the list:

A child, grandchild, great-grandchild, adopted child, stepchild, brother or sister, half brother or half sister, brother-in-law or sister-in-law, stepbrother or stepsister, father or mother, grandparent, father-in-law or mother-in-law, stepfather or stepmother, aunt or uncle, niece or nephew, son-in-law or daughter-in-law.

Note that a person who dies during the year and was a member of the household until death still meets the member-of-household test. In addition, a child who was born and died during the year also meets the test.

Note that space aliens who have come to earth and have been living with you for the last eight months as members of your family do not meet the member-of-household test, no matter how adorable they are and how much you love them.

Children of Divorced Parents

There are special considerations regarding children of divorced parents. We cover them a little later.

More Information

In conclusion, know that the dependent tests can get even more complicated than this. So if you have any additional questions, check out IRS Publication 501.

MARRIAGE

We tend to think of the many benefits of marriage, such as having someone around to cook meals or squash bugs. We may daydream about wedding gowns, honeymoons, children, and homes. But there's a dark side, too: the marriage penalty.

The Marriage Penalty

If you're new to the wonderful world of taxation, you may have heard the phrase "marriage penalty" but might be wondering what it means. It has nothing to do with toilet seats left up or nighttime snoring serenades. Instead, it refers to some negative consequences, tax-wise, of being married.

First, know that when you're married, you and your spouse can file your taxes in one of two ways: jointly ("married filing jointly") or separately ("married filing separately"). Both are legal and viable options and depending on your circumstances, using one is probably more advantageous than using the other.

Filing separately doesn't mean that you're filing exactly like a single person. Instead, you'll each be using the "married filing separately" status. Married filing separately tax brackets are exactly half of the married filing jointly brackets, but are still less favorable than the rates for single people. In other words, once married, you probably can't avoid the marriage penalty, but you can, through planning and strategizing, minimize it.

Many people believe that couples filing jointly end up paying less than those filing separately. Frequently, though, this is far from the truth. Exemptions for joint filers are not simply twice that for single filers.

Whenever both spouses work, they typically have to pay a higher "joint" tax rate on their total income than they would pay if each were filing as a single person. This usually happens when both spouses have relatively equal incomes.

For example, say that two taxpayers each had adjusted gross income of $33,000 in 1999, and assume that it would be double that ($66,000) on a joint return. With the standard deduction and no other deductions and/or credits, their married-joint tax under 1999 rules would amount to $9,328, but their single tax (on $33,000) would amount to $3,919 each (for a total of $7,838). Simple subtraction reveals that their marriage penalty amounts to $1,490. An additional $1,490 simply for the privilege of being married—no other reason.

Ouch!

Joint filers fork over an additional $1,490 in tax for a number of reasons. The standard deduction for the joint return is $7,200. This is considerably less than $8,600, which represents twice the standard deduction for a single return ($4,300). But the main driver of this "penalty" is the fact that in our example, the joint return filers will pay tax at a 28% rate on a much larger portion of income, while the singles would each pay at a top rate of only 15%.

Why?

Take a gander at the tax table for single filers, and you'll see that (in 1999) the 15% rate bracket tops out at a taxable income of $25,750. Common sense might suggest that the joint 15% bracket would then top out at twice that, $51,500. But taxes and common sense often don't go hand in hand. The actual top end of the 15% rate for a joint return is only $43,050. This is substantially less than twice the single top amount, which is why the joint return will pay tax at the 28% rate while the two single returns will never get above the 15% rate.

And it gets worse. At the high end of the scale, if each spouse had taxable income of, say, $150,000 (total of $300,000), the couple would pay almost $7,500 more tax than if each were single.

There are even more marriage penalties. These don't apply to everyone, or in every year, but they still mean more tax when they do hit. Here's a list of some of the more common ones:

• Quicker loss of itemized deductions: A married couple starts to lose their itemized deductions when their total combined adjusted gross income exceeds $126,600. If single, each could earn $126,600 (total of $253,200) before losing any itemized deductions. This is a big difference!

• Quicker loss of personal exemptions: A married couple starts to lose their personal exemptions at a combined adjusted gross income of $189,950. For singles, this point begins at adjusted gross income of $126,600 (total for two: $253,200).

• Lower capital loss deduction: A married couple can deduct capital losses up to $3,000 total. The same two persons, if filing separately, could deduct a total of $6,000 ($3,000 each).

• Reduced passive activity loss deduction for active rental real estate owner: A married couple that actively participates in renting out real estate property can deduct up to $25,000 of loss from the activity if their modified adjusted gross income is $100,000 or less. If single, each would get a deduction of up to $25,000 ($50,000 total) and each could earn $100,000 ($200,000 total).

By now, it's probably hard to imagine any benefit in filing jointly. Well, for many couples, joint filing is indeed the smart choice. This often is the case when there's a wide discrepancy in individual earnings.

A Call for Reform

Many point to the marriage penalty as glaring evidence of the need for a fairer and more logical tax code. A number of folks in the House and Senate have attempted to address this issue and correct it—obviously without success. So this is not an issue lost on your Federal representatives. Some proposed tax changes do address the marriage penalty, but in our opinion, the proposals don't go far enough. If you believe that the marriage penalty is nothing more than a way for Uncle Sam to reach deeper into your pockets, you might want to express your feelings directly to your congressperson or senator.

Married Filing Separately

Once you're aware of the many disadvantages of filing jointly, you might think to yourself, "Fine, then. We'll just file separately."

Hold on, though. That's not necessarily the right decision. There are many complications to this filing status that are not immediately apparent at first blush. As is often the case with tax questions, there is no clear-cut answer that we can recommend for you. It depends on your particular tax situation.

In general, your decision will depend on which filing status results in the lowest tax. But there is a very important consideration that you should take into account. If you and your spouse file a joint return, each of you is jointly and individually liable for the full amount of the tax and any interest or penalty due on a joint return. This means that if your spouse decides to take the cash out of the bank and run away to Costa Rica, you could be stuck with the total tax liability.

Therefore, regardless of which method results in less tax, you may choose to file a separate return if you want to be responsible only for your own tax. (This might be a particularly smart choice if you've seen a lot of travel brochures lying around the house and there's been no discussion of a romantic getaway or family vacation.)

In most cases, filing jointly offers the most tax savings, particularly when the spouses have different income levels. The blending effect of combining the two incomes can bring some of it out of a higher tax bracket. For example, if one spouse has $75,000 of taxable income and the other has just $15,000, filing jointly can save about $1,500 in taxes over filing separately.

There is also tax-saving potential to filing separately when one spouse has significant medical expenses, casualty losses, or "miscellaneous itemized deductions." The allowable amount of these deductions is affected by the adjusted gross income. Medical expenses, for example, are deductible only to the extent they exceed 7.5% of AGI. Casualty losses must exceed 10% of AGI. Miscellaneous itemized deductions, which include, for example, investment expenses (other than investment interest), nonreimbursed employee expenses, and tax return preparation costs, are deductible to the extent that their combined total exceeds 2% of AGI. (This is often referred to as the "2% floor.")

If these deductions are isolated on the separate return of a spouse, that spouse's lower (separate) AGI, as compared to the higher joint AGI, can result in larger total deductions. For example, if one spouse has $7,000 in medical expenses and the couple's joint income is $90,000, then only $250 is deductible on a joint return, because 7.5% of $90,000 is $6,750 (and $7,000 - $6,750 = $250). But if the income of the spouse with the medical expenses is only $15,000, the deduction increases to $5,875 on a separate return, because 7.5% of $15,000 is only $1,125 ($7,000 - $1,125 = $5,875).

Note, though, that the amounts you claim as a deduction for exemptions and for itemized deductions, including miscellaneous itemized deductions, are phased out (i.e., reduced) once your AGI goes above a certain limit, depending on your filing status. The limit is higher for joint returns than for separate returns.

For example, in the case of the phase-out of personal exemptions, the AGI threshold in 1999 for joint returns is $189,950 as compared to only $94,975 for separate returns. Thus, if you file a married-separate return, your deduction for exemptions is phased out beginning when your AGI exceeds $94,975. But if you and your spouse file a joint return, your deduction for exemptions doesn't begin to phase out until your AGI exceeds $189,950. This means a phase-out that might occur on a separate return may be avoided if you and your spouse file a joint return.

The amount of tax savings at stake will vary depending on how many exemptions are claimed and your income levels. Similar phase-out rules also apply for the reduction of your itemized deductions that may be affected by the married-separate decision. (Married folks filing jointly will enter phase-out ranges more quickly than will married folks filing separately.)

There are many other factors that should affect your decision of filing jointly or separately. For example, the child and dependent care credit, adoption expense credit, and Hope and Lifetime credits are only available to a married couple filing a joint return. And you can't take the credit for the elderly or the disabled if you file separate returns unless you and your spouse lived apart for the entire year. Nor can you deduct qualified education loan interest unless a joint return is filed. You may also not be able to deduct contributions to your IRA if either you or your spouse was covered by an employer retirement plan and you file separate returns. And a Roth IRA contribution or conversion is virtually out of the question. Nor can you exclude adoption assistance payments or any interest income from series EE savings bonds that you used for higher education expenses if you file separate returns.

In addition, Social Security benefits are in some instances more heavily taxed on a couple filing separately. The benefits are tax-free when modified AGI does not exceed $32,000 for a joint return, but the base amount is zero on a married-separate return.

The Impact on State Taxes

The decision you make for federal income tax purposes may have an impact on your state income tax bill, too, so the total tax impact has to be compared. For example, an overall federal tax saving by filing separately might be offset by an overall state tax increase, or a state tax saving might offset a federal tax increase. Obviously, this will depend on your state of residency and the laws of your state. But it's certainly an issue to consider before making your final decision.

Unfortunately, we can't give you any definitive rules of thumb for when it pays to file separately. The tax laws have grown so complex over the years that there are often a number of different factors involved in any given situation. The only real way that you can determine exactly which filing status is best for you is to "run the numbers." That is, prepare your tax returns using *both* methods, and then make your decision. It can be a difficult process. If you use tax preparation software, the preparation of these returns is less daunting—*if* you know the law and apply it correctly.

Finally, those of you residing in "community property" states have even more issues to deal with when trying to separate joint income and assets.

Community Property

Let's now take a look at the "nuts and bolts" regarding the married-separate filing status, especially when dealing with community property states.

In a separate property state, the computations for the married-separate filing are fairly simple. You report only your own income and deductions on your separate return. If you do have joint assets with your spouse, special consideration must be given to how those assets are split.

But in a community property state (AZ, CA, ID, LA, NV, NM, TX, WA, and WI), generally all earnings, while married, are considered "joint," even if they are deposited into separate accounts. Assets purchased with joint funds may also be considered "community" assets if they are purchased with community funds. Therefore, in these states it is much more difficult to identify "separate" property.

Inheriting Property

What would you do if your rich Uncle Bill left you all of his stocks when he died? Have a party? Probably—as Bill was pretty loaded. But have you considered how this windfall will affect you? After all, you don't know the cost basis of the shares or even if you have a gain or loss.

It's important to note the difference between a gift and an inheritance (received from someone's estate). There's a big difference between the two.

With a gift of appreciated stock or property, your basis (or cost, for tax purposes) is the same basis that the person who gave you the gift originally had. So with gifts, you need to attempt to trace the cost all the way back to the person who originally owned it and gave it to you. This can sometimes be difficult.

With an inheritance, you get what is called a stepped-up basis for tax purposes. What this means is that your basis (i.e., cost) is established at the fair market value of the stock on the date of death of the donor.

The estate's tax return should disclose the value of the stock at date of death. Alternatively, if you know the date, you can get the stock price online at various sources—or even by calling your broker or the company's investor relations department and asking. Once you determine the value, back up your findings with a letter from the broker or the shareholder relations department. You'll need that information just in case the IRS wants to double-check (read: audit) your tax return.

As noted above, if you file a separate income tax return, you would report only your own income, deductions, exemptions, and credits on your separate return. But if you live in a community property state, this means you and your spouse must each report half of your combined community income and deductions, in addition to your separate income and deductions. The way you figure these amounts is affected by the community property rules of your state. Federal income tax law recognizes these rules for tax reporting purposes.

You must first determine whether your income is community income or separate income, as determined under the laws of the state where you live. This classification is important because if you file a separate return, only half the community income is reported on your return while all of your separate income must be included on it.

Generally, community income is all income from community property (also determined under state law), as well as salaries, wages, and other pay for the services of either or both spouses during their marriage. Generally, income from a spouse's separate property (as determined under state law) is the separate income of that spouse. For those of you who live in Idaho, Louisiana, Texas, and Wisconsin, income from most separate property is treated as community income.

Whether income from real estate property is community income or separate income depends upon the laws of the state where the property is located. If you and your spouse bought property during your marriage with both community funds and separate funds, income from the property would be partly community income and partly separate income.

Gains and losses from property are characterized as separate or community depending on whether the property producing the gain or loss is separate property or community property. Thus, a casualty loss to your community property home would be deductible, with each spouse deducting half.

The way you split other deductions generally depends on whether the expenses relate to community or separate income. Deductions for expenses incurred to earn or produce community business or investment income would be divided equally between you and your spouse. Deductions for expenses relating to separate business or separate investment income would be deductible by the spouse who is taxable on the income. Itemized deductions, such as charitable contributions or medical expenses, are generally considered paid from community funds and spouses must split the deductions 50-50. (If it can be shown that these expenses were actually paid from separate funds, they would be deductible by the spouse who paid them.)

Identifying your community and separate income and deductions according to the laws of your state is a very complicated task. This is why untrained people who try to use the married-separate filing status frequently find themselves on the wrong side of tax laws and regulations. Therefore, before you try to file that return using the married-separate status, your *minimum* required reading should be IRS Publications 504 and 555. The time you spend now may well save you a bunch of hassles down the line.

The Kiddie Tax

Kids with investment income don't escape the notice of the IRS. For them, there's the "kiddie tax." This so-called tax is not really a specific tax at all. Instead, it refers to the limitations the IRS places on the ability of a child under the age of 14 to have unearned income taxed at the child's lower tax rate. (If you think "kiddie tax" is a silly term, you may prefer to use the full and proper name of the tax: "Tax for Children Under Age 14 Who Have Investment Income of More Than $1,400." What—you'd rather not? We didn't think so.)

For tax year 1999, the kiddie tax provisions work like this:

- The first $700 in unearned income (such as interest, dividends, capital gains, etc.) is not subject to tax, either at the child's rate or the parents' rate.

- Unearned income of more than $700 and up to $1,400 is taxed at the child's rate (generally 15%, and usually much lower than the parents' rate).

- Unearned income of more than $1,400 is taxed at an adjusted parents' rate. (Unless the child's rate is greater, that is. This isn't likely, but it's possible.)

The kiddie tax rules *do not* apply if:

- The child is under age 14 and neither parent is alive at the end of the taxable year; or

- The child is age 14 or over as of December 31 of the taxable year.

Filing the Tax

There are two ways to file and pay the kiddie tax. The child can file her own return and compute the tax on Form 8615, or the parents can report the child's income on their own tax return using Form 8814 ("Parents' Election To Report Child's Interest and Dividends"). But there are restrictions to reporting the child's income on the parents' tax return. Form 8814 can only be filed if:

- The child's income is from interest and dividends *only*. (Capital gains from sales of stock would violate Form 8814.)

- The child's gross income for the year is less than $7,000.

- No prior-year estimated tax overpayments are applied to the child's current-year return.

- No estimated tax or withholding tax has been paid in the child's name.

So be sure to keep these restrictions in mind when making your decision about how to file.

Deciding Which Filing Option to Use

Before the Small Business Protection Act passed in August of 1996, the best recommendation was almost always: "File the child's return alone, using Form 8615." But the 1996 Tax Act corrected the quirk in the law that provided a greater benefit for the child filing an individual return. Now that the parent and child are back on a more level playing field, you must determine the method that will be most appropriate for your situation.

Some advantages of filing the child's income on the parents' return:

• Avoids the hassle of filing a separate return for the child.

• The parents' net investment income may be increased, which may allow a larger investment interest deduction for the parent.

• The adjusted gross income ceiling for charitable contributions is higher, which may allow for an increased deduction for charitable contributions.

• The first $1,400 of the child's income is taxed on Form 8814 and is not included in the parents' taxable income. This may reduce state tax liability in states that base income tax on the federal taxable income.

• If the child files his own return, he could be subject to the Alternative Minimum Tax, but the AMT might not kick in when reporting on the parents' return.

But there are also disadvantages (of course) to reporting the child's income on the parents' tax return:

• The additional income, by increasing the parents' AGI, can reduce or eliminate the deductibility of some itemized deductions. These may include the medical expense deduction, the deduction for casualty and theft losses, and miscellaneous itemized deductions.

• The additional income can reduce the $25,000 rental loss allowable for active participation. (If you own rental property, you probably already know this. If not, you should read IRS Publication 527.)

• Because of the increase in the parents' AGI, the deduction for an IRA contribution may be phased out or eliminated. It's even possible that the additional income could prohibit a conversion from a regular IRA to a Roth IRA. This increase in the parents' AGI might also trigger other conditions that are based on AGI, such as the taxability of Social Security benefits.

TAX STRATEGY

How to Beat the System

First, if at all possible, keep the reported unearned income below $700 for each child until they reach age 14. Barring that, at least keep the income below $1,400 to avoid paying tax on the unearned income at the parents' adjusted tax rate (more on that rate later). How do you do this?

- Using series EE Savings Bonds is one option. Bonds are not very Foolish—especially for children—but you can elect that the interest on the bonds not be recognized until sometime after the child reaches age 14. Or, if the income is limited, you can elect to report the income even before age 14.

- Stocks outperform bonds in the long run and are the best vehicle for those who (like children) have a long investing horizon. Consider investing in growth stocks that don't pay dividends and that you won't sell until after the child reaches age 14. Many young and dynamic companies don't pay dividends, as they need any excess cash to fuel further growth. At the time of this writing, Microsoft and America Online were examples of this type of company. (These are merely examples. You won't run out and buy any company's stock because of a mere mention in a book—right?)

- Be careful with mutual funds. They are required to pay out dividends and capital gains regularly, resulting in... oops— unearned income. Instead of mutual funds, you might want to build a stock portfolio for your child.

And for goodness sake, don't invest in double tax-free municipal bonds or municipal bond funds until the taxable earned income is greater than $1,400 per year. The returns on these are generally significantly lower than your local bank's money market account or savings bonds. These are mainly used by high-income folks, not ordinary Fools.

- The additional income may reduce the earned income credit, the child tax credit, the dependent care credit, the Hope credit, the Lifetime Learning credit, and any other credits that are based on AGI.

- The additional income may result in higher state tax liability for states that base their income taxes on federal AGI.

The Tax Rate for Income Above $1,400 Per Year

The tax rate used in computing the kiddie tax is the rate that would apply to the parents if the child's net unearned income were added to the parents' taxable income. This could put the child's income in a higher tax bracket than the parents'.

The kiddie tax, while a valuable part of your tax strategy, can lead to some confusion. Keeping the above tips in mind while planning your child's investments will make this planning easier. Also helpful to the planning process is IRS Publication 929, "Tax Rules for Children and Dependents."

The Child Tax Credit

One of the changes enacted by the Taxpayer Relief Act of 1997 allows qualified taxpayers to claim a $500 tax credit each year for each qualifying child still under the age of 17 at the end of the tax year. Let's briefly look at this new credit.

How It Works

If your modified adjusted gross income is $110,000 or less (for married people filing a joint return), $75,000 (for single or Head of Household filers), or $55,000 (for married-filing-separately filers), and you have a qualifying child in your household, you will be able to claim a $500 credit for this child.

For a child to be deemed "qualifying," the child must have a tax identification number (normally a Social Security number) and must be all of the following:

• A dependent (or qualified for the dependency deduction)

• Related to the taxpayer (son, daughter, stepson, stepdaughter, or an eligible foster child)

• Under the age of 17 as of the end of the year. This means that if your child turns age 17 in 1999, the child is not eligible for the child tax credit for the tax year 1999. This is true even if his or her 17th birthday falls on December 31, 1999 (or any future tax year). If the child is 17 at any time during the year, he or she is not qualified for the credit.

• A citizen, national, or resident of the U.S.

So if your modified AGI is below the limits noted above, and you have a qualifying child, you will receive a $500 credit per qualifying child for 1999. Simple as that. No other computations will be required. No other forms to fill out. And remember that this is a credit against your tax—a direct dollar-for-dollar reduction of your actual tax liability. It is not a deduction (which is much less valuable), but an actual credit.

Example: Amy and Howard Waddell, who own a business that makes eyelashes for action figures, have modified AGI in 1999 of $65,000. They also have three qualifying children (Tim, James, and Jason). When they compute their 1999 taxes, they determine that their total tax liability (before any credits) amounts to $7,500. From this tax liability, they take their child credit in the amount of $1,500 ($500 per child). Their net tax liability is now just $6,000. (And no, they can't just send the government five hammers and a toilet seat!) They also have federal withholding of $7,500. When they apply their withholding against their net tax liability, they'll receive a federal refund of $1,500. For Amy and Howard, the child credit reduced their tax liability by almost 17%. That's a pretty big reduction.

Phase-Out Rules

As with most tax laws, it wouldn't be any fun without some complications. The first issue for this law is the phase-out of the modified AGI. If your modified AGI is below the levels noted above (also called the "threshold amounts"), you don't have any problems. But what if your income is greater than the levels noted? Do you simply lose the credit entirely? Not necessarily.

The amount of the total credit you can take is reduced by $50 for each $1,000 (or fraction thereof) of modified AGI exceeding the threshold amounts. Some simple math will tell you that if you are a Head of Household filer with one qualifying child, your full $500 child credit will be received when your modified AGI is $75,000 or less, and will be completely phased out when your modified AGI is more than $83,000. If your modified AGI falls between those amounts, you're in the "phase-out" range. The IRS provides worksheets in the instructions to Form 1040 that you should use to compute your partial credit.

Example #1: Jill Kianka, an armpit sniffer at a deodorant company, files as Head of Household and she has one qualifying child, Hanna. Her modified AGI for 1999 is $74,000. She will receive the entire $500 credit for 1999.

Example #2: Same facts as above, but assume that Jill's 1999 modified AGI is $90,000. She will not receive *any* child credit. Her AGI exceeded the threshold amount by $15,000. Therefore, her child credit must be reduced (but not below zero) by $50 for each $1,000 of AGI over the threshold amount. Jill's income is $15,000 over the threshold amount. To compute how much to reduce the credit, divide the $15,000 by $1,000. That equals 15. Multiply 15 by $50 to get $750. Since the credit is only $500, she will lose the entire credit.

Example #3: Same facts as above, but assume that Jill's 1999 modified AGI is $78,000. It exceeds the threshold amount by $3,000. She'll have to reduce her credit by $150 ($3,000 divided by 1,000 is 3; 3 multiplied by $50 is $150). Her credit will be $350 ($500 minus $150).

Note that the amount of the credit is based on the number of qualifying children, while the phase-out is based on the total dollar amount of the credit. So the more children you have, the greater your potential credit and the wider your phase-out range. By way of explanation, let's look at example #2 again, but add another qualifying child.

Example: Jill, filing under Head of Household status, has two qualifying children and a modified AGI of $90,000. She is still $15,000 over the threshold, and will still be required to reduce her child credit by the $750 computed above. But, since she now has two children, she will start with a base credit of $1,000 (2 times $500 credit for each child) and will receive the benefit of a $250 child credit ($1,000 minus the $750 reduction). In effect, if Jill has one child, her phase-out range is from $75,000 to $83,000. But if she has two children, her phase-out range is from $75,000 to $91,000. And if she has three children, her phase-out range is from $75,000 to $99,000. And so on, and so on, and so on. The computations work exactly the same for each filing status. (All of a sudden, having 24 children is looking attractive, right? What—it isn't?)

Remember that the child credit rules do not take the place of any other credits for which you may otherwise qualify—such as the earned income credit or the dependent care (i.e., child care) credit.

The rules get even more complex when you have more child credits than you have income tax liability. If you have one or two children and your child tax credit exceeds your tax liability, then any excess credit beyond your liability is simply lost. It can't be carried forward—or carried back.

Example: John and Dawn Starostka have two qualifying children. Their tax liability *before* taking the child tax credit amounts to $700. Their child tax credit amounts to $1,000. As we pointed out above, the child credit is non-refundable in most instances. This is one of those cases. John and Dawn will be able to reduce their tax liability to zero by using $700 of the child credits. The remaining $300 of "unused" credit is lost forever. It can't be applied to any past or future tax year.

A Break for Some Large Families

If you have three or more children and your credit exceeds your tax liability, you may qualify for an additional child tax credit, which may allow you to use your entire credit and make part of the credit refundable. How do you do this? You complete IRS Form 8812 to compute your additional child tax credit. You are able to use the expanded credit against any Social Security and/or self-employment taxes you paid during the year.

If you are in this situation, you must review IRS Form 8812 and the associated instructions to understand the computations. It's not easy, and can be a bit confusing. And the additional child tax credit does interact with the earned income credit, making computations even more difficult. But the impact of the credit may be well worth the work.

You should also know that for 1998 (and only 1998) the child tax credit was not subject to Alternative Minimum Taxes. It is very possible that Congress will extend this exemption to future years but, as of this time, the exemption from AMT tax computations was only in effect for tax year 1998.

DEPENDENCY EXEMPTIONS FOR CHILDREN OF DIVORCED PARENTS

Divorcing parents have a number of things to be aware of with regard to the dependent status of their children. (We discuss dependency exemptions in general earlier in this book.)

Current Rules

Before we begin, note that neither parent is entitled to the exemption unless both provide between them more than 50% of the child's support for the year. Support, for this purpose, includes the value of any

TAX STRATEGY

Avoid Refunds

Many of you will find that this credit generates a very large federal tax refund. While this may make you happy, it's not a good practice. Think about it. Why should Uncle Sam be holding on to that money of yours all year long? The government doesn't pay you any interest on those big federal tax refunds.

If you're receiving a hefty refund, you might want to consider revising your federal withholding form for 2000 now. If you anticipate a large refund this time next year due to the child tax credit, change your W-4 form now and get that extra cash in your pocket right away. A $1,000 child tax credit ($500 each for two children) for 2000 can increase your monthly take-home pay by almost $100 from now until the end of the year. We suspect that you can put that money to better use than Uncle Sam.

The payroll department at your place of employment will be able to supply you with a W-4 form and instructions that you can use to revise your federal withholding. Make sure that you get the full W-4 form, the one with the worksheets, so that you can make the proper computations. If your employer doesn't have the full W-4 form, you can download it from the IRS website.

housing (or other items) that the parents provide. Assuming the parents combine to meet this support test (and all of the other required support tests are otherwise met), the exemption goes to the parent having custody of the child unless the custodial parent releases his or her claim to the exemption.

The comparative amount of support provided by each parent isn't relevant. Nor is the amount of any child support paid. Essentially, therefore, the parents can decide between themselves who will claim the exemption. This issue is often negotiated between the parents, and made part of the divorce or separation agreement. The exemption can alternate between the parents on a year-by-year basis, if they like.

If each parent has custody for part of the year, the custodial parent is considered for these purposes to be the one who has custody for the greater portion of the year. Many people live in states that institute what is known as "joint custody," and assume that you are each considered to have the child 50% of the time. This is not true for tax purposes. While your divorce decree may mandate "joint custody," the dependency exemption will go to the parent with the greater physical custody for the year. If you're wondering what happens when physical custody is 50-50, our answer is that that would hardly ever happen. Because if each parent has had a child for six months, you need to count weeks, and then days and if necessary, hours and minutes. It's extremely unlikely that each parent will have had physical custody for exactly 4,380 hours or 262,800 minutes. To take advantage of the exemption, one parent must have had greater physical custody.

The custody rules apply where parents have lived apart (in different residences) at all times during the last six months of the year even if they aren't formally divorced and haven't entered into a written separation agreement.

Exemption Release

Remember that the custodial parent may "release" the dependency exemption to the noncustodial parent. That release can be executed (a) on an annual basis, (b) for one or more future years (e.g., for alternate years), or (c) for all future years. In many cases, the custodial parent is receiving child support or alimony payments from the other parent. The custodial parent might prefer granting the release only on an annual basis so that he or she can refuse to do so if the other parent is delinquent. The custodial parent should make the release on Form 8332. The completed form must be attached to the noncustodial parent's tax return each year that he or she claims the exemption for the child.

Pre-1985 Rules

The rules we've just described only apply to post-1984 divorces and separations. If your divorce took place before 1985, you should be living (and planning) under a completely different set of rules. For pre-1985 split-ups, the noncustodial parent receives the exemption if the divorce decree or agreement says he or she should— as long as he or she contributes at least $600 in support of the child. But remember that regardless of what state law may have to say about child support, custody, and visitation rights, the federal law regarding the exemption deduction is what controls.

The Big Divorce Picture

Divorce is as much an economic event as it is a personal and emotional one. The child exemption is only one of many tax considerations that must be reviewed during divorce negotiations. There are many other even more complex issues that may have an impact on your finances during a divorce. Make sure that your professional representatives, either legal or tax, have knowledge of divorce tax issues and advise you to act accordingly.

CHILD AND DEPENDENT CARE CREDITS AND FLEXIBLE SAVINGS ACCOUNTS

If you have a young child or children, you may qualify to take advantage of the child care credit. And if your employer offers Flexible Savings Accounts ("FSAs"—many times also called "cafeteria plans"), there's an important relationship between the two that you should understand. But let's first review what the child care credit is.

The Child Care Credit

It permits you to take as a credit an "employment-related" expense. In other words, the expense must enable *both* you and your spouse to work, and it must be for the care of your child (or other dependent) who is either under 13 or disabled. Paying the next door neighbor to baby-sit while you and your spouse take in a dinner and a movie does *not* qualify.

The typical expenses that qualify are payments to a day care center, nanny, or nursery school. Sleep-away and sports camps generally don't qualify. The cost of first grade or higher doesn't qualify because it's primarily an education expense and not a "care" expense. Surprisingly, the rules on kindergartens aren't clearly defined. Apparently, if the school offers a program similar to a nursery school's (more "care" than education), it can qualify. If it offers more of an educational program, it may not.

To claim the credit, you and your spouse must file a joint return and complete IRS Form 2441. You must include the name, address, and Social Security number of the care-giver (or tax I.D. number, if it's a day care center or nursery school). In addition, a day care center must be in compliance with state and local regulations. You also must include on the form the Social Security number of the child(ren) receiving the care. There's no credit without it. Omission of the Social Security numbers while still claiming the credit will result in a summary assessment of tax liability against you.

Limitations

Several limits apply. First, qualifying expenses are limited to the income you or your spouse earn from work, using the figure for whoever earns *less*. Therefore, if one of you has no earned income, you will *not* be entitled to any credit. (However, special rules essentially remove this limitation for a spouse who's a full-time student or who is disabled.)

Next, qualifying expenses for any year can't exceed $2,400 per year if you have one qualifying child, or $4,800 per year for two or more. In most cases, this limit will set the ceiling for you. (If your employer has a dependent care assistance program under which you receive benefits excluded from gross income, these limits are reduced by the excludable amounts you receive.)

Finally, the credit will be computed as a percentage of your qualifying expenses—in most cases, 20%. If your joint adjusted gross income is $28,000 or less, the percentage will be higher, but never above 30%.

There's a sliding scale involved, with the percentage of the credit falling between 20% and 30% depending on your AGI.

Example: Rick and Maria Munarriz both work and place their son, Kevin, in a day care center. Maria earns $65,000 but Rick earns only $6,000. They spend $8,500 annually on day care. As mentioned earlier, since Rick's income is the lower one, their qualifying expenses are limited to his income. That's just the first limitation. The second limits them further to $2,400 (since there is only one child involved). Twenty percent of this amount is $480, so that's their child care credit. If their expenses were for two or more children, their credit would be $960 (20% of the $4,800 limit).

Remember that a credit reduces your tax bill dollar for dollar. Therefore, in our example, Rick and Maria will pay $480 less in taxes by virtue of the credit. A $480 deduction might only save them $134 (28% of $480), but a $480 credit saves a full $480. Credits are *always* more valuable than deductions.

Dependent Care Flexible Spending Accounts

If your employer offers a dependent care flexible spending account (FSA), you may wish to consider participating in it instead of taking the child care credit. Under a dependent care FSA, you may contribute up to $5,000 on a pre-tax basis. The money is withheld by your employer from your paycheck and placed with a plan administrator in a noninterest-bearing account. As you incur dependent care costs, you submit a statement with the plan administrator substantiating the cost and receive reimbursement. Dependent care FSAs are generally more advantageous from a tax perspective than taking the tax credit. But your situation may well be an exception—run the numbers and see which strategy is best for you.

Let's see what would happen if Rick and Maria contributed the $5,000 maximum to a dependent care FSA. Their combined gross income of $71,000 would be reduced by the $5,000 contribution to $66,000. Assuming a $7,200 standard deduction (married filing jointly), and three $2,750 exemptions (one each for Rick, Maria, and their child) totaling $8,250, Rick and Maria will have taxable income of $50,550 ($66,000 - $7,200 - $8,250).

The 1999 tax on $50,550 for married taxpayers filing jointly is $8,558 (using the tax rate schedule). The 1999 tax for taxable income of $55,550 (Rick and Maria's taxable income if they hadn't excluded $5,000 under the dependent care FSA) would be $9,958. By using the FSA, they save $1,400 in federal income taxes as opposed to $480 by taking the child care credit. That's almost $1,000 extra. Think of all the boxes of Fruit Loops it'll buy!

Not only can participation in a dependent care FSA save you money on your income tax—it can also save on FICA (Social Security) taxes, because contributions to the FSA aren't counted as wages for FICA purposes. Consequently, you may save up to 7.65% of the amount contributed to the FSA depending upon your income and the taxable wage base for the year in which the contribution is made. In the example above, Rick and Maria would save an additional $382.50 in FICA taxes by contributing to the FSA as opposed to taking the child care credit directly.

And it can get *even better:* If you live in a state that imposes an income tax, it is possible that the contribution to your FSA will also be exempt from state income taxes, thereby reducing your tax liability even further.

But not all of the news is good: There are four major drawbacks to dependent care FSAs. First, money is deposited in an FSA on a use-it-or-lose-it basis. If you don't incur dependent care expenses that equal or exceed the amount you plopped into your FSA, you forfeit the surplus. Second, once you elect to participate in an FSA and elect the amount withheld, you may not change your election (except for a few limited exceptions). Third, it often takes several weeks to receive reimbursement for the expenses submitted. Fourth, if you *don't* otherwise qualify for the credit (such as only one spouse working), and you use the FSA option, you will be required to add your FSA contribution back into your income—thereby losing most of your tax savings. The FSA won't work if you don't qualify for the credit.

It's important that you review your options and the benefits provided by your employer in order to determine what is best for you. Upon review, you may find that an FSA saves you the most moolah. To learn about this and other child care issues in greater detail, see IRS Form 2441 and the associated instructions. See also IRS Publication 503.

THE EARNED INCOME CREDIT

The earned income credit (EIC) was enacted in 1975 as a means of targeting tax relief to working low-income taxpayers with children, providing relief from the Social Security tax for such taxpayers, and improving incentives to work. The emphasis here is on low-income taxpayers—but in many cases, the term "low-income" is really in the eye of the beholder.

If you have two or more qualifying children and your modified adjusted gross income is less than $30,580, you may qualify for the credit. At the other end of the spectrum, if you have no qualifying kids, your modified AGI must be less than $10,200 before the EIC kicks in. It's quite possible that you qualify for the EIC and don't even know it. If your income is greater than the thresholds noted above, you might want to just skip this section. But before you do, think for a second: Is it possible that any of your friends or relatives would qualify for the EIC? If so, you might want to take a few minutes to read more about it.

As mentioned above, the EIC was originally introduced to assist low-income working taxpayers with children. Subsequently, it has been expanded to include working individuals *without* children. So don't think that just because you don't have any qualifying children that you are not eligible for the credit. You may be.

General Requirements

In order to qualify for the EIC, you must meet *all* of the following requirements:

- You must have earned income. Earned income isn't just what shows up on your W-2 form. It also includes other stuff, such as Schedule C and F (Business and Farm) income, and other nontaxable income. We'll spend more time on the definition of earned income for EIC purposes later on.

- Your investment income *cannot* be more than $2,350 for 1999. How is investment income defined? We'll discuss that in more detail soon.

- Your filing status *cannot* be married filing separately. If you file separately, you will not be eligible to receive the EIC—regardless of your income status.

- You, your spouse (if you are filing jointly), and the qualifying child(ren) *must* all have Social Security numbers. As you may know, for dependent purposes you may use other identifying numbers (such as ITINs or ATINs). But for EIC purposes, these other numbers will not work.

• You or your spouse may *not* be the qualifying child of another person.

• You may *not* file Form 2555 or Form 2555EZ (the Foreign Earned Income exclusion forms). If you exclude foreign income, you will not be eligible for the EIC.

• If you are a nonresident alien for *any* part of the year, you generally can't claim the credit. But if you are a nonresident alien, check out IRS Publication 596—there are some limited exceptions that might help you out. These exceptions would also include special rules for military personnel stationed outside the U.S.

So if you meet all of the requirements noted above, read on... the news may be good.

Qualifying Children

If you have any children and wish to take advantage of the EIC, those children must be "qualifying" children. In order for a child to be considered a qualifying child, *all three* of these requirements must be met:

• Relationship Test: The child must be your son, daughter, adopted child, grandchild, stepchild, or foster child. A foster child is defined as a child cared for by you as your own child. Unlike the relationship test for dependents, the EIC test has a much more narrow scope. Because of the "foster child" definition, though, there is a large loophole that you might be able to slip through—even if the child in question may not be directly related to you. Remember that the term "foster child" does *not* mean a ward of the court, or placed by an adoption or foster agency. It's just a child that you care for as your own.

• Age Test: The child must be under age 19 at the end of the tax year. If the child is a full-time student, then he or she must be under age 24 at the end of the tax year. If the child is permanently and totally disabled at any time during the tax year, the child can be of any age.

• Abode Test: The child must have lived in your home for more than six months during the year. If your child is a foster child, that child must have lived in your home for *all* 12 months during the year. Generally, this home *must* be within the U.S., but remember that there are special exceptions for military personnel stationed outside of the U.S. Check out IRS Publication 596 for additional discussion on those exceptions.

So... if you are a qualifying taxpayer and you also have qualifying children, you may be in business for the EIC. There are just a few other requirements that must be met:

Your earned income and modified AGI must *each* be less than:

• $26,928 if you have one qualifying child, or

• $30,580 if you have two or more qualifying children.

In addition, you *must* attach Schedule EIC to your tax return in order to provide information about your qualifying children. And that's it. Well... almost. There is one important issue that you've got to remember when dealing with the EIC. You must know that if a child is a qualifying child for more than one person, only the person with the higher modified AGI is eligible for the credit.

Example: Peter and Mary are unmarried and lived together for the entire year. They care for Mary's 10-year-old son Paul. Since they are not married, they file separate tax returns. Peter's income is $50,000 and Mary's income is $12,000. Paul can be considered to be a qualifying child for *either* Peter or Mary. Can Peter or Mary choose who will receive the credit? Nope. In this situation, neither Peter nor Mary will be eligible for the credit. The credit has left on a jet plane without them.

Peter may be able to claim that Paul is his "foster" child. But the problem is that his income is well above the AGI limitations. And while Mary's income is well within the AGI limitations, she is not allowed to claim the EIC for Paul because of the law that says only the person with the higher modified AGI is eligible for the credit. In this case, that would be Peter.

Now, then... what would happen if Paul were not a qualifying child for Peter? Then Paul would only be a qualifying child for Mary, and Mary would receive the credit. So if you're thinking of living with your significant other without the benefit of marriage, be aware of this one little quirk in the EIC rules.

The EIC Without Kids

If you're a low-income taxpayer and have no children, you still get a bite (albeit a small one) of the EIC apple. If you do not have at least one qualifying child, you must meet all of the following requirements in order to claim the EIC:

- Your earned income and modified AGI must each be less than $10,200.

- You must be at least 25 years old but younger than 65 years old at the end of the tax year. If you are married, either spouse can meet this age requirement.

- You (or your spouse if married) *cannot* qualify as a dependent on any other person's tax return.

- Your main home must be in the U.S. for more than half of the year.

Note that you're *not* required to complete Schedule EIC if you don't have kids. That's only required for those with children.

So there you have it. If you meet all of these qualifications, you are eligible for the EIC. (Whoopee!) But think about this for a moment. At the beginning of this section, we noted that the EIC was written into the law in order to help the low-income working taxpayer. Don't these rules and regulations seem a bit complex for the "average" or "low-income" taxpayer to understand? We think so, too. It's nice to offer such a social program for low-income taxpayers. But does it have to be this complicated? The IRS estimates that millions of dollars in EIC payments to taxpayers are going unclaimed because of the complexity of the rules and requirements. The IRS is doing everything that it can to try to notify taxpayers that they may be missing out on EIC payments. But there are still people who fall through the cracks because of the complexity of the laws. (If you're dismayed by this, consider giving your congressperson a jingle and letting him or her know of your concern.)

Speaking of complications, let's now move onto some definitions. (If you didn't think the EIC rules were that complicated before, you might soon reconsider.)

Investment Income Limitations

As you'll recall, in order to qualify for the EIC, your investment income can not exceed $2,350 (for 1999). For the purposes of this discussion, investment income would include:

- Taxable interest and/or dividends

- Tax-exempt interest

- Net income from non-business rents and royalties

- Net capital gains reported on your Schedule D

- Net passive income

So, because of these limitations, it is very possible that your earned income is less than the required amount for EIC purposes, but your excess investment income will not allow you to be eligible for the EIC.

Example: Telephone sanitizer Mark Feldhousen Jr., has a qualifying child for EIC purposes, and has earned income of $15,000. Mark also has net capital gains of $2,500. Because of this excess investment income, he is not eligible for the EIC. Mark's total income is only $17,500—well under the AGI limitations—but since his investment income was over the limit, he loses his entire eligibility for the EIC. So keep this little fact in mind if you may otherwise qualify for the EIC, but have other income from investments.

Earned Income Defined

For purposes of the EIC, earned income includes *all* income from employment, even if this income is not taxable. Taxable earned income would include:

- Wages, salaries, and tips

- Union strike benefits

- Long-term disability benefits received prior to your minimum retirement age

- Net earnings from self-employment

Nontaxable earned income would include:

- Voluntary salary deferrals (deferred compensation)

- Voluntary salary reductions (cafeteria plans/Flexible Spending Accounts)

- Combat zone pay

- Basic and in-kind quarters/subsistence allowances from the U.S. military

- Meals or lodging provided by the employer for the convenience of the employee

- Housing allowance or rental value of a parsonage for the clergy

- Excludible dependent care benefits

- Anything else of value (money, good, or services) for services performed, even if not taxable

So remember, when dealing with the EIC rules, that earned income can include *more* than just your "normal" W-2 wages.

Modified Adjusted Gross Income

For EIC purposes, modified AGI would begin with your normal AGI as reported on your tax return *plus* all of the following:

- Your net capital loss from line 13 of Form 1040

- Any net loss from estates and trusts that you normally report on page two of Schedule E

- 75% of the net loss from non-farm sole proprietorships from line 12 of Form 1040

- 75% of the net loss from farm sole proprietorships from line 18 of Form 1040

- 75% of the net loss from other trades or businesses reported on Schedule E

- Net loss from non-business rents and royalties reported on Schedule E

- Tax-exempt interest

- Nontaxable distributions from pensions, annuities, and IRAs (except for a rollover or trustee-to-trustee transfer of an IRA or other retirement plan)

So if you have a complicated return, you'll have to take a close look at how all of the numbers are assembled in order to determine your correct modified AGI.

Computing the Credit

The most complicated issue regarding the EIC is probably the computation of the credit. If you read the law, trying to compute your EIC is a real head-scratcher. There are separate rates, AGI limitations, percentage limitations, and phase-out limitations. If you had to do these computations by hand, it would be likely that you would arrive at the wrong answer most of the time. But the IRS realized this early on, and provided an all-inclusive table. This and IRS worksheet that you must use to compute the EIC will make the process as painless as possible. Once you complete the worksheet, go to the tables and look up your EIC. You'll find that your EIC will be anywhere from a low of $1 to a high of $3,816, depending upon your personal situation, number of qualifying children, etc.

If all else fails, you can even have the IRS compute the credit for you, if you provide it with the necessary information as noted on the EIC worksheet.

One Final Thought

We know that none of the Fools reading this would ever, *ever* try to pull the wool over the eyes of the IRS and claim the EIC when they are not eligible. But, sadly, many people do. The IRS has determined that the EIC has been tremendously abused over the last number of years. It's easy to do—just about anyone with larceny in his or her heart can. Because of that abuse, the IRS has imposed some pretty tough penalties for those who decide to play fast and lose with the rules.

• Fraud: Any taxpayer who fraudulently claims the EIC is disqualified from taking the EIC for the next *10* years. That's in addition to any criminal prosecution that IRS may try to take.

• Reckless or intentional disregard of the rules: Any taxpayer who improperly claims the earned income credit with a reckless or intentional disregard of the rules is disqualified from taking the credit for the next *two* years. Intentional disregard does not mean a minor math or clerical error. If your credit is denied simply for a minor math or clerical error, you don't have to live in fear of this provision being enforced against you.

• Denial/reinstatement: If you are denied the EIC under either of the two provisions, you must apply for reinstatement by filing IRS Form 8862 "Information To Claim Earned Income Credit After Disallowance."

• Due diligence for tax preparers: Tax preparers are also under the gun. Under the Taxpayer Relief Act of 1997, a $100 penalty is imposed on any preparer who fails to meet "due diligence" requirements regarding the EIC. The IRS has issued procedures that tax preparers must follow to protect themselves from the penalty. So even if you decide to take your return to a tax preparer, be prepared for that preparer to ask you a number of pointed questions in order to shield himself from any potential penalty.

Are the rules complicated? Sure. Are they inordinately complicated? Probably. Is the IRS trying to do the best that it can to give the credit to as many qualifying individuals as possible? Absolutely. But there are some complications, and some concepts and rules that may be difficult to understand. We hope that by highlighting the issues surrounding the EIC you'll be able to more clearly understand the problems—and the solutions.

ADOPTION EXPENSE CREDITS

Before discussing children and related tax issues any further, we should address how you can actually *get* the little ones. No, this isn't going to be a talk about the birds and the bees—that's best left to your parents. But if for some reason procreation the old-fashioned way doesn't work for you, you have another option: adoption. Uncle Sam understands that adoption proceedings can be an expensive process, which is why the Small Business Job Protection Act created a nonrefundable credit for qualified adoption expenses and a new exclusion for employer-provided adoption assistance programs. Congress created these new tax benefits because of a belief that the financial costs of the adoption process should not be a barrier to adop-

TAX STRATEGY

The Advance EIC Pays Throughout the Year

If you are eligible to claim the EIC and have at least one qualifying child, you can receive part of the credit in your paycheck throughout the year. (Why wait for a large federal tax refund?) Apply for the advance EIC and put that money to use immediately.

In order to qualify for the advance EIC payment:

· Your earned income and modified AGI must be below the income limits ($26,928 if one qualifying child; $30,580 if two or more qualifying children), *and*

· You must complete IRS Form W-5 ("Earned Income Credit Advance Payment Certificate") each and every year that you are eligible, and that Form W-5 must be given to your employer.

Advance payments are limited to 60% of the maximum credit for a taxpayer with one qualifying child (up to $1,387 for 1999). Form 1040 (and not Form 1040A or 1040EZ) must be filed in order to report the advance EIC payments that you received during the year, and to report any additional EIC that you may be qualified to claim. So if you believe that you'll qualify for the EIC, make sure to look into the advance EIC payment in order to get those dollars into your pocket early.

tion and to encourage not only regular adoption, but also adoption of children with special needs.

The credit and exclusion are effective for taxable years beginning in 1997. But know that unless new laws are enacted, the exclusion for adoption assistance programs and the general adoption credit are due to expire on December 31, 2001. For 2002 and beyond, only the credit for the adoption of a child with special needs will remain. So if adoption is in your future, you may want to make sure that it's in your near future in order to jump on the adoption credit bandwagon.

Adoption Credit Overview

The law allows a credit for the amount of qualified adoption expenses that you pay during the tax year. The credit is limited to $5,000 of aggregate expenses for each child, or $6,000 per child with special needs. The dollar limitation is for adoption expenses for *each* child, cumulative over all taxable years. It's not an annual limitation. So this is really a child-by-child limitation. Adopt two children, and your limitation rises to $10,000 ($12,000 if both of the children have special needs), but the maximum credit you can take for each child is still $5,000 ($6,000 for a special needs child).

The year that the credit is allowed will depend on whether the child is a U.S. citizen or resident.

If the expenses of a *domestic* adoption are paid before the year the adoption becomes final, the credit is allowed for the taxable year *after* the year the expenses were paid. If the expenses of a domestic adoption were paid or incurred during or after the year the adoption becomes final, the credit is allowed for the year of payment. A credit for the expenses of a *foreign* adoption is not allowed until the tax year that the adoption becomes final. What does this mean exactly?

Well, let's say that Lee and Karen Burbage pay qualified adoption expenses of $2,000 in 1997, $1,500 in 1998, and $2,500 in 1999 for a domestic adoption. The adoption becomes final in 1999. Lee and Karen are allowed a credit of $2,000 in 1998 (representing the expenses paid in 1997). They will also receive a credit of $3,000 in 1999. The $3,000 represents the $1,500 of expenses paid in 1998, and the $2,500 of expenses paid in 1999—that are allowed to be claimed in 1999 because that was the year that the adoption became final. If you're reading carefully, you might have noticed that $1,500 and $2,500 add up to $4,000, not $3,000. What happened to the "lost" $1,000? Well, while Lee and Karen actually paid

$6,000 in qualified adoption expenses, only the first $5,000 is available for the credit. If they adopted a child with special needs, their 1999 credit would have increased to $4,000, since the total expense limitation for a special needs child is $6,000.

If Lee and Karen paid the same expenses for a foreign adoption, they would not have been able to take any of the credit until 1999—the year in which the adoption became final. And their dollar limitations would also be the same: $5,000 or $6,000 for a special needs child.

But the adoption credit is scheduled to end relatively soon. So remember that for *either* a domestic or foreign adoption, no credit is allowed for expenses paid before January 1, 1997, or after December 31, 2001, except for the expenses of adopting a special needs child. As the law is currently written, the credit for the expenses of adopting a special needs child does not have a scheduled ending date. Always remember: Congress giveth, and Congress can taketh away.

If you pay qualified adoption expenses but the adoption is not successful, you are allowed to claim the credit in the next taxable year following the year that the expenses were paid.

Before you begin to see adoption tax credit dollar signs dance before your eyes, note that this is a nonrefundable credit. As we explained in the first section, a nonrefundable credit will only reduce your taxes to zero—and not below. But all's not completely lost. If your credit exceeds your income tax liability, you can carry the excess credit forward for five years.

Some additional bad news: The adoption credit is not exempt from the Alternative Minimum Tax. So if you are in the AMT zone, your adoption credits may amount to much less than you might hope for. So make sure that you're familiar with your AMT status before you spend your credit savings on little Johnny's new highchair.

Qualified Adoption Expenses

In order for your expenses to be available for the adoption credit, they must be "qualified." The tax code defines qualified expenses as those that are reasonable and necessary, and that are directly related to the legal adoption of an eligible child. They would include court costs, attorney fees, and even traveling expenses while away from home. But be aware that qualified expenses do *not* include the costs of any surrogate parenting arrangement *or* the costs of adopting your spouse's child. Expenses are not qualified if they are paid in violation of federal or state law. And none of these expenses can be reimbursed under an employer adoption program or any other state or federal program.

Eligible Children

Not only must the expenses be qualified, but the *child* must also be "eligible." For this purpose, an eligible child must be either:

• Under age 18, *or*

• Physically or mentally incapable of caring for himself or herself

Again, remember that these standards only apply until December 31, 2001. After that date, only expenses paid for the adoption of a child with "special needs" will be applicable toward the credit. A child with special needs is defined as:

• A child who is a U.S. citizen or resident, *and*

• Who cannot or should not be returned to his/her parents' residence (as determined by the applicable state agency), *and*

• Who probably will not be adopted without assistance because of a specific factor or condition. Examples of those factors or conditions would include a child's ethnic background, age, membership in a minority or sibling group, medical condition, or physical, mental, or emotional handicap.

Marital Status

The adoption credit is available to single people and married couples alike.

If you're married, though, at the close of the tax year, you and your spouse must file a joint return in order to claim the credit. When one spouse dies during the year and a joint return is allowed for the survivor and deceased spouse, the credit is allowed only if a joint return is filed. A person legally separated under a decree of divorce or separate maintenance is not considered married. Certain individuals, while not legally divorced, may be considered unmarried for purposes of the credit. If you file a separate return for the year, maintain a household for a qualified individual for more than one-half of the year, and if your spouse is not a member of the household at any time during the last six months of the year, you will likely be considered unmarried for the purposes of the adoption credit.

Income Limitations

No tax law would be complete without deviations and limitations. The adoption credit is no exception. The credit is phased out for taxpayers with modified adjusted gross income over $75,000. The phase-out is complete at modified AGI of $115,000. So if you have income equal to or in excess of $115,000, you can't claim the credit. (These amounts apply to single people and married couples alike.) Seems simple enough, eh? Well, that's really only the start. Fasten your seatbelts for the next paragraph.

Here is the official explanation of the phase-out credit computation, directly from the Internal Revenue Code Section 23(a):

The amount allowable as a credit under subsection (a) for any taxable year (determined without regard to subsection (c)) shall be reduced (but not below zero) by an amount which bears the same ratio to the amount so allowable (determined without regard to this paragraph but with regard to paragraph (1)) as (i) the amount (if any) by which the taxpayer's adjusted gross income exceeds $75,000, bears to (ii) $40,000.

Huh? Well, let's try to look at it in another way. (Finally, some fun for the math majors reading this book!) To compute your credit when you are in the phase-out range, use this formula:

Allowable credit = QAE - [QAE x ((MAGI - $75,000)/40,000)]

Where:
QAE = Qualified adoption expenses for the year
MAGI = Modified adjusted gross income

If you're still scratching your head, we don't blame you. Let's put an example to work. In our earlier example, Lee and Karen had allowable expenses of $3,000 for 1999. Let's assume that their modified AGI amounts to $85,000. Their income is greater than $75,000, so we know right off the bat that their credit will be limited. But we also see that their modified AGI is less than $115,000—so we know that they'll get at least a partial credit. The credit is reduced by the ratio of $10,000 divided by $40,000, or 25%. (The $10,000 is the result of subtracting $75,000 from their modified AGI of $85,000.) Therefore the credit is reduced by $750 (25% times $3,000), to $2,250. Better?

To calculate modified AGI for the purposes of the adoption credit, disregard exclusions for foreign earned income and housing costs, income from specified U.S. possessions, and income from Puerto Rico sources. For most people, your modified AGI will be exactly the same as your normal

AGI. But if you have foreign earned income or exempted income from Puerto Rico, your computations are a bit more complex.

Reporting Compliance

A taxpayer claiming the adoption credit must file IRS Form 8839 with either Form 1040 or Form 1040A. You can't claim the credit when filing with Form 1040EZ. Another filing requirement is that you must identify all eligible children on your return, including, if known, the name, age, and taxpayer identification number (TIN) of each eligible child.

The Adoption Assistance Exclusion

Another nifty provision that adopting taxpayers should know about is the Adoption Assistance Exclusion. You may recall that normally, whenever your employer pays something on your behalf, you must add that value to your taxable income. Well, not so when your employer foots some or all of your adoption bill.

The Adoption Assistance Exclusion provides that your taxable income (assuming that you are a W-2 type employee) would not include amounts paid by your employer for qualified adoption expenses and furnished to you pursuant to an adoption assistance program established by your employer. You can exclude up to a cumulative $5,000 per child ($6,000 for a special needs child). But, as with the adoption credit, this income exclusion is effective for tax years beginning after December 31, 1996, and does not apply to amounts paid after December 31, 2001.

Since the adoption assistance exclusion is based upon a formal plan established by your employer, we'll not spend too much time with it here. Just know that there are income limitations and restrictions on the adoption exclusion—similar to the adoption credit. Make sure to check with your employer's human resources department to see if your employer offers such an adoption assistance program. In most cases, if your employer does maintain such a program, you would be financially better off using the employer program as opposed to the adoption credit. And in many cases, you can take advantage of *both* the credit and the exclusion! So check it out, Fool.

Coordination of Benefits

The adoption credit and the adoption assistance exclusion are coordinated so that you may claim both in relation to one adoption effort but may not claim both for the same expense. If you are within the AGI limitations, you can claim the (up to) $5,000 credit for qualified adoption expenses that *you* pay and exclude from income another $5,000 paid *by your employer* for other qualified adoption expenses. You just can't claim the credit for amounts paid by your employer, even if the payment is not made under a qualified adoption assistance program. And you also can't exclude from income amounts that you pay yourself. If you pay the expenses yourself, you're only eligible for the credit. The combination of both the credit and the exclusion can be a valuable tool when adoption expenses are substantial.

Look at the case of suburban bed-and-breakfast owners Rosy and George. Let's say that it costs them a total of $10,000 to adopt a child. They pay out-of-pocket qualified adoption expenses of $4,000. In addition, George's employer has a qualified adoption assistance program in place. The employer pays $6,000 of qualified adoption expenses directly. George will be able to exclude $5,000 of this assistance payment from his income. (It doesn't even show up on his W-2 as wages—it's completely ignored for tax purposes.) He will have to claim as income the "excess" employer assistance payment of $1,000—but that's still a good deal for him. And it gets better. That $4,000 that he and Rosy paid out-of-pocket for additional qualified adoption expenses? Those expenses are eligible for the adoption credit.

So if adoption is in your future, make sure that you understand how the law works and what is available to you. You can learn more about the rules by looking at IRS Form 8839 and the associated instructions. But if you

TAX TIP

Adoption Taxpayer Identification Numbers

Many people find it difficult to obtain a child's Social Security number while in the midst of an adoption. The IRS understands this and offers a way to obtain a temporary Taxpayer Identification Number in order to comply with the adoption credit reporting requirements. It's commonly called an Adoption Taxpayer Identification Number (or ATIN in tax-speak). This is a temporary ID number issued by the IRS to a child in a domestic adoption when the parents are unable to obtain the child's existing Social Security number or are unable to apply for a new Social Security number until the adoption is final. An ATIN can also be used to claim the dependent exemption for the child and also the child care credit. But it can not be used to claim the earned income credit.

An ATIN can be obtained by filing Form W-7A with the IRS along with a copy of legal placement documentation. The ATIN will remain in effect for two years. If you need to keep the ATIN in effect for a longer period of time, an extension is available. For more information, get Form W-7A from the IRS.

really want to get into the meat of the adoption rules, read IRS Publication 968.

FAMILY INCOME SHIFTING

Little ones enrich your life and make you realize how lucky you are to be a Fool. If you're a long-term investor, you'll spend time with your arms wrapped around your child, and not around a bunch of market-timing charts and graphs. Your youngsters will be your best friends and your companions on lazy Saturday afternoons. They'll drag mud—and lost animals—into the house. They'll even pull grandpa's finger (at least once). And for all the joy that they'll bring into your life, children are also important for a financial reason. And that is... because their tax rate is lower than yours.

If you can find ways to move income that would be taxable to you (at your higher bracket) to your children, the entire family will benefit in the long run. Heck—it's not even just the kids that can get in on the action. You may have parents whom you support in one way or another. This means that their tax bracket is likely also lower than yours. So if you can get some of your taxable income into their lower rates... well, you can see the positive impact for the family.

What you are doing is "shifting" your income from a higher bracket to a lower bracket. Is it legal? Sure, when done correctly. Does the IRS like it? Not necessarily, which is why the "kiddie tax" rules (among others) were put into place. But as long as you do all of the right things and stay within the law, Uncle Sam is at your mercy for a change.

Let's take a few minutes to discuss some of the most common income shifting techniques.

Employ Child Family Members

If you are a Schedule C or F business owner, one of the best shifting strategies is to pay wages to your child as an employee. Consider this (using 1999 tax rules):

- If you have $4,300 in business income, and are in the 31% bracket, you'll pay $1,333 in federal income taxes. If you pass that same income to your child in the form of wages, you'll reduce your tax by this same $1,333—

and your child will owe no income taxes on the income (assuming that the child has no other wages).

- If you have $6,300 in business income, and are in the 31% bracket, you'll pay $1,953 in federal income taxes. But if you pay wages to your child in the amount of $6,300, she'll pay zero income taxes on these wages—if she has no other wages and puts $2,000 into a deductible IRA.

And it gets even better! The wages that you pay your child will not be subject to any FICA or Medicare taxes as long as the child is under age 18. And not only that, if the child is under age 21, there won't be any Federal Unemployment (FUTA) taxes imposed on those wages, either.

And not only that, if your net Schedule C or F income is less than $72,600 for 1999, paying these wages to your child will also reduce your self employment ("SE") taxes. So if you can pay wages to your child in the amount of $6,300, and you're under the SE tax limit, you'll save an additional $964 in SE taxes. This means that you could save a grand total of $2,917 in income and SE taxes simply by paying wages of $6,300 to your minor child. Wow.

And, as an employee, your child may also qualify for other fringe benefits that your business may offer, including other retirement plans (such as a SIMPLE plan, a SEP plan, a Keogh plan, etc.). It just doesn't get much better than that.

There are some things to consider before you enter into this type of transaction, though.

- The child must actually perform the work and provide services. You can't put little Heathcliff on the payroll if Heathcliff doesn't show up for work.

- The work performed must be directly connected with your trade or business. You can't pay Heathcliff from your business for doing chores around the house.

- While there are no federal rules regarding the age of the child applicable to this provision, the payments to your child must be reasonable in relation to the services rendered. Don't expect to pay little Heathcliff $150 an hour and get away with it.

- You *must* follow the IRS rules and regulations when you put Heathcliff on the payroll. This means you'll need to apply for a Federal Tax ID number, file quarterly payroll tax reports, issue annual W-2 forms, and fork over any and all payroll taxes required. You can't simply call Heathcliff an "independent contractor" and give him a Form 1099 at the end of the year. It doesn't work like that. If you're going to do it, do it right.

- Remember that *earned* income is not subject to the kiddie tax rules. Which is why this gambit works so well. Even if Heathcliff is under age 14, as long as he has no other earned income, this little tax trick will work just fine. His earned income won't be subject to the kiddie tax.

This tax dodge is one that is a thorn in the side of the IRS. They may try to question you and your deductions. So make sure that you keep appropriate records and documentation showing the hourly wages paid, the work performed, the total hours worked, and on and on. The more documentation you have, the better you'll weather the storm should the IRS come calling. And you'll also want to check out your state and local employment laws. Some states have laws against "child" employment unless specific guidelines are met. So make sure that you are aware of those laws and comply with them.

Employing Adult Family Members

While not as powerful as the employment of children, this technique also works well. Even if your kids are older, or you decide to employ your parents in the business, you'll still save some tax dollars. The theory works the same, but some of the benefits may be lost in the following manner:

- If your family employee (either your child or parent) is age 18 or older, you'll have to deduct applicable FICA and Medicare taxes. In addition, you'll also have to match those FICA and Medicare deductions in the form of employer payroll taxes.

- You may have to pay Federal Unemployment (FUTA) on the wages paid to the family employee.

But even if you lose some of the impact of the tax savings because of the employment tax issues, the income tax savings are still there for the taking. Say that you pay your mother-in-law $15,000 to keep your business books. If this is her sole source of income (other than her monthly non-taxable Social Security benefits), she'll pay only about $1,193 in income taxes. This business deduction can save you about $4,650 in income tax savings if you are in the 31% bracket. Even factoring in the employment tax expenses, you'll still be way ahead of the game. And employing adult family members has other benefits:

- You can justify a higher salary for the work performed.

- Your adult family employees can participate in and receive even greater benefits from qualified retirement and benefit programs.

- While you'll be subject to employment taxes on the wages, those employment taxes are business expenses for your business, thereby reducing your income taxes even more.

There is no question that the payment of wages to family members is one of the most powerful ways to shift income to lower tax brackets and take care of the family at the same time. Make sure that you don't overlook it.

IRAs

Little Cletus works nights at the local burger shack from time to time during his high school years. He doesn't make much money, and all that he does earn is spent on the important things in life, such as cars and girls. There's no way that you can convince Cletus to put aside $2,000 for an IRA. What to do?

Consider gifting Cletus $2,000 at the end of the year to fund his IRA. While this isn't a direct "shift," it does get that $2,000 out of your asset base (which will eliminate the income tax on the earnings), and will allow Cletus to make an IRA contribution. You can decide to make a deductible IRA contribution for Cletus—or you might decide that the ultimate tax savings of the Roth IRA would be Cletus's best bet. Regardless, this is a method that will get Cletus on the savings bandwagon and will save you a few shillings at the same time.

Gifts of Stock

By transferring stock to family members in a lower tax bracket (such as your child or parent), you can reduce the tax liability on interest, dividends, and capital gains. We discuss this approach in more detail elsewhere in the book. Just realize that this is another "shifting" technique available to you.

Gifts

A parent (or anybody for that matter) can gift a child or parent up to $10,000 a year ($20,000 for married couples) without having to pay any gift taxes or file any gift tax returns. Again, this may not be a direct "shift," but it still removes the gifted funds from your asset base, and may allow the earnings on those funds to be taxed at a lower family member rate.

Many people dismiss this opportunity, thinking that real wealth can't be accumulated in such small chunks. They should think again.

• A gift of $10,000 (just one single $10,000 gift), compounded for 30 years at a rate of 10% will amount to more than $174,000. And if the rate is 17%, that little $10,000 gift will grow to more than $1 million over the same 30-year period. This is why compound interest is the Seventh Wonder of the Ancient World. (What? That was the Lighthouse at Alexandria? Well, then consider this the Eighth Wonder.)

• A gift of $2,000 annually (one $2,000 gift each year), compounded at 10% over a 20-year period will top $126,000 at the end of the 20-year term. Increase the rate of return to 20%, and the result amounts to more than $448,000 at the end of the 20-year term.

How can small amounts turn into such large amounts? It's due to the effects of compound interest in conjunction with time. And time is something that children have. Start them on their way early enough, and there should be plenty for them to pay for education, a new home, start a business, or even take a vacation to Europe. So don't kid yourself into thinking that you can't save enough fast enough. When you're dealing with kids, time is certainly on your side.

Tuition or Medical Gifts

As we noted earlier, the gift tax limitation is $10,000 per individual. But that limitation goes right out the window if the gifts are made for tuition or medical reasons, and the gifts are made directly to the education institution or medical facility. This is another way to facilitate an indirect "shift"—by taking considerable funds from your asset base, potentially reducing your estate taxes, and avoiding future income on those assets.

Consider your granddaughter Allegra. She was just accepted into Brown University's Egyptology Ph.D. program. Allegra doesn't have sufficient funds to pay for this education (she always seems to spend any extra cash on airfare, ending up at the Avenue of the Sphinxes in Luxor, Egypt). You can simply write a check for $25,000 (or another appropriate amount) toward Allegra's books, tuition, housing, and incidentals directly to Brown. Allegra doesn't have to report any of this gift as taxable income. And even though your gift was greater than the $10,000 annual gift exclusion, since it was used for educational purposes and given directly to the university, you'll have no gift taxes to pay or gift tax returns to file. Beautiful.

Contributions to a State Tuition Program

When you make contributions to a state tuition program, the earnings are usually tax-deferred until the year that withdrawals are made for the payment of college education expenses. The child will generally be taxed on the earnings, but at his or her lower rate. Again, this is another method by which you can "shift" income to a family member in a lower tax bracket. Why?

If we still haven't convinced you that income shifting might be beneficial to you, we'll give it one last try. By reducing your income, you also reduce your adjusted gross income. As we discussed earlier, many issues are based upon the size of your AGI. So if you can reduce your AGI, you may be able to get some additional goodies (such as deductions and credits) that are based upon a percentage or amount of AGI. Additionally, by reducing your AGI, you may be able to avoid many phase-out and exclusion limitations that are based on it. Here is just a partial list of the items that may be increased with a decrease in AGI:

• Itemized deductions (medical deductions are subject to a 7.5% floor, casualty losses to a 10% floor, and miscellaneous deductions to a 2% floor)

• Roth IRA contributions based upon phase-out rules

• Deductible traditional IRA contributions based upon phase-out rules

• Education IRA contributions under phase-out rules

• Amounts allowed for personal exemptions under phase-out rules

• Amounts allowed for itemized deductions under phase-out rules

• The $25,000 rental loss allowed under the passive activity rules

• The earned income credit

• The child and dependent care credit

• The child tax credit and additional child tax credit under phase-out rules

• The Hope Scholarship and Lifetime Learning credits under phase-out rules

• The amount of Social Security benefits that you can receive on a non-tax basis

As you can see, reducing your AGI might have a big impact on your overall tax situation. This is why income shifting is something that you should consider when forming your personal income tax reduction strategies.

A Word of Warning

Many people are hesitant to shift assets to their children for fear that the kids will no longer qualify for student aid. This is certainly a valid concern. If you think that student aid will be required for your child's college education, you have to think long and hard with respect to the issue of shifting assets and income to your child. We'll discuss this issue in more detail in a forthcoming section.

FOSTER PARENT ISSUES

Not everyone who has children is a natural or adoptive parent. There are untold thousands of people out there who are foster parents. And there are some special tax issues for those special parents. Here's a quick overview of some of these issues.

Foster Care Payments

Generally, foster parents receive payments from the applicable state, local, or other agency to be used for the care and needs of the child. If such payments are made by a state, political subdivision, or tax-exempt placement agency, and the care of a child under age 19 is provided by you in your home, the payments are generally not taxable. (Know that there are limits regarding the number of children and their ages.)

Difficulty-of-Care Payments

Additional payments to compensate for the additional work and care of physically, mentally, or emotionally handicapped foster individuals are not necessarily excluded from income. These are called "difficulty-of-care" payments, and they are made in addition to the normal care payments. These payments are taxable if they are made for more than 10 qualified foster individuals under age 19, or for more than five foster individuals age 19 or older.

Self-Employment Income

Foster care payments that don't qualify for the income exclusion must be reported on Schedule C as self-employment income. As such, these payments would also be subject to the self-employment tax.

On Call

Payments made to you for keeping a space open in the home, such as with an "on call" arrangement, do not qualify for the income exclusion, and must be reported as self-employment income on Schedule C.

Claiming an Exemption

You may claim an exemption for a foster child if *no* care payments are received, and the five dependency tests (discussed earlier in the book) are otherwise met. But if you are receiving payments, those payments prohibit you from claiming the dependent exemption.

Filing Status

Single foster parents can file as Head of Household if:

• The foster child may be claimed as your dependent, and

• You maintain a household which is the foster child's principal residence for the entire year, and

• You satisfy all of the other Head of Household filing requirements (as discussed earlier in the book).

Earned Income Credit

If the child lived with you for the entire year, and all of the other earned income credit requirements are met, you may be able to claim the earned income credit. We discuss the EIC in much greater detail elsewhere in the book. Check it out.

There are other twists and turns regarding foster parents and foster care issues. For additional reading, check out IRS Publications 17, 501, and 526.

FAMILY LOANS

It's probably just a matter of time before somebody in your family hits you up for a loan. But this doesn't necessarily have to be a bad deal. You can help a relative by lending the capital to start a business, make an investment, pay personal expenses, or even buy a home. And the interest stays in the family, rather than going to some cold, impersonal bank or finance company. When done correctly, it can very well be a "win-win" situation. If you decide to make the loan, there are some issues that you should understand relative to family loans and taxes.

As with any loan, a loan to a family member should be made in a businesslike manner. You should make sure that you create an enforceable note that shows:

• The loan amount

• A definite payment date or dates

• A stated rate of interest

• Collateral or security

Without a valid note, the IRS could make a claim that there was really no loan at all—that it was nothing more than a gift. If you are making the loan, this is the *last* thing that you want the IRS to do to you. And that is especially true if the loan goes bad at some time in the future.

Interest Issues

As the lender, you are required to report the interest that you receive on the note as income. Simple as that. Report your interest income on Schedule B.

But the borrower's rules are not so clear cut. How the loan is used will determine whether the interest that is paid will be deductible or not. For example, if the loan proceeds go to pay off personal debts and obligations, the interest paid on the loan will be nothing more than nondeductible personal interest. If the loan proceeds are used for business purposes, the interest paid will likely be a business expense, deductible on the appropriate business schedule. If the proceeds are used to purchase investments, then the interest would probably be considered investment interest, subject to the investment interest rules. If the proceeds are used to purchase or refinance a primary or secondary residence, it is quite possible that the interest would be considered deductible home mortgage interest (assuming that the property is secured by the note in the form of a mortgage or trust deed). So the interest rules regarding the borrower can get quite complex. If you're the borrower, make sure that you know how the rules will work for (or against) you.

Interest on Loans Between Related Parties

As a lender, it's usually best to charge the family member interest at the going rate. Why? Because an interest-free loan could be viewed by the IRS as nothing more than a gift. And not only that, the IRS might deem that you actually did receive the going rate of interest, and gave that interest back to the family member. So even if you don't charge or collect interest on the family loan, the IRS can step in and make you report interest income that you never received. This is why it is best for all concerned to simply charge interest on the note at a reasonable and normal rate.

But in many cases, related individuals make loans for less than the normal going rate. That's not unusual at all. The IRS understands that fact of life and has established minimum loan rates for loans between related parties. These rates (known as the Applicable Federal Rates or "AFR" in tax-speak) change on a monthly basis, and are basically tied to the yield on Treasury securities. The AFR is divided into three levels:

• Short-term (three years or less)

• Mid-term (more than three years but not more than nine years)

• Long-term (more than nine years)

The IRS publishes applicable federal rates each month in the Internal Revenue Bulletin that you can find at the IRS website. Or find the current AFR by pointing your Web browser to: http://www.netaxs.com/people/evansdb/afr.html.

Awwwwww... C'mon, Mom!

You explain to your child why you need to charge interest. And the line above is exactly what you hear in a loud and pitiful high-pitched voice.

When Bad Things Happen to Good Loans

Who cares if it's a gift or a loan? Does it really matter? Well, yes, it does. If you expect to be repaid, you're making a loan. If you're simply giving the money away, and repayment is the last thing on your mind, you're making a gift. If you want, expect, and demand repayment, and a loan is what you really have, make sure that all of your paperwork is in order. This is important because of that small chance that the loan goes bad and you're not repaid.

In such circumstances, if your paperwork is in order, you may be able to claim a non-business bad debt deduction (basically a short-term capital loss). But your paperwork must be in order, the loan must be real and enforceable, and there must be a bona fide debtor/creditor relationship. Uncle Sam isn't wild about you simply throwing money around to relatives and then trying to deduct the nonpayment at a later date as a bad debt. This is especially true when family members are involved. You'll have to be prepared to make reasonable efforts to collect the debt or foreclose on your security interest. Heck, you may even have to haul your relative to small claims court in order to make a valid and reasonable attempt at collection. If you're not prepared to do that, you shouldn't be prepared to claim a non-business bad debt deduction for the nonpayment of the loan.

For more information on the rules and requirements for the non-business bad debt deduction, review IRS Publication 550.

What's a mother to do? If you decide not to charge at least the applicable AFR interest on the loan, you may run afoul of the below-market loan rules. And you likely don't want to do that. Fear not! As usual, there are exceptions to the below-market loan rules.

The first exception is known as the $10,000 exception. The rules for below-market loans do not apply to loans of $10,000 or less, and for which the proceeds are not directly used to buy income-producing assets (such as stocks or bonds). So that clears the way for you to make a loan to a family member for $10,000 or less and not charge interest, as long as the proceeds are not used to purchase stocks, bonds, notes, or other income-producing property.

The second exception is (as usual) a bit more complicated. It's known as the $100,000 exception. It states that the loan must be for $100,000 or less, and the borrower's net investment income (loosely defined as interest, dividends, and short-term capital gains less any investment expense) does not exceed $1,000. If the borrower's net investment income exceeds $1,000, the lender will be required to report interest income in an amount equal to the net investment income of the borrower.

For example, Marilyn makes a loan to her daughter Jill so Jill can start a business as a past-life regression therapist. Using the AFRs, the annual interest would amount to $3,500. But Marilyn decides to simply forego this yearly interest in order to help Jill with her tight money problems. So far, so good. There are no gift tax implications to Marilyn because the foregone interest is less than the $10,000 gift tax annual exclusion. As long as Jill has net investment income of $1,000 or less, Marilyn will not have any interest income to report. Likewise, since the interest isn't paid, Jill has no interest expense to deduct.

But let's change the picture a little bit. Let's say that Jill's net investment income amounts to $2,000. In this case, because the net investment income is greater than $1,000, Marilyn will be required to report $2,000 as interest income, and Jill will have an interest deduction for $2,000.

The below-market rules can get a little tricky. So if you're contemplating a loan between family members or any other related party (such as employee-employer, an individual to his or her corporation or partnership, and many others), make sure that you have a firm grip on the rules. You can read much more about related-party transactions and the below-market interest rules in IRS Publication 550.

CUSTODIAN ACCOUNTS

So you've given little Keanu that first $10,000 gift. But now what? Since he's only three years old, he can't be expected to open up his own bank or brokerage account, can he? (He can't.) Someone else must help Keanu out with this little matter. This is where custodian accounts come into play.

Tax Issues

Remember that while you (or someone else) may be the custodian of this account, the account really belongs to the child. The custodian is simply involved in managing the account, protecting the assets in the account, and generating growth and/or income within the account. Since the account belongs to the child, so do any income or gains (and the associated taxes) generated by the account. This is one reason that custodian accounts are so very popular: The earnings and gains shift to the child and are (usually) taxed at a lower rate.

There are a few other issues that you'll want to be aware of. *You* can't simply use the funds generated by the custodian account to support the child. You have a legal obligation to support your child. The laws that deal with this precept may vary from state to state. Nevertheless, the message is clear: These funds are not meant for the general support of the child. So if you decide to take some of this income from the custodian account and use it for Keanu's general support (buying him food, clothing, and Teletubbies videos), you could subject yourself to taxes on that income. Certainly something to consider.

And let's not forget the kiddie tax. While this income still belongs to the child, some of it could very well be taxed at your personal tax rate via the kiddie tax rules. Obviously, having Keanu's income taxed at your individual tax rate will cancel some of the tax benefits of establishing a custodian account—so it's something that you'll want to manage as carefully as possible.

As we've discussed, in order to get the funds to Keanu, you'll normally make a gift of some sort or another. We'll discuss gift tax issues a bit later on. But know that, depending upon the type of account established for the child, there might be gift tax consequences if the gift isn't considered a "gift of a present interest." (That is, if the recipient can't enjoy it now.) This could really foul up your estate tax planning if you're not careful—so be careful. And speaking of fouling up your estate tax planning, a custodial account can do just that if you don't pay attention. Because if you're the custodian for your child's account, the value of that account will be included (and taxed) in your estate if you die before your child reaches the age of majority. If a substantial sum of money has been invested in a custodian account, this could cause some problems.

It's very important to remember—always—that these funds really do belong to the child. They aren't yours to do as you please. And when your child reaches the age of majority, look out. Because the money is all theirs, to do with as they please. Let that thought haunt you for a few minutes.

(We pause to permit the haunting...)

Okay, now let's look at the various kinds of custodial accounts that are out there. Two of the biggies are the UGMA and the UTMA. "Ugma? Utma." Gee, that sounds like a cave man asking a cave woman out on a date.

Uniform Gifts to Minors Act (UGMA) Accounts

One of the most popular custodian accounts is the UGMA. But it has certain limits. The rules are different from state to state, but generally the UGMA account can only be used for lifetime gifts (and not gifts made by a will). In addition, only certain kinds of property can be used to fund the gift. Those properties would include money, stocks or securities, life insurance, or annuities. Gifts such as your valuable collection of 40 years of *National Geographic* magazines, your "Earl of Swampscott" title, or your 1979 El Camino upholstered with velvet do not qualify.

As mentioned above, once the child reaches the age of majority (18 or 21, depending upon the state), the custodian no longer has control over the account. On his appropriate birthday, little Keanu can peer at you across the dinner table and scream "It's mine… aaaaaaallllll mine!" And there's not a darn thing that you can do about it. This is one of the drawbacks to custodian accounts.

Uniform Transfers to Minors Act (UTMA) Accounts

A second custodian account is the UTMA account. The UTMA is becoming more and more popular as people learn more about it. In fact, in many states, UTMAs have replaced UGMAs. UTMA accounts are more flexible than UGMA accounts in that UTMA accounts allow the custodian to maintain control over the account for a longer period of time than an UGMA. While an UGMA account requires control to pass to the child at the age of majority, an UTMA account permits postponing distribution of the account until age 18, 21, or in some situations, even 25, depending upon the state. So read up on UTMA accounts and learn what the limitations might be in your specific state.

In addition, UTMA accounts may be invested in real estate, royalties, patents, and paintings. Finally, the UTMA account allows the funds in the account to be used or spent for broader purposes (e.g. for the support of the child) than the UGMA account. It is for all of these reasons that the UTMA account has become quite popular and will likely grow even more in popularity in the years to come.

Custodian accounts can be very valuable—not only as savings vehicles, but also as tax reduction vehicles. But there are still some who are not keen on custodian accounts. Why? First is the control issue. Do you think that little Keanu will be able to handle a substantial account at 18? Or even 25? You may have a little angel at age 11. But when those hormones begin to kick in at age 16 or so, your Dr. Jekyll may turn into Mr. Hyde. These con-

Avoiding the Kiddie Tax

If you decide to use an UGMA or UTMA account for your child, consider your investment options carefully, so that you don't get tripped up with kiddie taxes and end up being taxed on some of the gains or earnings at your tax rate. One method is to invest primarily in growth stocks (many of which pay no dividends) until the child turns 14. Once the child turns 14, the kiddie tax no longer applies, and you can re-balance your portfolio and take gains and income at the child's lower tax rate.

Don't be afraid of taking at least a little income. Even for a child under age 14, you can receive a small bit of income or gains each year. For 1999, the first $700 of unearned income would be untaxed. The next $700 of unearned income would be taxed at the child's rate (which is still lower than yours, we assume). So if nothing else, try to keep your annual income and/or gains just below the maximum allowed under the kiddie tax rules. You'll be glad you did.

And finally, a short word on mutual funds. We don't much care for them, as you may have guessed. But if you invest in them, be careful when they're included in a custodian account. Remember that mutual funds must distribute virtually all of their earnings to their fund-holders at least once a year. If the fund does well, the distribution that you receive may put the income of the custodian account well above the kiddie tax ceiling that you are shooting for. This may be a very unpleasant surprise, especially when you have to compute some of the taxes on the gain at your higher tax rate. So if you insist on having mutual funds in your custodian account, make sure to keep a close eye on anticipated distributions.

trol issues are a valid concern. So take a long, hard look at your particular situation before you make a major commitment to a custodian account.

The second potential problem with a custodian account is that of financial aid. If little Keanu has substantial assets under his name and control, he probably won't qualify for the various financial aid programs out there. If you start planning for your child's educational future early enough, you may not have to rely on any type of financial aid. That would certainly solve the problem. But not everybody has the financial resources to make that happen, and financial aid ultimately may be required. Just realize that this can be a real problem and it might not rear its ugly head until it's too late, if you're not prepared. (For more information on financial aid issues, flip over to our "Education" chapter.)

Finally, what happens if you decide that you want to close a custodian account, and simply take the money back under your name and under your complete control? How does that work? Not very well, unfortunately. Some would say that you're stealing your child's money. And while that may be harsh, it is certainly closer to truth than fiction. Others would have you believe that closing a custodian account in this fashion would be tantamount to tax fraud. We're not so sure about that. There are many reasons that it may be necessary to close a custodian account. Circumstances may have changed. Financial resources may have dried up. Prospects may be bleak. Would those reasons be sufficient to close the custodian account with impunity? Perhaps not. You've certainly heard the old saw: You gotta do what you gotta do. And that's true here also. Intent will play a big part of the issue should the IRS (or lawyers for your now-estranged child) decide to question you about a custodian account that once was, but now no longer exists.

We don't have all the answers. We're not sure that anyone does. But if you'd like to read more, the best discussion dealing with the issues of closing custodian accounts can be found at the Fairmark tax site (http://www.fairmark.com). Kaye Thomas, a tax attorney, discusses all of the pros and cons, ups and downs, ins and outs of the custodian account conundrum. It's great reading. Take a look.

Finally, if and when you want to, where do you go to open an UGMA or UTMA account? Virtually every bank and brokerage firm (both full-service and discount) deals with these types of accounts on a daily basis. You should be able to set up an account almost anywhere.

GIFT ISSUES

Since we've already brought up the subject of gifting assets to your children or parents, now's the time to look at the main tax issues involving gifts. You may have heard about the "gift tax exclusion," and perhaps you're wondering how it works. You may be under the misconception that a gift is "deductible" by the person making the gift (the donor), and taxable to the person receiving the gift (the recipient). This is absolutely not true. Gifts (not to be confused with charitable contributions, which have their own separate rules and are discussed later in this book) are *not* deductible by the donor, or taxable to the recipient.

Each person is allowed to gift a specific amount that will *not* trigger any gift or estate tax issues. This specific amount is called the gift tax exclusion, and it is this exclusion that we'll briefly review here.

Why Give?

If you really need a reason to give, here's one. Gifting is a very effective way to transfer substantial amounts from your estate, free from gift and estate taxes, to your children or other loved ones. This technique of estate and tax planning can drastically reduce your taxable estate when you pass on, and may therefore reduce your associated estate taxes. Additionally, using gifts to shift income and assets can also be a valuable tax-planning tool.

The amount of the annual gift exclusion, which is currently $10,000, is adjusted for inflation annually. However, the amount of the exclusion will always be rounded to the next lowest multiple of $1,000, so the $10,000 amount won't increase to $11,000 until the inflation adjustment is at least 10%. At current levels of inflation, it may be several years before the exclusion rises to $11,000. For 1999, the amount remains $10,000. And it's very likely that the 2000 exclusion will also remain at $10,000. Inflation just isn't moving fast enough to increase the exclusion.

The Exclusion

The exclusion covers gifts an individual makes to each recipient each year. Thus, a taxpayer with three children can transfer a total of $30,000 to them every year free of federal gift taxes. (A married couple with three children can transfer a total of $60,000 annually.) If the only gifts made during a year are excluded in this fashion, there is no need to file a federal gift tax return. If annual gifts exceed $10,000, the exclusion covers the first $10,000 and only the excess is "taxable." Further, even "taxable" gifts may result in no gift tax liability thanks to the unified gift/estate credit (which we'll discuss soon).

At this point in time it should be noted that gifts made by a donor to his spouse are gift-tax-free under separate marital deduction rules. So if you are considering making a gift of property or cash to your spouse, understand that the annual $10,000 exclusion limit will not apply to you. You can exclude an unlimited amount of gifts between spouses.

Gift Splitting

If a donor is married, gifts to recipients made during a year can be treated as "split" between the husband and wife, even if the cash or gift property is actually given to a recipient by only one of them. By gift splitting, therefore, up to $20,000 a year can be transferred to each recipient by a married couple because their two annual exclusions are available.

Example: Bill and Blair White are a married couple with two married children, Maggie and Dalton, and two unmarried children, Nick and

Rebecca. They can transfer a total of $120,000 each year to their children and children-in-law ($20,000 for each of the six separate recipients).

Where gift splitting is involved, both spouses must "consent" to it. Consent should be indicated on the gift tax return (or returns) the spouses file. The IRS prefers that both spouses indicate their consent on each return filed. Since more than $10,000 is being transferred by a spouse, a gift tax return (or returns) will have to be filed, even if the $20,000 exclusion covers total gifts. So be aware that if you elect gift splitting, you'll need to file Form 709 (Annual Gift Tax Return) if more than $10,000 is being given to a single recipient in any year.

The Present Interest Rules

For a gift to qualify for the annual exclusion, it must be a gift of a "present interest." That is, the recipient's enjoyment of the gift can't be postponed into the future. For example, if you put cash into an account and provide that the recipient can receive the principal or income at any time, without restriction, the gift is of a present interest. But if you were to open an account that would restrict the income or principal into some future time (such as age 30 for a child), the gift is one of a "future" interest. The gift of the present interest qualifies for the annual exclusion because enjoyment of it is not deferred. However, the gift of a future interest will not qualify for the annual gift tax exclusion, and will therefore be a "taxable" gift in its entirety.

Also, since the recipient has to be able to immediately use and enjoy the gift, it may rule out children and incapacitated adults, unless there are arrangements for the gift to be formally managed by a guardian or custodian.

Gifts to Children

If the recipient of a gift is a minor and the terms of the account provide that the income and property may be spent by or for the minor before he reaches age 21 and that any amount left is to go to the minor at age 21, then the annual exclusion is available (that is, the present interest rule will not apply). These arrangements (called "Section 2503(c) gifts" because of the section in the tax code that permits them), allow parents to set assets aside for future distribution to their children while taking advantage of the annual exclusion in the year the trust is set up. The most common of these types of arrangements are Uniform Gifts to Minors Accounts and Uniform Transfer to Minors Accounts. But be aware that there are "Gift Trusts" being promoted that do *not* meet the exception to the present interest rule. These types of "Gift Trusts" therefore require the donor to file a gift tax return each and every year in which a gift is made, regardless of the amount of the gift.

The Unified Credit

Even gifts that are not covered by the exclusion and which are thus "taxable" may not result in a tax liability. This is so because a tax credit wipes out the federal gift tax liability on the first $650,000 of taxable gifts you make in your lifetime. (The $650,000 amount, which applies in 1999, will gradually rise to $1 million by 2006.) This credit, however, applies both for gift and estate tax purposes (that's why it's called "unified"). Thus, to the extent you use it against a gift tax liability, it is reduced (or eliminated) for use against the federal estate tax at your death.

Easy? Nope.

As you can see, using gifts in an overall estate plan can get complicated, and you should really consider using the services of a qualified tax/estate pro to assist you with your overall estate planning. But we hope that the above will clear up some commonly misunderstood issues regarding gifts and gift taxes. If you would like additional reading on gift and estate taxes, check out IRS Publication 950 at the IRS website.

Gifts of Stock

Gifting can be a great boon to many taxpayers. Instead of handing over cash, though, Foolish taxpayers should consider giving stock.

Let's look this gift horse in the mouth, shall we? First of all, know that if you receive (or give) stocks as a gift, you must know (or provide) the following information:

• The donor's tax basis (a.k.a. cost basis) for the stock.

• The fair market value of the stock at the date of the gift.

• The amount of the gift tax, if any, paid by the donor on the appreciation of the property.

Why do you need to know all of this? Because the recipient's basis in the gifted stock will depend upon the donor's basis and the fair market value on the date of the gift.

If the fair market value of the stock is more than the donor's basis at the time of the gift, then the recipient's basis is the donor's basis. If the donor was required to pay gift tax, your basis is increased by the amount of gift tax paid that is attributable to that gift.

Here's an example of gifting stock. Dad buys 100 shares of Remote Control Corporation (ticker: CLICK) stock for $5 per share on January 15, 1997. Then Dad gives the stock to you as a gift on April 4, 1999. On the date of the gift, the stock is valued at $15 per share. You receive the stock and then sell it on April 8 for $15 per share. Your capital gains are long-term, even though you only held the stock for a few days. This is because when you are given a stock gift, not only do you keep the donor's basis, but you also keep the donor's holding period. So this transaction would be reported on Schedule D, using a purchase date of 1-15-97, a sale date of 4-8-99, and a long-term gain of $1,000.

Imagine that for $20 per share, you bought 500 shares of International Alphabet Corp. (ticker: ABCDE), famous for its slogan, "We supply letters for languages around the world." The stock is now worth $30 per share. You want to help Mom buy a motorcycle, take piano lessons, pay off a loan—whatever—so you give her 300 of the shares. You have gifted stock worth $9,000 (300 times $30), so you're safely below the $10,000 limit. The basis of the shares in Mom's hands is $20 per share, your initial basis. If she turns around and sells the stock for $30, she will have a gain of $3,000 (300 times $10) that will be taxable to her.

This is a good example of "income shifting." It can really be effective if Mom is in a lower tax bracket than you (which is likely, if she's retired). By giving her stock and letting her sell it, she will receive much more money "after taxes" than if you gave her the cash after you sold the stock and paid your taxes. This type of income shifting also works well with children, but be aware of "kiddie tax" issues, which are discussed elsewhere in this book.

Gifts of Appreciated Property

The gifting of assets to a minor child or other family member may work out well for both parties, but remember that gifting must be viewed in the overall scope of a comprehensive estate plan. Depending on the age and health of the donor, cash or high-basis securities may be the best things to gift while you're still kicking, as higher bases are more advantageous for the recipients, who keep your basis. Low-basis assets in the estate can be passed through to beneficiaries upon your unfortunate demise. This takes advantage of the rule that lets the new basis be the fair market value of the securities on the day of inheritance.

You now know a bit more about the gifting of assets and how it works from a tax standpoint. But make sure you establish a complete estate plan before giving everything (or even anything) away.

Gifts of Depreciated Property

If the fair market value of some stock (or other property) that you plan to give to someone is less than your basis in it at the time of the gift, your best strategy might be to simply sell the stock and recognize a loss, which you can use to offset a gain. Then take the proceeds and give them away instead of the stock.

If you do want to give away stock that is now worth less than when you bought it, here's how it works. Let's say that you received shares of the Beehive Wig Co. (ticker: WHOAA) that have a fair market value of $8,000. The generous donor who gave them to you had a cost basis of $10,000 in them, though. These two numbers are key. If when you sell the shares they're worth more than the donor's basis ($10,000), the difference between the proceeds and the donor's basis is your gain. (Sell them for $11,000 and your gain is $1,000.)

On the other hand, if when you sell the shares they're worth less than their fair market value when you got them ($8,000), the difference between the proceeds and the fair market value upon receipt is your loss. (Sell them for $6,000 and your loss is $2,000.)

If when you sell the shares they're worth between the fair market value upon receipt and the donor's basis ($8,000 and $10,000), you have neither a gain nor a loss.

A final thing to understand about gifts is that once you give the stock or money, it's gone. You've lost control of it and cannot get it back. You can read up on gift tax issues in IRS Publication 950.

TAX RELIEF

Things Worse Than Doing Your Taxes

- Kidney stones
- Forgetting your parachute
- Accidentally biting down hard onto your fork
- Being hit by lightning
- Finding yourself in the path of a tornado
- Watching all episodes of *The New Love Boat*
- Nails on a chalkboard
- Waking up with a tattoo you can't remember getting
- Cleaning out the kitty litter box
- Getting pushed into a septic tank

Things Harder Than Preparing Your Tax Return

- Most math proofs
- Understanding actuarial information
- Learning computer programming code
- Hitting 500 home runs
- Performing open-heart surgery
- Becoming a movie star
- Rearing children well
- Learning Chinese
- Building a house

EDUCATION

Education costs money, but then so does ignorance.

—Sir Claus Moser

What you'll find in this chapter:
- Deducting Education Expenses
- The Hope Scholarship Credit
- The Lifetime Learning Credit
- The Education IRA
- Interest Deduction for Higher Education Loans
- Education Deductions and Credits: Interaction
- Financial Aid Issues

If it's been many years since you or anyone in your household has stepped foot in a classroom, cracked open a textbook, or basically taken any kind of course, and no one in your household is expected to incur any educational expenses for a long time to come, then you can skip this chapter. It won't apply to you.

If you don't fall into the category described above, then pay attention to this material, as it could save you a tidy sum of money. You largely have the Taxpayer Relief Act of 1997 to thank. It included many provisions that allow for expanded deductions and credits for qualified education-related expenses. We'll be looking at many of these provisions in much greater detail. But to kick off this chapter, let's visit an old friend that's been with us for a number of years: the deduction for education expenses.

DEDUCTING EDUCATION EXPENSES

The rules work like this: An education expense-related deduction is available if the education maintains or improves the skills related to your trade or business. Educational costs are also deductible if the education is required (by law or by your employer) to keep your current position or job.

On the other hand, educational costs are *not* deductible if the education is required to get into an occupational field (as opposed to staying in a field) or if it qualifies you for a new trade or business.

For example, you can't deduct basic law school costs because they are required to enter the legal field. Once you become a lawyer, however, any courses you take to keep current or to learn new techniques are deductible.

The expenses of becoming a specialist within a field may or may not be deductible. Let's consider Dr. Nick. If his goal all along was to become a psychiatrist and he went straight through medical school, an internship, and then into a psychiatric residency, all of the costs would be treated as required to enter the field and would not be deductible. But an internist who has already been practicing medicine for a period of time can deduct the costs of a psychiatric program he enters to improve his skills within his profession. See how the line can be a little bit hazy? And it can get even more confusing.

Many taxpayers take law-related courses to help them in their professions or businesses. Seminars and/or courses that you take within your profession on law-related issues are generally deductible since they improve your current skills. But law school courses leading to a degree (even if taken for the same "improvement" purpose) are generally not deductible because they lead to qualifying you for a new profession.

You can see how the "maintain and improve" standard may not be as cut and dried as you might hope. In many cases, some tax research may be needed to see if your unique situation would be deductible or not. And many times, if the situation is truly unique, or the money involved is substantial, the assistance of a qualified tax pro could be in your best interest.

But let's say that you meet the "maintain and improve" standard and determine that your education costs are deductible. You can not only deduct the education expenses, but you may also be able to include transportation costs. Transportation between home (or work) and the course location is deductible for education undertaken on a temporary or irregular basis. If the transportation is in the nature of a commute, it's not deductible. If you're away from home for deductible education, you can also include the full cost of travel, lodging, and 50% of the cost of meals. But, and this is a very big "but," travel as the educational vehicle itself (e.g., a French teacher's trip to France) is not deductible.

In the case of an employee, education expenses that are deductible under the above tests may be claimed as an itemized deduction, but only to the extent that they, along with other miscellaneous itemized deductions, exceed 2% of your adjusted gross income. And in the case of taxpayers with high AGI, miscellaneous itemized deductions are subject to a further overall limit. So, while your education expenses may be deductible, depending on how they must be reported on your tax return, you may find that you receive little or no actual tax benefit for those expenses. Before you undertake any deductible education, you might want to check your tax status to determine what positive tax impact these deductions may actually have.

What happens if you find that your education expenses are not deductible? Or you find that while the expenses are deductible, your tax situation is such that you receive very little (or no) tax benefit? Do you just hang your head, pay your taxes, and shuffle on? Not necessarily. Here's where many of the education provisions in the 1997 Tax Act kick in.

- Did you know that as of 1999, you may be able to claim a deduction for up to $1,500 in interest that you paid for qualified student loans—without even having to itemize your deductions? (This increases to $2,000 in 2000 and plateaus at $2,500 in 2001 and beyond.)

- Did you know that you may qualify for a Hope Scholarship Credit of up to $1,500 per year for the first two years of undergraduate education at an eligible educational institution?

- Did you know that you may qualify for a Lifetime Learning Credit of up to $1,000 per year for any post-high school education at an eligible educational institution?

- Did you know that your employer may be able to pay for some of your education-related expenses? (And that those payments would not be deemed taxable income to you?)

We'll discuss these provisions in greater detail in the following sections. And because they're all interrelated in some form or another, it will be important to identify the combination of deductions and credits that will offer you the greatest tax benefit.

One thing you'll have to decide is whether to take an itemized deduction for your education expenses. Itemized deductions reduce your taxable income, and therefore save taxes at your top tax rate. If you're not subject to the overall limit on itemized deductions, you may find that an itemized deduction for education expenses is most advantageous. If you don't itemize your deductions, you will generally want to claim the Hope/Lifetime Learning credits.

If your education expenses are not related to your current trade or business and are incurred to acquire new job skills, the education expenses would not be allowable as an itemized deduction. Those same expenses, however, may still qualify for the Hope/Lifetime Learning credit.

Confusing? It sure can be, which is why we want to take the time to shed some light on these issues. In the meantime, if you want to read more about deductible education expenses, check out IRS Publication 508.

THE HOPE SCHOLARSHIP CREDIT

Two major education provisions in the 1997 Taxpayer Relief Act are the Hope Scholarship Credit and the Lifetime Learning Credit. These are somewhat similar and are often discussed at the same time, but we'll break them down separately. First up, the Hope credit.

The Hope Scholarship Credit may allow you to convert part of the higher education expenses you pay for yourself, your spouse, or your dependents into tax savings.

The maximum Hope credit a taxpayer may claim is $1,500 per year per student for the first two years of undergraduate education at an eligible educational institution. The credit equals the sum of:

• 100% of the first $1,000 of qualified tuition and related expenses paid, plus

• 50% of the next $1,000 of qualified tuition and related expenses paid.

So if Max Lancaster's freshman tuition at Wartburg College in Waverly, Iowa, costs $15,000, he (or whoever claims him as a dependent) can claim the full $1,500 credit: 100% of the first $1,000 ($1,000) and 50% of the next $1,000 ($500). If Jenn Ravetto is attending a state school on a half-time basis and her expenses amount to $1,600 for the year, she can claim just $1,300: 100% of the first $1,000 ($1,000) and 50% of the next $1,000 (50% of $600 is $300).

Be aware that the maximum Hope credit amount will be adjusted for inflation after 2001. And note that the Hope credit is only available for the first two years of undergraduate education at an eligible educational institution. So this credit isn't for everybody.

Generally, eligible educational institutions are accredited schools offering credit toward a bachelor's or associate's degree or other recognized post-high school credential, as well as certain vocational schools.

The Hope credit is available only for the qualified tuition and related expenses of an eligible student, i.e., a student who is enrolled in a degree or certificate program on at least a half-time basis at an eligible educational institution. In addition, the Hope credit will be denied to any individual who has ever been convicted of a federal or state felony drug offense.

TAX STRATEGY

Watch the Clock!

If you find yourself about to pay for educational expenses at the end of the year (perhaps for a course that begins in January), stop and think for a moment. The Hope credit is only available for the year when payment was made. So if you pay now, you can only take the credit in this year. Check whether it might be more advantageous to take the credit next year. If so, see whether you can delay payment until the beginning of the next year.

The Hope credit isn't allowed for an expense that's claimed as an education deduction, and may not be claimed in a year when the student receives any tax-exempt distribution from an education individual retirement account. (That's an education IRA. We'll cover it shortly.)

Additionally, you should know that the Hope and Lifetime Learning credits may not be claimed in the same tax year for the same expenses, but each may be claimed for different expenses.

In order to be eligible for the Hope credit, qualified tuition and related expenses must be paid during that tax year for education furnished during an academic period that starts within that tax year or within the first three months of the following year. This is confusing, but it simply means that the academic period (let's use a semester for our example here) must begin within the tax year in which the expenses are paid or the semester must begin within the first three months of the following year.

For example, if a semester begins in October 1999 and the expenses are paid in September 1999, the credit is available (assuming all of the other requirements are met). But how about a semester that begins in February 2000? When can you pay and take the Hope credit for the expenses? In this happy situation, you can pay in 1999 or 2000, and take the credit in the appropriate year. Just remember that the credit can only be taken in the year when the payment is actually made—even if the education takes place in a preceding or following year. So for those with "academic periods" that begin early in 2000, you'll have a timing option to consider when claiming the credit.

The Hope credit is available for expenses paid after 1997 for education in academic periods starting on or after January 1, 1998.

The Hope credit can reduce regular income taxes to zero but *cannot* result in the receipt of a refund. If the expenses on which the Hope credit were based are later refunded (such as through a late payment of a scholarship), the credits may have to be recaptured and repaid back to Uncle Sam.

The Hope credit is based on the payment of qualified tuition and related expenses (such as academic fees) at an eligible educational institution. Qualified tuition and related expenses do *not* include the cost of books, student activity fees, athletic fees, insurance expenses, room and board, transportation costs, and other personal living expenses. They also don't include the cost of any course or education involving sports, games, or hobbies unless the course or education is part of the student's degree program.

The amount of qualified tuition and related expenses taken into account in computing the Hope credit must be reduced by tax-exempt scholarships and fellowships, certain military benefits, and any other tax-exempt payments of those expenses other than gifts or bequests. So if your qualified tuition and related expenses amount to $18,000 and you've been fortunate enough to receive $17,000 in scholarships, your Hope credit will be calculated based on just the remaining $1,000 in qualified expenses.

Unfortunately, you may have to abandon Hope, all ye who fall into certain categories.

The Hope credit is phased out ratably for married taxpayers filing jointly with adjusted gross income (with certain modifications) between $80,000 and $100,000. That is, the credit is reduced if the modified AGI is above $80,000 and is completely lost if it's $100,000 or more. For taxpayers who aren't married, the phase-out range is $40,000 to $50,000. After 2001, the phase-out amounts will be adjusted for inflation.

The Hope credit is not available for taxpayers who are married filing separately. In addition, it's also not allowed to an individual who can be claimed as a dependent on another's return. In this situation, the Hope credit is allowed only to the taxpayer claiming that individual as a dependent, and the credit is based on the total qualified tuition and related expenses paid both by the taxpayer and the student.

Note that the Hope credit *may* be used to reduce the Alternative Minimum Tax. When this legislation was originally passed, the Hope credit would reduce the regular tax, but not the AMT. But because of the recently passed Tax Relief and Trade Extension Act of 1998, the Hope credit can be used to reduce both the regular tax and the AMT... at least for 1998. We're waiting for Congress to make a decision for 1999 and future years. But as of this writing, no guidance has been forthcoming.

Finally, you should know that the eligibility for the Hope credit is subject to a number of technical requirements not discussed above. You might want to check with your local higher education institution for the additional details and requirements. Virtually all colleges and universities have information available to better explain the Hope credit. And, as always, if you have any specific technical questions on any of the Hope credit issues, you can always ask them online at the Fool.

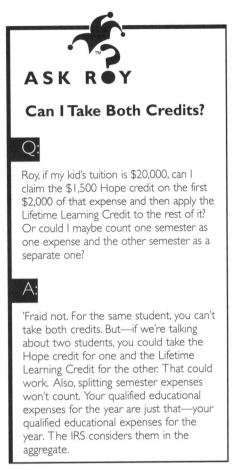

ASK ROY

Can I Take Both Credits?

Q:

Roy, if my kid's tuition is $20,000, can I claim the $1,500 Hope credit on the first $2,000 of that expense and then apply the Lifetime Learning Credit to the rest of it? Or could I maybe count one semester as one expense and the other semester as a separate one?

A:

'Fraid not. For the same student, you can't take both credits. But—if we're talking about two students, you could take the Hope credit for one and the Lifetime Learning Credit for the other. That could work. Also, splitting semester expenses won't count. Your qualified educational expenses for the year are just that—your qualified educational expenses for the year. The IRS considers them in the aggregate.

THE LIFETIME LEARNING CREDIT

The Lifetime Learning Credit has many similarities with the Hope credit, but a few major differences.

Here are the similarities:

• The school or college must be an eligible educational institution (including certain vocational schools).

• The credits are available only for qualified tuition and related expenses of an eligible student.

- The credits aren't allowed for an expense that was claimed as an education deduction, and may not be claimed in a year when the student receives any tax-exempt distribution from an education IRA.

- The credits cannot both be claimed in the same tax year for the same expenses. But each may be claimed for different expenses for different students.

- Neither of the credits is refundable, but they can be used to reduce the Alternative Minimum Tax, at least for 1998. As for 1999? Well, we just don't know. The legislation that allowed these credits was passed for only one year: 1998. At the time of this writing, Congress hadn't revealed any decisions regarding these credits and the AMT for 1999 and later years.

- The credits are not available for taxpayers who are married filing separately. In addition, the credits are not allowed to an individual who can be claimed as a dependent on another's return.

- The income "phase out" rules are also the same: The credits are phased out ratably for married taxpayers filing jointly with adjusted gross income (with certain modifications) between $80,000 and $100,000. For taxpayers who aren't married filing jointly, the phase-out range is $40,000 to $50,000. After 2001, the phase-out amounts will be adjusted for inflation.

So much for the similarities. Here are the significant differences between the Hope and Lifetime credits:

The Lifetime credit covers qualified education expenses paid after June 30, 1998, for academic periods beginning after June 30, 1998. (For additional information on how the "academic period" restriction works, review the preceding Hope section.)

The taxpayer may claim a Lifetime credit equal to 20% of up to $5,000 in qualifying tuition and related expenses. This credit applies to qualified expenses paid by the taxpayer for the taxpayer, his or her spouse, or any dependent. Therefore, the maximum Lifetime

TAX STRATEGY

Student Loans Count

Many people forget student loans or assume they don't apply when tallying up their educational expenses. In many cases, student loans count. If *you* took out the loan and *you* will be repaying it, then it counts as an educational expense of yours. Think of it this way: You *are* paying money toward education. You're just doing it via a loan.

credit that may be claimed is $1,000 (20% of $5,000). Starting in 2003, the maximum amount of qualified tuition and expenses that may be taken into account in determining the Lifetime credit for a tax year will increase to $10,000. That being the case, the maximum credit after 2002 will be $2,000 (20% of $10,000). You should know that these expense limits will not be indexed for inflation. (At least not according to the way they're currently structured.)

While the Hope credit is only available to students in the first two years of post-secondary education, the Lifetime credit (as the name implies) is available to all qualified students, for all qualified education, regardless whether the education is taken for an advanced degree or not. In addition, there is no limit on the number of years for which the Lifetime credit can be claimed. (Woo hoo!)

Also, while the Hope credit has a "half-time" enrollment minimum, the Lifetime credit does not. The Lifetime credit is available for the cost of courses at an eligible educational institution, regardless of whether the student is on a full-time, half-time, or less than half-time basis. If all these pluses aren't enough, here's one more: The Lifetime credit is available to either acquire or improve the student's job skills.

One advantage of the Hope over the Lifetime credit is that the maximum amount of the Lifetime credit that may be claimed on a taxpayer's return doesn't vary based on the number of students in the taxpayer's family. Therefore, unlike the Hope credit (which is computed on a per-student basis), the Lifetime credit is computed on a per-family basis. Let's look at an example.

Tony and Lee Miller are married, with an AGI of $35,000. They pay $5,000 in tuition and expenses for Tony, and also pay $2,000 in tuition and expenses for Lee. If they qualified for the Hope credit, they could claim a credit of $1,500 each, for a total Hope credit of $3,000. But if they don't qualify for the Hope credit, their maximum Lifetime credit would amount to only $1,000, even though they may both meet the eligibility requirements and have qualifying expenses. This is because for Lifetime credit purposes, the credit is determined on a per-family basis, and not on a per-student basis.

As you might remember, the Hope credit is denied to any individual who has ever been convicted of a federal or state felony drug offense. There is no such denial for the Lifetime credit. Why? We have no idea. We're just relieved that these credits aren't denied to people who wear funny velvet caps with bells.

Finally, as with the Hope credit, there are a number of technical requirements for the Lifetime credit that are not discussed above. For additional information, you might want to check with your local education institution.

THE EDUCATION IRA

We'll now look at yet another tax-saving education provision that was included in the 1997 Taxpayer Relief Act: the Education IRA.

An Education IRA (which really isn't an IRA at all, in the true sense of the word) is a custodial account or trust, usually maintained by a bank or financial organization, exclusively for the purpose of paying the qualified higher education expenses of the designated beneficiary. Education IRAs must accept contributions only in cash, and may not accept contributions for a beneficiary after the beneficiary turns 18. In addition, the Education IRA may not accept contributions of more than $500 total (except for rollover contributions) for any year. Also, unlike other IRAs, your contribution for an Education IRA must be made prior to the end of the calendar year. So if you want to make a 2000 Education IRA contribution, it must be done by December 31, 2000. With the Education IRA you do not have a "grace period" until April 15 of the following year to make the contribution.

Here's how it works: Jennifer and Theirrien Clark want to establish an Education IRA for their daughter Kaelyn. Jennifer wants to donate $500, Theirrien wants to donate $500, and even Grandpa wants to donate $500. Can't do it. Kaelyn (as the beneficiary) is limited to only one $500 contribution to her Education IRA account per year, regardless of the source of the funds. And she may only have *one* Education IRA account. Mom, Dad, and Grandpa can't each set one up for her.

Any individual may contribute a maximum of $500 a year to an Education IRA for the benefit of any person under age 18. But the $500 contribution limit is phased out ratably for contributors with modified adjusted gross income between $95,000 and $110,000 for single persons and between $150,000 and $160,000 for joint filers. What this means is that the full $500 contribution can be made if your modified AGI is less than $95,000 for single people ($150,000 for joint), but *no* contribution can be made if your AGI is $110,000 ($160,000 for joint). Within the phase-out ranges, the Education IRA contribution is reduced. For married-joint filers, the phase-out is between $150,000 and $160,000. For *all other* taxpayers (including married-separate filers), the phase-out range is between $95,000 and $110,000.

Another example: Kerah Cottrell, a single person, wants to establish an Education IRA for her favorite little guy, Jack. But her AGI is $100,000. Her maximum contribution to little Jack's Education IRA account would be only $333 because of the phase-out rules.

Note that unlike other IRAs, a person can make a contribution to an Education IRA even if that person has no compensation income for that tax year. This being the case, there is no reason that Kerah can't give a $500 *gift* to Jack. Jack can then turn around and open his *own* Education IRA account for the full $500, since he's well under the income limitations. (Well, we presume he is. If Jack is already raking in more than $95,000 per year, he may not be too interested in the benefits of the Education IRA.)

Distributions from an Education IRA are tax-free if the beneficiary's qualified higher education expenses for the year equal or exceed the Education IRA distribution for that year.

For example, let's say that Karen and Larry Kosoy contribute $500 per year to an Education IRA for their eight-year-old son Matthew for 10 years beginning in 1999. In 2009, when the account balance is $8,000 (including $3,000 in earnings), Matthew withdraws the entire $8,000 balance to pay part of his $10,000 qualified higher education expenses. Matthew's 2009 taxable income does not include the $3,000 in earnings from the Education IRA account.

Remember, though, that if a beneficiary excludes any amount of an Education IRA distribution for a tax year, neither a Hope nor a Lifetime Learning credit may be claimed for that beneficiary for that year. (By "exclude," we mean that the beneficiary reported the income but then elected to exclude it, treating it as nontaxable.) We'll discuss the interrelationship between these credits and the Education IRA in more detail a little later.

If distributions from an Education IRA exceed qualified education expenses, there is an additional tax of 10% of the taxable amount. But this 10% additional tax does not apply to distributions:

• Made after the death of the beneficiary;

• Due to the beneficiary's disability; or

• Made on a distribution that can be included in income solely because an election is made to waive the income exclusion (such as to take the Hope

When the Big 3-0 Approaches

Uh-oh. You're about to turn 30 and you have no educational expenses. (You don't have a spouse, either, but hey—matters of the heart can sometimes take a while.) Are you going to have to recognize the funds in your Educational IRA as taxable income (plus pay a 10% additional tax)? Not necessarily.

An Education IRA distribution not used for qualified education expenses is not taxable to the extent that it is rolled over into another Education IRA for the benefit of the beneficiary, or for the benefit of another member of the beneficiary's family. For this purpose, a family member includes: a son, daughter, or a descendant of either; a stepson or stepdaughter; a brother, sister, stepbrother or stepsister; a father, mother, or an ancestor of either; a stepfather or stepmother; a nephew or niece; an uncle or aunt; and a son-in-law, daughter-in-law, father-in-law, mother-in-law, brother-in-law, or sister-in-law. It would also include the spouse of any of those persons. But the new beneficiary of this rollover distribution must be under age 30 on the date of the rollover.

Let's see what this means. Andy Cross, a professional race car driver in Newport Beach, California, has not used all of his Education IRA and will soon turn 30. His account has a balance of $25,000, including earnings of $14,000. He has no educational expenses this year. Andy doesn't want to take the Education IRA as a distribution and pay the normal income tax and additional 10% tax on the $14,000 in earnings. Instead, he decides to roll over this $25,000 Education IRA to his nephew, who is only four years old. His nephew now has a *big* head start on his college savings!

or Lifetime credit as opposed to the tax-free treatment of the Education IRA).

Example: Using the example of Karen, Larry, and Matthew Kosoy above, let's say that Matthew decides to take his $8,000 Education IRA distribution and go to Europe in 2009, to "find himself." (Imagine Karen banging her head against a door frame in dismay.) Matthew doesn't incur any qualified education expenses for 2009. (No, the lesson he learned from missing a plane and wasting a $599 nonrefundable ticket doesn't count.) In this case, Matthew would have to report income of $3,000 (the earnings on the Education IRA) which would be subject to regular income tax. He would also have to pay an additional tax of $300 (10% of the taxable amount).

The beneficiary must have used up the Education IRA funds by the time 30 days have passed following his or her 30th birthday. Any funds remaining after that time will be deemed distributed to the beneficiary (whether actually distributed or not), and the earnings will be subject to regular income tax and the additional 10% tax if not used for qualified education purposes.

For the purposes of the Education IRA, "higher education expenses" include expenses for tuition, fees, books, supplies, and equipment required for the beneficiary's enrollment or attendance at an "eligible educational institution."

TAX STRATEGY

Qualified State Tuition Programs

Another tax-smart way to fund college education is through a qualified state tuition program. Certain states and agencies maintain programs that allow you to purchase certificates or make contributions to an account to pay for future education. Contributions to a qualified state tuition program are not deductible, but withdrawals used to pay for qualified education expenses will only be taxable to the extent that they are more than the amounts originally contributed to the program. So while you will eventually pay taxes on the earnings, all of the earnings will be tax-deferred until they are used for qualified education expenses.

Like an Education IRA, a qualified state tuition program will allow a rollover to another family member if the original beneficiary is unable (or unwilling) to use the funds for qualified expenses. But unlike the Education IRA, there is no limit to the amount of contributions that can be made to the tuition program in any given year. (Just be careful about the $10,000 annual gift exclusion.) And even better: There are no AGI phase-out limitations associated with qualified state tuition programs. This will allow many high-income taxpayers, who may be shut out of other tax breaks, to participate in this program.

State tuition programs have become so popular that many investment firms (such as Fidelity Investments) are offering special investment programs that allow you to make contributions to a fund that will qualify as state tuition program contributions—regardless of your actual state of residency. These are commonly called "Section 529" programs. So check with your favorite brokerage or investment firm for additional information on the plans that might be available to you.

For more information on a specific state tuition program, contact your local state agency that established and maintains the program. In addition, you may want to read more about this in IRS Publication 970. Also very helpful is a book called *The Best Way to Save for College*, by Joseph Hurley.

While there is no requirement that the beneficiary be enrolled on a half-time or greater basis, if the beneficiary *is* enrolled on a half-time or greater basis, some room and board expenses may also be considered a qualified education expense.

Again, as with most tax issues, there are other technical requirements that space does not allow us to deal with here and now. So before you begin your Education IRA, make sure that you've done your research. (Hey, we're sorry that we have to keep saying that, but few things are simple in the U.S. Tax Code. If we explained everything that could possibly be explained in this book, you'd have a hernia from lifting it by now.)

INTEREST DEDUCTION FOR
HIGHER EDUCATION LOANS

There's a new interest deduction introduced by the 1997 Taxpayer Relief Act—for interest on qualified education loans. It applies to loan interest payments due and paid after 1997, regardless of when the loan was originally taken out. Therefore, you may qualify for this deduction for interest that you paid after 1997 on existing education loans. The deduction is an exception to the general rule that interest on "personal" loans isn't deductible.

Here are the requirements for deductibility: The maximum amount of interest you can deduct is $1,500 in 1999, $2,000 in 2000, and $2,500 in 2001 or later. The maximum isn't adjusted for inflation. However, the deductible amount is reduced for certain high adjusted gross income taxpayers. We'll deal with those restrictions a bit later.

The interest must be for a "qualified education loan," i.e., for a debt incurred to pay tuition, room and board, and related expenses to attend a post-high school educational institution, including certain vocational schools. Certain post-graduate programs also qualify. Thus, an internship or residency program leading to a degree or certificate awarded by an institution of higher education, hospital, or healthcare facility offering post-graduate training can qualify.

But note: Only interest paid during the first 60 months that payments are required can qualify. Months in which payments aren't required, e.g., during a deferral or forbearance period, aren't counted against the 60-month period. In the case of an already existing loan, interest payments qualify for the deduction to the extent that the 60-month period has not yet expired. But months during which interest was paid before January 1, 1998, would count against the 60-month period. For this purpose, a loan and all refinancings of the loan are treated as a single loan. (Loan consolidators and refinacers, exclaim with us now: "Rats!")

Income limitations: If the taxpayer's status is married filing jointly, the deduction is only fully allowed for adjusted gross income of $60,000 or less. For taxpayers with AGI of $75,000 or more, no deduction is allowed. If AGI is between $60,000 and $75,000, the deduction is partially reduced, depending on how far above $60,000 the taxpayer's AGI happens to be.

Example: If AGI is $65,000, the deduction is reduced by 33 1/3%, since the $5,000 excess above $60,000 represents 33 1/3% of the $15,000 excess that would result in complete disallowance.

For other taxpayers, such as single taxpayers, a full deduction is allowed if AGI is $40,000 or less. No deduction is allowed if AGI is $55,000 or more, and a similar partial disallowance approach is taken when AGI is between $40,000 and $55,000. (For these purposes, AGI is computed with certain modifications. For example, the exclusion of income from U.S. savings bonds used to pay higher education costs isn't taken into account.) The $60,000 (and $40,000) "phase-out" beginning points discussed above will be adjusted for inflation for years after 2002.

Married taxpayers must file jointly or no deduction is allowed. Also, no deduction is allowed for a taxpayer who can be claimed as a dependent on the tax return of someone else. Where a deduction is allowed, it is taken above-the-line—subtracted from gross income to determine AGI. Because of this above-the-line treatment, the interest deduction can be used by everyone who qualifies for it, regardless of whether deductions are itemized or not.

Other requirements: The interest must be on funds borrowed to cover qualified education costs of the taxpayer or his spouse or dependent. The expenses must be for education furnished while the recipient was an "eligible student," i.e., at least a half-time student. Also, the education expenses must be paid or incurred within a reasonable time before or after the loan is taken out.

Let's take a closer look at the 60-month rule. While you can only deduct higher education interest during the first 60 months in which interest payments are required, those 60 months don't have to be consecutive. In addition, months in which the loan is in deferral don't count against the 60-month period. For example, after paying interest on a college loan for 25 months, Hubert decides to go back to school. Under the terms of the loan, payments are deferred during the time he is in school. When he resumes making loan payments after his schooling ends, he will still have 35 months of deductible interest remaining.

But remember that if you refinance a loan, the months that have elapsed on the original loan are

TAX TIP

Loan Timing Is Important

Say that you took out a loan to pay for your daughter Sally's qualified education. Sally was your dependent at the time that you took out the loan, but has since graduated, is working, and is no longer your dependent. You can still deduct the interest that you pay on the loan (assuming that you otherwise qualify to do so) because Sally was your dependent when you took out the loan. Many people incorrectly think that as soon as Sally is no longer a dependent, the interest is no longer deductible.

carried over to the new loan. For example, let's say that you have been paying off your qualified loan for the last 20 months, and you decide to refinance to take advantage of a lower interest rate. While the refinanced loan is "new," it is treated as a continuation of the original loan. This being the case, you will have only 40 months of remaining deductible interest.

And finally, remember that if you already have a higher education loan outstanding, you may *still* be able to deduct up to 60 months of interest, depending on when the loan payment began. In some cases, interest payments on loans taken out many years ago will still be deductible in 1999.

Example: You began paying off a higher education loan in July 1995, 42 months before January 1999. You will still be able to deduct a full 12 months of interest in 1999, and another six months in 2000 before your 60-month period expires.

So while these provisions can be a little tricky, it may be worth your while to look further into your ability to qualify for this deduction. If you have any additional questions or comments on these loan provisions, please post them online.

EDUCATION DEDUCTIONS AND CREDITS: INTERACTION

You now know all about various education credits and deductions. But, like prescribed medication, there may be some ugly results due to uninformed interaction between some of those deductions and credits. Let's look at some of those interactions and determine strategies to avoid potentially deadly (at least financially) combinations. This little section is full of some useful strategies.

Education IRAs and Hope/Lifetime Credits

If a beneficiary excludes from income any amount of an Education IRA distribution for a tax year, neither a Hope credit nor a Lifetime Learning credit may be claimed for that beneficiary for that tax year.

Example: Vince Hanks, a penguin tamer, qualifies for the Lifetime credit. He also has an Education IRA account. His qualified education expenses amount to $2,500. He wants to pay for these education expenses using $300 from his Education IRA account (tax-free), and the balance out of his own pocket.

In this example, Vince would not be able to claim the Lifetime credit. Why? Because he excluded $300 from his income via the Education IRA. So, Vince loses the benefit of the Lifetime credit just to save the taxes on the income from the Education IRA. If Vince is in the 28% bracket, his tax savings would amount to only $84 on his tax-free Education IRA distribution. Not a very good trade-off.

What should Vince do? He might want to waive the income exclusion for the Education IRA. He would then report the $300 Education IRA distribution as income (which would cost him an extra $84 in taxes). But, by waiving the tax-free nature of the Education IRA, he can claim the Lifetime credit and save $500 in taxes using that credit—a much better deal.

As a general strategy, whenever possible, students with Education IRAs should bunch distributions from their IRAs into years when no higher education credit is available. Or, at the very least, they should bunch distributions from Education IRAs into years when the value of the Education IRA exclusion would exceed the maximum available Hope/Lifetime credits.

Education IRAs and Qualified State Tuition Programs

A contribution made to a qualified state tuition program (established by a state to allow a person to purchase tuition credits or otherwise pay for higher education) for a beneficiary may cause any amount contributed to an Education IRA for that beneficiary to be subject to a 6% penalty excise tax.

What to do? Make sure, if you participate in a qualified state tuition program, that you don't make any contributions to an Education IRA in that same year for that same student. But there are no restrictions on making a contribution to a qualified state tuition program for one student and to an Education IRA for a different student. Additionally, there are no restrictions on making a state tuition program contribution (in year one), and an Education IRA contribution (in year two) for the same student.

Hope/Lifetime Credits and Education Deductions

Remember that the Hope or Lifetime credit cannot be claimed for any education expenses that are otherwise claimed as a business expense.

Example: Diane Vidoni, a traveling performer, is qualified to claim the Hope/Lifetime credit. She pays $1,750 in qualified education expenses that maintain or improve her current job skills. Diane can either claim a deduction for these expenses (as an itemized deduction), or she can take the Hope/Lifetime credit. But she can't claim both the deduction and the credit.

What should Diane do? She must closely review her tax situation and take the largest tax benefit available to her. Generally, a credit is much more valuable than a deduction. In addition, the education deduction would be subject to the 2% AGI limitation for miscellaneous itemized deductions. So it is very likely that Diane would benefit most from foregoing the education deduction and claiming the Hope/Lifetime credit instead. But only Diane (or her hired tax pro), after a close review of her personal tax situation, will be able to make that determination.

Hope Credit and Lifetime Credit for the Same Student

Remember that the Hope and Lifetime credits can't be claimed in the same tax year for the same student. But claiming the Hope credit in one year doesn't prevent a taxpayer from claiming the Lifetime credit for qualifying expenses of that same year for other tax years. In addition, if there are two students involved, there is no restriction from claiming the Hope credit for the first student and claiming the Lifetime credit for the second student.

Example: Captain Dick and Sharon Hegeman have two children in college. Graham is a freshman and Haley is a junior. Assuming that all of the other requirements have been met for each credit, Dick and Sharon may claim the Hope credit for Graham's expenses and the Lifetime credit for Haley's expenses.

Note that until 2003 (when the maximum Lifetime credit increases to $2,000), the Hope credit will always produce the larger credit. After 2002, the Lifetime credit will produce a larger credit than the Hope if qualified tuition and expenses for the tax year exceed $7,500. So plan the use of your credits accordingly.

Hope/Lifetime Credits and Drug Problems

Here we are, back to talking about drug interactions. Remember that while the Hope credit is not allowed for a student who has been convicted of a federal or state drug felony, there is no such restriction for the Lifetime credit. So, even if the Hope credit is not available to a student because of drug problems, he or she may still qualify for the Lifetime credit.

While there are other twists and turns regarding the interaction between the various education credits and deductions, these are the major issues that will affect most people. The key to claiming any education credits or deductions is understanding the law and making the best choices allowable.

FINANCIAL AID ISSUES

This section has absolutely nothing to do with taxes, at least not directly. We've pointed out earlier that some decisions that you make regarding income shifting and custodian accounts may affect future financial aid decisions and outcomes. So the least we can do is give you a brief overview of some of the financial aid issues and some resources that you can use to get yourself up to speed regarding financial aid.

Online Resources

If you're without computer access, try calling the Federal Student Aid Information Center at 800-4-FED-AID. Two of the most popular (and beneficial) brochures to request from them include "The Student Guide" and "Direct Loans"—which deals with government loans and grants.

If you're wired, you'll find a wealth of information a few mouse-clicks away. Here are a few major financial aid websites:

- www.ed.gov: This is the U.S. Department of Education's website. Once there, click on the "Student Financial Assistance" link and you'll soon be looking at a wealth of information on government student aid programs. You can even apply for some online, such as with the Free Application for Federal Student Aid (FAFSA). If you're willing to type a long URL into your Web browser, you can read the Department of Education's excellent handbook, "The Student Guide," online. It's at: http://www.ed.gov/prog_info/SFA/StudentGuide/.

- www.finaid.org: This site, the Financial Aid Information Page, has a little bit of everything, and is certainly a place to check out. You'll read about everything from scholarships to alerts on popular financial aid swindles.

- www.fastweb.com: FastWEB is a commercial (but free) site that will allow you to search a scholarship database in order to locate suitable sources of financial aid.

- www.fool.com/money.htm: This is our "Personal Finance" area. Scroll down through it and you'll see our "Paying for College" section. It offers numerous tips.

How to Get Yours

Now we get down to the crux of the matter. Many financial aid/scholarship programs (and all of the grant programs) are based upon financial need. The more you have, the less you need. A student is expected to contribute about 35% of his or her assets toward educational costs, while a parent is expected to contribute roughly 6% of assets. Basically, financial need is determined by the need of the student (based upon total educational costs), less the "expected family contribution" from both the student's and parents' assets.

It's easy to see that because of the disproportionate percentage applied to the student versus the parent, the greater the student's assets, the less likely the chance for financial aid. Keep this in the back of your mind when you begin your income shifting and custodian account strategies. The "expected family contribution" is based upon a number of complicated factors and formulas, which include:

• The parents' and student's assets

• Allowances for federal income, state income, and Social Security taxes paid

• The parents' tax return data

• Allowances based upon the number of total family members, and also the number of family members in college

• Special employment allowances if both parents work or if a single parent files as Head of Household or as a surviving spouse

If you've attempted to complete a financial aid package, you likely don't have fond memories of the process. Or perhaps even the outcome. Trying to help you to complete the financial aid package is well beyond the scope of this book, and could possibly be more difficult than putting the finishing touches on a Form 1040. Which is why we would like to see you in a position to fund your child's education on your own and bypass this entire process. But we do want you to understand that the student's assets are an important factor when determining need for financial aid programs.

Reducing Your Expected Family Income

Here are a few of the more popular methods that you might consider to reduce your "expected family income":

• If you have loans against a life insurance policy, consider taking funds out of your general assets to pay off that life insurance loan. This will reduce your general asset base for testing purposes, and the value of your life insurance contract will not be considered a part of your expected family income.

• Reduce the student's assets and income. If you've had Junior on the payroll, consider reversing that decision. If the student has assets that can be transferred or shifted back to the parent (kinda like a reverse shift), consider doing so. Determine if the student can reduce assets by buying an insurance or annuity contract or buying personal assets (such as a car, clothing, etc.).

• Reduce the amount of parental cash assets by paying off mortgage loans with existing cash or other assets. Parents can also reduce cash assets by purchasing an annuity or insurance contract or buying personal assets such as cars, furnishings, clothing, etc.

• Consider shifting assets to your business, if possible. For financial aid purposes, only 60% of the value of the business is considered an asset for expected family income purposes. So making a transfer of assets to your business can reduce your asset base by 40% without a real reduction in assets.

Do these sound like games that you don't really want to play? We don't blame you. Many of the solutions may be harsher than the problem. Why go out and spend

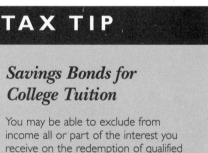

TAX TIP

Savings Bonds for College Tuition

You may be able to exclude from income all or part of the interest you receive on the redemption of qualified U.S. savings bonds during the year if you pay qualified higher educational expenses during the same year. This exclusion is known as the Education Savings Bond Program.

This program isn't too exciting to us Fools, as we believe that you can do much better than investing in series EE savings bonds. But you should know that it's available to you. In addition to the crummy rate of return that you'll receive on these bonds, there are a number of restrictions, requirements, and income limitations that must be overcome in order for you to exclude the interest from these bonds for education purposes.

For more information on this program, check out IRS forms 8815 and 8818 and the associated instructions. For a more complete overview of this program, check out IRS Publication 550.

TAX RELIEF

Acronym Glossary for Tax-Related Personal Ads

- MFJD: Married filing jointly and discreetly
- AMTP: Alternative Minimum Tax Payer
- NFE: Never filed extension
- NBA: Never been audited
- SHOH: Single Head of Household
- SNLD: Single, no longer a dependent
- LCGB: Lotsa capital gains, baby
- NNOL: No net operating loss
- NOLBTSTAS: Net operating loss, but things should turn around soon
- PMOT: Prepare my own taxes
- 396: AGI in the 39.6% tax bracket

money like a drunken sailor just to reduce your asset base in an attempt (perhaps an unsuccessful one) to qualify for student aid? We prefer saving, investing, and growing your assets—not spending willy-nilly to reduce your asset base. Some of the decisions that you make in an attempt to qualify for student aid may haunt you for many years to come. So don't take these suggestions as gospel. Give them a lot of thought before you proceed—or even consider proceeding.

Independence Day

You may believe that simply dropping your child as a dependent from your tax return and allowing him or her to file as an independent person will help in the federal aid application process. This isn't the case, according to information available. A student is considered a dependent of the parent and does not qualify for independent status unless one of the following requirements are met:

• The student is over age 24 by the end of the application year.

• The student is married.

• The student has a legal dependent.

• The student is an armed service veteran.

• The student is attending professional or graduate school.

• The student is an orphan or ward of the court.

So simply playing fast and loose with the dependents on your tax return may not solve the problem. Make sure that you know the rules, requirements, and restrictions for independent status, and are on solid ground before you start goofin' with your tax return.

FIVE

YOUR HOME

The place is very well & quiet & the
children only scream in a low voice.
—Lord Byron

What you'll find in this chapter:
- Home Sale Exclusion
- IRA Withdrawals for Homebuyers
- Moving Expense Deductions

When we think of investments, we don't always think of houses. (Many Fools, at least, are used to focusing intently on stocks, not letting our attention wander to other investments.) But the house you live in is very likely the biggest investment you'll ever make—so it deserves some consideration. It can also prove quite lucrative.

In the days of yore (those days preceding May 7, 1997), if you sold your primary residence for a profit, Uncle Sam offered you the opportunity to exclude up to $125,000 in gains from taxation. (In other words, you could essentially pretend that up to $125,000 of any gain on the house wasn't taxable income.) This was permitted only once in your lifetime and only if you were 55 or older and met some other requirements. If you couldn't use the $125,000 exclusion, you could purchase a property of equal or greater value with the proceeds of the sale and defer the gain into the new property.

Well, one of the most momentous changes in tax law in 1997 affected home sale exclusions, changing them significantly for the better. In fact, these new rules can amount to such an incredibly big deal for many Fools that we're left scratching our heads as to why so much fuss is being made about the Roth IRA. True, the Roth may prove to be quite beneficial in the long run (or not). But if you're selling a home in the near future, these new rules are likely to leave you with a *lot* of money in your pocket *right now*.

If you sold your principal residence after May 6, 1997, you may be eligible to exclude up to a whopping $250,000 from capital gains tax. Yowza. Excited? Wait—it gets even better. You only have to have lived in the residence for two of the five years preceding the sale. Unlike previous rules, you don't have to roll over any gains into the next residence you buy. You no longer have to be 55 or older. And best of all, you're no longer limited to taking advantage of this tax break only once in your lifetime. In fact, even if you already cashed in your once-in-a-lifetime ticket, that's forgotten and you get to play again.

This is a *very* big deal, Fool. If you're lucky enough to sell a home that has appreciated by $250,000 or more, you may get to enjoy a gain of a quarter of a million dollars, tax-free! And years later, you may be able to exclude another hefty sum. And again after that. And if you're married, you may be eligible for up to *$500,000* in exclusions each time. (We'll pause now, while you look for a paper bag to breathe into for a while.)

Think of that legendary old woman who lived in a shoe. Let's say that she bought the shoe in 1974 for $75,000 and lived in it with her many children for several years. In 1998, thanks to some Foolish investments in stocks, she could afford a bigger and better place—perhaps even a hip boot. The shoe itself had appreciated substantially; late in 1998 she sold it for $330,000. Her capital gain is the difference between her purchase price and the proceeds from the sale: $255,000. (Any money she's spent on improvements to the shoe can be added to her initial cost basis, thus decreasing her gain.) The old lady's timing is terrific. Not long ago, she would only have been able to exclude $125,000 of the gain from tax if she met all the requirements. This year, though, she gets to exclude a full $250,000. She gets to keep it tax-free and can spend it as she sees fit—on some other housing, on a trip around the world, or perhaps on skin care products she sees advertised on television late at night. Note that the remaining $5,000 of gain does get taxed, though, at the appropriate capital gains tax rate.

Now that we've informed you about this amazing new tax treat, you need to do a little self-evaluation. Have you, in fact, sold your primary residence after May 6, 1997? Do you plan to sell it in this current tax year? For most people, the answer is probably nyet. If you're in this group, then as exciting as the rest of this chapter is, it doesn't pertain to you right now. You may want to skip ahead—but reading the chapter now may help you in planning any future home sales.

Now, back to our new friend, the home sale exclusion. Are there any strings attached? Well, of course there are. Who ever heard of a tax law without any strings attached? (Traders of string futures in the commodities markets surely noticed the price of string skyrocketing in recent decades as the world supply of string dropped—concurrent with new tax legislation.) Let's jump in, shall we?

The Ownership and Use Rule

You (the seller) must have owned and lived in the home as your principal residence for at least two of the five years preceding the date of sale. The two years don't have to be consecutive, though. You could live in it for six months, live somewhere else for a year, move back into it for 18 months, and then sell it. That would work.

How, precisely, are you supposed to measure your time in the home? According to the IRS, you will meet the two-year test if you can show that you owned and lived in the property as your principal residence, or main home, for either 24 full months or 730 days during the five-year period ending on the date of the sale. And while short, temporary absences for vacations and other seasonal absences do count as periods of use, converting the property into a rental unit if you move to another primary home may jeopardize your use of the exclusion.

TAX TIP

Home Improvement

Remember adding that room to your house? Covering your home with aluminum siding? Remodeling your kitchen? Well, if you've got records of how much you spent on improvements to your house, they might save you a bundle when you sell it. The cost of improvements can be added to your purchase price, decreasing your gain upon sale. For example, imagine that you bought your home for $100,000, spent $30,000 on improvements, and sold it later for $200,000. If you ignore the improvements, your gain is $100,000. But the improvements (if you've kept those receipts!) mean you can increase your basis in the house to $130,000 and the gain is reduced to $70,000. With the new home sale exclusion described in this section, this might not make a difference, but in some circumstances it might make a big difference.

Remember, though, that we're talking real improvements here, not repairs. An improvement should add value to your property, last longer than a year, and remain attached to the property. Replacing a broken toilet paper rack doesn't generate any kind of tax windfall—sorry!

The Two-Year Rule

In most cases, you can only take advantage of this home sale exclusion once during any two-year period.

The Ownership and Use and Two-Year Rules for Married Folks

Here's some more good news. If you're married, you can exclude up to a mind-boggling $500,000 in capital gains from the sale of your principal residence. The bad news isn't even so bad—it's just that there are a few more strings attached. Below are the ownership and use and two-year rules as they apply to married people. Note that *all four* conditions must be met.

A married couple may exclude up to $500,000 of their home sale gain if:

• They file a joint return for the year of the home sale;

• Either spouse owned the home for at least two years in the five-year period ending on the sale date;

• Both spouses used the home as a principal residence for at least two years in the five-year period ending on the sale date; and

• Neither spouse had used the new exclusion on the sale of another residence within the two-year period ending on the date of the current home's sale.

Since this is such a big tax break, make sure you plan your home sale carefully to ensure that you qualify. This includes living in it for the required amount of time. Proper planning can save tens of thousands of tax dollars. Improper planning can cost you just as much.

Rollovers and Extended Holding Periods

If you "rolled over" a gain from a previous residence into the purchase of your current residence, you can tack on the time you lived in the earlier home to the time you lived in the later one, thus extending your holding period.

With the new law, there's no more rolling over of gains from one sale into another residence. For example, the little old lady cannot take her taxable $5,000 gain and exclude it from taxes by applying it to another home purchase. It's unavoidably taxable. A single person with a much larger total gain of $365,000, for example, will only be able to exclude $250,000 and will have to pay taxes on the remaining $115,000. (Uncle Sam is giving you a big break with the $250,000, but the Pentagon still needs to buy some $500 staplers.)

Reduced Exclusions

If you don't fully pass the ownership and use test, you're not totally out of luck. You might still be able to exclude part or all of your home sale if either of the following conditions exist. (That's right—either, not both.)

• You owned your residence on August 5, 1997, and sold it after that date but before August 5, 1999.

• You fail to meet the ownership and use qualification and/or the only once every two years qualification because you had to sell the home due to a change in your place of employment, health, or because of other unforeseen circumstances.

For example, imagine Kaiti Trimble, who works at Fool Global Headquarters. She bought a lovely new home in January of 1998, but a few months later she's informed that the company is sending her off to Antarctica to head up the new "Fool Antarctica" office. She sells her home in September of 1999, buys a jacket and a hat, borrows a *How to Cook Squid* cookbook, and makes a down payment on an igloo. Even though Kaiti didn't meet the ownership and use test, she will still be able to exclude part or all of her gain because the second exception above was met. (She had to sell her home because her employer changed her place of employment.)

If you qualify for a reduced exclusion, you need to calculate how much of your gain you can exclude. Here's the relatively simple math involved:

1. Determine the number of days that you (a) "used" the home as your principal residence and the number of days that you (b) "owned" the home as your principal residence. Use the *smaller* of (a) or (b) as your starting point.

2. Divide the result in number (1) by 730 days (730 is the product of multiplying 365 by two—it represents two full years of use).

3. Multiply the result in (2) by $250,000 (for a single person).

4. The exclusion will be the *lesser* of the gain on the sale of the property or the result in (3).

Looking back at the Kaiti's situation, let's assume that Kaiti owned and used her home for 615 days before it was sold, and she realized a gain of $220,000 on the sale of the property. She would divide the number of days used (615) by the two-year amount (730) to arrive at a result of 0.842466. She'll then multiply $250,000 by this result to arrive at a maximum exclusion of $210,617. So, while Kaiti realized a gain of $220,000 on her home sale, she can only exclude $210,617 of that amount. This means that she will be required to pay taxes on the remaining $9,383 gain.

ASK ROY

Q:

Exactly what are "unforeseen circumstances" when discussing the home sale exclusion?

A:

It's hard to pin this down—because the regulations that define the term "unforeseen circumstances" haven't been written yet. Without them, it's hard to get a flavor for what the IRS considers such a circumstance.

But does that mean that there are no "unforeseen circumstances" until the IRS tells us exactly what they might be? I'm not so sure. Is losing your job (as opposed to a "change in place of employment") an unforeseen circumstance? I would sure think so. How about a death in the family? Seems reasonable. Divorce? Possibly. A lousy winter (it was way too cold)? Probably not.

The point that I'm trying to make here is that if you don't otherwise qualify for the reduced exclusion because of health or job relocation purposes, all might not be lost. With any luck, the regulations will be out soon and we will all know what the IRS considers an unforeseen circumstance. But until then, you'll have a decision to make if unusual or extreme circumstances require that you make a move before your two-year period has expired.

Reduced Exclusions for Married Couples

Married couples who don't meet all the required conditions may still be able to claim a reduced exclusion on their home sale gain. It's just a matter of calculating how much using a formula devised by those merry mathematicians at the IRS. You can review the computations involved online at our tax area or in IRS Form 2119, or even in IRS Publication 523.

So there you have it—the new home sale exclusion rules, in a nutshell. Note that the rules can get even more complicated and technical if you use part of your home for business and/or convert your principal residence to a rental property. So if either of these issues apply to you, you might want to consult a qualified tax pro to help you with your computations and recognition of your exclusion.

IRA WITHDRAWALS FOR HOMEBUYERS

You generally can't take an early distribution from your regular (or Roth) IRA account and avoid the dreaded 10% penalty. But the 1997 Taxpayer Relief Act created an exception to the rule to help people become homeowners.

The new law allows individuals to receive distributions from their IRAs to pay up to $10,000 of first-time homebuyer expenses without incurring the 10% early withdrawal penalty that usually applies to withdrawals from an

IRA before age 59 1/2. Even though the penalty is waived, you will still be required to pay taxes (as applicable) on the IRA withdrawal itself.

Funny Definitions

In an odd twist of government logic (is there really such a thing as government logic, or is it an oxymoron?), you should know that a "first-time homebuyer" doesn't really have to be a first-time homebuyer, since the law defines the term as someone who has not owned a home for two years. So in addition to benefiting "first-time" homebuyers, the law also helps "not-recent" homebuyers.

In yet another twist of government logic, you can take advantage of the provision even if you are not the homebuyer. Huh? Well, the law states that the first-time homebuyer can be the IRA owner, his or her spouse, or any of his/her children, grandchildren, or ancestors. So maybe this provision should really be called, "Penalty-Free Withdrawal for Not-So-Recent Homebuyers and/or Relatives of an IRA Owner." You be the judge.

How It Works

The $10,000 limit is a lifetime limitation on the amount of withdrawals that can be pulled out of the IRA penalty-free under the first-time home-buyer provision. So don't think that you'll get this relief each and every time you want to buy another home. Once you use up your $10,000, you're done. And while the law isn't crystal clear, it seems permissible that, for example, a husband and wife helping one of their children scrape together a down payment could each withdraw up to $10,000 from their respective IRAs without incurring any penalty for early withdrawal. (Just remember that their total lifetime allowable withdrawal for this purpose is $20,000. They can't do this for each of their children.)

Know that any IRA funds distributed to you must be used to pay qualified acquisition costs before the close of the 120th day after the day you received the distribution—so this isn't a completely open-ended deal. You need to plan and time your purchase and your distribution carefully.

Also, know that qualified acquisition costs include the costs of buying, building, or rebuilding a home and any usual or reasonable settlement, financing, or other closing costs. So the distribution must be related to the purchase of the property and can't be used for other home-related expenses such as furnishings or general home repairs or maintenance.

Mortgage Interest Credit

A little-known tax savings related to home ownership is the mortgage interest credit. If you qualify for it, you'll be able to reduce your taxes *dollar for dollar* by the amount of the credit. A mortgage interest credit is available to first-time homebuyers whose income is generally below the median income for the area where they live. The credit is intended to help lower-income individuals afford home ownership. The tax credit is allowed each year for part of the home mortgage interest they pay.

To be eligible for the credit, you must get a mortgage credit certificate (MCC) from your state or local government. Generally, an MCC is issued only in connection with a new mortgage for the purchase of your main home.

The MCC will show the certificate credit rate you will use to figure your credit. It will also include the certified indebtedness amount on which the interest is eligible for the credit.

You must contact the appropriate government agency about getting an MCC *before* you get a mortgage and buy your home. Contact your state or local housing finance agency for information about the availability of MCCs in your area. If you believe that you may qualify for the mortgage interest credit, make sure that you and your lender discuss this issue before you actually purchase the property or enter into the loan.

To claim the credit, complete Form 8396 and attach it to your Form 1040. You'll also have to reduce your home mortgage interest deduction by the amount of the mortgage interest credit. This sounds harsh, but in virtually all cases, the credit is more valuable than the deduction.

Heads-up: Note that if you purchase a home after 1990 using an MCC, and you sell that home within nine years, you will have to recapture (repay) a portion of the credit. Learn even more about the credit in IRS Publications 523 and 530, as well as the instructions accompanying Form 8396. Go get 'em, Fool!

Finally, this benefit is only available for IRA accounts (either Roth or traditional)—not for 401(k) or 403(b) accounts or any other type of retirement instrument.

MOVING EXPENSE DEDUCTIONS

It's hard sometimes to think of any positive aspects of moving. Packing is a chore. Unpacking can be a drag. Things get lost, things get broken. But despite all this, there is a bright side: deductions.

Dwight Gibbs works for Raisin' Hell, a small but growing company in Fresno, California, that makes fiery snacks from raisins and habanero peppers. Business is bustling and the president wants him to set up the company's new branch in Providence, Rhode Island.

He's excited about the big move, of course. It should prove very beneficial to his bank account and résumé. It might offer him some tax advantages, as well—he may be able to deduct his moving expenses.

Let's get a move on and address the rules for this kind of deduction.

You can deduct the expenses for one trip (for you and your family) to the new home and for moving your furniture and household goods, if you satisfy the minimum distance and period-of-employment requirements. If you meet these two tests you will be able to deduct your moving expenses whether or not you itemize your deductions. That is, you can take an above-the-line deduction and still receive benefits from your moving expenses, even if you don't itemize your deductions. (Above-the-line: appearing before AGI is determined. Below-the-line items occur after AGI is calculated.)

But there are two tests that you must pass before you can deduct your moving expenses. (Remember—you must pass both of them.)

The Distance Test

The distance from your old residence to your new job location must be at least 50 miles more than the distance from your old residence to your old job location. In other words, the commute from your old residence to your new job must be at least 50 miles more than your previous commute (from old residence to old job).

For example, Chad's old job was three miles from his former home. In order to have deductible moving expenses, Chad's new job location must be at least 53 miles from his former home.

Minimum Period of Employment Test

As an employee, you must work full-time in the new general area for at least 39 weeks in the first 12 months after arrival there. (You start counting after your last trip before starting work full-time.) If you are self-employed, you must work full-time in the new general area for at least 39 weeks in the first 12 months and at least 78 weeks in the first 24 months after arrival there. Either you or your spouse can satisfy this requirement (but weeks worked by one can't be added to weeks worked by the other).

Leave or vacation time counts as employment time, and so do involuntary absences because of illness, strikes, shutouts, and natural disasters. Further, off-season periods of less than six months in a seasonal-basis employment count if covered by your employment contract. (For the self-employed: Off-season periods of less than six months count if you perform services both before and after off-season.)

This minimum-period-of-employment requirement is waived if, after you get a job in which you could have reasonably satisfied the test, you are laid off or fired other than for willful misconduct or if you're transferred by the employer for the employer's benefit. The minimum period is also waived if you die or are disabled.

What Can Be Deducted

If you meet the above two tests, you can deduct the following expenses for moving yourself and the members of your household (but not tenants or employees) to the new location:

• The cost of moving household goods and personal effects. This includes the cost of packing, crating, transporting, storing, and insuring belongings (storing and insuring for any consecutive 30-day period after the move). It also includes connecting and disconnecting utilities, and shipping the car and household pets. Expenses of moving household goods or personal effects from a place other than the old residence are deductible only to the extent of what it would cost you to move them from the old residence. The cost of moving items bought en route isn't deductible—sorry.

• Expenses of travel (including lodging but not meals) from the old residence to the new. The cost of a single trip for you and for members of your household is allowed, but you needn't travel together at the same time. If you use your car for travel, you can deduct either the cost of gas and oil (accurate records must be kept) or a standard mileage rate (currently 10 cents per mile), plus parking fees and tolls. General maintenance, repairs, insurance, or depreciation aren't deductible.

• Lodging expenses for the day you arrive in the new area, plus the cost of lodging in the old area within one day from the time you couldn't live in the old home anymore because the furniture had been moved. Note that pre-move expenses and living expenses while house-hunting aren't deductible.

A Few More Rules

There's no dollar limit on the amount of the expenses, but you can only deduct reasonable costs. That means the expenses can't be lavish or extravagant. Excessive deductions might draw the attention of auditors at the IRS, so expense embellishment is not recommended.

Also, you must move by the shortest, most direct route available by the conventional mode of transportation used and in the shortest time commonly required to travel that distance. Side trips, for example, aren't deductible. So, don't plan to move from Ohio to Oregon via Hawaii!

The expenses must generally be incurred within one year from when you start working at the new location, but expenses may be postponed for a reason such as allowing your child to finish school.

The expenses should be deducted in the year(s) in which you pay them. Even if you haven't satisfied the minimum employment period by tax return time, you may deduct them. If you later can't satisfy the requirement, you must either include in income the amount you deducted, or file an amended return for the year of the deduction with the deduction eliminated. You also can wait and claim the deduction on an amended return or a refund claim when you have satisfied the minimum employment period.

TAX TIP

More Home-Related Tax Savings

For more information on home-related tax issues, pop into our "Itemized Deductions and Miscellaneous Credits" section. There we explain how you can minimize your tax burden even further, by accounting for things such as property taxes and mortgage interest payments.

If you are reimbursed by your employer for your expenses or if your employer pays them directly, then you're out of luck regarding deductions. You shouldn't claim any reimbursed amounts as deductions. (As a small bonus, you also don't have to claim them as income. Yes, they may have arrived as checks to you, like a paycheck—or perhaps in your paycheck. But the reimbursement amounts do not represent income.)

Many employers will reimburse you for moving expenses that don't qualify for the deduction. These will show up on your annual W-2 form as income to you. The IRS views these payments as income.

If you and your employer are accounting for everything properly, your reimbursed and excludable expenses won't be included in "wages" or any other taxable amounts on your Form W-2. Instead, they'll appear for information purposes only in the 'Other' box (Box 13) of the W-2 as Code P.

To support your deduction, it's important that you keep records of distances from your old and new residence to your old and new job, dates of travel and arrival to the new area, employment periods, and records and receipts for your moving expenses. For additional detailed information, check out IRS Publication 521 and Form 3903 (and instructions).

TAX RELIEF

Presidents on Taxes

The tax which will be paid for education is not more than the thousand part of what will be paid if we leave the people in ignorance.—Thomas Jefferson

The wisdom of man never yet contrived a system of taxation that would operate with perfect equality.—Andrew Jackson

I can't make a damn thing out of this tax problem. I listen to one side and they seem right— and then I talk to the other side and they seem just as right, and here I am where I started. God, what a job!—Warren G. Harding

Unless we wish to hamper the people in their right to earn a living, we must have tax reform. —Calvin Coolidge

To the extent that some people are dishonest or careless in their dealings with the government, the majority is forced to carry a heavier tax burden.—John F. Kennedy

I want to be sure that he is a ruthless son of a bitch, that he will do what he is told, that every income tax return I want to see, I see.—Richard M. Nixon (on the kind of IRS Commissioner he wanted)

The federal income tax system is a disgrace to the human race.—Jimmy Carter

The taxpayer—that's someone who works for the federal government but doesn't have to take the civil service examination.—Ronald W. Reagan

Read my lips. No new taxes.—George Bush

I wish I could promise you that I won't ask you to pay any more.—Bill Clinton

SIX

YOUR HOME OFFICE

The brain is a wonderful organ; it starts working the moment you get up in the morning and does not stop until you get into the office.

—Robert Frost

What you'll find in this chapter:
• Home Office Deductions
• Travel Expenses and the "Tax Home"

It can be great to work out of your home. You get to work in a robe and bunny slippers, if you like. Or in a full suit of medieval armor, if you prefer. There's no one there to ask you to stop singing the theme from *Star Trek* so loudly. No one to mentally utter "tsk tsk" at your lunch of Slim Jims and Oreos. (Unless you're working in your mom's basement, that is.)

But every silver lining has a cloud. Home offices do make life a little more complicated, at least in regard to taxes. The extra work you put into your taxes in regard to your home office can pay off, though, in the form of handy deductions. Here's the scoop on the subject.

HOME OFFICE DEDUCTIONS

You may deduct your home office expenses if you meet any of the following three tests:

• The separate structure test

• The place for meeting patients, clients, or customers test

• The principal place of business test

You may also deduct the expenses of certain storage space if you qualify under the rules described further below.

If you do qualify, you compute your home office deductions on Form 8829, and report them above-the-line on Schedule C.

Here are the tests:

- Separate structure: This is the easiest test to meet. It allows a deduction for the costs of a separate unattached structure on the same property as your home—for example, an unattached garage, artist's studio, work-shop, or office building that is used as a home office. To qualify for the deduction, the separate structure must be used exclusively and on a regular basis in connection with your business.

- Home office used for meeting patients, clients, or customers: Alternatively, you may deduct your home office expenses if you use the home office exclusively and on a regular basis to meet with patients, clients, or customers in the normal course of your business. The patients, clients, or customers must be physically present in the home office. Telephone calls to them from your home office won't do the trick. (Sorry.)

- Principal place of business: In addition, you may deduct your home office expenses if you use your home office, exclusively and on a regular basis, as your principal place of business.

What's a Principal Place of Business?

The meaning of "principal place of business" has been the source of many disputes between the IRS and taxpayers. The current rules for determining a taxpayer's principal place of business were laid down by the Supreme Court in its January 1993 decision in *Commissioner v. Soliman,* which was widely reported in the media. (Soliman was an anesthesiologist who spent about 30 to 35 hours per week with patients at several hospitals. He also spent two to three hours a day in his home office on administrative and other work. The court determined that the home office was not Soliman's principal place of business.) But the Taxpayer Relief Act of 1997 has altered some aspects of the "principal place of business" test in favor of taxpayers starting in 1999.

According to the Soliman decision, there are two primary considerations in determining a taxpayer's principal place of business: (1) the relative importance of the activities performed at each location where the taxpayer's business was conducted, and (2) the amount of time spent at each place. The IRS says that it will first apply the "relative importance" test by comparing the activities performed at home with those carried on elsewhere. If this comparison clearly shows where the principal place of business is, there's no need to look further. When the "relative importance" test doesn't give a clear answer, says the IRS, the "time" test comes into play. However, these tests may not clearly reveal that any location is the taxpayer's principal place of business. In that case, the taxpayer will be treated as not having a principal place of business.

Under a provision in the Taxpayer Relief Act of 1997 which went into effect in 1999, a home office will now qualify as the taxpayer's principal place of business if the taxpayer uses the home office to conduct administrative or management activities of the business, so long as the taxpayer doesn't have another fixed location where substantial administrative or management activities of the business are conducted. However, according to the IRS, the office must be used exclusively, and on a regular basis, for the administrative or management activities.

Storing Products at Home

If you're in the business of selling products at retail or wholesale, and if your home is your sole fixed business location, you can deduct home expenses allocable to space that you use regularly to store inventory or product samples. The space doesn't have to be used exclusively for business purposes, and you can do business at the fixed locations of your customers (e.g., retail stores, if you're a wholesaler) and nonfixed locations (such as flea markets or craft shows).

Imagine "Mad Dog" Yergeau, who has signed up to sell high-tech hampers to friends and neighbors through a multi-level marketing outfit. If he's filled half of his two-car garage with boxes of hampers, he is eligible for the home office deduction.

"Exclusive and Regular Use"

As noted earlier, when you claim to be using your home office under any of the tests outlined above (except the "storage space" test for retailers and wholesalers), the home office must be used exclusively and on a regular basis in connection with your business. (For storage space used by retailers or wholesalers, the space must be used regularly for business purposes, but doesn't have to be used exclusively for those purposes.)

The exclusive use requirement means that you must use your home office solely for the purpose of carrying on your business. Any other use will result in loss of all deductions for your home office expenses.

For example, a professional musician's home studio that's used only for rehearsal, recording demo tapes, etc., passes the exclusive use test. But a caterer's living room that's used to meet with clients and potential clients, as well as for family entertainment and gatherings, won't pass the test. Neither will a spare bedroom that's used to work in and store business records, but that's also used by occasional overnight guests.

The regular basis requirement means that you must use the home office in carrying on your business on a continuous, ongoing or recurring basis. Generally, this means a few hours a week, every week. A few days a month, every month, may do the trick. But occasional, "once-in-a-while" business use won't do.

Specific Deductions and Allowances

So, now that you've determined that you do indeed have a legitimate home office, what exactly can you deduct?

Well, if your home office is your principal place of business, the costs of traveling between your home office and other work locations will be deductible in full, regardless of whether the other work location is regular or temporary, and regardless of the distance. So what for other people might simply be nondeductible commuting costs are deductible transportation expenses for you!

A qualifying home office also means that you may take business expense deductions for the following:

• The "direct expenses" of the home office, such as the costs of painting or repairing the home office and depreciation deductions for furniture and fixtures used in the home office, *and*

• The "indirect" expenses of maintaining the home office. These include the properly allocable share of utility costs, depreciation, insurance, etc. for your home, as well as an allocable share of mortgage interest, real estate taxes, and casualty losses.

Amount Limitations on Deductions

The amount you may deduct as a home office expense is subject to limitations based on the income attributable to your use of the home office. Also having an impact are your residence-based deductions that aren't dependent on use of your home for business (e.g., mortgage interest and real estate taxes) and your business deductions that aren't attributable to your use of the home office. (What? You didn't get that? Then let's review an example.)

Say you operate your business out of a home office that occupies 20% of the space in your home. This year, your business grosses $50,000. The mortgage interest and real estate taxes on your home total $20,000, $4,000 of which is allocable to the home office. You have $5,000 of additional home office expenses (depreciation, utilities, etc.), and your business has $30,000 of expenses that are not associated with the use of your home office (secretarial and bookkeeping services, legal and accounting fees, advertising expenses, etc.). To figure out whether you can deduct your home office expenses, you first subtract the home office portion of the mortgage and real estate taxes ($4,000) from the business's gross income. This leaves you with $46,000. Then, from this, you subtract your business expenses that aren't attributable to your use of the home office—$30,000. This leaves you $16,000. If this figure exceeds the amount of your remaining home office expenses ($5,000 in our example), you can deduct all of those expenses. If this figure is less than your remaining home office expenses, your deduction is limited.

Just remember that the business use of home costs for insurance, repairs, utilities, and depreciation are limited to the net income from the business activity. While mortgage interest and real estate taxes can create a net loss on the Schedule C, these other expenses cannot. But if you find that your deductions are limited because of your net Schedule C profit, don't panic completely. Any home office expenses that can't be deducted because of the limitations may be carried over and deducted in later years.

Note that the same interest and taxes can't be deducted on both Schedule A (itemized deductions) and Schedule C. Only the remainder of the interest and taxes, after subtracting the amount attributable to the home office, is to be deducted on Schedule A.

Computers and Related Equipment

If your use of the home office qualifies under any of the rules discussed earlier, you may be able to use the "expensing" provisions of Section 179 of the tax code to deduct the cost of computers and related equipment that you use in the home office. In addition, those deductions will not be subject to the "listed property" restrictions that would otherwise apply. We discussed this in greater detail in Chapter 1 in the section on putting your computer to work.

ASK R●Y

Maternity Leave Deduction

Q:

My wife is a commissioned salesperson who gets a W-2 form each year and is going on maternity leave in October. She can work out of our home on a limited basis and not lose clients if we forward her work phone line to the house, install a desk system with a modem link to her company's computer, and add a fax machine. This home office equipment is not just a convenience, but is essential to competing in the world of sales with a babe in arms. Without trying to write off the space in our home, can we deduct these expenses from our taxes?

P.S. I have a letter from the president of her company that states that these items are necessary to the continuation of her job during maternity leave and that the company cannot provide them to her.

A:

It sounds like she's going to buy a desk, chair, files, a modem, and so on, and that she'll also need to pay for some telephone installation and monthly line charges. I also assume that she will be using an existing computer to modem link to the job.

Certainly all of the charges that you mention are deductible as business expenses, subject to the 2% floor for itemized deductions. The desk, chair, etc. must be depreciated, but you can elect the Section 179 expensing option to take the entire cost in the year purchased. The monthly call forwarding expense is deductible. The monthly telephone expense attributable to business and the installation of the new phone line are also deductible. The new modem must be depreciated, but once again, you can use the Section 179 election to expense. None of this has to do with the home office, since you are *not* claiming an "office in the home" deduction. See the difference?

You already have the required letter from the employer indicating that these expenses are required for her job and will not be reimbursed. So you're already over that hump. Nice job. All of these expenses are ordinary and necessary and are certainly deductible.

Now then, let's talk about the home office rules just for a second, on the off chance that they apply to you. If the home office is used exclusively for business purposes and is for the convenience of your wife's employer, you may also qualify for home office deductions.

Caution: Home Office Deductions Can Affect Home Sale Exclusions

Know that if you claim any home office deductions with respect to a portion of your principal residence, when you sell the residence, any profit attributable to the portion used as a home office may not be eligible for the otherwise available $250,000/$500,000 exclusion for gain on the sale of principal residences.

Another rule you should be aware of is that the gain from the home sale representing the post-May 6, 1997, depreciation you claim on the home office is not eligible for the home sale exclusion.

For More Information

As you can see, the office-in-home rules can get pretty ugly... and complicated. You really need to know that you are on firm ground before you consider claiming this deduction. You'll find much more information on the office-in-home rules in IRS Publication 587.

TRAVEL EXPENSES AND THE "TAX HOME"

Can you deduct travel expenses when you travel for business? Well, as you might have suspected by now, the answer is: "It depends." First, you need to determine your "tax home."

You can deduct travel expenses when business is conducted away from your "tax home." Your tax home is the entire city or general area where your place of business, employment, or post of duty is located. The location of your family home does not matter, although in most cases the tax home will be the same as the family home. The only way that you can have deductible travel expenses is to first have a tax home.

Our friends at the IRS use three tests to determine whether a taxpayer is considered to have a tax home, or a "regular place of abode," for determining allowable travel expenses.

• Whether the taxpayer performs a portion of his/her business in the vicinity of his/her claimed residence and uses the residence for lodging while performing such business there.

• Whether the taxpayer incurs duplicate living expenses while on business travel.

• Whether the taxpayer:

> • Has not abandoned the vicinity in which his/her historical place of lodging and his/her claimed residence are both located, or

- Has family members currently residing at his/her claimed residence, or

- Taxpayer frequently uses the claimed residence for lodging.

If *all three* of the tests are satisfied, the IRS will assume there is a tax home and the taxpayer's away-from-home travel expenses will be deductible.

If only two of the three tests are satisfied, the IRS will closely examine the facts and circumstances to determine whether there is a qualified tax home.

If only one or none of the tests are satisfied, none of the taxpayer's work-related travel expenses will be allowed by the IRS.

In addition, while expenses for *temporary* employment away from home are deductible, expenses for *indefinite* employment are not. If you're away from home at a single location for more than one year, the travel will be considered indefinite, not temporary, regardless of the circumstances.

Also, know that employer reimbursements for any nondeductible expenses must be included in the employee's gross income.

If you have any additional questions on how the issues of a tax home affect travel expenses, refer to IRS Publication 463, "Travel, Entertainment, and Gift Expenses."

TAX RELIEF

Buying Civilization

I like to pay taxes. With them, I buy civilization.

—Oliver Wendell Holmes

It might make you feel better about paying taxes if you think about what you get for your money. After all, our dollars do provide some rather nifty things. (And if Uncle Sam didn't waste any of the money, life would be even sweeter.)

- Public schools
- Public libraries
- People to respond to your 911 call in the middle of the night
- People to respond when your house catches fire
- $435 hammers and $640 toilet seats for the military
- A court system
- Police officers to prevent and address crime
- Roads and highways
- Prisons
- Public parks
- National parks
- Fireworks displays
- Public and industrial safety programs
- Social services
- Space exploration
- The protection of a military force
- Water and sewage treatment plants
- Lots of free public museums in Washington, D.C.

Economists at the Tax Foundation (www.taxfoundation.org) have estimated that the price of American civilization in 1998 was $9,939 for every man, woman, and child in the country. That's the nation's total tax revenue for the year, divided by the population. The federal government took $6,810 of it, while state and local governments grabbed the remaining $3,129.

This might not seem *that* bad, until you learn that between 1900 and 1917, the average annual tax bite per person (in 1998 dollars) was just $366. (Interestingly, state and local taxes made up the majority of this amount.) Of course, we're paying for more services and, arguably, more civilization these days.

ITEMIZED DEDUCTIONS AND MISCELLANEOUS CREDITS

Homer: *I need some deductions. Deductions...Okay, Marge—if anyone asks, you require 24-hour nursing care, Lisa's a clergyman, Maggie is seven people, and Bart was wounded in Vietnam.*
Bart: *Cool!*

—"The Simpsons"

What you'll find in this chapter:
- Medical Expense Deductions
- Deductions for Taxes Paid
- Deductions for Interest Paid
- Mortgage Interest
- Investment Interest and Margin Interest
- Charitable Contribution Deductions
- Casualty and Theft Loss Deductions
- Miscellaneous Itemized Deductions
- Miscellaneous Credits

As we've discussed earlier, deductions and credits are similar... but different. They both allow you to reduce your tax liability. But credits are much more efficient than plain old deductions—especially when you're talking about itemized deductions. And itemized deductions are what we'll be looking at in this section. Most of the credits that are important to you have been reviewed in other sections of the book. But we'll use this section to mention a few other credits you should be aware of.

As you know, there are many different types of deductions. Some take place to offset income (above-the-line deductions). But others, itemized deductions, are a bit easier to quantify and understand. They're below-the-line deductions, and they live in their own little world... a world called Schedule A.

Itemized Deductions—A View From the Top

Remember that itemized deductions are applied against your adjusted gross income, thereby allowing you to arrive at a lower taxable income... and a lower income tax (yippee!). But itemizing your deductions is something that you're allowed to do, not necessarily something that you *must* do. If your situation is such that you have itemized deductions greater than your standard deduction, you can report your itemized deductions. But if you don't have any or many itemized deductions, you're allowed to take the "standard" deduction. You get the standard deduction simply for being you—an enriched and happy Fool. So it's your choice, your decision. You basically compare your itemized deductions to your standard deduction, and use the larger of the two results to reduce your taxable income. The concept is really pretty simple.

Yet there are some common misconceptions about itemized deductions. Many believe that they can't itemize their deductions unless they're home-owners paying large amounts of deductible interest expense. That's simply not true. While mortgage interest may be the largest itemized deduction on any given tax return, it's certainly not the *only* itemized deduction. All of your itemized deductions build on top of one another. You may not have one specific type of deduction that is necessarily large. But when smaller deductions are added together, you may well find yourself "over the top" of your standard deduction. Even non-mortgage holders have a tremen-dous opportunity for itemizing deductions. Think about the folks who live in states that impose a relatively high rate of state income taxes. Simply by using the state income taxes that they pay—and nothing more—many peo-ple can qualify to itemize their deductions. Consider the businessperson with a bunch of unreimbursed business expenses. Or even the unfortunate few who may have lost property because of a flood or fire. And those peo-ple who make substantial charitable contributions year after year. Those contributions alone may allow for the use of itemized deductions. So don't discount good old Schedule A. Each and every year you should take at least a few minutes to review Schedule A and see if your circumstances will allow you to itemize your deductions.

Finally, note that you can only itemize deductions if you file Form 1040. Itemization is not permitted with Form 1040A or 1040EZ.

What Are They?

Have we piqued your interest yet? Want to learn a bit more about itemized deductions? Great, because we want to tell you more about them. Basically, itemized deductions can be broken up into six major categories. They include:

• Medical Expense Deductions

• Tax Deductions

• Interest Deductions

- Charitable Contribution Deductions

- Casualty and Theft Loss Deductions

- Miscellaneous Deductions

Within each of those major categories you may find additional sub-categories to deal with. We'll look at each of these major categories and give you highlights on what they are and how they work. In no way will this section of the book be the last and final word on itemized deductions. If we wanted to do that, we'd add another 500 pages to the book—and you'd be snoring by page 50. So we'll simply introduce you to itemized deductions, let you know that they're out there, and show you how they work—with maybe a tax tip or two along the way.

Limits on Itemized Deductions

Now that we've got you all revved up on itemized deductions (is that possible?), let's get the bad news out of the way first. Even if you find that you *can* itemize your deductions, you may find that your overall itemized deductions are limited.

The Revenue Reconciliation Act of 1990 added a section to the IRS code that limits the amount of itemized deductions allowed to certain "high-income" taxpayers. The limit will apply to you (regardless of whether you believe you're a "high-income" taxpayer or not) if your AGI is in excess of $126,600 ($63,300 for a separate return filed by a married individual) for tax year 1999. If you're subject to this limitation, you're required to reduce the overall amount of your allowable itemized deductions by the lesser of:

- 3% of the excess of adjusted gross income over the applicable amount; or

- 80% of the amount of otherwise allowable itemized deductions.

Of course, to make things complicated, this limit doesn't apply to all deductions. Here's which ones count and which ones don't.

Deductions subject to the overall limit:

- Taxes paid

- Interest (except investment interest)

- Charitable contributions

- Job expenses

- Most miscellaneous deductions

Deductions not subject to the overall limit:

- Medical (and dental) expenses

- Investment interest expense

- Non-business casualty and theft loss

- Gambling loss (to the extent of gambling winnings)

In addition, there's another kind of limitation on these deductions: Various categories of itemized deductions have threshold (or "floor") limits. For example, there's a 7.5% threshold for medical deductions, a 10% floor for casualty losses, and a 2% floor for miscellaneous deductions. The floors are in respect to AGI. Here's what this means.

Imagine Carleen Murchison, accountant to the stars, who has an AGI of $40,000. Her floor for miscellaneous deductions is 2%. This means that she can only deduct those qualifying items that exceed 2% of $40,000, or $800. If she has $700 in miscellaneous deductions, she's out of luck. If she has $900 of miscellaneous deductions, she can deduct $100—the amount by which she exceeds the floor.

As you can see, the hurdle is higher for medical deductions. Carleen will only be able to deduct those medical expenses that exceed 7.5% of her AGI—in her case, $3,000.

MEDICAL EXPENSE DEDUCTIONS

We're about to jump into medical expense deductions. If you and everyone who lives in your household or appears on your tax return are in the pink of health, you may be able to skip this entire section. But don't be too hasty. You might end up saving a lot of tax dollars via medical deductions if you keep reading. Deductions are available even if you spent some money tending to someone *else's* health.

In general, you're allowed to deduct unreimbursed amounts paid for your own medical care and the care of your spouse and/or dependents. "Paid" is the key word here, since, with very few exceptions, you are allowed the deduction only in the year that you pay the medical expense. The scope of medical care includes the diagnosis, cure, mitigation, treatment, or prevention of disease, procedures affecting a structure or function of the body, related transportation, qualified long-term care services, and medical insurance. But it does *not* include expenses paid for the benefit of overall general health or well-being. We'll discuss this in a bit more detail soon, but let's move on and talk about the bad news associated with the medical expense deduction.

The medical expense deduction is allowed *only* to the extent that the expenses exceed 7.5% of your adjusted gross income. So unless your AGI is small, or your medical deductions are large, it's unlikely that you'll receive any real benefit from the medical expense deduction. But with some clever planning, you might be able to maximize your medical expenses. Howzat? Take a look at Nabil Makar, a space traffic controller in the galaxy of Zebulon-9. (We'll have to assume, of course, that Zebulon-9 happens to use the current U.S. tax code.)

Nabil has $40,000 of AGI and $3,000 of unreimbursed medical expenses in 1998 as well as $3,000 in 1999. His medical expenses save him no taxes in either year, because in neither year do they exceed 7.5% of AGI. But watch closely. If Nabil would have paid only $1,000 of medical expenses in 1998, and then paid $5,000 of expenses in 1999, he would have paid the same amount of total

TAX STRATEGY

Bunch Your Other Deductions

In this chapter we describe how to "bunch" medical expenses to help make them deductible. But bunching doesn't have to stop with medical expenses. The same strategy will work with miscellaneous itemized deductions, which have a 2% floor based upon your AGI. By bunching your deductions into one year, rather than spreading them out over two years, you may be able to eke out a valuable deduction.

Consider bunching as many of your taxes, medical expenses, charitable contributions, and any other itemized deductions you might have over a two-year period into one year. Doing this means that every other year or so, you may be able to claim a deduction. On alternate years, the standard deduction may be your best bet.

Still don't quite get it? Well, let's look at an example.

Say that Mary Ann, a single person, has no other itemized deductions during the year, but she annually makes charitable contributions in the amount of $4,000. Since her standard deduction is $4,300, she will never exceed the standard deduction in any given year. But what if she decides to bunch her deductions? In 1999, she doubles up on her contributions, contributing a total of $8,000 (perhaps $4,000 in January and $4,000 in December). She'll then be able to itemize her deductions for 1999. In 2000, she'll make no contributions, but will still receive the benefit of her standard deduction. So over a two-year period, she has still made $8,000 in total contributions, but she's picked up more than $3,700 in additional deductions. If Mary Ann is in the 28% tax bracket, this bunching strategy will save her more than $1,000 in taxes over a two-year period. Not bad for some simple planning, eh?

So if you have itemized deductions that are just under the standard deduction allowance, don't overlook the tax savings that bunching your deductions might allow.

medical expenses ($6,000), but would have generated a medical expense deduction in 1999—the year that he "bunched" his medical payments. So this is something to keep in mind, especially near the end of the tax year. Will "bunching" your medical deductions get you over the 7.5% AGI hump in order to generate a medical deduction? If so, you might want to consider this technique.

Medical Expenses of Dependents

As we noted in the introduction to this section, medical expenses that you pay for you, your spouse, and your dependents qualify for the deduction. Think about this for a second. This is one of the few areas of the tax law in which *you* may claim a deduction for the payment of another person's expenses.

Anyway, we're sure you know who *you* are. And if you are married, we're quite certain that you know who your spouse is (unless perhaps you're a polygamist who's taken things to extremes, in which case you might have some problems). But who exactly is your dependent? You might think that the answer to this question would be: a dependent is somebody that I claim as a dependent on my tax return. That would be a logical assumption. But it's dead wrong.

You may be allowed to deduct medical expenses paid for a dependent even if you're *not* allowed to claim that person as a dependent on your tax return. Here's the deal: In order to deduct medical expenses, you must provide more than half of the support of the dependent.

Take the example of Laura Knopf. She paid $3,000 in dental expenses for her dear granddaughter Ethel. The problem is that Ethel lives with her parents, and her parents provide more than half of Ethel's support. Since Laura does *not* provide more than half of Ethel's support, Laura is not entitled to the medical expense deduction. And unfortunately, Ethel's parents are also not entitled to the deduction, because they didn't pay for the expenses. So it's a no-win situation for everybody involved.

Another example. Joann Floyd, a beauty consultant, has a son named Benjamin. Benjamin earned $10,000 in wages before illness forced him to leave his job at the astronaut food factory. Joann is not allowed to claim a personal exemption for Benjamin, since he fails the gross income test. Nevertheless, Benjamin is still Joann's dependent for medical expense purposes. As such, Joann is entitled to deduct the medical expenses paid on her son's behalf.

In an odd twist, a child of divorced or separated parents who is in the custody of one or both for more than half of the year, and receives more than half of his or her support from either or both, is considered to be the dependent of both for purposes of the medical expense deduction. That's right—the same person may be treated as a dependent (for medical expense deduction purposes) by either or both parents.

Take the case of Tory and Kenny Coleman, who happen to be divorced trapeze artists. Their child Ann lives with Tory, but is actually supported by support payments made by Kenny. During 1998, Ann had medical expenses of $3,000. Kenny paid $2,000 of those expenses, and Tory paid the remaining $1,000.

TAX STRATEGY

Give Two Gifts at Once

Recall our example of Laura, who paid $3,000 for her granddaughter's dental expenses but couldn't deduct the amount. If you ever find yourself in a similar situation, there's a nifty tax strategy you can employ.

Since Laura doesn't provide sufficient support to claim the medical expense deduction for Ethel, instead of paying the medical bills directly, Laura could have given a gift of this money to Ethel's parents. Ethel's parents could have then paid the medical expenses and claimed the deduction. Laura is really out nothing, since she can't get the deduction anyway. She's forked over the same amount of money. But Ethel's parents might realize additional tax savings by now having the ability to claim the medical deduction. So Laura has really given two gifts! Sometimes a dollar is more than a dollar.

For tax purposes, Ann is generally the dependent of Tory, since she is the custodial parent. But for purposes of the medical expense deduction, Ann is considered to be the dependent of *both* Kenny and Tory. That being the case, Kenny may deduct the $2,000 of medical expenses that he paid, and Tory may deduct the $1,000 of medical expenses that she paid—subject to their own individual AGI limitations.

One final thought to keep in mind: In order for you to claim a deduction for medical expenses paid for a spouse or dependent, that person must be your spouse or dependent *either* at the time the medical services were rendered *or* at the time you actually make the payments for them. Confused? Let's look at more examples.

Grumpy's wife underwent an expensive medical procedure in 1998. Grumpy and his wife were divorced later that year. Grumpy paid for the procedure in 1999. He may claim the medical expense as a deduction for 1999 since the patient was his wife at the time the treatment was received, even though she wasn't when he paid for it. See how it works?

Sneezy's fiancée underwent an operation five months before their marriage in November 1998. Sneezy paid for the operation in 1999. Sneezy may claim the medical expenses that he paid as a deduction in 1999. Why? Because the patient was his wife at the time the expenses were paid, even though she wasn't when the treatment was received.

Medical Care—What Is It?

The IRS has acknowledged that a number of expenses may qualify as medical expenses, from the typical visit to a doctor or dentist, to the costs of medical insurance. In addition, the IRS has allowed "amounts paid for operations or treatments affecting any portion of the body, including obstetrical expenses and expenses of therapy or X-ray treatments," as well as the expenses of "hospital services, nursing services (including nurses' board where paid by the taxpayer), medical, laboratory, surgical, dental and other diagnostic and healing services, X-rays, medicine and drugs... artificial teeth or limbs, and ambulance hire." Acupuncture also qualifies, but the cost of illegal operations or treatments is specifically nondeductible.

So far, so good, right? Not so fast. There remains a gray area of procedures, treatments, and health regimens that are neither clearly inside nor clearly outside the scope of medical care, and a large body of litigation and rulings has grown around the question of what is medical care. It's not our intention to try to define each and every type of medical expense here in this book. But we'll point out some general issues that address common questions.

Medical Care—An Overview

The expenses of medical care generally include amounts paid for:

• The diagnosis, cure, mitigation, treatment, or prevention of disease, or for the purpose of affecting any structure or function of the body

• Qualified long-term care services (for amounts paid after December 31, 1996)

• Transportation primarily for and essential to medical care

• Insurance covering medical care

It's not as clear as it appears, though. One of the most often litigated questions in the area of medical expenses is whether an expenditure benefits a particular ailment of the taxpayer, or is merely beneficial to his or her general health, or, worse yet, is simply a personal expense unrelated to health. Expenditures in the first category are deductible; those in the latter two are not.

For example, consider the interesting case of Julieta Stack, flotation director for the Women's Professional Golf Organization blimp. Julieta paid $300 to enroll in a karate class to help her lose weight and improve her general health. While sparring one night in the class, however, she suffered a cracked rib, which she paid her doctor $200 to treat. The $200 paid to the doctor is a qualified medical expense. But the $300 paid for the karate class is not.

In order for an expense to qualify for the medical expense deduction, it's necessary to show the "present existence" or "imminent probability" of an illness as well as to demonstrate that the expense was incurred "primarily" for the treatment of the illness. So you really need to be careful when you claim "iffy" medical deductions that might be construed as nondeductible general health expenses—and this can be a difficult line to draw. This is why medical expenses have been often litigated and outlined by IRS regulations and procedures. Let's take a few minutes to discuss various types of expenses and highlight whether those expenses are deemed to be deductible medical expenses or nondeductible personal expenses.

Drugs

Amounts paid for medicine and drugs are deductible only if paid for a prescribed drug or for insulin. A prescribed drug is "a drug or biological" that requires a physician's prescription for its use by an individual. However, amounts paid for a controlled substance, illegal under federal law, are not deductible as medical expenses, even if legal under state law. Remember the medical marijuana issue that was recently passed in some states? While state law may allow for the purchase of marijuana for medical purposes, Uncle Sam won't allow the expense of that purchase to qualify as a medical deduction. Heck, the IRS has even ruled that the costs of nicotine gum and nicotine patches are not deductible medical expenses because they contain a drug (other than insulin) and do not require a physician's prescription.

Remember that in order for the expense to qualify, a "physician" must prescribe the drugs. The term "physician" includes legally authorized doctors of medicine and osteopathy, dentists and dental surgeons, podiatrists (limited to services which they are authorized under state law to perform), optometrists (limited to services related to the condition of aphakia), and chiropractors (limited to treatment by means of manual manipulation of spine to correct subluxation which has been demonstrated by X-ray to exist). So make sure that your drug expense qualifies as such before you record that expense on your tax return.

Medical Service Providers

The expenses of doctor or dentist services are deductible in the vast majority of cases. But even if your doctor doesn't have "MD" after his name, amounts paid for medical services rendered by chiropractors, psychologists, psychotherapists, and others providing similar services may still be deductible—even when the practitioner is not licensed. However, an expense that is merely beneficial to you is not deductible simply because your doctor recommended it. Expenses for cosmetic surgery, absent congenital abnormality, personal injury, or a disfiguring disease are not deductible.

In addition, medical care includes nursing services. Accordingly, a nurse's wages and any related payroll tax expenses may be deductible. If you pay for a nurse's meals, that expense may also be deductible, as well as any lodging costs in excess of those which you would have otherwise incurred. But if your nurse does double duty around the house, those expenses related to the cook/housekeeper function are nondeductible personal expenses.

The cost of nursing services is an expense of medical care even if the person who provides the services is not trained as a nurse. In general, the determination of what is medical care depends on the nature of the services rendered, not on the experience, qualifications, or title of the person rendering them. Services may constitute medical care even if they are provided by people with no medical training. But be careful. While the nature of the services rather than the training of the person providing them is primary, the lack of special training on the part of the provider is often mentioned in court cases in which the court denies a deduction based on a finding that the services were not medical in nature. Also, note that services of a nurse who cares for a healthy child do not constitute medical care, and the expense is not deductible.

It's possible that you can claim a medical deduction for what the IRS describes as "unconventional practitioners." You may deduct medical care provided by Christian Science practitioners and Navajo medicine men. But no deduction is allowed for the expense of an "audit" performed by representatives of the Church of Scientology. The IRS has privately ruled that amounts paid to an "unauthorized psychologist" to "deprogram" a taxpayer's son, who had been a member of a religious cult, were not deductible because they were not in the nature of medical care.

How about the services of completely nonmedical personnel? As with most issues regarding medical expenses, the rulings have been mixed. A deduction was allowed for payments to an individual to accompany a taxpayer's blind child to school for the purpose of guiding the child through the halls. The services of the guide constituted medical care because they alleviated the condition of blindness. A deduction was similarly available for amounts paid to an individual who took notes for a deaf person attending college. Also deductible was the expense of hiring a nonprofessional individual to assist some taxpayers in giving their child physical therapy.

But taxpayers have not been successful in attempting to deduct the cost of a chauffeur as a medical expense. The expenses of babysitters have also consistently been held to be nondeductible personal expenses, even if they are paid for watching children while a taxpayer visits his or her physician. Taxpayers attempting to claim the expenses of their children's day care as medical expenses have fared no better, even when the services are provided in a hospital day care center. A deduction was also denied for the expense of sending children to a boarding school on the advice of a physician so that their mother, who was suffering from throat cancer, would be able to rest her voice.

Institutional Care

Naturally, the cost of in-patient hospital care and hospital services is deductible. But the expenses of care received in an institution other than a hospital may or may not qualify as a deduction, depending on your condition and the nature of the services that you receive.

If the availability of medical care in an institution is "a principal reason" for your presence in it, and meals and lodging are furnished only because they are incidental to the medical care, then the cost of medical care, meals, and lodging at the institution is generally deductible as a medical expense. Similarly, if special services furnished by a school for the mentally or physically handicapped are a principal reason for an individual's presence in the school, then the expenses of attending the school are medical expenses, including the cost of ordinary education which is incidental to the school's special services. For example, a blind individual is enrolled in a special school for the blind principally in order to receive the special training for the blind. The school also offers classes in English, history, and mathematics. But the entire cost of attending the school is an expense of medical care.

On the other hand, if the availability of medical care in an institution is not a principal reason for someone's presence there, only the costs of actual medical care received are deductible. The expenses of meals and lodging in the institution are not deductible.

Lodging

The cost of lodging while away from home when it's "primarily for and essential to medical care" may be deductible. If the medical care is provided by a physician in a licensed hospital or equivalent facility, and there is "no significant element of personal pleasure, recreation, or vacation" in the travel away from home, the expenses may be deductible. But there are limitations on the amount of the lodging expense that may be deducted:

• It may not be "lavish or extravagant under the circumstances," and

• It may not exceed $50 per night per individual

Also, if the person receiving treatment is unable to travel alone, the lodging expenses of the person accompanying him or her are also deductible. Other expenses related to their stay, such as food, are not deductible. Expenses of the stay should be distinguished from expenses such as meals and lodging while in transit.

Remember that the lodging expenses of a taxpayer who is away from home merely for the benefit of a more congenial climate are not deductible.

Birth Control

The IRS has ruled that the following birth control measures *are* deductible:

• Oral contraceptives prescribed by a physician

• Legal abortions

• Vasectomies

• Female sterilization

Cosmetic Procedures

In tax years beginning before 1991, the IRS and the courts generally looked favorably upon taxpayers' attempts to improve their appearances. The expenses of a "face lift" qualified for deduction even if the procedure was not undertaken on the recommendation of a physician. Surgical hair transplants also qualified, as did the cost of a wig recommended by a physician for a woman who had lost all her hair. Hair removal by electrolysis was also deductible. But the line was drawn at tattoos and ear piercing, the cost of which is a nondeductible personal expense.

But all of that has now changed. For tax years beginning in 1991, the costs of "cosmetic surgery" and other similar procedures are not deductible medical expenses unless the surgery or procedure is necessary to ameliorate a deformity arising from, or directly related to, any of the following:

• A congenital abnormality

• A personal injury resulting from an accident or trauma

• A disfiguring disease

"Cosmetic surgery" is defined as any procedure that is directed at improving the patient's appearance and that does not meaningfully promote the proper function of the body, or prevent or treat illness or disease. So at the moment, the only way that you can deduct that elective nose job is with the use of a time machine.

ASK ROY

Laser Eye Surgery

I have heard a lot lately about laser surgery to correct vision. It seems to be more and more popular and well regarded. If I undergo it, can I deduct any of the cost as a medical deduction?

While there have been no specific rulings regarding laser surgery, it's really quite similar to radial keratotomy (which is a different kind of eye surgery to correct nearsightedness). This issue has not been decided by an actual court case or IRS regulation, but instead by a Private Letter Ruling (PLR) 9625049 provided by the IRS to a specific taxpayer. The taxpayer was concerned that the IRS would rule that radial keratotomy was "cosmetic" (and therefore nondeductible), so the taxpayer asked the IRS the question directly. The IRS basically responded that the benefit of improving the taxpayer's appearance (by removing the need for eyeglasses) was only secondary. The primary reason for the surgery was to correct a part of the body—the taxpayer's bum eyes. Because of that, the surgery was ruled a valid medical expense, and was not cosmetic. Now, we can't rely specifically on PLRs as an official IRS position for everybody. The IRS position in a PLR is only applied to that specific taxpayer. But PLRs do give us a hint of where the IRS stands on various issues. And based upon this PLR, it seems rather certain that laser eye surgery will qualify as a valid medical expense.

Counseling

The expenses of counseling by psychiatrists, psychologists, and psychiatric social workers are generally deductible. However, where psychoanalysis is undertaken by students attending psychoanalytic training institutions, and the analysis is required as part of their training, the cost is a nondeductible personal expense. But if the analysis is undertaken primarily for a patient's mental health, the cost is deductible even if the treatment also qualifies the patient for admission to psychiatric training.

Psychiatric treatment received at a hospital on an outpatient basis by a husband and wife for sexual inadequacy and incompatibility has been ruled deductible, but no deduction was allowed for the closely related expense of marriage counseling by a clergyman, or for counseling constituting spiritual guidance.

If the extent of your counseling expenses amounts to several beers bought each week at a local watering hole for a buddy who gives you lots of great advice about the perplexing opposite sex, then sorry. No deduction.

Treatments for Drug, Alcohol, and Smoking Problems

Amounts paid to maintain a dependent in a therapeutic center for drug or alcohol abuse are deductible as expenses of medical care, including the cost of meals and lodging incidental to the treatment. Additionally, the cost of a program to help a taxpayer stop smoking is deductible. But remember that amounts paid for drugs (other than insulin) not requiring a prescription, such as nicotine gum and certain nicotine patches, are not deductible. The IRS position on smoking programs is relatively new. In 1999 it reversed its position on smoking cessation programs and advised taxpayers to file amended returns for refunds if such programs were paid for in recent years or if such expenses would put the taxpayer's medical expenses above the 7.5% limitation.

Special Diets

Generally, the costs of special food or beverages do not qualify as a medical expense. If you're on a prescribed diet to treat a specific health condition, the amount by which the cost of the special foods exceeds the amount you would otherwise spend is deductible. But remember that the special diet must be related to a specific health problem in order to be deductible.

In an unusual twist of logic (or perhaps not so unusual), a taxpayer was allowed to deduct the cost of a device for adding fluoride to his home water supply when the installation was undertaken on the advice of a dentist. But a taxpayer who wanted to avoid fluorinated water was denied a medical expense deduction for the cost of bottled distilled water purchased to avoid drinking fluorinated water supplied by the city.

Weight Reduction Programs and Recreation

The cost of weight reduction programs has been ruled to be medical expense when the programs are undertaken on a physician's recommendation for the treatment of specific medical conditions related to a taxpayer's obesity. When the program is primarily for a taxpayer's general health, however, the cost is nondeductible. So your aquatic kick-boxing classes probably don't qualify.

Most memberships in health clubs or fitness centers are acquired to benefit the member's general health, and thus the costs of the membership are not deductible. The IRS has ruled, however, that the club fees may be deductible when a physician prescribes the treatments offered and substantiates, by statement, that the treatments are necessary for the alleviation of a physical or mental defect or illness of the individual receiving them.

Taxpayers have been uniformly unsuccessful in attempting to claim the expense of dancing lessons as medical expenses. The following expenses relative to dance lessons and instruction have been denied:

• Upon a doctor's recommendation to correct postoperative weakness in the taxpayer's abdominal and leg muscles

• Upon the recommendation of a psychiatrist, who believed that the taxpayer would benefit from the social atmosphere of the dance studio

• Upon a doctor's recommendation as therapy for arthritis

• Upon a doctor's recommendation to treat curvature of the spine

• To help cure varicose veins.

In addition, the cost of playing golf was held not to be a medical expense. This was decided even though a taxpayer's physician had been recommending the sport as a means of treating the taxpayer's emphysema. It wasn't shown that some less expensive form of exercise, such as walking, could not have offered the same medical benefits.

Education

While ordinary education is not medical care, the costs of attending a special school for a mentally or physically handicapped individual are medical expenses if the school's resources for alleviating the individual's condition are a principal reason for his or her being there. Thus, the cost of special instruction or training, such as speech and lip-reading, designed to alleviate the loss of speech due to deafness or to compensate in part for a deaf person's loss of hearing is a deductible medical expense. Also permitted as deductible was the tuition of a deaf person who attended "regular" college and took special classes in speech correction and aural rehabilitation, as well as English classes that improved her lip-reading, comprehension, and oral communication. Her room and board, however, were nondeductible personal expenses.

The cost of special education for a mentally retarded individual is also an expense of medical care when the availability of medical care is a principal reason for the individual attending the school. A deduction has also been allowed for the tuition of a special school for a child with psychological and emotional problems that prevented her from functioning normally in a public school. Also deductible have been clarinet lessons recommended by an orthodontist to alleviate a congenital defect causing a severe malocclusion of a taxpayer's son's teeth.

But no deduction was allowed for the expense of sending a child to military school in the hope that the disciplined environment would have a salutary effect on his social adjustment. Likewise, no deduction was allowed for the expense of sending a blind child to a college preparatory school, where the school made no special accommodations to the child's condition.

Special education as a medical expense can be a very tricky deduction. Make sure that you are on solid ground before proceeding. In most cases, additional tax research will be required.

Legal Expenses

Legal expenses may also be medical care expenses if they are incurred to establish the right to proceed with a course of treatment. No deduction was allowed, however, for the legal expenses of a divorce, even when a taxpayer's psychiatrist recommended it. Additionally, no deduction was allowed for the legal costs incurred by a taxpayer in attempting to put an end to the campaign of harassment launched against him by his wife, who suffered from a form of mental illness known as "conjugal paranoia." In both cases, the legal expenses were held to have been incurred primarily for personal rather than medical reasons.

Capital Improvements and Expenses

Capital expenditures (those things that have a useful life of more than one year) that are primary to the medical care of you, your spouse, or your dependents may be deducted in full in the year that they are paid. Unlike most other capital expenditures, they are not required to be depreciated. But be aware that there are limitations for expenses that are permanent improvements to your property.

Examples of fully deductible capital expenditures include:

• The cost of a wheelchair

• Payments for eyeglasses, hearing aids and component parts, and artificial teeth and limbs

• The cost of acquiring, training, and maintaining a dog to assist a deaf person or a blind person

• The cost of crutches or an inclinator

• The cost of a reclining chair, where it was shown that the chair was prescribed by a doctor, served no purpose other than mitigation of the patient's condition, and was not to be used generally as an article of furniture

• The cost of a detachable air conditioner purchased solely for the use of a sick person

In addition, special aids purchased to prevent further deterioration of the eyesight of a person who is afflicted with an eye condition, or to alleviate that condition, also qualify for the deduction. But only the excess expense over what would have normally been spent (if the medical condition were not present) would be deductible. For example, assume that Stevie Wonder, who is blind, buys Braille editions of books costing $150. Regular printed editions of the same books cost $60. The amount of Stevie's medical expense would amount to $90.

A deduction was allowed for special equipment enabling a deaf person to communicate over the telephone—as well as its repair costs. Deductions were also allowed for the extra cost of a special television with a visual display of the audio portion for the deaf over the cost of a conventional set of the same model. And even the cost of an adapter for a conventional television set was deemed deductible. Deductions have also been allowed for the extra cost of specialized equipment installed in cars and vans to accommodate the taxpayer's medical condition. But when a taxpayer couldn't show that the equipment was medically related, the deduction was denied. Other items for which a deduction was not allowed include a vacuum cleaner and a dust elimination system purchased for a taxpayer allergic to house dust to decrease the amount of dust in the taxpayer's household.

If a capital expenditure for medical care also constitutes a permanent improvement or betterment of your property, then the expenditure is deductible only to the extent that it exceeds the increase in the property's value. Let's take Mr. French's case. Acting on the advice of his physician, Mr. French installs an elevator in his house so that his wife, who is afflicted with a heart disease, will not be required to climb stairs. The elevator costs $1,000 to install, and the value of the house is increased by $700. The medical expense is $300.

If the asset purchased is so specialized that it does not increase the property's value, then the expenditure is deductible in full. The Senate Finance Committee has indicated its belief that this approach should be taken with regard to modifications to the residence of a physically handicapped individual for the purpose of accommodating his or her condition.

The expenses of operating and maintaining a capital asset are deductible if its primary purpose is the medical care of a qualifying individual. These expenses may be deductible in full even if none or only a portion of the asset's original cost qualified for the deduction. But understand that the expenses are deductible only as long as the medical condition that required it persists.

So be careful if you plan to install a pool or spa for "medical" purposes. That pool or spa will likely increase the value of your property, at least in the eyes of assessors and the IRS. And the medical deduction may be very small indeed. You probably won't get away with deducting the entire cost of the pool or spa. In fact, this entire issue of capital improvements can get really messy. So do your homework before you make any improvements to your property for medical purposes.

Transportation

Transportation costs are deductible if the transportation is primarily for, and essential to, medical care. Those costs, however, do not include the expenses of meals and lodging while at the away-from-home location, unless they are paid as part of a hospital bill.

If you travel merely for the general improvement of your health, none of the related expenses are deductible. For example, at the end of tax season last year, Roy took a trip. He needed a break from the stress and pressure of all of his tax work (trying to learn and implement all of these tax laws, rules, and regulations). Roy decided to take a cruise to the Bahamas. He returned rested and invigorated, convinced that the trip saved him from a nervous breakdown. Alas—the expenses of the trip were not deductible.

In addition, if you choose to undergo prescribed treatment in another locality for purely personal reasons, the transportation costs are not deductible. For example, Zsa Zsa is required to undergo surgery. After the surgery, she will be required to take two weeks off work to recuperate. Zsa Zsa is convinced that the recovery period would be more pleasant in Hawaii than at home, so she arranges to have the operation in Honolulu. She spends $2,000 on her round-trip plane ticket, $4,000 for her hospital stay, and $3,000 in hotels and restaurants after being released from the hospital. Sadly, only Zsa Zsa's $4,000 hospital bill is deductible. (Sorry, Zsa, Zsa. At least you've got the memories and a tan!)

Medical expense deductions were allowed for the following transportation costs:

• A trip to Arizona for a child suffering from "deep bronchitis bordering on pneumonia"

• A trip prescribed for an arthritis sufferer

• A trip to Florida during the winter for a taxpayer who, following a larynx operation, suffered spasms of coughing and ruptured blood vessels in the lungs in cold weather

• Transportation to Alcoholics Anonymous meetings

• Transportation to a swimming pool for the purpose of allowing a child with arthritis to exercise

• Transportation to special schools

Deductions may also be taken for cab and bus fares incident to trips to a doctor's office. Medical transportation, however, does not include ordinary commuting expenses, even if they were larger than they otherwise would be due to the taxpayer's medical condition.

Finally, if you use your own car for medical transportation, you may compute that deduction either on the basis of your actual expenses (which is very difficult and time consuming), or using a standard mileage rate plus parking fees and tolls. The mileage rate is 10 cents per mile for 1998. The 1999 rate isn't out at the time of this writing, but we expect it to remain the same. Know that a controversy exists as to whether the costs of meals and lodging incurred while en route to receive medical care are included in the expenses of "transportation." The Sixth Circuit held that they are, but the IRS has continued to adhere to its position that they are not.

Long-Term Care Services

Effective for expenses paid on or after 1997, medical expenses include unreimbursed expenses for "qualified long-term care services." Qualified long-term care services are necessary diagnostic, preventive, therapeutic, curing, treating, mitigating and rehabilitative services, and maintenance or personal care services required by a chronically ill individual and that are provided under a plan of care prescribed by a licensed healthcare practitioner.

A chronically ill individual is anyone who has been certified within the preceding 12-month period by a licensed healthcare practitioner as generally meeting one of the following two tests:

• Being unable to perform, without substantial assistance from another individual, at least two activities of daily living, such as eating, using the toilet, moving about, bathing, dressing, and continence, for at least 90 days, due to a loss of functional capacity, or

• Requiring substantial supervision to protect such an individual from threats to health and safety due to severe cognitive impairment.

A licensed healthcare practitioner is a physician, a registered professional nurse, or a licensed social worker. Maintenance or personal care services refer to care the primary purpose of which is providing needed assistance with any of the disabilities as a result of which the individual is a chronically ill individual. They include protection from threats to health and safety due to severe cognitive impairment. No deduction is allowed for the cost of long-term care provided by a spouse or relative unless the spouse or relative is a licensed professional with respect to those services.

But don't confuse long-term care expenses with those expenses dealing with living in a continuing care or life-care facility. They have separate tax problems and issues. Life-care communities usually require large upfront entrance fees as well as monthly fees thereafter. Some of those fees (both the monthly and upfront) may qualify as medical expenses if there is an agreement that requires a specific fee payment as a condition for the home's promise to provide lifetime care that includes medical care. So make sure that you know the differences between facilities, and make sure that you are aware of the tax consequences.

Insurance

The cost of insurance covering medical care and transportation for medical care, and the cost of qualified long-term care insurance contracts (up to the amount of eligible premiums) are deductible as medical expenses.

Note that if you're a participant in a Section 125 ("Cafeteria Plan") for health insurance, you can't deduct those insurance premiums on Schedule A. This is due to the fact that the amount is deducted from your pay prior to expenses.

Determination of insurance premium costs, however, can be difficult when the policy covers more

TAX TIP

Medical Insurance for the Self-Employed

Self-employed individuals are allowed to claim a percentage of the amount paid during the taxable year for insurance that's for medical care for themselves, their spouses, and their dependents as an above-the-line deduction (as an adjustment to income).

For taxable years beginning in 1997 and thereafter, the allowable deduction for health insurance of self-employed individuals is:

1997: 40%

1998: 45%

1999 through 2001: 60%

2002: 70%

2003 and thereafter: 100%

The deduction, however, may not exceed the taxpayer's earned income derived from the trade or business with respect to which the plan providing the medical care is established. Furthermore, the deduction is not available to taxpayers who are eligible to participate in subsidized health plans maintained by their employers or their spouses' employers. Amounts deductible above-the-line by self-employed taxpayers can't be used to reduce their self-employment tax. Neither can the same above-the-line deductions be claimed a second time as an itemized deduction for medical expenses. But the excess of the actual expense over the amount that can be claimed above-the-line may be claimed as a medical deduction. So if you're self-employed and you're paying medical insurance, there may be a valuable deduction for you. As with most tax issues, though, there are various requirements and restrictions. To read more about this deduction, check out IRS Publication 535.

Medical Savings Accounts

If you're self employed, or work for a "small employer" (generally 50 or fewer employees), you may be eligible to participate in a Medical Savings Account (MSA). MSAs were developed to help improve competition in the healthcare services market by giving individuals control over their healthcare expense decisions.

You can purchase a low-cost health insurance policy that has a high annual deductible. You can then make a tax-deductible contribution to an MSA, which is an IRA-like savings account. When you incur medical expenses, the amount not covered by insurance can be withdrawn tax-free from the MSA account to pay for those expenses. If you don't incur any medical expenses during the year, the contributions remain in the MSA account and are available for future use.

Because this is *not* a "use it or lose it" type of plan, the incentive is for the participant to shop for lower healthcare prices, and incur healthcare expenses only when absolutely required. Is it working? Well, this was originally a pilot program and the response has been less than overwhelming. Many employers are finding it difficult to find a proper MSA account custodian (such as a bank or brokerage firm). Lately, though, more financial institutions are warming up to MSAs, so you might have some luck finding a custodian.

There are many more rules and requirements attached to MSAs. So if this is something that looks interesting to you, read more about MSAs in IRS Publication 969.

than medical care and payment is made with a single premium. An insurance policy may provide an indemnity for lost income during a period of illness, or for loss of life, limb, or sight. The cost of this additional coverage is not deductible. If an automobile insurance policy covers the medical expenses of the insured arising out of an automobile accident, as well as the usual property and liability coverage, only the cost of the medical coverage is deductible as a medical expense; the basic automobile insurance coverage is not. If an insurance contract covers other items besides medical expenses, then the premiums are not deductible unless the amount allocable to medical coverage is separately stated in the contract, or furnished to the policyholder by the insurance company in a separate statement. Even amounts separately stated as allocable to medical coverage are not deductible if they are unreasonably large in relation to the total charges under the contract. The determination of whether an amount separately stated as allocable to medical coverage is unreasonably large is made by considering the relationship of all the coverage under the contract, together with all the facts and circumstances.

Effective for tax years beginning in 1997, medical expenses include unreimbursed amounts paid for "any qualified long-term care insurance contract" to the extent that the premiums do not exceed specified dollar limits. For 1999, the *annual* dollar limitations are:

- Age 40 or less: $210

- Age 41-50: $400

- Age 51-60: $800

- Age 61-70: $2,120

- Age 71 and over: $2,660

These annual amounts are indexed for inflation annually.

There are certainly other requirements and restrictions when dealing with long-term care insurance. So if this is something that might be of interest to you, make sure that you read more about the deduction of these premiums in IRS Publications 525 and 535.

Medical Deductions and the Alternative Minimum Tax

For purposes of the regular income tax, unreimbursed medical expenses are deductible to the extent that they exceed 7.5% of your adjusted gross income. But for AMT purposes, the floor is raised from 7.5% to 10% of AGI. This means that it's harder to secure an AMT deduction for medical expense than it is for regular tax purposes. If you are in the AMT zone, you may find that your medical expenses are much less valuable than you initially thought.

Tired Yet?

After reading all of this, are you ready for some medical treatment? If so, at least you're probably now familiar with what's deductible and what isn't. Even after pages and pages of information, we have really only scratched the surface of the medical expense deduction. If there are potential medical expense deductions in your future or actual ones in your recent past, you can (and should) read much more about this topic in IRS Publication 502.

DEDUCTIONS FOR TAXES PAID

Deductions for taxes paid are a bit more straightforward than those for medical expenses. Sure, there are twists and turns, but not as many as in the previous section. Following are highlights of many of the common itemized deductions dealing with taxes.

Real Estate Property Tax

A real property (or "real estate property") tax is a direct tax on interests in real estate, in contrast to a tax on occupancy or possession rights. To be a deductible real property tax, the tax must be imposed by a political subdivision against all real estate in the taxing district, other than property exempt for constitutional, religious, charitable, or similar purposes.

A real estate property tax is not deductible if it's assessed against local benefits of a kind tending to increase the value of the assessed property or is in the nature of a capital expenditure. In addition, the fact that the tax is a real property tax does not mean that whoever pays it is entitled to the deduction.

We could get really bogged down here with more definitions and legal descriptions. But a better way to handle the issue might be through a series of examples.

Example #1: A residential construction tax is imposed by a school district on each newly constructed residential unit and on units converted to residential use. This is a tax on the exercise of an incident of ownership (i.e., making residential use of real property) rather than the ownership of real property. Accordingly, it is not a real property tax.

Example #2: A state transaction privilege tax is imposed on a contractor who builds and sells homes. The purchaser of the home pays a price that reflects the tax. The tax is not a real property tax and is not deductible by the purchaser since the purchaser does not pay it.

Example #3: A "renter's tax" is imposed by a county on all renters. It's measured by a percentage of rent paid for occupancy of a multifamily dwelling unit. This is not a tax on the ownership of real property but on the exercise of an incident of ownership, namely, the occupancy of real property. It is not imposed on the property owner or against the renter's leasehold interest, but is the personal liability of the renter. Accordingly, it is not a real property tax.

Simply understand that a real estate tax can only be deducted by the owner of the property upon which the tax is imposed. In addition, a deduction is not allowed when a buyer of property pays the delinquent real estate taxes of the seller. Instead of a deduction, the buyer must treat these tax payments as an addition to the cost of the property. (At least it raises the cost basis of the property, eventually decreasing the gain upon sale.)

Real property taxes are deductible for any and all property that you own. There is no restriction on the number of properties for which you can deduct real estate taxes.

Real Property Refunds and Rebates

If you receive a refund or rebate of real property taxes in 1999 for taxes that you paid in 1999, you'll simply reduce the real estate tax deduction on Schedule A by the amount of the refund or rebate.

But if you receive a refund or rebate in 1999 of real estate taxes paid in an earlier year, you can't simply reduce the real estate tax deduction on Schedule A. Instead, the refund or rebate must be reported on the "other income" line of Form 1040. But note that income is required to be reported only to the extent that the real estate taxes were used as a deduction that reduced your tax liability in an earlier year.

Co-ops

Mortgage interest and property taxes allocated to a tenant-stockholder in a cooperative housing corporation are generally treated the same as those paid by other homeowners, providing that the following conditions are met:

• The corporation has only one class of stock outstanding.

• Each stockholder has the right (but is not required) to occupy a dwelling unit solely because of the ownership of the stock.

• No stockholder can receive any distribution of capital, except on liquidation of the corporation.

• The corporation must receive at least 80% of its gross income from tenant-stockholders.

Your deductible percentage of interest and taxes paid by the corporation is allocated based on the number of shares that you own versus the total number of shares outstanding. Co-ops will normally issue year-end statements showing your share of the total amounts.

Special Assessments

You aren't allowed to deduct the principal and interest paid on "special assessments" as interest. If they're deductible, they're deductible as real property taxes.

Generally, the principal is not deductible if it tends to increase the value of the property. Examples of nondeductible assessments would include the construction of streets, sidewalks, sewer, water, and curb/gutter assessments. Instead, the principal amounts assessed are added to your cost of the property.

The interest on assessments are deductible as real property tax if the interest is based on the specific property, such as "per front footage" or "square footage," and you (as the owner of the property) can show the allocation of the amounts assessed.

But if the assessment is for maintenance and/or repairs, both the principal and interest is deductible as real property tax. An example would be an assessment to repair sidewalks, or resurface the street/alley.

State Income Tax

State and local income taxes are deductible in the year paid—and not necessarily in the year that the taxes are assessed. These taxes may be paid either through withholding, estimated payments, or payments for prior year(s)' state tax returns.

Remember that you can't simply go wild regarding the prepayment of state taxes. The IRS may disallow deductions for large estimated state income tax payments made solely to increase itemized deductions. And not only that, any state tax refunds that you receive may be required to be reported as additional income in the following year.

TAX STRATEGY

Prepayment of Estimated State Income Taxes

One of the most overlooked tax "loopholes" concerns the prepayment of fourth-quarter state estimated taxes. (If you live in a state that doesn't impose a state income tax, you may want to skip this section.)

The fourth-quarter estimated payment for federal taxes is due by January 15 of the following tax year. Generally, the corresponding state estimated tax payment is also due at that time. But remember that if you itemize your deductions, one of those deductions is for state taxes *paid*. So why wait until January 15 of year two to make those final state estimated tax payments for year one (and wait 15 months to get any federal benefit for them), when you can make them in December of year one and generate a federal tax deduction in the same tax year? This also works if you don't normally make any state estimated tax payments, but have had a good year and estimate that you *will* have a hefty state tax balance due on April 15. Why wait to make the payment? Make an estimated tax payment in December of year one instead and claim the deduction on your federal tax return.

For example, consider Dayana Yochim, a demolition and decoration consultant. She's in the 28% tax bracket, and has a $500 state estimated tax payment to make on January 17, 2000. If Dayana, who itemizes her deductions, makes this final state estimated tax payment on December 30, 1999, she will generate an additional $500 federal tax deduction. And that deduction will save her $140 in federal taxes for the 1999 tax year.

It's true that Dayana would still get that $140 benefit if she made the payment in January 2000. And if she makes the state payment in December rather than January, she'll be losing the use of that $500 payment for about 16 days. But she'll be gaining the use of the $140 refund for almost 16 months.

Note that state taxes are a preference item for Alternative Minimum Tax purposes. So if you're in a situation where the AMT may kick in, the early prepayment of these state taxes may not be of any real benefit to you.

Personal Property Taxes

A personal property tax is an "ad valorem" tax imposed on an annual basis on personal property, based upon the value of the property. To qualify, the tax must meet three tests:

• It must be "ad valorem"—that is, substantial in proportion to the value of the personal property.

- It must be imposed on an annual basis, even if collected more frequently or less frequently.

- It must be imposed in respect to personal property.

The most popular personal property taxes are vehicle license fees. But they can be a little bit tricky. If the tax is based partly on value and partly on weight (or horsepower, or size, or some other factor), only the tax attributed to the value is deductible. Many state motor vehicle registration fees are not based on value, and are therefore not deductible. But other states and localities do impose value-based personal property taxes on motor vehicles—these are deductible.

Some states impose taxes that are a combination of value and some other test. For example, imagine Thom Unger, who's employed as a coffee filter folder. Thom's state imposes an annual registration fee based on 1% of the value of the vehicle, plus five cents per pound of the vehicle. The portion of the tax based on the 1% tax on the value of the vehicle would be deductible, while the tax imposed on the weight would not be deductible.

Nondeductible Taxes

There are a number of taxes that are simply not deductible on Schedule A under any circumstances. They include:

- Federal income and excise taxes

- Social Security, Medicare, and railroad retirement taxes

- Custom duties

- Federal estate and gift taxes

- Sales taxes

- License fees (such as driver's licenses, marriage licenses, dog licenses)

- Fines/penalties for violation of the law, such as parking and/or speeding tickets

So don't try to deduct these expenses as taxes on your Schedule A. These birds won't fly.

Learn More

Schedule A taxes can get a bit more complicated than presented here. For additional information, read IRS Publications 530 and 535.

DEDUCTIONS FOR INTEREST PAID

Interest is what you agree to pay for the use, forbearance, or detention of money. Taxpayers often attempt to create interest deductions by making payments made for other reasons resemble interest payments. However, the determination of whether a payment is interest does not depend on labels the parties attach to it. Instead, the substance of the transaction is the controlling factor.

Kinds of Interest

You might think that interest is interest. And as such, *it must* be deductible somewhere… most likely on Schedule A. But that's not actually true. There are several categories of interest. Let's begin by reviewing them, and where you'll likely deduct the interest:

- **Mortgage interest** is the interest that you pay on your primary or secondary home. It may also include "points" that you pay on the loan. You deduct this interest and points on Schedule A.

- **Business interest** is the interest that you pay for debts incurred in a trade or business. You deduct this interest on Schedule C or F.

- **Investment interest** is the interest that you pay to hold investment property. It's generally deductible up to the amount of net investment income, and it's reported on Schedule A (via Form 4952). (Margin interest falls in this category.)

- **Passive activity interest** is interest on debts incurred in a passive activity other than investment interest (such as interest paid on rental property you own). The rules regarding passive activities will govern the deductibility of this interest. It's likely that you'll report this interest on Schedule E (via Form 8582).

- **Interest paid on tax-exempt investments** is the interest that you pay to hold tax-exempt securities or bonds (such as municipal bonds). This interest is specifically not deductible.

- **Personal interest** is the interest that you pay on personal (non-business) assets. These would include car loans, credit card interest, personal debt purchases, etc. This interest is specifically not deductible.

In short, the way that you use the loan proceeds will determine what kind of interest you have, how you must account for it, and how it can be deducted. And while the interest rules can be varied and complicated depending on how the interest is deducted, for the rest of our discussion we're going to stick with interest that's deductible as an itemized deduction on Schedule A. And we're simply going to hit the highlights. So if any of these issues are important to you, you'll want (and need) to do some additional research.

MORTGAGE INTEREST

In this section we'll discuss a number of home-related interest expenses. To learn more about other key home-related tax issues, head to the "Your Home" chapter.

Home Mortgage Interest

Home mortgage interest is the debt incurred to acquire, construct, or substantially improve your main or second home. And there are rules and restrictions attached to this general rule.

- The mortgage interest rules only apply to your main and second home. If you have a third (or fourth, or fifth) home, that interest is likely non-deductible personal interest unless the home is business or investment property that you don't use for personal purposes.

- The loan must be secured (in the form of a lien, mortgage, or trust deed) by the home(s).

- The total indebtedness is limited to $1 million. If the mortgage loan exceeds $1 million, not all of the interest that you pay on the loan will be deductible. This $1 million limitation is applied separately to each of your main and second homes. If your filing status is married filing separately, then your limitation drops to $500,000.

- If you refinance your original acquisition debt, the refinanced debt is considered original acquisition debt to the extent that the new loan balance doesn't exceed the principal outstanding on the old loan immediately before the refinancing.

There are also separate rules for mortgages incurred before October 14, 1987. If your loan began before that time, you should check out IRS Publication 936 for some additional information on the rules that may apply to you.

Home Equity Loans

Schedule A mortgage interest also includes qualified interest that you pay on a home equity loan. In order for a home equity loan to qualify as mortgage interest:

- The debt must be secured by the home. This can be either the first or second home. And the debt must exceed the original acquisition indebtedness.

- The home equity debt is limited to the lesser of:

  - The fair market value of the home less the total acquisition indebtedness on that home *or*

- $100,000 (or $50,000 if you're married filing separately).

TAX STRATEGY

Convert Nondeductible Interest Into Home Mortgage Interest

Are you saddled with nondeductible personal interest, such as interest you're paying on your auto, credit cards, or some other personal debt? Then you might consider a home equity loan to turn that nondeductible personal interest into deductible home mortgage interest. The tax savings could be substantial. In addition, it's likely that your interest rate on a home equity loan will be much less than the loan rate you're paying on your auto loan or credit card loan.

The downside is that you may be financing these debts over a much longer period of time, and paying much more in total interest. Not only that, if you find that you can't make your payments on your equity loan, your home is now at risk of foreclosure. There's also the risk that you'll run up your credit cards and other personal debt soon after you take out the equity loan. That would put you in an even more precarious position. So this isn't something that you want to do without some thought. But if you're disciplined and can manage your finances, the income tax savings can be significant.

This $100,000 limitation is cumulative for both your first and second home. You don't get to claim $100,000 against your main home and another $100,000 against your second home. The limitation is $100,000, no matter how it's sliced between your first and second home.

Points

Points on a loan are deductible in full in the year paid if *all* of the following requirements are met:

• The settlement or loan statement must clearly identify the amount of the points. They may be called "loan origination fees," "maximum loan charges," "loan discount," "discount points," or simply "points."

• The points must be computed as a percentage of the principal amount of the loan.

• The amount paid as points must not exceed the normal rates charged in the area. Any additional amount paid must be deducted (amortized) over the life of the loan. This would include "buying down" the interest rate on your loan by paying additional points. The normal points would be deductible, while the additional points would be deducted (amortized) over the life of the loan.

• The points must be paid on a loan to purchase or build your *principal* residence. Not only that, the loan must be secured by that residence. So if you pay points to purchase a second residence, those points must be deducted (amortized) over the life of the loan—they can't be deducted all in the year paid.

• The points must be paid directly with your own funds. They can't be financed. But understand that down payments, escrow deposits, earnest money, and any other funds paid at the closing will count as payment of points as long as these amounts are as much or greater than the points charged. If the points are paid from the loan proceeds, they must be deducted (amortized) over the life of the loan.

• You must use the cash method of accounting (which virtually all of us use).

You should also be aware that "loan origination fees" designated as such on VA (Veterans Administration) and FHA (Federal Home Administration) loans qualify as deductible points if the requirements above are met.

Home Improvement Loan Points

Points paid on a loan to improve your principal residence are also fully deductible in the year paid if the requirements above are met. For example, if you take out a new or additional loan to improve your principal residence (not your second residence), then the points that you pay (and don't finance) can be fully deductible in the year paid as long as the general point requirements are met.

Seller-Paid Points

Homebuyers are allowed to deduct seller-paid points as an itemized deduction on Schedule A. The seller is treated as having paid the amount of the seller-paid points to the buyer, who in turn is treated as having paid the points charged by the lender. There are, of course, restrictions to this general rule:

In order to qualify as deductible seller-paid points, all of the six requirements noted above for normal points must be met. In addition, the closing statement must clearly indicate a credit given for points paid by the seller.

Refinance Points

If you refinance a loan to get a lower interest rate, it's likely that you'll get hit with points. These loan points must be deducted (amortized) over the life of the loan. It makes no difference if you actually pay or finance the loan points—they will still be required to be amortized.

But if you refinance your loan and borrow additional funds, and you use some of those additional loan proceeds to substantially improve your primary residence, a portion of the loan points paid may be deductible in full in the year that they are paid.

Take the case of Emily and Joe Noradounkian, asparagus and artichoke farmers in Rhode Island. Their mortgage loan balance was $42,000. They decided to refinance the original loan and borrow an additional $18,000 to put a second story on their principal residence. They paid $2,000 in points on the refinancing. Since they actually paid the points (and didn't finance them), they will be allowed to deduct 30% of the total points (or $600) in full in the year that the points were paid. The remaining $1,400 in points would be required to be deducted (amortized) over the life of the loan. The 30% factor was arrived by taking the amount of the loan used to improve the property ($18,000) divided by the total amount of the new loan ($60,000).

Home Equity Line of Credit Points

Points paid for a line of credit or "equity line," which is secured by the home, are deductible over the period of time that the credit line is in effect. However, like other points, if the funds from a line of credit are used for improvements on your primary home, they are fully deductible in the year that they are paid.

Construction Loans

Construction loans or loans to buy a lot on which you'll construct your primary or second residence will qualify as fully deductible mortgage interest if the following requirements are met:

• You can treat interest paid on the construction loan as home mortgage interest for a 24-month period ending when the property is ready for occupancy.

• If the construction period exceeds 24 months, only 24 months of interest qualify for the mortgage interest deduction.

• The loan proceeds must be used specifically for home construction expenses—including the purchase of the lot.

If your construction period exceeds the 24-month allowable period, you may have some options as to which 24 months you can elect to use to qualify for the mortgage interest deduction. If this applies to you, read more about how it works in IRS Publication 936.

Timeshares

Timeshares can be considered second homes for the mortgage interest deduction. Depending upon the type of the timeshare, interest deductions are available under the mortgage interest rules. But you must make sure that you have "fee simple" ownership in the unit in order to qualify for the mortgage interest deduction. If you have a "right to use" timeshare, you really only have a lease on the unit. You don't actually own it. Any interest on this type of "right to use" arrangement will be considered nondeductible personal interest and will not be eligible for the mortgage interest deduction.

Boats and Motor Homes

Interest paid on a boat or motor home used as either a primary or secondary residence can be deductible as home mortgage interest.

The boat or motor home must have basic living accommodations, such as a sleeping space and cooking and toilet facilities. You must also be sure that local law allows for such use. For example, a houseboat moored at a marina that prohibits overnight sleeping would not qualify as a primary or secondary home. So if your Uncle Billy decides to park (and leave for the foreseeable future) his motor home in front of your house, you might want to check your local zoning codes. If you find that living in a motor home is not allowable in your neighborhood, you might remind Uncle Billy that he's going to lose his mortgage interest deduction. That might get him to leave—fast!

Prepaid Mortgage Interest

If you decide to prepay your mortgage interest at the end of the tax year, you may be in for an unpleasant surprise. Prepaid interest on your home mortgage loan is generally not deductible in the year that you prepay the interest, but only in the year that the interest is actually due. The prepayment of interest is not like the prepayment of property or state taxes—the laws are completely different. So don't trick yourself into paying for a deduction that you can't take.

Seller-Financed Loans

If you pay your mortgage to an individual because you committed to a seller-financed mortgage, you are still allowed the interest deduction as long as you follow the proper rules. On Schedule A, you're required to report the seller's name, address, and tax identification number (usually the seller's Social Security number). So if you're paying interest on a seller-financed mortgage, you need to make sure that you have all of this information. In addition, the seller should be providing you with IRS Form 1098 that reports to you the mortgage interest that you paid during the year. But even if Form 1098 is not provided to you by the seller, you can still take the deduction—just be prepared to provide the appropriate information.

On the other hand, if you're the seller, you're required to report the mortgage interest income on your Schedule B, and you should issue Form 1098 to the person paying the mortgage.

INVESTMENT INTEREST AND MARGIN INTEREST

Investment interest is interest paid on loans to hold investment property. But investment property doesn't just mean property such as real estate. It can also be stocks or other securities—any type of investment property, either real or personal.

Many investors are familiar with "margin" interest. That's the interest that your broker charges you when you borrow against your brokerage account. You might think that margin interest has its own set of rules, but it really doesn't. Margin interest is nothing more than a type of investment interest, and is subject to all of the rules and regulations regarding investment interest. Note, though, that someone with a brokerage account can borrow on margin and use the money for a non-investment purpose, in which case the margin interest would *not* be investment interest.

Investment interest is deductible up to the amount of net investment income received and is reported on Schedule A using Form 4952 as a back-up computation. The definition of net investment income includes short-term capital gains, so margin interest can generally be deducted against short-term gains. With respect to long-term capital gains, an additional decision must be made.

You can stick with business as usual and have your long-term capital gains taxed at their preferential rate. If you do so, you can't use any gains as investment income in order to offset investment interest expense. Or...

You can elect to treat all or some of your long-term capital gains as investment income. The upside is that it can then be used to offset investment interest. The downside? It's not taxed at the preferential capital gains tax rates.

TAX TIP

No Deduction for Tax-Free Investment Interest

If your investment interest is due to money you borrowed for a tax-free investment (such as tax-exempt bonds), you can't deduct it. You can only deduct it if the investment generates taxable income.

If you're confused now, we're not surprised. This is a tricky thing to understand. Let's take a closer look.

Net investment income doesn't normally include long-term capital gains income (i.e., gains from capital assets held for more than one year). But you're allowed to elect to treat all or part of your long-term net capital gains as investment income—provided you reduce the amount of net capital gain eligible for the capital gains rate by the same amount. (In other words, if you elect to treat X dollars of long-term capital gain as investment income, you must decrease your long-term capital gains by X dollars.)

This is an important choice that you have to make.

Here's an example. Consider Spice Girl Nutmeg, who is a single person and has the following income and expenses for 1999:

Wages $80,000

Interest Income...................................$3,000

Long-Term Capital Gains $6,000

Investment Interest Expense $5,000

Other Itemized Deductions $4,000

If Nutmeg does *not* treat any capital gains as investment income, her investment interest expense deduction is limited to the amount of her net investment income (in this case, it's her interest income). So she deducts $3,000. Her tax, using the 1999 Schedule D worksheet, amounts to $16,114. What happens to the rest of the investment interest expense, beyond the $3,000? Nutmeg will carry forward that $2,000 to the next tax year.

Note that Nutmeg ends up losing the ability to deduct that last $2,000 on her current tax return. In order to avoid this, she can elect to treat $2,000 of long-term capital gains as investment income. Doing so means the full $5,000 of investment interest expense is deductible, and her tax according to the Schedule D worksheet is $15,714. No investment interest expense is carried to the next year. So the election saved Nutmeg $400 in taxes for the year. (The $2,000 would have been taxed at 20%, amounting to $400.)

Would it have been more beneficial for Nutmeg to not make the election, and simply carry over the $2,000 of investment interest to the following year? It would depend upon a number of factors, including her anticipated net investment income and long-term capital gains in the next year. While making the election may save you tax dollars in the short run, it may cost you tax dollars in the long run. Your best bet is to gaze deeply into your crystal ball in order to see what the future may bring. Just don't for-

Reduce Your Gains With Margin Interest? Not!

Under *no* circumstances can you take your margin interest and add it to the cost basis of your stock. Or reduce the sale price of your stock by the margin interest that you paid. Or claim this interest as a miscellaneous itemized deduction on Schedule A. Or use it to reduce your interest income on Schedule B. These are the only places where investment interest can be claimed: on Form 4952 and/or on Schedule A.

get that in many cases, a bird in the hand really is worth more than two in the bush.

For much more information on the investment interest expense deduction, see IRS Publications 550 and 535, and IRS Form 4952 and the associated instructions.

Still Holding Your Interest?

The rules for interest deduction can be complicated—especially if the transactions involved are complicated. And if the interest is other than Schedule A interest, the rules can get even more complicated. You'll have to deal with interest tracing rules and interest reallocation rules. As we told you when we began this chapter, this is certainly not the last and final word regarding interest deductions—not even for Schedule A interest deductions. We simply wanted to point out some general issues that you might not be aware of regarding Schedule A interest issues. You should read much more about the interest expense rules before you take your deduction. You can do so with IRS Publications 535, 936, and 550 for interest issues relative to Schedule A interest deductions.

CHARITABLE CONTRIBUTION DEDUCTIONS

If you're a Fool's Fool, you probably not only try to build significant wealth for yourself, but you give some of your wealth away, as well. If you make donations to charities or certain other organizations for philanthropic purposes, you may be eligible for an income tax benefit in the form of a deduction for charitable contributions. But the amount deductible in any taxable year depends on the value and type of the property contributed, the form of the gift, and the nature of the recipient organization. While charitable gifts should rarely, if ever, be made solely for tax purposes, if you do decide to make such a contribution, you'll want to make sure that it's carefully timed and structured to take advantage of the tax savings opportunities offered by the deduction. In this section we'll review some of the more common issues relative to the charitable contribution deduction.

Charitable Organizations

In order to be allowable as an itemized deduction, charitable contributions must be given to qualified organizations. These organizations include:

- Churches, temples, synagogues, mosques, and other religious organizations

- U.S., state, and local governments as long as the contribution is solely for public purposes

- Public parks and recreational facilities

- Nonprofit schools, hospitals, and volunteer fire companies

- Other charitable organizations such as the Red Cross, Goodwill Industries, United Way, Salvation Army, CARE, Boy and Girl Scouts, Boys and Girls Clubs, etc.

- Veterans' organizations

Types of Contributions

Money and property are what is usually given—and we'll talk about those a bit later. But there are other ways to claim a charitable contribution deduction. Some of these would include:

- **Travel related to charitable activities.** You can deduct travel expenses such as transportation (either using actual expenses or a standard mileage rate—14 cents per mile for 1998), meals, and lodging if there is ot a significant element of personal pleasure, recreation, or vacation in the travel.

- **Volunteer expenses.** If you have out-of-pocket expenses when serving for a qualified organization, you may also have a contribution deduction. For example, Boy/Girl Scout leaders can deduct the cost of uniforms purchased for performing donated services which are not suited for outside wear.

- **Exchange students.** You can deduct up to $50 per school month for housing an exchange student (grade 12 or lower) sponsored by a qualified organization. While the student doesn't necessarily have to be a foreign student, the student must become a member of your household under a written agreement between you and the charitable organization.

- **Delegates.** You can deduct the unreimbursed expenses of attending a church (or similar organization) convention. But you must be an official delegate of the convention, and not simply attending in an unofficial capacity.

Nondeductible Contributions

There are a number of organizations that might be "nonprofit," but that are not charitable. There's a big difference between the two. Not only that, there are certain things that you might give that will not be deductible—even to an appropriate organization. So you've got to be careful when anticipating your charitable giving. Some of those items that are not considered charitable contributions include:

- Money or property given to

  - Groups that are run for personal profit

  - Homeowners associations

  - Political groups or candidates for public office

  - Civic leagues

  - Social and/or sports organizations

  - Groups whose purpose is to lobby for law changes

  - Labor unions

  - Chambers of commerce

  - Foreign organizations

  - Individuals

TAX TIP

Miles and Miles and Miles

Don't let us confuse you by citing different amounts of money you can deduct for mileage. The truth is that the deductible amount varies depending on the situation. Moving expense deductions are $0.10 per mile. Medical deductions are also $0.10 per mile. Charitable deductions are $0.14 per mile. Business-related deductions allow $0.315 per mile. Note that these are all 1998 rates—the 1999 rates aren't out yet.

- The cost of raffle, bingo, or lottery tickets

- Tuition

- Dues, fees, or bills paid to country clubs, lodges, fraternal orders, or similar groups

- Value of the time or services that you may provide to an organization

- Value of blood given to a blood bank

Deduction Limits

Could you give all of your annual earnings away to charity and not pay any income taxes? Nope. There are limits to the percentage of charitable contribution deductions that you're allowed to claim relative to your income. The limits are based on the type of donation (cash or property), and the type of organization receiving the donation.

- **50% AGI Limitation:** If you give cash or unappreciated property to a publicly supported organization, you will be allowed to deduct a charitable contribution up to 50% of your AGI. Examples of publicly supported organizations would include religious organizations, educational organizations, hospitals, medical research organizations, and other organizations that receive a substantial amount of support from the general public or governmental units. In short, these are the normal charities that we discussed earlier in the section.

- **30% and 20% AGI Limitation:** There are situations where your maximum contribution is limited to 30% or 20% of your AGI. These mainly deal with contributions of appreciated property and/or contributions made to other than publicly supported organizations (such as veterans' organizations, fraternal societies, nonprofit cemeteries, and certain private foundations). If you are contributing this type of property, or making contributions to these organizations, check IRS Publication 526 for more details regarding the 30% and 20% limitations.

Carry-Forward of Excess Contributions

If your contributions exceed the AGI limitations, you can carry over the excess to each of the five succeeding tax years. Those carryover contributions will be subject to the original percentage limits that were applicable in the year of the original contribution. And your carryover contributions are deducted after deducting allowable contributions for the current year.

Substantiation Requirements

If you make a contribution (of either cash or property) of $250 or more, you must obtain substantiation of the contribution from the charity in order to secure your deduction. The substantiation must consist of a written acknowledgement of the donation from your organization. If the donation is made in cash, the acknowledgement should state the amount. If the donation is of property, it's sufficient to simply describe the property without having to estimate its value.

There is no required format for the acknowledgement. It can be made by postcard, letter, or computer-generated form. It can even be taped to a coconut and tossed onto your porch. But at a minimum it should contain the name of the donor, the name and address of the organization, the date of the donation, and the amount of cash donated or a description of any donated property. The IRS requires that you receive the acknowledgement before you file your tax return for the year in which the contribution was made. That being the case, the organization should provide the acknowledgement at least by the end of the year.

If the organization provides some tangible benefit to you in return for your contribution, the value of that benefit must be included on the acknowledgement form. For example, if the organization gave you a crystal tea set in return for your contribution, the acknowledgement form must include the value of the tea set—and the cost of the tea set would not be deductible. But there are three exceptions to this rule:

• The first is for intangible religious benefits (such as the right to attend religious services in return for a contribution).

• The second is when the item has only a token value. (If you really want to know, for 1999, an item is of token or insubstantial value if the fair market value is the lesser of: 1) $72, or 2) not more than 2% of the amount of the payment, or 3) the payment is at least $36 and the cost of the item is no more than $7.20.) The IRS annually adjusts the value of these items, and you can read more about their definition in IRS Publication 526.

• The third exception is when you receive membership privileges for a contribution of $75 or less. Such privileges would include free admission to events, free parking, and discounts on member purchases.

You're not required to aggregate contributions in determining if your contributions have reached the $250 threshold. Each contribution is viewed separately, even if it is made as part of a series of payments, such as monthly or weekly pledge payments. All contributions made on the same date, however, should be combined for purposes of determining if you have exceeded your $250 level. What does this mean exactly?

Let's look at Charlie Armstrong, a Foolmobile racer, who makes weekly contributions of $75 to his church. At the end of the year, his total contribution will amount to $3,900. But since each individual contribution was less than $250, no official acknowledgement from the church will be required. Charlie's cancelled checks will do just fine. But Charlie also makes one cash contribution of $300 annually to the local Humane Society. Because this one contribution is greater than the $250 limitation, Charlie will have to receive written substantiation in order to deduct this charitable contribution.

TAX STRATEGY

Spread Out the Contribution

If you're contemplating making a contribution of more than $250 and don't want to bother with required substantiation, consider breaking it up. Let's say that you plan to donate $800 to the Wettlaufer Spill Prevention Society, an environmental outfit determined to rid the world of spills large and small—oil spills and tipped-over soda cans alike. If you write a check for $800, you'll have to receive substantiation of the donation from the charity.

But you could spread out your donation over a wide period of time, perhaps deciding to give quarterly instead of annually. Write a check for $200 today, another one for $200 in three months, and so on—and you'll be in the clear. If the checks are dated very close together (such as a few days apart), the IRS will suspect that your intention isn't to really give $200, but to sneak around the rules—so be careful.

Quid Pro Quo Contributions

You may attend fundraising events where you receive something of value in return for your donation. This is sometimes known as a "quid pro quo" contribution. Examples of these types of contribution would include auctions of donated goods, or attending a charity dinner-dance function. But as the law reads, any time you make a contribution of $75 or more and you receive something of value in return, the IRS requires that the organization must provide a disclosure statement to you.

The disclosure statement is required to inform you that the deductible amount of your contribution is limited to the excess of the amount of the contribution over the value of the goods or services received in return. The organization must also provide a good faith estimate of the value of such goods or services so that you can determine the proper amount of this deduction. The disclosure statement should include your name and the name and address of the charity organization.

Contributions of Property With a Value of More Than $5,000

For contributed property (other than publicly traded securities) with a claimed value exceeding $5,000, you must obtain a qualified appraisal to substantiate the value of the property. A qualified appraisal is an appraisal prepared by an independent appraiser that contains specific information about the property, the value of the property, the valuation method, and the qualifications of the appraiser. A summary of the qualified appraisal, which must be signed by the appraiser and a representative of the charitable organization, is required to be attached to your tax return. Less stringent substantiation requirements are imposed in the case of gifts of publicly traded securities and gifts of property not exceeding $5,000 in value. The question of valuation of contributed property should not be taken lightly. Be prepared to substantiate your contributions. If the claimed value is excessive, you may be subject to an overvaluation penalty, as well as other sanctions.

Non-Cash Charitable Contributions—IRS Form 8283

Any time that you make total contributions of property in excess of $500, you'll be required to complete IRS Form 8283 and attach that form to your tax return. Form 8283 is to be completed when the aggregate of the property contributions exceed $500, even though no one single property contribution was greater than $500.

For example, opera diva Ksenia gave clothing with a fair market value of $200 to the Salvation Army. She also donated a pet carrier with a fair market value of $100 to the Humane Society. And finally, she gave her celebrity toenail clippings collection, with a value of $150, to a local museum. Even though no single property contribution was greater than $500, all of them combined exceed $500. That means Ksenia will be required to file IRS Form 8283 with her tax return.

Form 8283 simply asks you a bunch of questions about the contributions, how you received the donated property, when you purchased it originally, how you arrived at the fair market value of the contribution, your original cost of the property, and a few other things. Don't let this form dissuade you from taking the property deductions that you're allowed to take. It may be a bit of a hassle to complete the document, but it's not super-complicated and the tax savings may well be worth the bother.

Charitable Contributions of Stock

While donating money to worthy causes is something we think is great, it can be greater still to donate appreciated stock instead of cash. The tax advantages can be worth it. Here's how it works.

The first thing you need to do is evaluate how long you've held the stock. Stock held for one year or less falls in the short-term category, while stock held for more than a year is long-term. Next, figure out the stock's fair market value. This is what you would receive from the sale of the stock on the day you make the charitable contribution. It doesn't mean you have to sell the stock then—just figure out its value on that date.

With stock held for the short term, you can claim it as a contribution and deduct the fair market value less the amount it has appreciated since you've held it. In most cases, this means that your deduction is basically your initial cost basis for the stock. For example, if you bought shares of New Jersey-based Hair Volumizer Inc. (ticker: BOUFF) for $800, held them for a year or less, and then donated the bundle when it was worth $1,000, you're looking at an $800 deduction.

If the sale of the stock on the day of the contribution would result in a long-term capital gain, you can generally deduct the full fair market value, up to 30% (not 50%) of your gross income. For example, if you've held 100 shares of Rent-to-Own Underwear (ticker: EWWWW) for more than one year and the shares are worth $20 each on the day you donate them, you can probably deduct $2,000—no matter at what price you bought them. Consider that if you bought the shares long ago at a split-adjusted $5 per share, your capital gain would be in the neighborhood of $1,500, and by donating the stock, there's no gain on which to be taxed. At 20%, the tax on $1,500 would have been $300, so in a sense you're getting credit for a $2,000 donation but are saving $300 with it, so it's really just costing you $1,700. Not bad!

To donate stock, you just have to transfer ownership of the shares. Your broker can help you with that, as can the charity to which you're planning to contribute. Remember, though, as with all tax-related issues, there are always details to consider that relate to your particular situation. You'd be well advised to consult IRS Publication 526 or a tax professional.

TAX STRATEGY

Which Stocks to Give?

If you're planning to donate stock, choose carefully which shares you give. The factors that should most influence your decision are how long you've held a given share and whether it's appreciated or not (and by how much).

If a stock has actually fallen in value, for example, you're probably better off selling it so that you can claim the capital loss. Then, if you wish, you can donate the proceeds of the sale in order to generate a contribution deduction.

If the stock you donate has appreciated considerably, you'll realize a large charity deduction. Great. But remember that your total deductions for this type of charitable contribution are limited to 30% of your AGI. And even though you can carry over any excess contribution, you won't receive the most bang for your buck if you over-contribute.

Remember that making a contribution of a stock rids your portfolio of that stock. Is that what you want to do? You might consider making a contribution of a stock that has not only appreciated, but has also fallen out of (your) favor because the fundamentals of the company have changed. Contributing a stock that you really love can be a not-so-great idea, as you'll miss out on any future appreciation. The charity will likely sell the stock that you donate as soon as they receive the shares. So giving it some little gem that you found, thinking that the charity will benefit from its future growth, may not do as much good as you hope, and might also not be healthy for your portfolio. It's all part of the process of managing your investments and maximizing your contributions. It's a balancing act.

Finally, if you *do* have a winner that you think is going to be a bigger winner in the future, you may still make a contribution of that stock and keep it in your portfolio. How? Simply buy it back after you make the charitable contribution. It'll cost you real live dollars to do it, but you may still benefit greatly in the long run. And you don't even have to wait more than 30 days before buying it back, as wash sale rules don't apply to contributed stock (because you're not taking any loss).

A Charitable Close

We believe that charitable giving is just another part of a Fool's life. And it's a good life. Part of being a Fool is helping others... and charitable contributions do just that. We hope that this section will help you structure your giving in such a way that it will also benefit you from a tax standpoint. If done correctly, the only loser is Uncle Sam... and he probably isn't all that upset about being a loser here. These deductions are granted by legislative grace because the government realizes that we're all better off when many of us make contributions to our favorite charities. So if you can do good things with your contributions, and save yourself tax dollars at the same time, it's certainly something to consider.

Remember that this section is really an overview of the entire charitable contribution issue. If you're interested in delving deeper into the tax aspects of charitable contributions, then you should read IRS Publication 526, which you can download at the IRS website at www.irs.gov. While you're at the website, you might want to make sure that the organization you're giving to is a qualified organization, allowed to accept such contributions and give you an itemized deduction in return. IRS Publication 78, "Cumulative List of Organizations," lists hundreds of thousands of tax-exempt organizations that qualify for purposes of a charitable contribution deduction. At the IRS website, you can easily search a database of such organizations. Make sure that your charity is on the list before you make your contributions. You may be glad you did.

CASUALTY AND THEFT LOSS DEDUCTIONS

Sometimes... well... bad things happen. If so, you may be entitled to an itemized deduction for the loss that you suffer. The problem is, the restrictions associated with the deduction of casualty and theft losses are pretty severe. It almost adds insult to injury. So don't rely on Uncle Sam to step in and make you whole if you get hit with a casualty or theft loss. You may have a quite unpleasant surprise.

Before we look at what a casualty or theft loss might actually be, let's look at the rules regarding the deduction—or at least the potential deduction. Remember that when you're dealing with casualty and theft losses, the rules are basically similar for both. Instead of writing "casualty and theft" over and over again in the following sections, we'll just use the word "loss." So when you see "loss," think "casualty or theft."

The Bigger, the Better... Kinda

First and foremost, a loss must exceed $100 to even have a chance at a deduction. The law requires that you reduce each loss by $100 (by "a floor" of $100, in proper tax-speak). But this floor applies to each separate event, and not necessarily each separate loss. Take the case of Job, who has had a really bad month.

A few weeks ago, Job had his money clip stolen. Several days later, his laptop computer was struck by a very small meteor and melted. Then, only a week later, a volcanic eruption damaged his house, his garage, and his car. How many $100 limitations does Job have to deal with? Three. The theft of the money clip and the destruction of the laptop were two separate incidents, so the $100 limitation is applied to each event. But the volcanic eruption was one event, even though there were three separate losses. So only one $100 limitation would be applied to this event.

If you can get over the $100 hump, you still have one more big hurdle to overcome: the adjusted gross income limitation. In order to be claimed as an itemized deduction, your total losses must exceed 10% of your AGI. So, in effect, your losses must exceed 10% of your AGI plus the $100-per-loss floor. You can quickly see that this means your losses may have to be large—in many cases *very* large—in order for you to receive any tax relief. The larger your AGI, the smaller your deductible loss. Or, if you want to look at it in a more skewed light, the larger your loss, the larger your potential deduction. But that's almost like wishing for a larger, more painful canker sore.

Looking at Job again (although you might not find him, since he's now curled up in a hotel bed with the covers pulled over his head), let's try to figure his loss deduction. He had $75 in his money clip when it was ripped off. His loss on the laptop amounted to $1,500. And his combined loss for the damage caused by the eruption weighed in at $4,500. For the year in question, Job had AGI of $50,000.

Regarding the cash, it didn't exceed the $100 floor—so we can just forget about it. The loss on the laptop would be reduced by $100, for a net loss of $1,400, and the eruption losses would also be reduced by $100 for net losses of $4,400. Job's net losses before AGI testing amount to $5,800. Ten percent of Job's AGI is $5,000. Reducing his net losses by his AGI limitation leaves him with a deductible loss of $800. If Job is in the 28% bracket and can otherwise itemize his deductions, his tax savings will amount to about $224. Not much of a recovery, eh? And just when you thought you got to the end of the bad news, we've got a bit more to give you.

What's My Loss?

A casualty or theft loss equals the *lesser* of:

• The decrease in the fair market value of the property as a result of the casualty or theft, or

• Your cost basis (or adjusted basis) in the property before the casualty or theft *minus* any insurance or other reimbursement that you received or expect to receive.

In effect, if the property has increased in value, the only loss that you're going to receive is your cost in the property. You'll generally not receive a loss for any uninsured increase in value of the property. (In other words, if something you paid $1,000 for was worth $5,000 when you lost it, your loss is still just $1,000.) If the property has decreased in value, you'll only generate a loss of its fair market value at the time of loss. (In other words, if it cost you $5,000 and its fair market value was $1,000 when you lost it, your loss is $1,000.)

Take Job and his meteor-melted laptop. He originally purchased it for $2,000. But because of normal wear and tear, it was only worth $1,500 at the time of the meteor hit (according its fair market value, or FMV). Immediately after the hit, the FMV was zero. So Job's decrease in the FMV of the laptop amounted to $1,500. His cost basis in the property was $2,000. But his loss is determined to be the *lesser* of the decrease in FMV *or* the cost of the property. Using this standard, Job has a casualty loss of $1,500. Instinctively, you may think that Job's loss was really $2,000—the amount he originally paid for the laptop. But the IRS isn't interested in allowing you to claim your original cost when the actual FMV of the property is less than the original cost. So in most cases, your deductible loss will be less (perhaps much less) than what you originally paid for the property. Ouch. It can't get any worse… right? Wrong.

Insurance, Anyone?

As noted above, any insurance reimbursement that you receive must be factored into the loss computations. You'll reduce your loss by the amount of the insurance that you receive (or expect to receive). Once again, let's look at poor Job and his problems to illustrate an example of how insurance reimbursement works.

Job's original cost basis in the house, garage, and car amounted to $40,000. The FMV of this property before the eruption was $60,000, but was only $25,000 after the eruption. Therefore, the decrease in FMV because of this loss amounted to $35,000. But Job had the sense to insure this property, and received an insurance reimbursement in the amount of $30,500. So he's required to reduce his loss of $35,000 by the amount of the insurance reimbursement of $30,500. This leaves him with a net loss after insurance of $4,500 (before his $100 floor and AGI limitations), and that's what Job reports on his tax return. So Job won't be able to double dip—taking the insurance money and trying to claim the full loss in FMV on the property. The IRS won't allow it.

One other twist with respect to the insurance issue: If the damaged property is covered by insurance, you must file an insurance claim and take the insurance that you are legally entitled to. If you simply decide not to submit the claim, you receive no loss deduction—regardless of the amount of the loss.

Take Dana for example. Her driving record isn't the best—she tends to run into things occasionally. One afternoon, she swerved to avoid hitting a chicken crossing the road, and ran smack into a tree. The good news was that neither Dana nor the chicken were injured. The bad news was that her car suffered severe damage. Dana was concerned that if she turned in another claim to her insurance company, her rates would skyrocket—or even worse—her insurance might be cancelled. So she decided to simply repair the damage herself with her own money, and left the insurance company out of the entire situation. Even if the amount of the loss exceeds the $100 floor and the 10% AGI limitations, Dana has no loss. Since the car was covered by insurance, and Dana decided not to submit the claim, no loss will be allowed.

Here's a last twist. What if Dana had this accident just after passing a "Chicken Crossing" sign? This is where things get murky. On the one hand, the turn of events is no longer quite so unexpected. On the other hand, the IRS is still likely to call it an accident, as it does most auto mishaps. It can be hard sometimes to determine exactly what a casualty loss is.

Casualty... Casually

So what's a casualty? The Internal Revenue Code allows a deduction for losses of property if such losses arise from fire, storm, shipwreck, or other casualty. Apart from the terms "fire," "storm," and "shipwreck," neither the Code nor the regulations define the term "casualty." Thus, the task of further defining this term has been left to the IRS and the courts.

"Casualty" has been defined as "the damage, destruction, or loss of property resulting from an identifiable event that is sudden, unexpected, or unusual," such as an "accident, a mishap, [or] some sudden invasion by a hostile agency." Property that is lost or misplaced does not give rise to a casualty loss unless it results from an event that is (1) identifiable, (2) damaging to property, and (3) sudden, unexpected, or unusual in nature.

In order to claim a loss, you must prove not only the existence of a casualty, but that the identifiable event caused the loss sustained. In this connection, the IRS has stated that an "accident or casualty proceeds from an

Pop Quiz

Can you guess which losses qualify as casualties in the eyes of the IRS? First, quickly cover up the answers that are in fine print at the bottom. Then jot down "yes" or "no" for each situation and see how many you guessed right.

1. Losses caused by a hot water boiler bursting in a home due to an air obstruction in the water pipes that prevented the proper flow of cool water into the boiler.

2. Losses caused by a water heater bursting from rust and corrosion.

3. Losses resulting from rust and water damage to rugs, carpets, and drapes caused by a bursting water heater.

4. The household cat broke a vase during the course of "extraordinary behavior" (its first fit).

5. A household servant accidentally broke glass and chinaware in the course of cleaning.

6. A husband activated a garbage disposal unit after inadvertently depositing the contents of a glass, which contained his wife's engagement ring, into the drain. (His wife had placed the glass near the sink.)

7. Furniture dropped 16 floors by movers while transferring a taxpayer's property from one apartment to another.

8. Loss of an automobile that unexpectedly fell through the ice and sank to the bottom of a lake while a taxpayer was ice fishing.

9. Trees destroyed within five to 10 days after a massive southern pine beetle attack in an area not known for such massive attacks.

10. Damage over an extended period of time to the basement wall of a residence as a result of heavy pressure exerted on the walls due to improper drainage of storm water and the nonporous nature of the clay backfill.

11. Suffocation of trees due to improper grading.

12. Timber loss due to abnormal and unexpected drought conditions.

13. Damage to the exterior of a taxpayer's home caused by unusually severe smog, containing an unusually high concentration of chemical fumes and lasting one day.

14. Losses incurred due to a sonic boom.

15. Losses sustained when a vandal broke into a house under construction and damaged new appliances that the taxpayers had placed on the premises.

Answers:

Casualties: 1, 3, 6, 7, 8, 9, 12, 13, 14, and 15
Not casualties: 2, 4, 5, 10, and 11

unknown cause, or is an unusual effect of a known cause." Either the cause or the effect may be said to occur by chance or unexpectedly. Thus, the term casualty is deemed to encompass such events as hurricanes, tornadoes, floods, storms, shipwrecks, fires, or accidents. The determination of whether a casualty has been incurred by a taxpayer for purposes of the loss deduction has been the subject of numerous court cases and IRS pronouncements.

What may or may not constitute a casualty is a very large issue. The courts and the IRS have dealt with these questions over the years. There are thousands of decisions, rulings, and court cases—far too many to discuss here in any detail. You know which "biggies" (such as fires, storms, hurricanes, earthquakes, vandalism, tornadoes, etc.) qualify for loss deductions, but there are many other incidents that may also qualify. What doesn't qualify would include mislaid or lost property, termite or moth damage, progressive deterioration, disease and insect damage to trees and other plants, and accidental breakage or damage done by a pet.

So if you have a loss from property in what might seem to be an unusual situation, you'll want to check it out in much more detail. You may find that your unusual situation has already been identified and ruled on by either the IRS or the courts. You may not be happy with the ruling, but you might as well know about it going in.

Theft

You might think that a theft loss is pretty straightforward. But that's not entirely true. It can get complicated. Generally, you deduct a theft loss in the year that it was discovered—and not necessarily when the theft actually took place. In addition, theft losses are deductible if they result from illegal acts under the applicable state law and if they're done with criminal intent. This could be another gray area, and the courts and the IRS have been busy dealing with issues regarding what may or may not be theft—especially cases that deal with fraud and embezzlement. So again, if your theft issues are complicated, make sure to check out the IRS publications, regulations, and court cases. You may very well find direction in regulations and/or court cases that deal with your specific issues.

Loss of Additional Explanations

Casualty and theft losses are difficult. We've just shown you the tip of the iceberg with this section. Business casualty losses have their own rules. Insurance reimbursement issues can get complicated. Losses involving presidentially declared disaster areas are subject to other rules (and tax opportunities). You can read much more about these issues in IRS Publication 547 and the workbook that the IRS provides in Publication 584. You'll report your losses, if any, on IRS Form 4684—so you might want to review that form and its instructions, also. If you've suffered a casualty or theft, then read these publications for additional information and guidance.

MISCELLANEOUS ITEMIZED DEDUCTIONS

Miscellaneous itemized deductions include all deductible items that don't fall into the other Schedule A categories (such as medical expenses, taxes paid, interest paid, charitable contributions, or casualty losses). But they generally can't be personal in nature. They're required to be associated with your business or investment activities, or the collection and/or production of taxable income.

And there are literally thousands of 'em.

IRS Publication 529 will give you information on these deductions. We recommend reading that publication to get a clearer idea of what you may be dealing with. We'll cover some of the basics here, to give you an introductory overview. So make sure that you learn more about these deductions before you attempt to use any of them.

There are two types of miscellaneous deductions:

• Those that are deductible in full (assuming that you otherwise qualify to itemize your deductions); and

• Those which are deductible only to the extent that they exceed 2% of your adjusted gross income.

In Full

The miscellaneous expenses that are deductible in full are few in number. The most popular would be gambling expenses. But remember that gambling expenses are only deductible up to the amount of gambling income. You may hit the jackpot for $1,000 in winnings. Because you feel lucky, you'll continue to gamble... and you may end up losing $3,000. Your gambling loss deduction will be limited to $1,000. And this loss will *only* be allowed if you are otherwise qualified to itemize your deductions. If you take the standard deduction, you have effectively lost your gambling loss deduction. Wave bye-bye. Adios.

So don't go to Las Vegas thinking that any money you lose will be deductible. It won't. And, as of this writing, "day-trading" hasn't been defined as gambling. (Perhaps it should. But that's an issue for another day.)

Other miscellaneous items that are deductible in full include:

• Special job-related expenses of the handicapped

• Estate taxes already imposed on the same taxable income (income with respect to a decedent)

• Unrecovered costs of an annuity (on a decedent's final return)

• Repayments of income (in some cases)

Other than the gambling expense issues, the other deductions are pretty narrow in scope and affect very few people on a daily basis. But if any of these things seem to ring a bell with you, make sure to check out the rules in IRS Publication 529.

The 2% Test

All other qualified itemized deductions can only be deducted if they meet the 2% test. If you've been reading this book cover to cover, you already know how the test works. If not, then understand that the 2% test means the deduction is only allowed to the extent that it exceeds 2% of your AGI. Take the case of Larry McCloskey, CEO of online meringue manufacturing and delivery company eMeringue.com. Larry's AGI amounts to $45,000. He has miscellaneous itemized deductions of $1,000, subject to the 2% limitation. Some quick math will show you that 2% of Larry's AGI amounts to $900. Since his deductions are limited to that amount in excess of his AGI, his miscellaneous itemized deduction will be limited to $100 ($1,000 in total deductions less the 2%-of-AGI amount of $900). So, similar to the case of medical expenses and casualty losses, your deductions may not be significant unless your deductions are large or your AGI is small—or a combination of the two.

Common Deductions

Some (but certainly not all) of the most common miscellaneous itemized deductions that are subject to the 2% of AGI limitation include:

• Appraisal fees (for charitable donations or casualty losses)

• Clerical assistance in order to maintain investments

• Depreciation on business assets

• Unreimbursed employee business expenses

• Expenses to collect interest or dividends (collection fees)

• Hobby expenses—to the extent of hobby income

• Work clothes and uniforms if they are required by your employer and not suitable for outside wear

• Tax preparation fees and/or other tax assistance expenses

• Legal fees for collecting or producing taxable income, keeping a job, or obtaining tax advice

• Professional fees for obtaining investment advice

• Investment expenses in general and some investment travel

• Job-hunting expenses

• Safe-deposit box fees

• Cost of a home safe to retain tax/investment papers

• Small tools and supplies used in your trade or business

• Retirement custodial fees paid directly (such as IRA, Keogh, SIMPLE, etc.)

• Job-related educational expenses

• Medical examinations required by your employer

• Professional and union dues

- Repayment of income (in some cases)

- Service charges on dividend reinvestment plans

- Trust administration fees

- Long-distance business calls

- Books, magazines, and other publications dealing with investments or taxes (such as the cost of this book!)

- Legal fees for the collection of alimony

- Office-in-home deduction

- Office-in-home expenses

- Job dismissal insurance

- Extra cost of a phone installed in your home for business use

- Cleaning and maintenance of work clothes (if done professionally)

- Business-related travel and entertainment

Again, this is only a very short list. There are hundreds of other miscellaneous expenses that may or may not apply to you. IRS Publication 529 will help you identify them. In addition, some of these "one-liners" are much more complicated and require additional research. We'll cover a few of them shortly.

But before we move on, let's take a look at a list of items that are *not* considered miscellaneous itemized deductions. There are many misconceptions regarding what is and isn't deductible in this section of Schedule A (which is why IRS Publication 529 is required reading). But here's a brief listing of many of the most commonly misunderstood items that *don't* qualify as miscellaneous itemized deductions:

- Personal living expenses

- Commuting expenses

- Funeral expenses

- Home repairs and improvements on your personal residence

- Legal fees for divorce (other than for tax planning)

- Parking tickets and other fines that are payments for illegal activities

- Political contributions

- Sales tax (except when added to the cost of a business asset)

- Telephone expenses of the first line for basic local residential service (even if a portion of the use is for business purposes).

- College tuition

- Education expenses that qualify you for a new trade or business

- Club dues (except for certain business or public service organizations)

- Gambling losses in excess of gambling winnings

- Licenses and fees (such as marriage licenses, animal licenses, driver's license, etc.)

- Life insurance

- Losses from the sale of your personal residence

- Cleaning of your work clothes if you wash them yourself (not professionally)

- The cost of travel that is primarily a form of education

- Costs directly related to buying or selling an investment (such as broker purchase and sale commissions)

- Expenses and costs of attending investment seminars or conventions

- Expenses to attend a company's annual stockholder meeting—even if you own stock in that company (unless you're organizing a hostile takeover)

- Estate planning advice (except for the portion related to tax advice)

- Legal costs and expenses relating to child support and custody

As we noted, there are a number of miscellaneous itemized deductions that have their own set of rules and requirements. While we won't take the time to discuss them all in detail here, we'll offer a brief overview of some of the major topics.

Job Costs and Expenses

IRS Publication 463 deals with unreimbursed expenses regarding your employment. Topics would include business-related insurance, job-hunting expenses, business telephone expenses, and uniforms and work clothes. With any luck, your employer will cover all of the ordinary and necessary expenses required for you to perform your job. But if not, check out IRS Publication 463 for additional details.

Education Costs

IRS Publication 508 will give you a rundown of what qualifies as deductible education expenses and what doesn't. You can also learn more about education-related tax issues in our "Education" chapter.

Investment Expenses

IRS Publication 550 will fill you in on expenses that you incur in association with your investment activities. Make sure you review our "Investor Tax Basics" chapter, as well, for the lowdown on various investment-related tax issues. (Investment interest and margin interest are addressed earlier in this chapter.)

Legal Fees

If you want to understand more about legal and other professional expenses and how they may relate to you, read IRS Publication 529.

Business-Related Travel and Entertainment

IRS Publication 463 will take you down the right road. You'll also want to entertain the idea of reviewing IRS Publication 1542 for a look at per-diem rates.

Business Use of Home

IRS Publication 587 will give you the rules, restrictions, and requirements. We've already covered the basics of the home office deduction in the "Your Home Office" chapter of the book. Head there for additional information.

MISCELLANEOUS CREDITS

When we began to draft this section of the book, we realized that it would be very small. Not necessarily because there are so few credits. Rather we found that we would be discussing many of the credits that you'd be interested in elsewhere in the book. We decided that we really didn't want to bore you with some of the more exotic credits (such as the Orphan Drug Credit or the Enhanced Oil Recovery Credit). So we'll just stick with a few of the credits that you might see in your day-to-day life that haven't been discussed elsewhere.

Electric Vehicle Credit

As an incentive to promote electric and clean-burning vehicles, a credit is available if you purchase a qualified electric car. Your credit is 10% of the cost of the vehicle, up to a maximum credit of $4,000. Report this credit on IRS Form 8834. The beauty of this credit is that it's available to you regardless of whether the vehicle is used for business or personal purposes.

In order to qualify, the electric vehicle must be:

• Manufactured for use on public roads, with at least four wheels

• Powered primarily by an electric motor

• Purchased new, not used.

• Acquired for your own use, and not for resale

You can read more about this credit in IRS Publication 535.

Disabled Access Credit

The disabled access credit is a nonrefundable tax credit for an eligible small business that incurs expenses to provide access to persons who have disabilities to comply with the Americans With Disabilities Act of 1990. If you're not a business or commercial property owner, this may not mean much to you. But for those who qualify, this can be a very valuable credit. You're allowed to report as a credit 50% of your eligible access expenses, to a maximum credit of $5,000. There is really no IRS Publication that deals specifically with this issue. But you'll report the credit on IRS Form 8826—and you'll find that this form and its associated instructions will provide you with all of the information that you'll need to take the credit.

The Foreign Tax Credit (Even if You Never Left Home!)

Don't think that this would ever apply to you? Think again. Even if you never travel beyond the borders of the good old U. S. of A., you may still get hit with a foreign tax. How? Well, perhaps on foreign investments such as stock, mutual funds, or partnership interests. With such investments, foreign taxes may have been paid on your behalf as a shareholder.

If you do get hit with foreign tax (usually withheld from the source country from your interest, dividends, or partnership distributions), what can you do? Well, you can either claim the foreign tax as a credit against your U.S. income tax, or you can take a deduction for the foreign taxes paid as an itemized deduction on your Schedule A. But you can't take both a credit and deduction for the same foreign taxes paid. Generally, the credit saves you more tax dollars, but the Schedule A deduction is allowed for certain taxes that don't qualify for the foreign tax credit due to boycott provisions or other limitations provided by the Internal Revenue Code. So don't be afraid to figure your taxes both ways (either using the credit or taking the deduction) and elect the treatment that saves you the greatest amount of U.S. tax.

In the not too distant past, computing and reporting the foreign tax credit was a monumental pain in the pencil. You were required to file IRS Form 1116, prepare a number of computations and calculations, and attach Form 1116 to your tax return. But no longer. If you qualify, you can simply report the foreign tax directly on Form 1040 (but only Form 1040, not Form 1040EZ or 1040A) in the credit section of the Form 1040 on page 2. Because of this change, taking the credit has never been easier.

You will be allowed to bypass Form 1116 and report your foreign tax credit directly on Form 1040 if:

• Your total foreign taxes paid during the year don't exceed $300 for a single filer, $600 for a married-joint filer.

- All of your foreign income is from "passive" sources, such as interest, dividends, annuities, rents, or royalties. The foreign income can't be from an active trade or business.

- All of the foreign income is reported on Form 1099DIV, 1099INT, or other similar statements.

- Foreign taxes from the current year can't be carried to any other tax year, and foreign taxes from any other years can't be carried to the current year.

If you pay foreign taxes, you can read more about how to claim the foreign tax credit or the deduction for foreign taxes on Schedule A by reading IRS Publication 514. Form 1116 and its instructions will also give you substantial information on how to compute and report the credit.

And that's the end of our credit review!

DEDUCTIONS AND CREDITS AND YOU

There was a lot of information in this section. In most cases, though, we've only really scratched the surface. We wanted you to have an idea of what was out there in the form of deductions and credits, and provide you with an overview of some tax issues that you might not otherwise have been aware of. So don't get silly and take any deductions or credits simply from the information provided here. It wasn't our intent to deal intimately with each type of itemized deduction or credit. To do so would have added about 100 pages (and about a pound) to this book. Instead, treat this section like an introduction... like a first date. Understand that there is still a lot that you'll want (and need) to know—and we've given you the resources to do just that. As with love, becoming more and more familiar can be the best part of the entire relationship. (Or not—we are still dealing with taxes here.)

TAX RELIEF

On Taxation

Isn't it appropriate that the month of the tax begins with April Fool's Day and ends with cries of "May Day!"—Robert Knauerhase

Taxation with representation ain't so hot either.—Gerald Barzan

The art of taxation consists in so plucking the goose as to obtain the largest possible amount of feathers with the smallest possible amount of hissing.—Jean B. Colbert

The Rosetta Stone... whose text in hieroglyphics, dometics, and Greek was the key to revealing the stories of ancient Egypt, was in fact a grant of tax immunity. Which is why, of course, it was engraved in stone and not on papyrus.—Alvin Rabushka

Death and taxes are both certain.... But death isn't annual.—Anonymous

If the Lord had meant us to pay income taxes, he'd have made us smart enough to prepare the return.—Kirk Kirkpatrick

The income tax created more criminals than any other single act of government.
—Barry M. Goldwater

Income tax has made more liars out of the American people than golf.—Will Rogers

All the Congress, all the accountants and tax lawyers, all the judges, and a convention of wizards all cannot tell for sure what the income tax law says.—Walter B. Wriston

The Eiffel Tower is the Empire State Building after taxes.—Anonymous

Income taxes are the most imaginative fiction written today.—Herman Wouk

A dog who thinks he is man's best friend is a dog who obviously has never met a tax lawyer.—Fran Lebowitz

We don't pay taxes. Only the little people pay taxes.—Leona Helmsley

RETIREMENT INSTRUMENTS

I am a free man. I feel as light as a feather.
—Javier Pérez de Cuéllar

Retirement plans play a crucial role in providing a source of income in our later years. We've all seen or heard about "the three-legged stool" that shows Social Security, our personal lifetime savings, and company retirement plans as the triad from which we'll draw the funds to pay for our expenses after we retire. (If your nest egg is resting on a two-legged stool, you probably have a little more planning to do!)

These plans serve many purposes for employers and employees alike, and they come in many shapes and sizes. Unfortunately, few of us really understand the plans we have, despite the critical function they fulfill in our lives. To help increase that understanding, we offer this overview of common retirement plans. We'll go into considerable detail for some of the more common ones, such as IRAs and 401(k)s.

Qualified Retirement Plan

A qualified retirement plan is one that meets the numerous requirements of the Internal Revenue Code (IRC) and the Employee Retirement Income Security Act of 1974 (ERISA). Plans meeting these requirements qualify for four important tax benefits:

- Employers may deduct allowable contributions in the year they were made on behalf of plan participants.

- Plan participants may exclude contributions and all earnings thereon from their taxable income until the year they are withdrawn.

- Earnings on the funds held by the plan's trust are not taxed to that trust.

- Many times participants and/or beneficiaries may further delay taxation on a plan's benefits by transferring those amounts into another tax-deferred vehicle such as an Individual Retirement Account (IRA).

A qualified retirement plan falls into one of three general categories: a defined benefit plan, a defined contribution plan, or a hybrid plan (combining characteristics of the first two categories).

Nonqualified Retirement Plans

A nonqualified retirement plan is one that does not meet the requirements of the IRC or ERISA. These plans may be "discriminatory" in their application, meaning that they're not necessarily open to everyone and participation might be subject to some plan-specific criteria. They're typically used to provide deferred compensation to key employees. Because these plans allow a broader flexibility to the employer, they do not receive the same favorable tax treatment that permitted qualified plans get. Employers receive no tax deduction until the employee receives proceeds from the plan. On receipt, the proceeds are taxed to the employees and are ineligible for transfer to an IRA. In some situations, the employee may face immediate taxation on the benefit even when the funds will not be received until much later.

Defined Benefit Plans

A defined benefit plan is the traditional company pension plan. It's so named because the ultimate retirement benefit, the amount you'll receive when you retire, is definite and determinable as a dollar amount or as a percentage of wages. In short, it's defined. To determine these amounts, defined benefit plans usually base the benefit calculation on a combination of years of employment, wages, and/or age. These plans are funded entirely by the employer, and the employer bears the responsibility for the payment of the benefit as well as all risk on monies invested to fund the benefit.

Benefits typically are not payable until normal retirement age and usually are paid in the form of a lifetime annuity. (But a large minority of plans permit lump sum payments at retirement.) Lifetime annuity payments are taxed at ordinary income tax rates and are ineligible for rollover to an IRA. Lump sum payments may be transferred to an IRA to defer immediate taxation. Once transferred to an IRA, though, the proceeds are subject to IRA rules and regulations.

After January 1, 2000, five-year forward income averaging for lump sum payments is eliminated. However, persons born on December 31, 1936, or earlier retain the option to use 10-year forward averaging based on 1986 tax rates and to use the 20% long-term capital gains rate on benefits attributable to service prior to 1974. (For more information on forward averaging, read IRS Publications 554 and 575. And while you're there, also check out IRS Form 4972 and the associated instructions. It's complicated stuff.)

People younger than 55 who receive retirement benefits as income in a form other than a lifetime annuity are subject to an excise tax based on a premature distribution from a qualified retirement plan. The excise tax will continue until the retiree reaches age 59½. If you're in this unfortunate camp, you'll be taxed on that benefit at ordinary rates and will be assessed an additional 10% early distribution penalty, as well. Hmm... perhaps you might want to rethink that plan to retire at age 50.

Defined Contribution Plans

While defined benefit plans used to be the norm, times have changed. It's no longer so common to see someone spend most of his or her working life at one company. It's also less common to see employers offering defined benefit plans. Many have shifted the burden of risk onto the employee. It's now more typical to see companies offering defined contribution plans. This means that employees need to be much more informed about these plans and about financial planning in general.

A defined contribution plan is a qualified retirement plan in which the contribution (the amount going into it) is defined, but the ultimate benefit to be paid (the amount coming out of it) is not. In such plans, each participant has an individual account. The benefit at retirement depends on the amounts contributed and on the investment performance of that account through the years. In such plans, the investment risk may rest solely with the employee because of the opportunity to choose from a number of investment options. These plans take many forms and are known by various names, such as 401(k), 403(b), money purchase, or profit sharing plans.

Annual contributions by the employee and/or employer are limited to a maximum of $30,000 or 25% of compensation, whichever is smaller. At retirement, benefits are typically paid in installments or as a lump sum; however, they may also be paid as an annuity. Income tax ramifications and rollover options are the same as those described above for defined benefit plans. Installment payments for a period of less than 10 years are eligible for transfer to an IRA, while those lasting for a period of 10 years or more are not.

We'll now plunge into discussions of the many types of retirement instruments that may be available to you. First up, the traditional IRA (also known as the "regular" or "normal" IRA).

THE TRADITIONAL IRA

You probably already understand the concept of the Individual Retirement Account. Assuming you qualify, you sock away up to $2,000 a year ($4,000 for married folks) in a tax-deferred account and most likely withdraw it during retirement. It seems that only about 5% of Americans take advantage of IRAs, though, suggesting that most people haven't thought through their many benefits.

Many Fools may think that just plopping their money into a brokerage account or mutual fund is good enough. This might not be the case, though, as IRAs offer three compelling advantages over regular investments:

- There's an up-front tax break, which is essentially a government subsidy to your savings. For example, if you contribute $2,000 and you deduct that from the income on which you're taxed, you'll be saving $560 that you otherwise would have shelled out to the IRS (assuming a 28% tax rate). You can take that $560 and invest it. In 25 years, growing at 11%, it'll be $7,608—all because you took advantage of that IRA.

- The deferral of taxes permits these savings to accumulate more rapidly since they aren't subject to capital gains taxes over the years. In other words, the stocks and/or mutual funds you buy and sell in your IRA don't generate taxable gains. This is a huge difference from your mutual funds, where you end up paying Uncle Sam every year for capital gains. Instead of taking two steps forward and one step back, IRAs permit you to keep moving forward until you're ready to withdraw funds.

- When the money is finally withdrawn after age 59½, it's taxed as regular income. By then, though, an investor may be in a lower tax bracket. So while you might have paid 28% or 36% or more on the $2,000 of income that you diverted into an IRA, you may end up paying only 15% on it at retirement. This even tops the 20% capital gains rate.

By now you're surely convinced that IRAs are for you. Slow down, Fool—there are still some limitations to address. For starters, there's a 10% penalty for early withdrawal (prior to age 59½). Also, if you participate in an employer-sponsored retirement plan, you may not be able to enjoy full deductibility of the $2,000 annual contribution. For 1999, if you're covered by a 401(k) or other pension plan, IRA contributions remain fully tax-deductible only if your annual income is below $31,000 ($51,000 for married couples). Incomes between $31,000 and $41,000 ($51,000 and $61,000 for married couples) are in a "phase-out" range, where only part of a $2,000 IRA contribution would be deductible. If your annual income is above these limits, you're not exactly out of luck. You can still plunk your pesos into an IRA to take advantage of the tax-deferred accumulation of assets—you just can't deduct the contribution from this year's income.

Things are looking even better for IRA investors. New tax laws are hiking up the income limits and easing the restrictions on withdrawals. By 2007, folks with annual income near $100,000 will be able to participate. And importantly, IRA savings can now be withdrawn without penalty to buy a first house or pay for education expenses.

IRS Publication 590 can give you more information on IRA rules, restrictions, and phase-out computations.

IRA Deduction Limitations

There have been massive changes made recently to the rules limiting deductible contributions to Individual Retirement Accounts. The limits apply to taxpayers who are active participants in employer-sponsored retirement plans. The changes may allow you a deductible IRA in future years that may not have been permitted in the past. Let's take a few minutes to understand these changes.

First, recall that in general, up to $2,000 a year in deductible IRA contributions can be made by a taxpayer, as long as he earns compensation at least equal to the contributed amount. For married couples filing jointly, up to $4,000 can be contributed, as long as their combined compensation at least equals the contributed amount.

The Old Rules

Under the old rules, if a taxpayer was a participant in an employer-sponsored retirement plan, the amount that could be deducted for an IRA contribution was limited (or completely eliminated) depending on the taxpayer's adjusted gross income. For single taxpayers, no deduction was allowed if AGI was $35,000 or more. If AGI was between $25,000 and $35,000, the $2,000 maximum deduction was reduced, with the reduction amount increasing ratably as AGI crept upward toward $35,000. For married taxpayers filing jointly, the same approach was taken but the figures were different: No deduction was available if AGI was $50,000 or more, and the deduction was phased out for AGI between $40,000 and $50,000. Additionally, and more importantly, even if only one spouse participated in an employer's plan, the limitation applied to both spouses. To the extent the deduction limitation applied, the $2,000 maximum IRA contribution could still be made: It just was not fully deductible (or deductible at all, depending on AGI).

The New Rules

Beginning in 1998, the rules have been eased in two respects. First, for married couples filing jointly, if only one spouse is a participant in an employer's plan, the limitation only applies to that spouse. However, the maximum deductible IRA contribution for an individual who is not an active participant, but whose spouse is, is phased out for taxpayers with AGI between $150,000 and $160,000. Second, the amounts triggering the limitations have been increased starting in 1998, both for single taxpayers and married couples filing jointly. For single taxpayers, the limitation range increased to $31,000-$41,000 for 1999 (i.e., the maximum IRA deduction is reduced if AGI exceeds $31,000 and is zero if it is $41,000 or more). For 2000, the range increases to $32,000-$42,000; for 2001 to $33,000-$43,000; for 2002 to $34,000-$44,000; for 2003 to $40,000-$50,000; for 2004 to $45,000-55,000; and for 2005 and later years to $50,000-$60,000.

For married couples filing jointly for 1999, the maximum IRA deduction starts being reduced at an AGI of $51,000 but only reaches zero for AGI of $61,000 or more. That is, for married couples the "phase-out range" is lengthened to $10,000, so as AGI increases above $51,000 (to $61,000) the maximum allowable IRA deduction is reduced more slowly. For 2000 the range increases to $52,000-$62,000; for 2001 to $53,000-$63,000; for 2002 to $54,000-$64,000; for 2003 to $60,000-$70,000; for 2004 to $65,000-$75,000; for 2005 to $70,000-$80,000; for 2006 to $75,000-$85,000; and for 2007 and later years to $80,000-$100,000. But note: For married couples filing separately, the phase-out range remains at zero to $10,000, as before.

Let's look at an example: Speke and Julia Wilson, operators of a drive-through hypnosis center, file jointly in 1998 with joint AGI of $75,000 (mainly compensation income). Speke is an active participant in his employer's plan but Julia is not. Any IRA contribution Speke makes is not deductible, but Julia can deduct up to $2,000 in IRA contributions. Why? Because Speke is a participant in his employer's plan, and his joint AGI is greater than $60,000. But Julia, who is *not* a participant in her employer's plan, is available to make a deductible $2,000 IRA contribution because her joint AGI is less than $150,000. Julia's deductible IRA contribution is no longer "tainted" just because Speke is a participant in his employer's pension plan.

Note that in this example, if the joint AGI were $55,000 instead of $75,000, Speke would be able to deduct up to $1,000 in IRA contributions. Since their AGI is only halfway between the $50,000-$60,000 range, the deduction limitation would only be reduced 50%: from $2,000 to $1,000. Julia would still be able to deduct her entire $2,000 contribution, since the joint AGI would be under the $150,000 limitation.

As you can see, many more people can now make deductible IRA contributions. This is something that you should be giving consideration to *now* in order to plan for the years ahead.

Next up, our new friend, the Roth IRA.

THE ROTH IRA

It seemed like such an easy concept when it was first introduced back in 1997: Put some money away for a while and then take those funds and earnings out tax-free at some time in the future. But like most tax issues, the Roth IRA has turned into a monster. While the concept is still easy to understand, the actual rules and regulations have become very complex.

The Basics

Beginning January 1, 1998, you can make an annual nondeductible contribution to a Roth IRA up to the excess of:

• The lesser of $2,000 or 100% of your earned income, minus

- The aggregate amount of contributions for the tax year to all other regular IRAs.

What this means is that your combined contributions for the tax year to a regular IRA and a Roth IRA can't exceed $2,000 in total. So you'll want to determine which savings vehicle is best for you (Roth or regular IRA), and place that $2,000 contribution in the appropriate IRA. While the law certainly doesn't prohibit you from splitting your contribution, perhaps placing $500 in a Roth IRA and $1,500 in a regular IRA, the administrative hassles and fees with this type of arrangement may be more than you're willing to bear. But for some folks, because of the Roth IRA phase-out rules (which we'll discuss soon), splitting your $2,000 IRA contribution into a regular IRA and a Roth IRA may be necessary if you want to make a full $2,000 contribution.

A few distinctions to note:

- It's important to understand that you can fund a Roth IRA and a SEP, SIMPLE, and/or Education IRA at the same time. The $2,000 restriction is only applicable to the combination of regular and Roth IRAs. So if you're in a situation where you can fund a Roth IRA and a SEP, SIMPLE, and/or Education IRA, the law does allow you to do so.

- Remember also that you can fund a Roth IRA even if you're covered by a company retirement plan (such as a pension plan, profit-sharing plan, or 401(k) plan).

Example: Swimming pool lap counter Teresa Allen is a single taxpayer. In 1999 she will make $50,000 in earned income. She is also a participant in her company's pension plan and will contribute the maximum amount to its 401(k) plan. In her spare time, Teresa has a consulting job and will earn additional business (Schedule C) income in the amount of $15,000. She will make a maximum SEP IRA contribution based upon her net business income. (We're not done yet—Teresa is very industrious!) She also makes an Education IRA contribution for the benefit of her niece. Even with all of these tax-deferred savings and investment vehicles, Teresa can still make a $2,000 Roth IRA contribution for 1999.

It should also be noted that any amounts rolled over to a Roth IRA in a "qualified rollover contribution" are *not* counted toward the $2,000 annual contribution limit. So, in the example above, even with everything Teresa has going on, she could make a "qualified rollover contribution" and still have the choice of making a $2,000 Roth IRA contribution for 1999.

Income Limitations

And now for the bad news—some individuals may not be eligible for the Roth IRA. Limitations based upon your tax filing status and AGI are listed below:

- Single and Head of Household:
  Income: AGI = $95,000 or less
  Rule: $2,000 contribution to a Roth IRA is fully allowable (assuming that the earned income rules are met). When AGI rises above $110,000, no Roth IRA contribution is allowable. Between the $95,000 and $110,000 "phase-out" range, only a partial Roth IRA contribution will be allowed.

- Married Filing Jointly:
  Income: AGI = $150,000 or less
  Rule: $2,000 contribution to a Roth IRA for each of the joint filers is fully allowable (again, assuming that the earned income rules are met). When AGI rises above $160,000, no Roth IRA contribution is allowable. Between the $150,000 and $160,000 "phase-out" range, only a partial Roth IRA contribution will be allowed.

- Married Filing Separately:
  For married persons filing separate returns, the AGI limitation is so severe as to virtually prohibit a Roth IRA contribution. For married-separate filers, the "phase-out" range is between $0 and $10,000. This means that a married-separate filer will never be able to make a full Roth IRA contribution, and when AGI rises above $10,000, no Roth IRA contribution is allowed whatsoever.

Phase-Out Ranges

If you fall into the phase-out ranges listed above, your Roth IRA contribution is limited on a pro-rata basis, depending upon how far your AGI moves into the phase-out range.

Example: Ann Margaret Dodd, a single person and baseball umpire, has AGI of $105,000, earned income of at least $2,000, and is not a participant in her employer's pension/profit sharing plan. Since she is two-thirds into the phase-out range, she is only allowed a one-third contribution to her Roth IRA. Therefore, her maximum Roth IRA contribution would amount to $666.67 (which she can round up to $670). Since her Roth IRA was limited, can she make a regular IRA contribution? Sure—in the amount of $1,330 ($2,000 less $670). Will that IRA contribution be deductible? That will depend upon her circumstances. In our example, Ann isn't a participant in her employer's pension/profit-sharing plan, so her regular IRA would be fully deductible. If she were a participant, her deductible IRA contribution would also be limited. If you're unsure about the regular IRA deduction issues, read more in our regular IRA section.

Finally, be aware that there are no age limits on contributions to a Roth IRA. A young child with earned income can make a Roth IRA contribution if it is deemed appropriate. Not only that, unlike a regular IRA, persons over the age of 70½ can still make Roth IRA contributions as long as they have earned income and are not otherwise restricted by the AGI limitations. And finally, unlike a regular IRA, a Roth IRA is not subject to the rules that require minimum distributions when you turn age 70½.

Roth IRA contributions for a tax year must be made no later than the due date of your tax return, not including extensions. So if you are qualified to make a 1999 Roth IRA contribution, that contribution must be made no later than April 17, 2000—the due date of your tax return.

Conversion From a Regular IRA to a Roth IRA

A conversion from a regular IRA to a Roth IRA is possible if certain provisions are met. First, the conversion must be "qualified." The term "qualified rollover" can get a little complex, but it's basically a rollover that meets the 60-day rollover time period, and is not in violation of the "one-year" rollover rules. For additional information regarding qualified rollovers, check out IRS Publication 590.

Assuming that you meet the qualified distribution rules, you still have one other hurdle to overcome: the adjusted gross income limitations. The law states that if your AGI is greater than $100,000, you may *not* convert from a regular IRA to a Roth IRA. This $100,000 limitation applies not only to single filers, but also to married people filing jointing, and Heads of Households. But don't think that you can beat the AGI limitations by filing a married-separate tax return. You can't. The law specifically states that if you are a married taxpayer filing a separate tax return, you may *not* convert your regular IRA to a Roth IRA—regardless of your AGI.

(Note: But what can you do if you made a Roth conversion in January 1999 and now find that your AGI will exceed the $100,000 limitation? Don't panic, since you have the ability to "recharacterize" your Roth IRA back to a regular IRA without penalty if you follow a few simple steps.)

AGI limitations are computed without regard to the amount of the conversion.

Example: Meredith Asenath Tiedje, a single person (and quality supervisor at a spork factory), has 1998 AGI of $75,000. She also has a regular IRA in the amount of $60,000 that she wants to convert to a Roth IRA. For AGI limitation purposes, Meredith's conversion threshold is $75,000 (the amount of her "normal" AGI, without regard to the conversion amount), and *not* the total of her "normal" AGI and her "conversion" amount. Meredith's AGI for income tax purposes *will* change if she decides to make this conversion, but that's an issue we'll discuss in detail soon.

Conversion Taxation Issues

Okay. You've determined that you *can* make a Roth conversion. Now you need to know more about the tax issues involved in making the conversion.

The funds converted from the regular IRA to the Roth IRA that would have been taxable had the distribution not been part of a qualified conversion will be subject to income tax at your normal tax rate.

If your IRA consists only of prior deductible contributions and the earnings thereon, the total amount of the conversion will be subject to taxation. If part of your IRA consists of prior nondeductible contributions (money you added after having been taxed on it), those will not be taxed again at the time of the conversion. And if your IRA consists of funds from a prior rollover from another qualified pension plan (such as a pension/profit-sharing plan, 401(k) plan, 403(b) plan, Keogh plan, SEP plan, etc.), all of the funds will be taxable to you at the time of the conversion.

This income *will* have an impact on any and all tax issues that are based upon AGI, except for any current or future Roth contribution and/or conversion issues. Affected will be your medical expenses (subject to the 7.5% AGI floor), miscellaneous deductions (2% AGI floor), taxability of Social Security (based upon AGI), passive loss limitations (based upon AGI), and many other tax provisions that use AGI as a guidepost. In some cases, these may be severely affected. So this must all be taken into consideration when you decide whether you want to make a Roth IRA conversion at all.

With qualified conversions, the 10% penalty for an early withdrawal from an IRA account will *not* be imposed. But should you decide to remove these converted funds early from the Roth IRA, you may be subject to a penalty.

Let's look at the example of Ginger, who works at a mouse pad factory. Ginger's 1999 AGI is $75,000, and she wants to make a $60,000 conversion from her regular IRA to a Roth IRA on or before December 31, 1999. For 1999, her AGI for income tax purposes will be $135,000 (her regular AGI of $75,000 plus all of her conversion income of $60,000).

Ginger will add an additional $60,000 to her normal AGI, and will pay tax on that income at her normal tax rate. This spiked income will have an impact on all of the tax issues that use AGI for a benchmark (medical deductions, miscellaneous deductions, taxability of Social Security, etc.). She will *not* be hit with a 10% early withdrawal penalty on the amount of the IRA converted to the Roth IRA (assuming she doesn't take the funds out of her Roth IRA early).

In effect, Ginger is trading tax dollars now for the tax-free status of the Roth earnings in the future. Is that appropriate? Perhaps for Ginger, based upon her personal situation, the answer is yes. But it is certainly *not* appropriate for everybody. In fact, for some people, the conversion of a regular IRA to a Roth IRA may actually cost them tax dollars in the long run. This is why the Roth IRA conversion debate has now become very heated.

The decision to make this conversion is very personal, based upon your status, goals, age, intentions, etc. The "convert or not" question can only be answered by you, based upon your personal, financial, and tax situation. Online you can find various "calculators" to help you with your decision. You can also check out other sites that deal with Roth conversion decision issues. Two of the best would include the Fairmark tax site (http://www.fairmark.com) and the Roth IRA site (http://www.rothira.com). Before you make your final conversion decision, take some time to read what these sites have to say about the pros and cons.

We've just reviewed the provisions in the law regarding Roth IRA contribution and eligibility rules (the stick). We'll now review the tax treatment of qualified distributions from the Roth IRA (the carrot).

Qualified Distributions

Any qualified distribution from a Roth IRA is *not* included in gross income for individual tax purposes. Simple as that. In effect, a qualified distribution from a Roth IRA is tax-free—no taxes due on the principal, no taxes due on the earnings—no taxes due, period.

To be qualified, the distribution *must* be:

• Made on or after the date you become age 59½ or;

• Made to your beneficiary, or to your estate after you die, or;

• Made to you after you become disabled within the definition of the IRS code, or;

• Used to pay for qualified first-time homebuyer expenses.

But, and this is a very big but, even if one of the qualifications above is met, the distribution is *still* not qualified if it is made within a five-tax-year period. We'll explain how to compute the five-tax-year holding period a bit later. Just know that five *tax* years are not necessarily the same as five *calendar* years. (What, you're not surprised at this revelation?)

So there are really two sets of rules that must be met before a Roth IRA distribution becomes qualified, and therefore tax-free: The distribution rules and the five-tax-year rules. Unless both sets of rules are met, the distribution will *not* be qualified, and the earnings will be subject to tax, and possibly penalties.

Many people are under the impression that as long as the Roth IRA funds are maintained in the Roth IRA account for more than five years, *any* distribution after that time will be treated as tax-free. Nothing could be further from the truth.

Example #1: Firefighter Austin Fowler, who is 25, makes a Roth IRA contribution of $2,000 in 1999. In 2006 (well beyond the five-tax-year period), Austin closes his Roth IRA and takes a distribution in the total amount of $4,500 (representing the original $2,000 contribution and $2,500 in earnings). He is not disabled, nor does he use these funds to pay first-time homebuyer expenses. Since Austin is *not* over age 59½ when he takes the distribution, the distribution is *not* qualified. He will owe income taxes on the $2,500 of earnings. Additionally, Austin may be assessed a penalty on this $2,500 of earnings. Ouch.

What this really means is that once the five-tax-year holding period is met, any distribution from the Roth IRA will be a qualified distribution (and therefore excludable from income tax) if it is made after age 59½ or if it meets one of the other requirements. This is true even if you later add a contribution or conversion to that same Roth IRA account. The *first* contribution or conversion controls, and begins, the five-tax-year clock ticking. Let's look at ...

Example #2: David Siegel, a 58-year-old duck decoy buoyancy engineer, makes a $2,000 contribution to a Roth IRA for 1999. In 2002, he converts $20,000 to his Roth IRA from his regular IRA. In 2004, when the value of his Roth IRA account is $35,000 ($22,000 of contributions/conversions and $13,000 of earnings), David withdraws the entire amount in his Roth IRA account. The entire distribution is a qualified distribution, and no part of it will be subject to tax or penalty. Why? Because at the time of the withdrawal, David is over age 59½, and the five-tax-year period was met.

Here's another interesting twist regarding the Roth. Under the Roth IRA rules, and unlike the rules for a regular IRA, you *can* remove your principal contributions without tax or penalty. Note that we said "contributions." The rules for removing your conversion amounts are a bit different (and we'll discuss that later). But let's go back to example #1 above. If Austin decided to take a withdrawal of only $2,000, this withdrawal would be treated as a distribution of original contributions, and would *not* be subject to taxes or penalties. This only makes sense, since the original contributions were not deducted from income when they were originally made. This same rule applies to multiple Roth IRAs that do *not* contain conversions. Roth IRAs that contain both conversions and regular contributions fall under a completely different set of rules which may require the payment of penalties on the "early" withdrawal of conversion amounts. We'll discuss those rules soon.

The Five-Tax-Year Rule

The waiting period for a qualified distribution may be shorter than five calendar years, especially if a contribution is made after the close of the tax year for which it is recognized. Remember that you have until April 15 of the following year to make a contribution for the current tax year. And, according to the law, the first year that is counted is the year for which the contribution is made, not the calendar year in which the contribution is actually made. So the smallest period of time that can pass before a "normal" (i.e., no special issues such as death or disability) qualified Roth IRA distribution could possibly be made would be less than four years! The following example will bring this point home:

Example #3: Scott Shrum, a 57-year-old fortune cookie stuffer, makes a $2,000 contribution to his Roth IRA on April 15, 1999, for tax year 1998. On January 2, 2003, Scott withdraws $3,000 from his Roth IRA (when he is past age 59 ½). Of the $3,000 withdrawn, $2,000 represents the original contribution, and $1,000 represents the earnings. This entire distribution is qualified, and is therefore not included in Scott's income since it meets the requirements for qualification. For purposes of the five-tax-year rule, 1998 counted as the first tax year (beginning on January 1, 1998), and the five-tax-year period ended December 31, 2002. So even though Scott had his funds in his Roth IRA for less than four calendar years, he has met the five-tax-year rules, and his distribution is qualified. Because of the five-tax-year rules, the absolute earliest that a qualified Roth IRA distribution can be made would be sometime in year 2003.

Under the *old* Roth IRA rules, contributions and conversions had different five-tax-year start times. It was because of these staggered start times that the IRS suggested that contributions and conversions be maintained in separate Roth IRA accounts. That suggestion was made to various financial institutions, and the institution passed that information on to their clients. But with the changes made to the Roth IRA rules by the Tax Reform Act of 1998, the need for these separate accounts has been made moot. It is now certainly acceptable to commingle your Roth IRA conversions and contributions, since the same five-tax-year rules apply to both. So if your broker still insists that you segregate your conversion funds and contribution funds, make sure to tell him (or her) of the new law which removed the segregation restrictions.

Sure, it's a bit complicated. But it's certainly better than under the old law. Thank heaven for small favors. Next up, taxation and penalty issues of nonqualified (or "early") Roth IRA distributions.

Penalties on Earnings From Contributions

Unless an exception applies, any distribution from a Roth IRA taken before an individual reaches age 59½ will be subject to an "early withdrawal penalty" of 10% of the amount of the distribution required to be included in your gross income. Be very careful *not* to confuse the early withdrawal penalty with the taxes imposed on a nonqualified distribution (discussed earlier). A nonqualified distribution imposes a tax on the distribution, but the early withdrawal penalty will be imposed in addition to the tax.

Example: Bernie Dietz, a 30-year-old soup technician, makes a Roth IRA contribution of $2,000 in 1998. In 2005, his Roth IRA has a balance of $3,500. Bernie decides to close his Roth IRA in a nonqualified distribution in 2005. Since the distribution is nonqualified, he will owe taxes on his Roth earnings of $1,500, and will pay tax on this amount at his marginal tax rate. In addition, since the distribution took place before he reached age 59½, and since he did not meet any of the exceptions, he will also be assessed a 10% early withdrawal penalty on the earnings. If Bernie is in the 28% marginal tax bracket, he will pay $420 in tax on the earnings, and will pay a penalty of $150 on the early distribution.

Anyone considering an early withdrawal should run the numbers. If the earnings in your Roth account are substantial, the penalty could be a very steep price to pay.

Exceptions

The 10% early withdrawal penalty does *not* apply to the following distributions:

• To a beneficiary because of the death of the Roth IRA owner

• Due to the IRS-defined disability of the Roth IRA owner

• That are part of a series of substantially equal periodic payments made at least annually for the life (or life expectancy) of the Roth IRA owner or the joint life (or expectancies) of the Roth IRA owner and the beneficiary

• To the extent that the distributions do not exceed the amount allowable as an itemized medical deduction (regardless of whether you itemize your deductions or not)

• To unemployed individuals for the purchase of health insurance premiums

• To pay higher education expenses

• To pay for qualified first-time homebuyer expenses

• For distributions after December 31, 1999, to pay a levy under Code Section 6331 on the IRA

These are similar to the penalty exceptions that apply to a regular IRA. For an additional discussion of these penalty exceptions, read IRS Publication 590.

Penalties on Conversions From a Regular IRA to a Roth IRA

The penalty rules regarding rollovers are a bit different from contributions. Remember that with contributions, you can withdraw your "principal" contribution at any time, and it won't be subject to taxes or penalties (as noted in Bernie's example above).

But an early withdrawal of a prior conversion has a different twist. The early withdrawal penalty applies to a distribution from a Roth IRA of a prior conversion but:

• Only if the distribution is made within the five-tax-year period starting with the year that the conversion was distributed from a regular IRA; and

• Only to the extent that the distribution is attributable to amounts that were able to be included in gross income as a result of the conversion.

Example: Kim Tipple, a warden at a minimum security prison, makes a $20,000 conversion from her regular IRA to a Roth IRA in 1998. The entire amount converted can be included in her income for 1998. She makes no additional contributions or conversions in later years. In 2001, before she is age 59½, Kim withdraws $10,000 from the Roth IRA. While she will have no tax to pay on this withdrawal, she *will* have to pay a 10% penalty ($1,000) unless one of the exceptions apply.

Why? For one very important reason: Kim didn't keep the conversion amount in her Roth IRA for the required five-tax-year period. Because of this, Kim will owe the penalty (but not the tax) on the converted funds subsequently distributed. This is true regardless of Kim's age at the time of the distribution. If you don't keep your conversion amount in your Roth IRA for the required five-tax-year period, you'll pay a penalty. This is one reason you might not want to make a conversion if you're near age 59½ and will need some of your IRA funds in the very near future. With a traditional IRA, you could withdraw funds without penalty as soon as you are older than 59½. But if you convert your traditional IRA to a Roth IRA, you'll be stuck with the five-tax-year holding period to avoid the 10% penalty.

If you're going to take funds early from your Roth IRA, weigh your conversion decision very carefully—especially if you made nondeductible contributions to your original IRA. (Remember, those are contributions of post-tax money.) If you did so, you'll be worse off by converting to a Roth IRA and taking the funds early than you would by simply taking the funds from the regular IRA. Why? Because a pro-rata part of all withdrawals from a regular IRA is treated as coming out of nondeductible contributions. But amounts withdrawn from conversions to a Roth IRA are treated as coming out of income taken into account on the conversion first. We'll cover this in more detail when we discuss the "ordering rules."

For example, Will Somers is a cheerleader for the Washington Warthogs indoor soccer team. He has $12,000 in a regular IRA, half of which is from deductible contributions and earnings and the other half from nondeductible contributions. He's contemplating converting it to a Roth IRA. He also wants to withdraw $4,000. Here are Will's options. He can leave the money in the regular IRA and take out the $4,000. He'll be taxed on half of it ($2,000) because half of the account is composed of deductible contributions and earnings—and he'll pay a 10% penalty, too, but just on $2,000. The other $2,000, coming from post-tax, nondeductible contributions, is his free and clear. But if he converts the entire account to a Roth IRA and then withdraws $4,000, he'll get hit with a 10% penalty on the distribution because of the ordering rules. He won't have to pay taxes on the distribution (because the income taxes were already paid in the year of the conversion). But by planning his distribution in this fashion, Will caused himself to pay an additional $200 in penalties.

If you're reasonably young (perhaps under age 50), and expect to need to withdraw funds from an IRA after five years (and can't use any exceptions to avoid the 10% penalty), you may be better off converting funds in your regular IRA to a Roth IRA now. Why? If the rollover amount isn't withdrawn until *after* the five-tax-year period, the 10% penalty won't be imposed, even if the withdrawal from the Roth IRA occurs before you turn age 59½ and no other exception to the penalty applies. This is because for a Roth IRA you have met the five-tax-year exception, and therefore dodge the 10% penalty. But there is *no* five-tax-year exception for a regular IRA. So while you would still pay tax on the earnings in either case, you would dodge the 10% penalty by converting to a Roth IRA.

As you can see, the tax planning implications are numerous—too numerous to mention here. Just be careful when making your Roth IRA decisions.

Income Acceleration

Those who converted their regular IRA to a Roth IRA in 1998 had an additional decision to make. They could recognize the amount of the entire conversion as income in the year of the conversion—or they could elect to spread out the income over four years. (Today the first option is the only one available to those who convert.)

If you converted your IRA in 1998, chose to spread out the income, and have now decided to remove those funds early from your Roth IRA, how do you deal with the income and penalty issues? Well, you'll get hit with "income acceleration." Here's how it works.

The law says that if you withdraw converted amounts in any tax year *before* the last year of the four-year spread, you'll have to include in income any amounts withdrawn that have not yet been subject to tax. The rules are a lot more technical than this simple sentence, but the following example will give you the theory behind the law.

Sarah Williams, a professional focus group participant, has a regular IRA with a value of $40,000, consisting of $10,000 in nondeductible contributions and $30,000 of earnings. Sarah converted this regular IRA to a Roth IRA in 1998, and decided to use the four-year income spread. Sarah is required to report $7,500 in income for each of the four years beginning with 1998 ($30,000 divided by 4 = $7,500). In early 1999, Sarah makes a withdrawal of $10,000. In 1999, Sarah will have to include $17,500 in her gross income. This $17,500 amount consists of the $7,500 normally required to be reported in 1999 (because of the four-year income spread) plus the $10,000 withdrawal. In 2000, Sarah will be required to include $5,000 in her gross income, since that is all that is left of the original four-year spread amount ($7,500 reported in 1998, $17,500 reported in 1999, with $5,000 to be reported in 2000... amounts to the initial $30,000 on which tax was due). In 2001 (the fourth year under the four-year spread), Sarah will *not* be required to include any additional amounts in her gross income, since the taxable amounts were previously reported and taxed because of the early withdrawal. And, with respect to penalties, Sarah would pay an additional $1,000 in penalties on the $10,000 distribution taken in 1999, assuming that she doesn't qualify for any of the exceptions to the penalty.

So, if you decide that you'll pull a fast one on Uncle Sam by taking the four-year income spread, and then taking a distribution early in 1999, you can just forget about it. Uncle Sam will pull a fast one on you!

IRS Ordering Rules

Here's another complication in the life of a Roth IRA account holder. What if you have contributions, conversions, and earnings all mixed up in the same account and you decide to take a distribution? What are you really taking? Well, the IRS has deemed that Roth IRA distributions *must* be withdrawn in the following order:

- First, from contributions to the Roth IRA (other than conversion amounts)

- Second, from conversion contributions, on a first-in, first-out (FIFO) basis

- Third, from earnings

Who cares? You might—especially if you find that you have to take an early withdrawal. Let's look at another example:

Mrs. Livingston is an FBI language specialist (specializing in Tagalog and Armenian). She converted $80,000 from a regular IRA to a Roth IRA in 1998. Of the amount converted, $20,000 represented nondeductible contributions and $60,000 represented earnings. Mrs. Livingston decided to spread her taxable income attributable to this conversion over the four-year period (as was permitted in 1998), including $15,000 in income for each of the next four years, beginning with 1998. In 1998 she also made an annual contribution to the Roth IRA in the amount of $2,000. In 1999, the value of the Roth IRA was $92,000 ($80,000 converted, $10,000 in earnings on the converted funds, and $2,000 in contributions). At that time, Mrs. Livingston withdrew $25,000 from the Roth.

Of the amount withdrawn, $2,000 was treated as a tax-free (and penalty-free) withdrawal of the $2,000 contribution she made in 1998. The next $23,000 was treated as coming from the converted funds.

In 1999, Mrs. Livingston has to include $38,000 in her gross income. Why? Because of the income acceleration rules. The $38,000 includes the $15,000 required from the normal income spread and the $23,000 taxable withdrawal itself. In 2000 she'll report $7,000 as the remaining taxable portion of the original $60,000 income spread. In 2001 she won't be required to report any additional income under the four-year-spread rules (since these amounts were accounted for in previous years).

With respect to penalties, Mrs. Livingston would get hit with a penalty of $2,300 (10% of the taxable withdrawal) in 1999.

So there you have it. The moral to the story: Keep your hands off of your Roth IRA funds. Just kidding there. But seriously, you can see how complicated the reporting can become. So unless you're able to do a *lot* of reading on the Roth IRA distribution rules, you might just want to leave the account alone.

No Minimum Distribution Rules

Unlike a regular IRA, a Roth IRA is not subject to the minimum distribution rules. This means that you will not be required to remove any of your Roth IRA funds in the year in which you turn age 70½. This being the case, a Roth IRA will allow you to continue to build up the value of the IRA for the benefit of your heirs—free from all income taxes. And while estate taxes may have to be paid on the value of the Roth IRA upon your death, no part of the Roth IRA will be taxed as income to your beneficiaries. This is completely different from a regular IRA. The value of a regular IRA will be included in your estate. But regular IRA earnings will also be taxed as income to your beneficiaries. This could cause a very large combined estate/income tax to be assessed against your loved ones. A Roth IRA can eliminate much of these taxes. This might be an enormous estate tax issue for you, so it's something to understand and consider in your estate tax planning.

Spouse as Roth IRA Beneficiary

As with a regular IRA, if your spouse is your Roth IRA beneficiary, and you happen to go to the great beyond, your spouse can treat your Roth IRA as his or her own. The Roth IRA can be kept intact. Your spouse will not have to deal with any required distribution rules, and will have all of the normal rights and privileges which would accrue to a Roth IRA account.

Non-Spouse as Roth IRA Beneficiary

If you decide to have a non-spouse as your Roth IRA beneficiary, your rules will be a little different.

First of all, if you elected the "four-year spread" of income, and you pass on before the four years have expired, any remaining unreported spread-out income on your final tax return (i.e., the tax return that will be required to be filed in the year of your death) will have to be accelerated.

Example: Tom is single, and made his Roth IRA conversion in 1998. The income attributable to the Roth IRA conversion amounted to $40,000. Tom decides to spread this income over the allowed four-year period (1998, 1999, 2000, and 2001). So Tom decides to report $10,000 in his income for 1998.

In 1999, Tom meets an untimely demise. Tom's Roth IRA beneficiary was his brother Jerry. When the executor of Tom's estate completes Tom's final individual income tax return for 1998, she will have to include the remaining unreported conversion income. In this case, the executor would be required to report the remaining $30,000 in Tom's final individual income tax return. As you can see, this $30,000 was the amount of the income "spread" that was not previously reported in prior tax years.

If Tom had been married, and had named his spouse as beneficiary of his Roth IRA, his spouse could have continued the income spread over the remaining years. But she also would have had the option to take the remaining income in the year of Tom's death. Completely her decision based upon her tax issues.

A big issue for non-spouse beneficiaries is that of the distribution of the account after the death of the Roth IRA owner. As we noted earlier, if the surviving spouse is the beneficiary, there are no required distribution rules. But if the beneficiary is not a spouse, that beneficiary *must* take the Roth IRA distributions either:

• By the end of the year containing the fifth anniversary of the account owner's death, *or*

• Over the life expectancy of the beneficiary, starting no later than December 31 on the year following the year in which the account owner died.

This isn't necessarily a bad thing. Think about it. Any distribution in the year that includes the fifth anniversary of the owner's death would have to be made after the five-tax-year period restrictions on contributions/conversions had expired. Therefore, no part of the distribution would be included in the beneficiary's income. So while the account must be eventually liquidated by the beneficiary, Uncle Sam has allowed for a method by which, if the beneficiary does the right thing, none of the Roth IRA proceeds will be subject to tax or penalty. Of course, if the beneficiary is greedy, and wants to take the Roth IRA distribution immediately after the death of the Roth IRA owner, there may be taxes to pay. So, in this case, patience is rewarded in the form of tax-free income.

On the other hand, if distributions are made over the life expectancy of the beneficiary starting no later than December 31 of the year following the year in which the owner died, it is very possible that some of those distributions would be included in the beneficiary's income. Why? Because the five-tax-year holding period may not have been met. But since distributions are treated as being made out of contributions first, the chances are that most distributions made before the end of the five-tax-year period would be made out of contributions, and would not be subject to tax.

Regardless of how the beneficiary decides to take the Roth IRA distributions, and regardless of the taxability of the distributions (if any), none of the distributions would be subject to the 10% early withdrawal penalty. If you reread the section on Roth IRA penalties, you'll find that the death of the Roth IRA holder will avoid the 10% penalty on the beneficiary.

Example: Shirley converts her regular IRA to a Roth IRA in 1998. She includes all of the required conversion income in her 1998 income, and reports it in full on her 1998 tax return. She also makes a $2,000 Roth IRA contribution for 1998 and 1999.

In 2000, Shirley passes away. Her Roth IRA beneficiary is her daughter Laverne. Laverne can take the entire Roth IRA distribution immediately, but will be subject to some taxes (because she will have taken the distribution before the five-tax-year holding period had expired on the original conversion). But even if Laverne has taxes to pay on the Roth IRA distribution, there will be no penalties imposed.

According to the rules, though, Laverne can wait as long as "the end of the year containing the fifth anniversary of the account owner's death" to remove the funds. Since Shirley died in 2000, Laverne must remove the funds from the Roth IRA account no later than December 31, 2005. The five-tax-year holding period would be met in 2003. So if Laverne waits until sometime in 2003 to take the distribution, none of the Roth IRA funds would be included in her income. The five-tax-year holding period was met, and the account assets were distributed before the required distribution date (12-31-2005).

As you can see, even though a non-spouse beneficiary is much more restricted with respect to the inherited Roth IRA account than is a spousal beneficiary, the rules are flexible enough to allow for the beneficiary to dodge taxes and penalties.

IRS Form 8606—For Both Roth and Traditional IRAs

In the past, Form 8606 was mainly used to report your "basis" in an IRA account. To put it another way, if you had made nondeductible traditional IRA contributions in prior years or in a current year, Form 8606 was required to report (and keep track of) those nondeductible contributions. That only makes sense, right? Since they were nondeductible when you made the contributions, you received no tax benefit for the contributions, and should not have to pay taxes on the contributions when you take a distribution from the IRA account or convert the IRA account to a Roth IRA. Form 8606 did that for you, creating a record of the contributions.

Form 8606 was significantly expanded for 1998. And it will likely continue to expand for 1999. It's now used not only to report your nondeductible contributions to a traditional IRA, but also if you have made a conversion of your traditional IRA to a Roth IRA, or if you have "recharacterized" your IRA during the year.

Who Files Form 8086?

The law says that you *must* file Form 8606 if any of the following apply to you:

- You made nondeductible contributions to a traditional IRA for 1998. (If this applies to you, you'll focus on Part I of Form 8606.)

- You received distributions from a traditional IRA in 1998 *and* you made nondeductible IRA contributions in any prior years. (This is where you'll want to make sure that you don't get taxed twice for those prior year nondeductible contributions. You'll also be dealing with Part I of the form.)

- You converted part or all of the assets in a traditional IRA to a Roth IRA during 1998. (If this is you, use Part II of the form.)

- You recharacterized amounts that were converted to a Roth IRA. This basically refers to those who originally converted their traditional IRA to a Roth IRA, and then later determined that their adjusted gross income was greater than the law allowed. Or it could be that you performed a recharacterization from a Roth IRA back to your traditional IRA, and then a reconversion back to a Roth IRA in order to dodge some taxes. (Regardless of the reason, Part II of Form 8606 was designed just for you.)

- You received distributions from a Roth IRA in 1998. And don't forget that some recharacterizations are considered Roth IRA distributions.

- You are the beneficiary of an Education IRA *and* you received distributions from it in 1998. Again, it's not likely, but if this applies to you, you'll want to complete Part IV of Form 8606.

If *any* of the above apply to you, IRS Form 8606 is in your immediate future, and must be completed and attached to your tax return. Remember that the above rules and requirements are based upon the Form 8606 instructions as they stood in 1998. We'd love to give you the additional rules for 1999, but neither the form nor the instructions have been published as we write this. But there's no reason to believe that Form 8606 will "shrink" substantially for 1999. If anything, it will be expanded to cover issues such as tracking nondeductible Roth IRA contributions and distributions. But never fear: We'll provide the updated rules for the 1999 Form 8606 with our update to this book.

If you're required to complete this form, make sure that you carefully read the instructions and follow both its computations and logic. And if you use a tax professional or tax software to prepare your tax return, make sure that *they* have completed Form 8606 correctly. The only way that you can do that is to understand the form and double-check their work. It may be a bit of a pain, but the taxes you save may be your *own*.

Roth IRA Conversion Issues

You may be wondering, "How may times can I convert, then un-convert, then re-convert my IRA to a Roth IRA, and vice-versa?" Until recently, that answer was not clear. Now it is.

During the summer 1998 doldrums in the market, after a number of IRAs had been converted, many people decided to "un-convert" their Roth IRA back to a regular IRA, and then "re-convert" back to a Roth IRA in order to save substantial tax dollars.

Example: In June 1998, Neil, a miner with a heart of gold, converted his regular IRA #1 to a Roth IRA #1 when the value of his IRA portfolio was $60,000. Since he had no basis in his IRA, he was required to include $60,000 in his 1998 income. But because of the summer market drop, Neil found the value of his portfolio reduced significantly—all the way down to $35,000. Because of this decrease, he faced the possibility of paying taxes on gains that he no longer had. He decided to "un-convert" (or, in tax lingo, "recharacterize") his Roth IRA#1 back to a regular IRA #2. Then he took Regular IRA#2 and re-converted it to Roth IRA #2 when the value of his IRA portfolio was $35,000. Voila! Just like that, simply by moving these funds around, Neil saved tax dollars on the difference between his first conversion ($60,000) and his reconversion ($35,000). Obviously, this could be a substantial tax-saving technique. And Uncle Sam wasn't too pleased about it.

Part of the problem was the fact that the original law did not contemplate this transaction. The recharacterization rules which were put into place with the 1998 tax law changes were addressed to provide relief to those people who converted their Roth IRAs early in 1998, and subsequently found that their AGI would exceed the $100,000 limitation. The lawmakers hadn't realized that some people would make these recharacterizations simply to save tax dollars. (Wow... how out of touch can the people in Washington really be?)

But in a recent notice (Notice 98-50, 1998-44 IRB), Uncle Sam finally recognized that some individuals might just arrange their affairs in order to reduce their taxes and addressed this very issue. Under this notice, a taxpayer who converts a regular IRA to a Roth IRA during 1998 and then shifts the amount back to a regular IRA using the recharacterization procedure, may reconvert the regular IRA back to a Roth IRA *only once* after October 31, 1998, and before January 1, 1999. In addition, the taxpayer is allowed only one reconversion in 1999. Any additional reconversions that take place during that time are considered "excess reconversions," and are subject to special rules. But any reconversions made before November 1, 1998, aren't treated as "excess reconversions," no matter how many of them actually took place.

While we realize that 1998 has long since passed, the recharacterization issue was one that confused a lot of people. In fact, there are probably a number of people out there who violated the 1998 rules and may not even know it... yet. For that reason, we've touched on the rules as they existed in 1998—just in case you had one (or a number) of recharacterizations and reconversions in 1998. You might want to check back to see if you did 'em all correctly. If you did, you get a gold star for the year. If you didn't, an amended tax return may be in your future.

But how about the rules for 1999? Well, it's really pretty simple: The regulations state that an IRA owner who converts an amount from a traditional IRA to a Roth IRA during 1999 and then transfers that amount back to a traditional IRA by means of a recharacterization may reconvert that amount once (but no more than once) on or before December 31, 1999.

For example, let's consider Ursula, who has a traditional IRA. And before we go any further, it might be helpful to point out that you'll need to pay close attention to the wording ahead. Understand that a "conversion" is different from a "reconversion." And a "recharacterization" is a third beast. Generally speaking, a recharacterization is when a Roth IRA is transformed back to a traditional IRA and a reconversion is when a traditional IRA becomes a Roth IRA once more. Got it? On to the example:

- In March 1999 Ursula converts her traditional IRA to a Roth IRA.

- In July 1999, for whatever reason, she recharacterizes it back to a traditional IRA.

- In October 1999 she then reconverts the traditional IRA back to a Roth IRA.

- In November 1999, the market takes a substantial dump. She wants to make a second recharacterization of her Roth IRA back to a traditional IRA and then immediately make a second reconversion back to a Roth IRA.

While Ursula can certainly make the second recharacterization (in November) back to a traditional IRA, she is barred from making any additional reconversions—at least until January 1, 2000. She's already made her one allowed reconversion for 1999 (in October). But if Ursula did decide to ignore the rules and make an additional reconversion before January 1, 2000, it would be treated as an "excess reconversion," and would be subject to those rules.

There are even more new rules for 2000. If you make a conversion from a traditional IRA to a Roth IRA in 2000 or later, and then recharacterize it back to a traditional IRA, you may not reconvert that amount from the traditional IRA to a Roth IRA before the *later* of:

- The beginning of the year following the year in which the amount was originally converted to the Roth IRA; *or*

- The end of the 30-day period beginning on the day on which you transferred the Roth IRA back to a traditional IRA by means of a recharacterization.

Any reconversion made before the later of these two dates would be deemed a "failed" reconversion, and would be subject to the failed reconversion rules, described below.

Example: Aileen has a traditional IRA that she converts to a Roth IRA in May 2000. She then recharacterizes that Roth IRA back to a traditional IRA on August 10, 2000. She now wants to make a reconversion back to a Roth IRA. But she has restrictions. She can't make that reconversion until the later of:

- January 1, 2001 (the beginning of the year following the year in which the amount was originally converted to the Roth IRA); or

- September 10, 2000 (the end of the 30-day period beginning on the day on which she transferred the Roth IRA back to a traditional IRA by means of a recharacterization).

Since she must wait until the later of these two dates, Aileen has to hang on until at least January 1, 2001. If she decides to go ahead and make the reconversion before January 1, 2001, it will be treated as a "failed" reconversion and will be subject to the failed reconversion rules.

Excess Reconversions

If you violate the excess reconversion rules, you effectively ignore any of those conversions deemed "excess" for tax purposes. The taxable conversion amount would be based on the last reconversion that wasn't considered an excess reconversion. Even though an excess reconversion will be ignored for tax purposes, it will still be treated as a valid Roth IRA conversion. You simply won't receive the benefit of a lower tax on the conversion.

Let's review Ursula's case again. Assume that when she made her original conversion to the Roth IRA in March 1999, the value of the account was $30,000 (and was all subject to tax). When she recharacterized her Roth IRA back to a traditional IRA in July 1999, the value was $25,000. In October, when she makes her first reconversion, the value of her traditional IRA is $24,000. In November (after the recharacterization back to a traditional IRA), when the value of her traditional IRA was $18,000, Ursula contemplates a reconversion. She realizes, because of the rules noted above, that she must wait until January 1, 2001, to make this reconversion. But she decides to cast her fate to the wind and makes the reconversion anyway in November 1999 when the value of the traditional IRA is $18,000. As we pointed out earlier, this is an "excess" reconversion. The law says that while the new (November) Roth IRA is valid and in force, her tax savings on the "excess" reconversion are not. So while the value of her Roth IRA account is now only $18,000, Ursula will still have to report the last reconversion that wasn't considered an excess reconversion for her 1999 income tax purposes. Therefore, Ursula's taxable income on the conversion is $24,000. For all intents and purposes, the "excess" (November) reconversion is simply ignored for tax purposes, and all of her fancy footwork was for naught.

Failed Conversion Rules

Remember that one of the requirements that you must meet in order to make a Roth IRA conversion is that your AGI doesn't exceed $100,000.

So what happens if you make your Roth IRA conversion early in the year, and later in the year you find out that your AGI will exceed $100,000? What you have is a "failed" conversion. It failed because your AGI exceeded the $100,000 limitation. In this case the law allows you to call a time-out and recharacterize your Roth IRA back to a traditional IRA. But there is just one catch: The recharacterization must take place on or before the final due date for your tax return—including extensions. For just about all of us, this date would be October 15 of the following year. And not only that, IRS Announcement 99-57 states that the October 15 recharacterization deadline remains valid, even if you filed your actual tax return prior to October 15.

For example, look at Karin. She converted her traditional IRA to a Roth IRA in January 1999. In November 1999, she was told by her employer to expect a very big year-end bonus. Karin knew that this bonus would kick her AGI above the $100,000 limitation and she would no longer be able to make the Roth IRA conversion. But that conversion actually took place months before... so what now? Well, Karin realized that she had a "failed" conversion. She also knew that she would be able to recharacterize her Roth IRA back to a traditional IRA by October 16, 2000 (because October 15 falls on a Sunday). And she also knew that she could make this recharacterization back to a traditional IRA with no tax or penalty consequences.

You essentially treat a failed conversion as if the original conversion never happened in the first place—as long as you recharacterize the account back to a traditional IRA no later than October 15 of the following year. No tax. No penalty. Nothing. But just don't confuse a "failed" conversion with an "excess" reconversion. As you can see, the rules are quite different.

Simple? Nope. Easy? Not quite. Understandable? Hardly. All we can hope is that if you have played the "conversion" game with your IRA/Roth IRA, you now understand the rules. If not, you could be in for a very, very rude awakening come tax-filing time.

So, Should I Convert My IRA to a Roth IRA?

Bet we know what you're thinking. Is it anything like: "Well... what should *I* do? You've given me everything except the answer to my question. You've told me all about the Roth IRA, how the conversions work, the taxes I would have to pay, and how I could get my money out... but you haven't told me if I *should* make the Roth IRA conversion."

You're right. We haven't. And we won't. It's not that we don't want to. It's just that the conversion issue is really a personal one. There are both tax

Top 10 Roth IRA Questions

Because of the general confusion regarding the Roth IRA, Fools Dave Braze and Roy Lewis prepared these answers to questions they're often asked regarding it. Dave is our resident retirement and mutual fund expert, and Roy is, as you know, our tax demystifier. Without further ado... (drum roll please).

Q. I want to contribute to my Roth IRA, but my custodian says that I can't put annual contributions into an account that has been converted. Is this true? And if so, what should I do?

A. There's no reason for you to separate your contribution and conversion funds into separate accounts. Under the *old* Roth IRA rules, contributions and conversions had different five-tax-year start times. It was because of these staggered start times that the IRS suggested that contributions and conversions be maintained in separate Roth IRA accounts. That suggestion was made to the various financial institutions, and the institutions passed that information on to their clients.

But with the changes made to the Roth IRA rules by the Tax Reform Act of 1998, the need for these separate accounts has been negated. It is now acceptable to commingle your Roth IRA conversions and contributions, since the same five-tax-year rules apply to both. So if your broker still insists that you separate your conversion funds and contribution funds, make sure to tell him or her of the new law that removed the segregation restrictions. And if that doesn't work, consider finding a new broker.

Q. I converted my regular IRA to a Roth IRA back in January. I've just discovered that my adjusted gross income will exceed the $100,000 conversion limitation this year. What should I do?

A. You can "recharacterize" your Roth IRA conversion back to a regular IRA without any penalty or tax. You've just got to do it prior to October 15 of the following year. You're also required to "un-convert" not only your original conversion amount, but also any of the earnings generated by that original conversion. So, just because you go over the AGI limitation, all is not lost. Contact your broker and he should be able to help you with the recharacterization back to a regular IRA account.

Q. My daughter is 16 years old. Can she make a Roth IRA contribution?

A. Age is not a determining factor. As long as your daughter has earned income with which to open the Roth IRA account, and as long as she is under the AGI limitations, she may make an IRA contribution regardless of her age.

Q. My father is 73 years old. Can he convert his regular IRA to a Roth IRA?

A. As noted above, age is not a determining factor. If your dad's AGI is under the $100,000 limitation, he's eligible to make the conversion. Be aware, though, that your father is in the period of minimum required distributions (MRD) from his traditional IRA. Therefore, before he converts that regular IRA to a Roth, he must receive his MRD for that year. Whatever that amount is, it cannot be transferred to the Roth.

Q. I'm retired and drawing Social Security. Can I contribute part of my Social Security benefits to a Roth IRA account?

A. Nope—sorry. In order to make a Roth IRA contribution, you must have earned income. Earned income is generally income that you receive from working—as compensation for your labor in one form or another. It's reported to you on a W-2 form, or you report it on Schedule C (Business Income) or Schedule F (Farm Income) with your normal tax return. Earned income generally does not include Social Security benefits, pensions, interest, dividends, rental income, or capital gains. (Or gifts, or quarters found in pay phones, or money discovered beneath the cushions of your sofa.)

Q. I intend to retire at age 50. When I do, I'll need income. Can I take money from my Roth IRA without paying any taxes or penalties?

A. Potentially, yes. Under the IRS ordering rules, you are allowed to remove your original contributions at any time without tax or penalty. In addition, after you've waited at least five tax years, you're able to withdraw your original converted amounts without taxes or penalties. It's only when you get to the earnings generated by the original contributions and conversions that you will have a tax and/or penalty problem.

Even if you do determine that you'll have to break into the earnings prior to age 59 ½, you may still avoid the penalty (but not necessarily the tax). If you remove the funds from your Roth IRA account using a distribution method that is part of a scheduled series of substantially equal periodic payments made over your life expectancy (and the life expectancy of your beneficiary), you may still be penalty-free.

Q. When I convert my regular IRA to a Roth IRA, do I have to pay the taxes all at once?

A. 'Fraid so. If you decide to make a Roth IRA conversion in 1999 or later, you'll be required to report the entire conversion income in the year of conversion. For conversions occurring in 1998, the income could have been spread out over several years.

Q. If I convert my IRA to a Roth IRA, will that income increase my adjusted gross income for the current year?

A. Absolutely. This income *will* have an impact on any and all tax issues that are based upon AGI—except for any Roth contribution and/or conversion issues. But any tax provisions that use AGI as a guidepost will be affected—including medical expenses (7.5% AGI floor), miscellaneous deductions (2% AGI floor), taxability of Social Security (based upon AGI), passive loss limitations (based upon AGI), and many others.

In some cases, your AGI may be severely affected. This must be taken into consideration when you decide whether you want to make a Roth IRA conversion.

Q. If I have a large tax balance due next April because of my Roth IRA conversion, will I be able to avoid the underpayment penalties related to estimated taxes?

A. No. There is no exception to the underpayment penalty just because the balance due was caused by a Roth IRA conversion. There are other exceptions to the underpayment penalty that you might want to review that may allow you to dodge the penalty, but there is no "safe harbor" simply because the underpayment was caused by a Roth IRA conversion.

Q. I've heard from a friend that the Roth IRA AGI limitation is $100,000. I've heard from other friends that the actual AGI limitation is much greater. Which is it?

A. It depends on whether you're talking about a "conversion" or "contribution."

If you're talking about converting your regular IRA to a Roth IRA, then the AGI limitation is $100,000 for all filing categories. (Except for married filing separately folks, who are effectively prohibited from making a conversion regardless of the size of AGI, unless the couple is separated and has lived apart for the entire tax year.)

But if you're talking about making a contribution, then the rules are a bit different. The AGI limitations vary based upon your filing status. You can check them out earlier in the Roth IRA section under "Income Limitations."

and non-tax issues to consider. Only *you*, with the proper study and understanding, can really make that decision. You might be able to make the decision on your own. Or you might require the assistance of a qualified tax pro and/or financial planning pro. Regardless, *you* have to be intimately involved. (Sorry, that's just the way it is.)

There are places that you can do additional reading on the pros and cons of converting your traditional IRA to a Roth IRA. One of our very favorites would be Kaye Thomas's Fairmark Press site (http://www.fairmark.com). You'll find a wonderful series of discussions there dealing with all sides of the issue. Tax issues. Non-tax issues. Investment issues. The entire gamut. You may also want to check out the Roth IRA site (http://www.rothira.com), where similar discussions take place. Heck, you can even check out our own Fool's School area at The Motley Fool site (www.fool.com). That's the home of our Tax Strategies area.

And while this might be a lot of reading, there are some issues that virtually all financial professionals probably agree upon regarding the Roth IRA conversion:

• **Paying the Tax:** When you make a Roth IRA conversion, there will obviously be taxes due on those converted funds. Do you have other funds available with which to pay those conversion taxes? If not, it is likely that conversion is not for you. If you must remove funds from the IRA account to pay the conversion taxes and you are under age 59 ½, you'll be subject to an additional 10% early distribution penalty on the funds withdrawn to pay the taxes. Certainly not a good thing. About the only time that paying the conversion taxes out of your IRA makes sense is when your traditional IRA is funded primarily by nondeductible contributions. While the 10% penalty will still apply, it will apply on a much smaller taxable distribution.

• **Pay Now... Save Later:** When you make a Roth conversion, you'll be paying your taxes now on that conversion. That simply rubs people the wrong way. Why pay taxes now when you can defer those taxes to some time in the future? Remember that, given the same principal amounts, a Roth IRA is much more beneficial than a traditional IRA. Why? Because while the traditional IRA's earnings are tax-deferred, the Roth IRA's earnings are tax-free. Just think about it. Which would you rather have: a $20,000 traditional IRA or a $20,000 Roth IRA? Most people would take the Roth IRA in a heartbeat, because it will be growing tax-free. The traditional IRA will also grow, but at some point in time either the account holder (or beneficiaries) will have to pay taxes on the distributions. No so with a Roth IRA. So in many cases, paying the tax on the conversion now will save you lots of tax dollars in the long run.

- **What's My Rate?** One of the potential disadvantages to conversion now is that you're now probably in a much higher rate than you will be in your retirement years. But this argument can be more fiction than fact. If this were a perfect world, and you could predict your future tax rate with absolute certainty, and you determined that you would be in a much lower bracket in the future, then a current conversion might not be best for you. But there are two problems that normally crop up with this argument. First, take a look at some of your retired friends and family members. Have their tax rates dropped? After years of saving and investing Foolishly, many of your retired friends and neighbors probably have virtually the same tax rates that they had when they were working. Next, think about our friends in Congress. How many tax rate changes have we had since 1986? Certainly a few. There's even current legislation to change some of the brackets again. Can you really believe that you can count on Congress to keep the general tax rate structure as it currently exists? Over the next 10, 20, 30, or even 40 years? Through no fault of your own, you may find your rates twisted upon retirement. So don't let this argument scare you away from conversion if all of the other factors point in that direction.

- **State Issues:** Two of the most valid reasons for not making the conversion have to do with the legal environment of your state of residence. Your traditional IRA may enjoy protection from creditors. That's certainly a nice thing to know if you run into a financial jam. But in many states, the law is not clear regarding similar protection for a Roth IRA. So if you think that you'll need this creditor protection, give the conversion another thought. In addition, most states have conformed to the federal Roth IRA rules regarding not taxing future Roth IRA issues. But there may still be a few states out there that have not made the decision one way or another yet. So you'll have to check out the tax laws of your particular state. If you find that they don't conform to the federal IRA laws, you might want to carefully consider not making a Roth conversion.

- **Minimum Distributions:** One of the most powerful reasons to convert to a Roth IRA is that you won't be bothered with minimum distribution rules. As you know, in a traditional IRA, you're required to withdraw funds from the IRA once you turn age 70½. And these funds are taxable to you at the time of the distributions. With a Roth IRA, there are no such minimum distribution rules. If you anticipate that you have sufficient other non-IRA assets to see you through your golden years, avoiding the required minimum distributions could allow you to leave substantially greater wealth to your children or other beneficiaries. If this is your situation, coughing up taxes now on a conversion may end up being a very small price to pay for passing substantial tax-free wealth to your children or grandchildren in the future.

- **Speaking of Beneficiaries:** As you likely know, *somebody* will pay the taxes on a traditional IRA. Either you'll pay taxes on the distributions while you're alive, or your beneficiaries will pay taxes on your IRA distribution after you pass on (to the great tax-free zone in the sky). Either way, Uncle Sam will get his pound of tax flesh out of the traditional IRA. But that's not the case with a Roth IRA. You are able to take tax-free distributions in the future. And even if you go to the great beyond prior to using up your entire Roth IRA, your beneficiaries will also be able to take those Roth IRA distributions on a tax-free basis after your death. So again, paying a conversion tax now may save many more tax dollars in the future.

As you can see, there are many issues surrounding the Roth IRA conversion question. What may be right for one person may not be right for another. Which is why we can't give you an off-the-rack answer in a custom-fit world. We've tried to give you something to think about, and places to go to get additional information.

401(k) PLANS

Also known as a cash or deferred arrangement (CODA) plan, a 401(k) is a qualified defined contribution plan that takes its name from the section of the Internal Revenue Code that prescribes the rules under which it operates. (That's not a particularly imaginative way to name such a major plan. We think something like the "Golden Nest Egg" plan would have been better, but no one asked us.)

In a 401(k), an employer permits an employee to defer receipt of part of his or her compensation by contributing that part to a 401(k) account. Deferred contributions are made on a pre-tax basis, and those contributions and all earnings remain untaxed until withdrawn from the plan. The 401(k) may also permit voluntary, after-tax contributions by employees. Earnings on after-tax contributions accumulate tax-free until withdrawn.

Many 401(k) plans include a matching contribution from the employer according to a set formula (e.g., 50% of the employee's contribution up to a maximum of 6% of compensation). Employers may also make contributions to an employee's account independent of the employee's contribution, and these contributions may be tied to a firm's profits as part of a profit-sharing plan. Participant's pre-tax contributions are limited to the lesser of a maximum percentage of pay or $10,000 (as adjusted periodically for inflation) per year. The percentage limitation varies from employer to employer depending on a number of factors, but generally ranges from 12% to 25% of annual compensation.

A 401(k) plan generally offers participants an opportunity to direct their account contributions to a broad range of investment options from conservative risk to aggressive risk. These options may include institutional or mutual funds investing in the money market, bond market, or stock market; annuities; guaranteed investment contracts; company stock; and self-directed brokerage accounts. A typical plan will offer a selection of a money market fund, a bond fund, and a stock fund.

In general, a 401(k) plan limits withdrawals of assets to five occasions: termination from employment, disability, reaching the age of 59½, retirement, death. Additionally, the plan may include provisions for loans and/or hardship withdrawals.

State and local governments are prohibited from offering 401(k) plans to their employees. This was once true of private, tax-exempt employers as well; however, as of January 1, 1997, the latter may now establish a 401(k) plan for their qualified employees.

TAX STRATEGY

Consider Not Rolling Over Your 401(k)

Unlike an IRA, where you must wait until you're at least age 59½ to remove your funds without penalty, 401(k) funds can be removed without penalty once you turn age 55 and separate from service (i.e. leave your job). Keep that in mind if you're in your 50s and are thinking of leaving your current employment (either voluntarily or involuntarily). Many times people simply take their 401(k) funds and transfer them to an IRA account once they separate from service. It's almost a knee-jerk reaction, but it might prove regrettable.

But let's consider John Wilen for a second. At age 54, he decides to quit his job as a manager at a sprocket factory and travel to Spain to train for the running of the bulls. Sure, he can take his 401(k) funds out of his employer's hands and roll them over to an IRA account. But why? If he leaves them with his employer, he will be able to take distributions without penalty in just a year—once he turns 55. But if he rolls those 401(k) funds over to his IRA, he'll have to wait until age 59½ before he could get his hands on the cash—an additional 4 ½-year wait. So by not rolling those funds over to an IRA account, John can get his hands on his retirement funds much earlier—in order to buy some sneakers and shin guards.

401(k) Tax Issues

While IRAs allow a Fool to invest up to $2,000 in a tax-deferred account, 401(k) plans permit even more substantial wealth building. With the basic 401(k) plan, you designate the percentage of your salary you'd like to have shifted into the 401(k) account and your employer complies with your wishes. The money is not counted as part of your income and is therefore not taxed—at least not now. It'll be taxable years down the line when you withdraw it. So if your salary is $40,000 and you divert $5,000 into your 401(k) account one year, your taxable salary will effectively be only $35,000. The $5,000 won't be taxable until later, when you withdraw funds from your 401(k). (Note: This section applies to Fools with 403(b) plans, as well.)

The benefits of the 401(k) are much the same as with the traditional IRA: decreased taxable income and tax-deferred capital appreciation. Plus, you're likely to be in a lower tax bracket when you withdraw funds.

401(k) plans are even more appealing if your employer matches your contribution to any degree. In fact, if this is the case, they pretty much become no-brainer investments in which you better consider participating. Let's say that one year you contribute 8% of your $40,000 salary, which amounts to $3,200. If your employer matches your contribution by chipping into your account 50 cents for every dollar you contribute up to 10%, that means you'll be receiving $1,600 from your generous employer. Think about what this means. You invested $3,200 and have already earned $1,600—you're sporting a 50% return from the get-go! Where else can you get a guaranteed 50% return?

401(k) plans are not without their disadvantages, though. For starters, they typically only permit you to invest in mutual funds. Not too Foolish. Even worse, many such plans don't even offer the glorious S&P Index fund—which has left most other mutual funds in the dust. Want a little proof of that? According to Lipper Analytical Services, from June 30, 1994, through June 30, 1999, only 4.3% of all open-ended equity mutual funds outperformed the S&P 500. From June 30, 1989, through June 30, 1999, about 10.4% did. If your plan is missing an S&P 500 Index fund, ask your plan administrator why and urge her to consider adding one. Quote her some Lipper statistics, to prove your point.

If your employer does not match your contributions to any degree and your investment choices include several lackluster mutual funds and no S&P 500 Index fund, you should think twice before maxing out investments into your 401(k) plan. This doesn't mean you shouldn't take advantage of it at all—for there are certainly some appealing tax advantages. But if you're a savvy Foolish investor, earning some 16% to 20% with the Dow Dividend Approach and perhaps doing as well or better with individual stocks you pick, it might not be smart to be using a 401(k) plan that only offers poorly performing mutual funds. Run some numbers and compare to see which choice is best for you—perhaps you'll settle on dividing your investment money between options.

If your plan does offer an S&P 500 Index fund, it might be worth it for you to contribute the maximum allowed amount to it, which in 1998 was $10,000. An important thing to note here is that since the contribution can be as high as $10,000, it can significantly reduce your taxable income, offering you a big tax boon.

When the time comes for you to withdraw funds from your 401(k) account (at age 59½ or if you experience one of several qualifying events such as disability), the withdrawal is usually counted and taxed as ordinary income. Early withdrawals face a 10% penalty in addition to taxes. (Note: If you leave your employer after age 55, you can withdraw your 401(k) funds without penalty. You don't get the benefit of this rule, though, if you terminate employment before age 55 and then wait until 55 to take the money out.)

403(b) PLANS

A 403(b) plan is a defined contribution plan that's also known as a tax-sheltered or a tax-deferred annuity program. This plan is for educational, religious, and charitable (i.e. 501(c)(3)) organization employees. It operates under similar maximum contribution rules and withdrawal privileges as a 401(k) plan. Like the 401(k), pre-tax contributions and all earnings remain tax-free until withdrawn.

There are two principal differences between a 401(k) and 403(b) plan. First, unlike the 401(k) plan, investment options in the 403(b) plan are limited to annuities and mutual funds only. Second, the 403(b) plan permits additional contributions under certain conditions that would otherwise exceed the normal annual limit of $10,000, as indexed. These additional contributions are to allow participants to "catch up" contributions for years in which they didn't participate, a feature not found in a 401(k) plan.

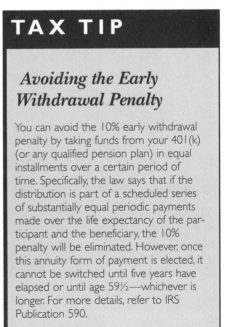

TAX TIP

Avoiding the Early Withdrawal Penalty

You can avoid the 10% early withdrawal penalty by taking funds from your 401(k) (or any qualified pension plan) in equal installments over a certain period of time. Specifically, the law says that if the distribution is part of a scheduled series of substantially equal periodic payments made over the life expectancy of the participant and the beneficiary, the 10% penalty will be eliminated. However, once this annuity form of payment is elected, it cannot be switched until five years have elapsed or until age 59½—whichever is longer. For more details, refer to IRS Publication 590.

SIMPLE PLANS

Effective for tax years beginning after 1996, Congress added a significant incentive designed to help employees, particularly those of smaller companies, save for retirement on a tax-favored basis. This is the "SIMPLE" plan (short for "Savings Incentive Match Plan for Employees"). The features of it discussed below should be of interest if you're self-employed, a small business owner, or a small business employee.

What Is a SIMPLE Plan and What Are Its Advantages?

A SIMPLE plan is a type of simplified retirement plan for small businesses. Because of its streamlined features, it is not subject to the complex qualification requirements associated with tax-qualified retirement plans. Administrative and legal costs, therefore, are minimized.

Some other key advantages of SIMPLE plans, from an employer's standpoint, are that they are subject to simplified reporting requirements and that the employer (and any other plan fiduciary) will not be subject to fiduciary liability resulting from the employee or the employee's beneficiary exercising control (direction) over the assets in his or her SIMPLE account.

Who Can Adopt a SIMPLE Plan?

Your business is eligible to adopt a SIMPLE plan if it (a) employs 100 or fewer people, at least one of whom earned at least $5,000 in compensation for the preceding tax year, *and* (b) does not maintain another employer-sponsored retirement plan. If your business is eligible to establish a SIMPLE plan but later becomes ineligible, your company will have a two-year grace period during which it may continue to maintain the plan.

And remember—self-employed people, even if they have no employees, are still eligible to open a SIMPLE plan.

How SIMPLE Plans Work

A SIMPLE plan allows employees to make elective contributions from their salary to an individual retirement account on a tax-deferred basis. Employee contributions must be based on a percentage of their compensation and cannot exceed $6,000 per year (which is indexed for inflation). The employer also contributes to the employee's account.

As an employer, your business would have to satisfy one of two contribution formulas:

• Under the matching contribution formula, your company generally would be required to match employee contributions dollar-for-dollar up to 3% of each participating employee's compensation. A special rule allows you to elect a lower percentage matching contribution for all employees (but not less than 1% of each employee's compensation). You cannot, however, elect to use a lower percentage for more than two out of any five years.

• Instead of making matching contributions, your company could elect to make a 2% contribution on behalf of each eligible employee who earns at least $5,000 in compensation for the year.

Here's an example: You're a business owner with two eligible employees. Employee Jeanie Mac makes $30,000 per year and elects to contribute 5% of her annual salary (or $1,500) to the SIMPLE plan. Your employee Chris Rugaber, however, who is an eligible employee with an annual wage of $40,000, decides that he does not want to make any contributions to the SIMPLE plan. You, as the employer, have a number of options regarding matching contributions:

• You can elect to match Jeanie's contribution up to 3% of her wages. If you elect this method, your contribution match would amount to $900. Since Chris doesn't participate in the SIMPLE plan, you are not obligated to make any contribution on his behalf.

• You can match Jeanie's contribution at a rate less than 3% (but not less than 1%). But remember that this lesser match cannot be used more than two out of any five years. So if you decide on the lesser match, you'll have to keep an eye on the calendar. As in the first option, you are not required to make any SIMPLE contributions on behalf of Chris.

• You can choose to make nonelective contributions of 2% for all eligible employees. In this case, you would owe a contribution of $600 on behalf of Jeanie (2% of her wage base of $30,000) and you would also owe a contribution of $800 on behalf of Chris (2% of his wage base of $40,000). Even though Chris is not participating in the SIMPLE plan, if you decide to go with the 2% nonelective contribution option, you are obligated to cover each and every eligible employee... even if that employee is not making any wage deferrals.

So, your choice will be predicated on how many employees you have, how many of them participate, their wage bases, your employee turnover, etc. But the nice thing is that each year's matching contribution is available for that year only, and can be changed for the following year. Your options are completely flexible from year to year.

Remember that no contributions other than employee elective contributions and required employer-matching contributions (or, if option #2 above is elected, required employer contributions) can be made to a SIMPLE plan.

Eligible SIMPLE Plan Participants

Generally, any employees who received at least $5,000 annually in compensation from your company during any two prior years and who are reasonably expected to receive at least $5,000 in compensation from your company during the current year must be eligible to participate in the SIMPLE plan. Self-employed individuals can also participate. All contributions to an employee's SIMPLE account must be fully vested.

There is no limitation on the percentage of salary that the employee can elect to defer, just on the dollar amount per year (currently $6,000). If an eligible employee has a salary of $6,000, he can elect to defer 100% of it. This won't have any impact on the employer contributions, but it gives the employee substantial flexibility regarding the amount of compensation to defer.

TAX STRATEGY

A SIMPLE Solution?

If you employ family members, such as your younger children, a SIMPLE plan can be extremely beneficial. If they decide to defer a large percentage of their wages, you, as their employer, receive tax deductions for their wages and the matching contributions that you are required to make, and they end up with little or no substantial income on which personal income taxes have to be paid.

Taxation of SIMPLE Contributions and Distributions

As an employer, your contributions to an employee's SIMPLE account are generally deductible, within limits. However, matching contributions are deductible in a given year only if they are made by the due date (including extensions) for your company's federal income tax return. Contributions to a SIMPLE account are excludable from employees' income and the assets of a SIM-PLE account, like those of a qualified retirement plan, grow tax-free.

Distributions from a SIMPLE plan are generally taxed under the rules applicable to IRAs, and tax-free rollovers can be made from one SIMPLE account to another. A SIMPLE account can be rolled over to a traditional or Roth IRA on a tax-free basis after a two-year waiting period that starts the day the individual first became a participant in the SIMPLE plan. If an employee is no longer participating in a SIMPLE plan (e.g., the employee has terminated employment), and two years have passed since she first participated in it, her SIMPLE account is treated as an IRA.

Early Withdrawal Penalties

Early withdrawals by an employee from his or her SIMPLE account are generally subject to the 10% early withdrawal penalty applicable to IRAs. Additionally, if the withdrawals are made during the two-year waiting period that begins on the date that the employee first became a participant in the SIMPLE plan, the early withdrawal penalty increases to a whopping 25%. So be careful!

Employment Taxes

Employer-matching and nonelective contributions to a SIMPLE account are not subject to employment taxes when made. This means that you can make matching contributions for your employees free from employment taxes such as FICA and Medicare.

But, if you are self-employed and file a Schedule C, you should know that any and all matching and/or nonelective contributions that are made to your own personal SIMPLE plan account *are* subject to self-employment taxes. So the tax treatment for your employees is a bit different than it is for you as the self-employed business owner.

Employee Contribution Rules

An eligible employee can elect, within the 60-day period before the beginning of any year (or the 60-day period before first becoming eligible to participate), to participate in the employer's SIMPLE plan and to modify any previous elections regarding the amount of contributions.

As an employer, you're required to contribute employees' elective deferrals to their SIMPLE accounts within 30 days after the end of the month to which the contributions relate. Employees must be allowed to terminate participation in the plan at any time during the year.

A SIMPLE plan can provide that an employee who terminates participation cannot resume participation until the following year. A SIMPLE plan also can permit an individual to make other changes to his or her salary reduction contribution election during the year. Your company may designate a SIMPLE account trustee to which contributions on behalf of eligible employees are made. Many mutual fund companies, for example, are now providing these services to small businesses.

If Your Business Currently Maintains a SARSEP

The SIMPLE plan replaces the Salary Reduction Simplified Employee Pension plans (SARSEPs) that are still in existence for certain small employers under current law. If your business established a SARSEP before January 1, 1997, it can continue to make contributions under the old SARSEP rules. Employees hired after December 31, 1996, can become participants in such pre-existing SARSEPs and be covered under the old rules, too. A business, however, cannot establish a new SARSEP after December 31, 1996. Furthermore, since a SARSEP is a type of employer-sponsored retirement plan, an employer cannot maintain both a SARSEP and a SIMPLE plan.

SARSEPs, like SIMPLE plans, are subject to simplified qualification, administration, and reporting requirements. Even if your business currently qualifies to maintain a pre-existing SARSEP, however, you might want to consider switching to a SIMPLE plan, depending on the circumstances. For instance, although it is now possible, under certain limited circumstances, for SARSEPs to permit employees to defer a greater dollar amount than under SIMPLE plans, this advantage will fade away as the $6,000 employee contribution limit is indexed for inflation. Also, SARSEPs are subject to special nondiscrimination testing, are limited to employers with 25 or fewer eligible employees, and are only available if 50% or more of the eligible employees elect to participate. SIMPLE plans are not subject to these constraints. (By nondiscrimination, we mean that the employees should be on the same footing as employers. A plan that benefits an owner disproportionately compared to her employees would fail the nondiscrimination test.)

This should give you an idea about the basics of the SIMPLE plan and its potential as a cost-effective, easy-to-administer retirement savings arrangement for you and/or your employees. If you would like to read more about SIMPLE plans, check out IRS Publications 560 and 590.

OTHER RETIREMENT PLANS

Profit-Sharing Plans

The most popular type of a qualified defined contribution plan is the profit-sharing plan. It permits employers to make a discretionary annual contribution of up to a maximum of 15% of pay or $30,000 to each employee's account, whichever is smaller. Originally designed to encourage productivity and to reward employees with part of a firm's annual profits, today employers may make contributions even when the business earns no profits in the year. However, no contribution by the employer is required during any year, profitable or not. These plans are often coupled with a 401(k) arrangement to allow voluntary pre-tax contributions by employees from their wages. Contributions and earnings accumulate tax-free until withdrawn by the participant.

Money Purchase Plans

Also a qualified defined contribution plan, a money purchase plan is one in which the employer is required to make an annual contribution to each employee's account regardless of the firm's profitability for the year. Contributions are usually specified as a percentage of annual compensation and are capped at the lesser of $30,000 or 25% of an individual's annual salary. Contributions and earnings accumulate tax-free until withdrawn by the participant.

Target Benefit Plan

While technically a defined contribution plan, a target benefit plan is actually a hybrid plan. The employer sets a target benefit for employees. Each year contributions are made to the employee's account based on actuarial assumptions that project the annual funding needed to reach that benefit. In that sense, the target benefit plan mimics a defined benefit plan. However, the actual earnings on the individual accounts may differ from the estimated earnings used in the assumptions. Thus, because the benefit actually received cannot be determined in advance, the target benefit plan is like a defined contribution plan. Regardless, contributions and earnings accumulate tax-free until withdrawn by the participant.

Employee Stock Ownership Plan (ESOP)

An ESOP is a qualified defined contribution plan in which the assets are invested mostly in qualifying employer stock. Usually, purchases of this stock are funded by employer contributions made to the plan based on total employee compensation. Purchase of stock by employees may be permitted as a plan option. When combined with a 401(k) plan, an ESOP is sometimes called a KSOP. (We're not sure what the "K" in KSOP stands for, but we sure hope it isn't "kombined.") Upon leaving the firm through separation or retirement, the participant will receive all vested interests in the form of the actual shares in the account. Alternatively, he or she may demand a cash distribution in lieu of the shares.

457 Plans

A 457 plan is a nonqualified retirement plan established for the benefit of state and local government employees or the employees of tax-exempt organizations. Participants may defer up to $8,000 in wages per year in a 457 plan. Until withdrawn, these contributions and all earnings remain untaxed. The 457 plan assets of tax-exempt employers are subject to the claims of the employer's creditors, but those of plans sponsored by government entities are not. Plan distributions may occur at retirement, on separation from employment, as the result of an unforeseeable emergency, or at death.

Distributions may be taken as a lump sum, in annual installments, or as an annuity. Regardless of how the money is distributed, on withdrawal it is subject to immediate taxation at ordinary income tax rates. Plan proceeds are ineligible for transfer to an IRA.

Keogh (HR-10) Plans

A Keogh plan is a qualified retirement plan established in law by the Self Employed Individuals Tax Retirement Act of 1962, otherwise known as the Keogh Act, or HR-10.

Keogh plans may be set up by self-employed persons, partnerships, and owners of unincorporated businesses as either defined benefit or defined contribution plans. As defined contribution plans, they may be structured as a profit-sharing, money purchase, or a combined profit-sharing/money purchase plan. Contributions are limited to the smaller of $30,000 or 25% of taxable compensation per year for employees, and to the smaller of $30,000 or 20% of taxable compensation for owner-employees.

Keogh plans may not authorize loans. Contributions and all earnings accumulate free of tax until withdrawn, generally at retirement. Withdrawals prior to age 59½ typically are subject to a 10% premature distribution penalty in addition to ordinary income tax; however, distributions are eligible for transfer to an IRA.

Simplified Employee Pension (SEP) Plans

A SEP is not a qualified retirement plan, except for deductible IRA contributions. It's a plan designed for self-employed persons, partnerships, sole proprietors, independent contractors, and owner-employees of an unincorporated trade or business. However, it may be set up by any type of business. The SEP offers an easy way for a small employer to establish a retirement plan for employees without the complex administration and expense found in qualified retirement plans. In fact, an employer may establish a SEP only if that employer has no qualified retirement plan in effect.

Under a SEP, the employer may make a contribution of up to the lesser of 15% or $30,000 of compensation to an IRA established in each employee's name. Hence, such an arrangement is known as a SEP-IRA. When made, these contributions are owned in their entirety by the employee, and they may be withdrawn and/or transferred by the employee at any time. Contributions to a SEP by the employer are discretionary, but must be deposited into each eligible employee's IRA when made. Because these accounts are IRAs, the amounts therein are subject to all IRA rules regarding transfer, withdrawal, and taxation.

Moving On

That pretty much concludes our tour of the main retirement instruments. Before we close out this chapter, let's take a quick look at another retirement-related topic of widespread interest: Social Security.

TAXATION OF SOCIAL SECURITY BENEFITS

You may have wondered whether your Social Security benefits (regular, disability, or survivor) will be subject to taxation. The answer is a definite *maybe*. Why maybe? Because the answer depends on the amount of your adjusted gross income and the total amount of your Social Security benefits.

If you're a single person, your benefits will not be taxable for 1999 unless the total of your modified AGI plus one-half of your Social Security benefits exceeds $25,000. If you are married and file a joint return, your modified AGI plus one-half of your combined Social Security benefits would need to exceed $32,000 before taxes kick in. If you're married and filing a separate return, and you lived with your spouse in 1998, your threshold is actually *zero*, and your Social Security benefits may be taxable from dollar one.

You'll note that we refer to "modified" AGI above. For the purposes of the Social Security limitations, modified AGI generally means your AGI for regular tax purposes *plus* any tax-exempt interest that you may have received. So investing in tax-exempt bonds in your later years will not help you dodge taxes you may owe on your Social Security benefits.

Example: Retirees Bob Bobala and Anna Regina Santiago-Bobala have regular income (such as interest income, dividend income, capital gains income, etc.) of $15,000. They also have tax-exempt interest income of $12,000. Together, they receive total Social Security benefits of $20,000. Since their modified AGI ($27,000) plus half of their Social Security benefits ($10,000) exceeds the $32,000 threshold, they will have to pay some taxes on their Social Security benefits.

Now that you know how to figure whether any of your benefits are taxable, your next question just may be: "So how much of my benefits will be subject to taxes?" Well, depending on your total income, it could be as much as 85% of your benefits.

Having 85% of Social Security benefits subject to taxes will apply only to married persons filing jointly with income that exceeds $44,000 (the adjusted base amount) or, for everyone else, income that exceeds $34,000. However, married persons living together during the year but filing separate returns have an adjusted base amount of zero.

Example: Let's compute the taxable amount of Bob and Anna Regina's benefits. As noted above, they have provisional income of $37,000 (their modified AGI of $27,000 plus $10,000 representing one-half of their benefits). From this amount, they would subtract their threshold limit of

$32,000. This gives them a result of $5,000.

The law says that you must include the *lesser* of 50% of your benefits (in this case, $10,000) or 50% of the above result ($2,500) as additional income subject to tax. So Bob and Anna Regina would be required to include $2,500 of their Social Security benefits as additional income subject to tax. This means that if they're in the 15% marginal tax bracket, they'll pay about $375 (15% of $2,500) in taxes on their total benefits of $20,000.

Had Bob and Anna Regina's provisional income exceeded $44,000, up to 85% of their benefits could have been subject to taxation. The computations required to determine the exact percentage are fairly complicated, too much so to go into here. Just know that as your income increases, so will the portion of your Social Security benefits subject to taxation.

Disability and Survivor Benefits

Please note that the rules above also apply to Social Security disability and survivor benefits. Many people are under the mistaken impression that disability and/or survivor benefits are not subject to the rules regarding taxability of Social Security benefits in general. This is, sadly, not the case.

TAX STRATEGY

Limiting Your AGI

Since your taxable Social Security benefits are based on your AGI, many folks receiving benefits try to find investments that will increase their wealth but not their AGI. Some people turn to annuities to do just that. Annuities generate tax-deferred income, which doesn't increase your AGI on an annual basis—as long as you don't take any distributions from the annuity. But there is a judgment day. When you take distributions from the annuity, your AGI will be affected, and your Social Security benefits will be taxable. Still, using annuities may allow you to manage your other income and deductions in order to minimize the tax on your Social Security benefits in any given year.

But Fools aren't too keen on annuities (even variable annuities), for a variety of reasons. So you might consider investing in non-dividend-paying stocks instead, to accomplish the same goal. You can control the year in which you cash in your stocks, and you may be able to manipulate your other income and deductions to allow you to minimize the tax impact on your Social Security benefits. In addition, as you know by now, long-term capital gains are given a preferred tax rate—whereas distributions from annuities are taxed at ordinary income rates.

Make sure to view your investments and investment returns with an eye on the impact they'll have on the taxability of your Social Security benefits.

Also, remember that in the case of disability and survivor benefits, many of those benefits are paid to dependent children. While you may deposit those funds and use them for the benefit of the kids, those benefits will not

Tax Affirmations

When you're stressing out about taxes, repeat the following affirmations to yourself. Or shout them from your rooftop—whichever works best.

- I'm the wind beneath many people's wings. I'm valued and loved by my friends and family. I'm smarter than the average bear. I can tie my own laces. I can ride buses by myself. I can count past 200. I can add and subtract, multiply and divide. I can copy numbers into boxes. I can find line 39. I can push buttons on a calculator. I can do my own taxes without freaking out.

- I am a vital and indispensable part of the ever-flowing river of humanity. I have been blessed to live on this good Earth and I bless the Earth with my gifts. When I return to dust, I will leave behind my legacy: descendants, furniture, my CD collection, letters I wrote, my car, three dozen t-shirts I rarely wore, and tax forms I filed. Historians and archaeologists will welcome the record of my existence with open arms!

- I am all that I can be when I tackle my taxes. I am the master of my financial destiny. I can plan effectively and save lots of money. I can take deep breaths when I stress out about it. People will turn their heads and admire me, uttering, "Wow—a person who understands taxes!" Adults will flock to me for advice and wisdom. Children will flock to me for gum and candy.

- I'm a strong and confident person. I'm not afraid of the dark. I'm not afraid of some little booklets and forms. I am rock and scissors; tax forms are paper. I can pound them and cut them up, if I want to. I am tax preparer—hear me roar!

be treated as your benefits for tax purposes. They are actually benefits paid to the children. If you don't believe that, check the form you receive from the Social Security Administration at the end of the year (Form SSA-1099). You'll receive separate statements for yourself and your children. And the kids' benefits will be reported under their separate Social Security numbers. Whatever you do, don't include the kids' Social Security benefits in the computations you do to determine your own taxable benefits.

If some of your Social Security benefits may be taxable, you need to refer to IRS Publication 915. It offers much more detail regarding the taxation of Social Security benefits and provides a number of worksheets you can use for the computations required.

IRS PROCEDURES & HOW TO DEAL WITH THEM

Death and taxes and childbirth! There's never any convenient time for any of them!
—Margaret Mitchell

What you'll find in this chapter:
• When You Don't Have the Money
• Extensions
• Audits

WHEN YOU DON'T HAVE THE MONEY

You've assembled all of your records and are putting the finishing touches on your tax return. You finally get down to the bottom line, and the balance due to Uncle Sam is much more than you expected. In fact, it's more than you can afford to pay. You've asked your friends, relatives, and your local bank for a loan, and all you got was $26.55 and a lot of good wishes. You've done everything that you possibly can to secure the funds without success. What now?

First and most importantly, don't let your inability to pay your tax liability in full keep you from filing your tax return properly and on time. Include as large a partial payment as you can. Simply filing your return, even if you don't include full payment, can save you substantial amounts in late filing penalties. Not only that, but you can keep the IRS wolves at bay with some payment extension procedures and installment payment arrangements. This will keep the IRS collection division from instituting its collection process.

Too many taxpayers hide their heads in the sand when they run into financial difficulties and fail to file their tax returns. But tax liabilities don't go away if ignored. It's very important that you file a properly prepared tax return even if full payment cannot be made. If you don't cooperate with the IRS, you can expect escalating penalties, plus the risk of having liens assessed against your assets and your income. Down the road, the collection process could also include seizure and sale of your property. In many cases, these tax nightmares can be avoided by taking advantage of arrangements readily offered by the IRS.

Head over to our online tax area to learn more about the penalties involved, whether you might qualify for a hardship extension, and how to arrange for installment payments. (Form 9465 is what you'll need to request installment payments.) Also, for anybody who may have payment problems with Uncle Sam, IRS Publication 1 is a must-read.

EXTENSIONS

Maybe you bought this guide on April 13, thinking that since you haven't begun to prepare your tax return, you'll just file for an extension. Or maybe you completed your tax return, but find that you have a balance due and don't have the funds available to pay; so you say, "No problem. I'll just file an extension."

Our advice to you is: Don't do it! Extensions are valid for the filing of the tax *forms* only, not the paying of the bill. An extension does *not* allow you to delay making your tax payment. If you find that you have a balance due and simply try to file an extension without the required payment, you could find yourself in the middle of a nightmare.

Don't file for an extension unless you really must. But if you really must, here's what you need to know.

Form 4868, "Application for Automatic Extension of Time to File U.S. Individual Income Tax Return," is the form that you need to use. You can obtain an automatic four-month extension to file your tax return by completing and filing Form 4868 by April 15. But in order for Form 4868 to be valid, you *must* make a reasonable effort to determine your tax liability and pay any anticipated tax balance due.

If you don't include payment with the extension or if the IRS determines that you didn't make a reasonable effort to estimate your tax liability, your extension can be denied—retroactively. You might also be slapped with a late return penalty and interest charges.

Here's a grisly example of what might happen. Assume you owe $1,500 in tax and you file your return on June 5. Your extension is retroactively denied. Your late filing penalty will amount to $225, and your failure-to-pay penalty would amount to $22.50. Add interest to these amounts, and you'll find that you could be paying an effective annualized interest rate of close to 100%! Egads.

Make every effort to file your return on a timely basis, or at least make a valid effort to compute your balance due and pay that balance due with the filing of Form 4868. If you overpay with Form 4868, you can get a refund or apply the overpayment to next year's taxes, but if you underpay, you could buy yourself some big problems.

Another thing to be aware of is that a number of elections on your tax return are required to be made by "the due date of the return, including extensions." This includes, for example, contributions to some retirement plans.

If you find, even after the additional four-month grace period, that you still can't complete your return, file IRS Form 2688, "Application for Additional Extension of Time to File U.S. Individual Income Tax Return," by August 15. That will buy you an additional two months (until October 15) in order to file your return. But this extension is not automatic, and you'll be required to provide a "reasonable cause" statement with the application. The IRS will then review your statement and determine if your cause is actually reasonable. They will notify you if your additional extension is approved or denied. Make sure that your statement shows a reasonable cause (generally, something beyond your control). Don't try the old "my pot-bellied pig ate my W-2 form" excuse. The additional extension is not there simply for your convenience.

AUDITS

In 1993, some 1 million tax returns were audited. This may seem an alarming number, but it's actually significantly lower than it has been in the past. In 1963, there were about 3.5 million audits. That's an encouraging sign to Fools who have their fingers crossed that they won't be audited. Another positive development is Congress's 1998 overhaul of the IRS, which among other things has shifted the burden of proof from the shoulders of the taxpayer to the shoulders of the IRS. Before this change, if you were audited, it was up to you to prove your return correct. Now, it will be up to the IRS to prove that there is a problem (assuming that you cooperate and furnish required records).

Of course, the chance that you'll be audited still exists. Returns are chosen to be audited for various reasons, as well as at random. Things that might trigger an audit include any unusual entries, hints pointing to unreported income, abnormally large deductions, and deductions for bad debt. You shouldn't lose much sleep worrying about it, though. There are steps you can take to decrease your odds of being audited. And if you do draw the short straw, it very likely won't be too painful.

To reduce your chances of being audited, make sure you include all your sources of income on your return. The IRS routinely cross-checks income reported to them by you and payments reported to them by those who have paid you. (Alimony, for example, needs to be included.) List your deductions clearly and in detail, so that the IRS can easily see what each item is. "Miscellaneous" just raises questions. In fact, make sure your entire return is very clear. If anything warrants a little explanation, attach a sheet providing the explanation. It's also a good idea to fill out a clean return. Perhaps, once you've got it all done correctly, you could copy it onto a fresh, blank form. If the IRS sees a lot of things crossed out or erased, it might draw a little too much attention (not that there's anything wrong with corrections). Finally, make sure that you're honest in your reporting. If you do get audited, you don't want to end up in trouble. All these preventive measures may still not be enough, though; the IRS does regularly select some returns at random to audit.

There are several types of audits: the office audit (conducted at an IRS office near you), the correspondence audit (conducted, as you might guess, via the postal service), and the field audit (conducted at your home or place of business). In addition, you might at some point receive a "CP-2000" form. This is simply the IRS's way of letting you know that after cross-checking your numbers and looking for discrepancies, it thinks there was some mistake. The CP-2000 might bill you for some more tax and interest (and possibly a penalty). If you think that the IRS is wrong and you're right, write back, enclosing documentation supporting your return. Be prompt. Keep copies of all correspondence with the IRS and consider sending your response by certified mail, as well.

When dealing with an audit, here are some things you might keep in mind:

- Remain unruffled. As long as you prepared your return to the best of your ability and have the necessary documentation to support it, you have little to fear. The IRS probably just has some questions to ask. They may end up pointing out something you missed and then charging you some back tax and interest—but that's very often all that happens. It's very possible that they'll accept your explanation and you'll escape with your wallet intact.

- You'll usually learn if you're being audited 12 to 18 months after filing your return.

- The IRS has three years from when you file your return to audit you (six if you underreported your income by 25% or more).

- When you know what questions the IRS is raising, do some research. Read appropriate IRS publications. See what tax laws are involved.

- You can have a qualifying tax professional accompany you or even go in your place.

- You only have to produce documents and offer information relating to the questions the IRS has raised. If the audit letter you received questions your medical expense deductions, you don't have to answer questions about the capital gains you reported. Remember that the audit is limited in scope. Don't offer more details than you're asked for and don't bring more records than you need to bring. Offering more information gives the IRS the right to ask questions about it.

- If the auditor raises new questions at your meeting, ask that they be sent to you in writing and say that you'll respond to them afterward.

- If the IRS plans to tape-record a meeting, they should alert you at least 10 days beforehand and they should offer to sell you a copy of the tape. If you want to tape-record the meeting, you must give the IRS 10 days' warning. Know, though, that it may make you look suspicious.

- The IRS should inform you of your rights. If you're impatient to learn about them, get IRS Publication 1, which covers them. You should have received it with your audit notice.

- You can ask for explanations. If you don't understand what the auditor is saying, ask to speak with his supervisor.

- You can't refuse to cooperate or provide information. This is not a criminal investigation, where the Fifth Amendment applies. (Of course, if you decide *not* to cooperate, a simple audit could soon turn into a criminal investigation.)

TAX RELIEF ™

Ways to Get That Tax Monkey Off Your Back

- Move to the Cayman Islands.

- Earn and receive no income each year. Survive on the kindness of family and strangers.

- Mow lawns and babysit in exchange for room and board.

- Learn how to minimize your taxes and prepare your report painlessly. Armed with knowledge and experience, it won't be much of a hassle.

- Join "the Family."

- Hire an accountant.

- Invest well. Paying the taxes will be less painful.

- Have your spouse do it.

- That's no tax monkey, that's my husband!

• After the audit, the IRS will either hand or mail you an "examination report" on Form 4549. If you agree with the IRS's "adjustments" (or just want to be done with the whole matter), sign and return Form 870, including a check for the amount due, if any.

• If you disagree with the IRS's findings, you can always appeal them in court.

TEN

CLOSING THOUGHTS

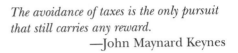

The avoidance of taxes is the only pursuit
that still carries any reward.
—John Maynard Keynes

The unprincipled and unscrupulous among us might interpret the words above as encouraging tax evasion. Heaven forfend!

These words of economics heavyweight John Maynard Keynes ring very true to our ears, simply because the tax-savvy Fool should indeed be spending some time and mental energy trying to avoid taxes—legally. We hope that this book has opened your eyes to the kinds of choices you have to make with your money and the tax implications that come with them. By effectively planning and timing the purchase and sale of investments, for example, you can avoid paying some taxes. You're not cheating the government or engaging in any nefarious behavior; you're simply doing what you're legally able to do to minimize your tax liability.

We've done our best to give you a basic understanding of tax issues that relate to you as an investor with a full life (family, home, retirement plan, etc.). To get answers to any questions lingering in your mind, drop by our online tax area at www.fool.com. We hope that having read this book, you now feel a lot more informed about taxes and you're prepared to plan, strategize, and make smart decisions to minimize your taxes. To help you, you'll find in the appendix, among other things, a handy tax calendar that features a list of what you need to do when.

In closing, if, despite your increased knowledge, you still find the world of taxes frustratingly complex, consider the following quotation and rest assured that you're in good company.

The hardest thing in the world to understand is income tax.

—Albert Einstein

APPENDIX

A FOOL'S TAX CALENDAR

Anytime or All Year 'Round

File a new Form W-4 to change your employer's tax withholding if you can claim a new exemption or if you need to remove one.

Are you buying or selling a major investment? Stop and think through the tax implications. Make sure that you're planning effectively, to minimize your tax burden.

As the year begins and progresses, occasionally run through the numbers and estimate what your taxes will be. Make sure that if it looks like you'll have to pay estimated taxes throughout the year that you plan to do so. If your income situation changes any time during the year, run through the numbers again. (Tax preparation software can be extremely handy for this purpose.)

January 2000

Energize yourself for an exciting year of tax planning with a trip to the annual Cowboy Poetry Gathering. It's held during the last week in January in Elko, Nevada.

January 17, 2000

Deadline for paying the last installment of your 1999 estimated tax (Form 1040-ES). If you miss it, penalties may be avoided by filing your final 1999 return and paying the balance of your 1999 tax by February 2, 2000.

January 31, 2000

Deadline for filing 1999 tax return (Forms 1040, 1040A) if you missed your January 17 estimated payment and want to avoid paying a penalty.

You should receive your W-2 and 1099 forms any day now. Don't lose them! (In fact, you might put them to use immediately. Start calculating your tax now—if it looks like you'll be due a refund, prepare and submit the paperwork as early as possible. Shouldn't that money be earning interest in your account and not the government's?)

April 17, 2000

THE BIG DAY! Your federal tax return is due today, and your state return is probably due, as well. We wish you many happy returns.

What? You're not done with your tax return? Then make sure you file for an automatic four-month extension. You'll need Form 4868 and you'll actually have to pay what you expect you'll owe... or face a penalty. Form 1040 or 1040A will be due by August 15. If you file for this extension, the deadline for contributing to a Keogh or SEP plan will also be extended.

Those filing estimated payments: Your 2000 first-quarter estimated tax payment is due today.

1999 income and self-employment tax returns and calendar-year partnership returns are due today.

This is also your last chance to set up and contribute to an IRA for 1999. Regardless of whether or not you file for an extension, this is still the deadline for IRAs.

If you have self-employment income and are not extending your return, make your Keogh or SEP plan contribution.

If you were a generous Fool and gave away more than $10,000 (per recipient) in taxable gifts, you'll need to file a gift tax return for the year (use Form 709 or 709-A) and pay any tax due. (You can use Form 4868 to file for an automatic four-month extension on this.)

May 2000

You've filed your taxes! If you feel like jumping for joy—or banging on a can—head to New York City, which is holding its annual "Bang on a Can" festival, celebrating the work of "musical inventors, misfits, and pioneers."

June 15, 2000

Second-quarter estimated tax payments for 2000 are due today.

Tax return deadline for citizens living overseas and nonresident alien individuals who are not subject to withholding.

June 30, 2000

Do you have signature authority over certain bank accounts, securities or other financial accounts in a foreign country? If so, you need to file Form TDF 90.22.1 by today.

July 8-9, 2000

It's time to take a break from all these tax issues. Head to Talkeetna, Alaska, for the annual Moose Dropping Festival, which features events like the popular Moose Nugget Toss.

August 15, 2000

If you filed for an extension by April 17, your reprieve has just ended. Your return is due today. If you just can't do it, file Form 2688 for an additional two-month extension. (This applies to gift tax returns, as well.) If you're filing now, this is your last chance to make a Keogh or SEP plan contribution. If you file for an extension, your Keogh and SEP contribution deadlines are also extended.

September 15, 2000

Third-quarter estimated tax payments are due today.

Fall

Start looking over your income and investments and estimate what your tax for the year is likely to be. You still have time to make some decisions that can lower your taxable income or increase your deductions. This is the time to consider whether you want to offset some capital gains with capital losses by selling certain holdings. A little planning now can be very profitable.

October 2000	Take your mind off your taxes for a little while. Fly to Maralal, Kenya, for the annual Camel Derby. After witnessing the winning dromedary crossing the finish line, take a short safari to see giraffes and warthogs in their natural habitat.
October 16, 2000	Deadline for filing your tax return if you got a second extension. It's also the deadline for making a Keogh or SEP plan contribution if you got the extensions. Note that this is the last, final, ultimate deadline for filing your tax return. There are no other extensions available.
December 29, 2000	Last day to establish a Keogh (but not SEP) plan for 2000.
January 15, 2001	Fourth-quarter estimated tax payments for 2000 are due today.

Calendar note: Deadlines for fishermen and farmers are not included on the chart above.

RESOURCES

Key Websites and Phone Numbers

- Internal Revenue Service: http://www.irs.gov
- The IRS main phone number: 800-829-1040
- For IRS tax forms: 800-TAX-FORM (800-829-3676)
- The Motley Fool Tax Strategies area: http://www.fool.com/school/taxes
- FoolMart, our online store: http://www.foolmart.com

General Tax Information Websites

- 1040.com: http://www.1040.com
- Essential Links to Taxes: http://www.el.com/elinks/taxes
- Fairmark Press Tax Guide for Investors: http://www.fairmark.com
- Federation of Tax Administrators' state tax resources: http://www.taxadmin.org/fta/FORMS.html
- Quicken's tax section: http://www.quicken.com/taxes
- Roth IRA information: http://www.rothira.com
- Tax and Accounting Sites Directory: http://www.taxsites.com
- The Tax Foundation (featuring many tax facts): http://www.taxfoundation.org
- Tax History Project: http://www.taxhistory.org
- Tax Resources Site Seeker: http://www.kentis.com/siteseeker/taxlink.html
- TaxWeb: http://www.taxweb.com
- Tax World: http://www.taxworld.org

State Tax Resources

Alabama
- For assistance: 334-242-1000
- For forms: 334-242-9681
- Department of Revenue: http://www.ador.state.al.us
- Income tax information: http://www.ador.state.al.us/incometax/Mainitindex.htm

Alaska
- For assistance: 907-465-2320
- For forms: N/A
- Department of Revenue: http://www.revenue.state.ak.us
- Income tax information: http://www.revenue.state.ak.us/iea/index.htm

Arizona
- For assistance: 602-255-3381
- For forms: 602-542-4260
- Department of Revenue: http://www.revenue.state.az.us

Arkansas
- For assistance: 501-682-7250
- For forms: 501-682-7255
- Department of Finance and Administration: http://www.state.ar.us/dfa
- Income tax information: http://www.state.ar.us/dfa/taxes/ind_tax/Individual_Income_tax_index.html

California
- For assistance: 800-338-0505
- For forms: 800-852-5711
- Franchise Tax Board: http://www.ftb.ca.gov/index.htm

Colorado
- For assistance: 303-232-2446
- For forms: 303-232-2414
- Department of Revenue: http://www.state.co.us/gov_dir/revenue_dir/home_rev.html

Connecticut
- For assistance: 860-297-5962
- For forms: 860-297-5962
- Department of Revenue Services: http://www.state.ct.us/drs

Delaware
- For assistance: 302-577-8200
- For forms: N/A
- Division of Revenue: http://www.state.de.us/revenue

District of Columbia
- For assistance: 202-727-6104
- For forms: 202-727-6170
- Office of the Chief Financial Officer: http://www.dccfo.com
- Income tax information: http://www.dccfo.com/Taxpayers/taxpayers.html

Florida
- For assistance: 850-488-6800
- For forms: 850-922-9645
- Department of Revenue: http://sun6.dms.state.fl.us/dor

Georgia
- For assistance: 404-656-4071
- For forms: 404-656-4293
- Department of Revenue: http://www2.state.ga.US/Departments/DOR
- Income tax information: http://www2.state.ga.us/departments/dor/inctax/index.shtml

Hawaii
- For assistance: 800-222-3229
- For forms: 800-222-7572
- Department of Taxation: http://www.state.hi.us/tax/tax.html

Idaho
- For assistance: 208-334-7660
- For forms: 208-334-7660
- State Tax Commission: http://www2.state.id.us/tax/home.htm

Illinois
- For assistance: 800-732-8866
- For forms: 800-356-6302
- Department of Revenue: http://www.revenue.state.il.us
- Income tax information: http://www.revenue.state.il.us/taxinformation/income/individual.html

Indiana
- For assistance: 317-232-2240
- For forms: 317-486-5103
- Department of Revenue: http://www.state.in.us/dor

Iowa
- For assistance: 515-281-3114
- For forms: 515-281-7239
- Department of Revenue and Finance: http://www.state.ia.us/government/drf/index.html
- Income tax information: http://www.state.ia.us/government/drf/rfaqs.html

Kansas
- For assistance: 785-296-0222
- For forms: 785-296-4937
- Department of Revenue: http://www.ink.org/public/kdor

Kentucky
- For assistance: 502-564-4581
- For forms: 502-564-3658
- Revenue Cabinet: http://www.state.ky.us/agencies/revenue/revhome.htm

Louisiana
- For assistance: 504-925-4611
- For forms: 504-925-7532
- Department of Revenue: http://www.rev.state.la.us

Maine
- For assistance: 207-626-8475
- For forms: 207-624-7894
- Revenue Services: http://janus.state.me.us/revenue

Maryland
- For assistance: 410-974-3891
- For forms: 410-974-3891
- Comptroller of the Treasury: http://www.comp.state.md.us
- Income tax information: http://www.comp.state.md.us/individual/default.asp

Massachusetts
- For assistance: 617-887-6367
- For forms: 617-887-6367
- Department of Revenue: http://www.state.ma.us/dor

Michigan
- For assistance: 800-487-7000
- For forms: 800-367-6263
- Department of Treasury: http://www.treas.state.mi.us
- Income tax information: http://www.treas.state.mi.us/faqs/indvtax/incometx.htm

Minnesota
- For assistance: 800-652-9094
- For forms: 800-652-9094
- Department of Revenue: http://www.taxes.state.mn.us
- Income tax information: http://www.taxes.state.mn.us/indiv.html

Mississippi
- For assistance: 601-923-7000
- For forms: 601-923-7000
- State Tax Commission: http://www.mstc.state.ms.us

Missouri
- For assistance: 573-751-4450
- For forms: 573-751-4695
- Department of Revenue: http://dor.state.mo.us

Montana
- For assistance: 406-444-2837
- For forms: 406-444-0290
- Department of Revenue: http://www.state.mt.us/revenue

Nebraska
- For assistance: 402-471-5729
- For forms: 800-626-7899
- Department of Revenue: http://www.nol.org/home/NDR

Nevada
- For assistance: 702-687-4820
- For forms: 702-687-4820
- Department of Taxation: http://www.state.nv.us/taxation

New Hampshire
- For assistance: 603-271-2186
- For forms: 603-271-2192
- Department of Revenue Administration: http://www.state.nh.us/revenue/revenue.htm

New Jersey
- For assistance: 609-588-2200
- For forms: 609-588-2525
- Division of Taxation: http://www.state.nj.us/treasury/taxation
- Income tax information: http://www.state.nj.us/treasury/taxation/freqqiti.htm

New Mexico
- For assistance: 505-827-0700
- For forms: 505-827-2206
- Taxation and Revenue Department: http://www.state.nm.us/tax

New York
- For assistance: 800-225-5829
- For forms: 800-462-8100
- Department of Tax and Finance: http://www.tax.state.ny.us

North Carolina
- For assistance: 919-733-4684
- For forms: 919-715-0397
- Department of Revenue: http://www.dor.state.nc.us/DOR
- Income tax information: http://www.dor.state.nc.us/DOR/taxes/individual

North Dakota
- For assistance: 701-328-2770
- For forms: 701-328-3017
- State Tax Department: http://www.state.nd.us/taxdpt
- Income tax information: http://www.state.nd.us/taxdpt/faq_individual_income_tax.html

Ohio
- For assistance: 614-846-6712
- For forms: 614-846-6712
- Department of Taxation: http://www.state.oh.us/tax
- Income tax information: http://www.state.oh.us/tax/assist/faqs-it.htm

Oklahoma
- For assistance: 405-521-3160
- For forms: 405-521-3108
- Tax Commission: http://www.oktax.state.ok.us
- Income tax information: http://www.oktax.state.ok.us/oktax/incomtax.html

Oregon
- For assistance: 503-378-4988
- For forms: 503-378-4988
- Department of Revenue: http://www.dor.state.or.us/default.html

Pennsylvania
- For assistance: 717-787-8201
- For forms: 717-787-8094
- Department of Revenue: http://www.revenue.state.pa.us

Rhode Island
- For assistance: 401-222-1040
- For forms: 401-222-1111
- Division of Taxation: http://www.doa.state.ri.us/tax

South Carolina
- For assistance: 803-898-5000
- For forms: 803-898-5599
- Department of Revenue: http://www.dor.state.sc.us
- Income tax information: http://www.dor.state.sc.us/tax/ind.html

South Dakota
- For assistance: 605-773-3311
- For forms: 605-773-3311
- Department of Revenue: http://www.state.sd.us/revenue/revenue.html

Tennessee
- For assistance: 615-741-2594
- For forms: 615-741-4465
- Department of Revenue: http://www.state.tn.us/revenue

Texas
- For assistance: 512-463-4600
- For forms: N/A
- Comptroller of Public Accounts: http://www.cpa.state.tx.us

Utah
- For assistance: 801-297-2200
- For forms: 801-297-6700
- State Tax Commission: http://www.tax.ex.state.ut.us

Vermont
- For assistance: 802-828-2865
- For forms: 802-828-2515
- Department of Taxes: http://www.state.vt.us/tax

Virginia
- For assistance: 804-367-8031
- For forms: 804-236-2760
- Department of Taxation: http://www.tax.state.va.us
- Income tax information: http://www.tax.state.va.us/it_wmf.htm

Washington
- For assistance: 800-647-7706
- For forms: 800-647-7706
- Department of Revenue: http://dor.wa.gov

West Virginia
- For assistance: 304-558-3333
- For forms: 304-344-2068
- State Tax Department: http://www.state.wv.us/taxdiv

Wisconsin
- For assistance: 608-267-9420

- For forms: 608-266-1961
- Department of Revenue: http://www.dor.state.wi.us
- Income tax information: http://www.dor.state.wi.us/faqs/indiv.html

Wyoming
- For assistance: 307-777-7961
- For forms: 307-777-5200
- Department of Revenue: http://revenue.state.wy.us

Tax Preparation Software

- Kiplinger TaxCut: http://www.taxcut.com
- MacInTax: http://www.macintax.com
- TurboTax: http://www.turbotax.com

INDEX

G

Gambling losses, deductibility of, 230, 279-280, 283

General business credits, 9-10

General Explanation of Tax Legislation, online, 88

Georgia state tax resources, 349

Gifts
  of appreciated property, 179-180
  to children, 177-178
  cost basis for, 132
  of depreciated property, 180
  and family income shifting, 163-164
  gift splitting, 176-177
  gift tax exclusion, 176
  holding period for, calculation of, 66
  of medical treatment, for deduction eligibility, 233
  of mutual funds, cost basis and, 51-52
  present interest rules, 177
  reasons for making, 175-176
  to relatives, vs. loans, 170
  of stock, 178-179
  unified credit, 178

Graduated tax rates, 5-7

Gross income, definition of, 2

Gross income test, for dependents, 124

H

Handicap expenses, deductibility of, 280

Hawaii state tax resources, 349

Head of household
  graduated tax rates for, 6
  exceptions for married individuals, 122
  requirements for, 120-122

Hedging
  one-sided, and constructive sales rules, 88-89
  Taxpayer Relief Act (1997) and, 81-92

Help with IRS problems, taxpayer advocate and, 339

Hobby expenses, deductibility of, 281

Holding periods, calculation of, 64-66

Home(s). *See also* Real estate property tax
  business use of, deductibility of, 285
  improvements to, recordkeeping for, 17, 20
  motor home loans, deductibility of interest, 261
  moving expenses, deduction of, 212-216
  purchase of, IRAs withdrawals for, 210-212
  sale of

capital gains tax exclusion for, 205-208
  and home office deductions, impact of, 222-223
  reduced exclusion, qualifications for, 208-210
  and IRS Restructuring and Reform Act (1998), 33
  losses from, deductibility of, 283
  recordkeeping for, 17
  taxes on, 29
  timeshare expenses, deductibility of interest, 260

Home computer expenses, deduction of, 99-102, 109, 221

Home equity line of credit, points, deductibility of, 260

Home improvement loans, points, deductibility of, 258-259

Home office expenses
  deduction of, 100, 109, 217-223
  amount limitations on, 220-221
  computers and related equipment, 99-102, 109, 221
  exclusive and regular use requirements, 219-220
  home sale exclusions, 222-223
  for maternity leave, 222
  specific deductions, 220
  and Tax Relief Act of 1997, 30

Home repair expenses, deductibility of, 282

Hope Scholarship Credits, 29, 185, 186-189
  and drug problems, 200
  and education deductions, interaction of, 199-200
  and education IRAs, interaction of, 198-199
  income phase-outs in, 190
  and Lifetime Learning Credit, 190-192, 200

House. See Home

HR-10 (Keogh) retirement plans, 332-333

Hurley, Joseph, 195

I

Idaho state tax resources, 349

Illinois state tax resources, 349

Incentive stock options (ISOs), 94-95
  strategies for, 95-96

Income. *See also* Adjusted gross income
  gross, definition of, 2
  reporting of, 2
  taxable, definition of, 3

income limitations, 297-298
and IRS Restructuring and Reform Act
(1998), 32
and minimum distribution requirements,
321
penalty for early withdrawal, 302
on converted funds, 305-306
exceptions, 303
proposed changes in, 38
and SEP IRAs, 296
and SIMPLE IRAs, 296
rollover from, 329
and taxes, 322
websites on, 348
SEP, 296, 333
and Taxpayer Relief Act of 1997, 29
withdrawals for home purchase, 210-212
IRS (Internal Revenue Service)
collection of taxes by, changes in (1998),
35
information-by-phone service (Tele-Tax),
23
restructuring of, and IRS Restructuring
and Reform Act (1998), 35
website and phone, 348
website for, 20-21
IRS publications
on adoption, 159-160
on alternative minimum tax, 93
on business use of home, 285
on calls, 97
on casualty and theft losses, 279-280
on charitable contributions, 273
of stock, 271
on constructive sales, 91
on deductions, 282
of education expenses, 284
of entertainment, business-related,
284
of home computer expenses, 102
of investment expenses, 264, 284
of job expenses, 284
of legal fees, 284
of medical expenses, 249
miscellaneous, 279, 280
for taxes paid, 255
of travel, business-related, 284
on dependents, definition of, 126
on education expenses, deduction of,
284
on Education Savings Bond Program, 203
on entertainment, business-related, 284
on estimated tax penalties, 103
on forms and schedules, 11
on forward averaging, 291

on foster parent tax issues, 168
on investment expenses, deduction of,
264, 284
on IRAs, 293
on job expenses, deduction of, 284
on legal fees, deduction of, 284
on mark-to-market trading, 110-111
on medical deductions, 249
on medical savings accounts, 248
on minors, taxing of, 14-15
on miscellaneous itemized deductions,
279
on mortgage interest credits, 212
on puts, 97
on recordkeeping, 17
on reduced capital gains exclusion qualifications, on sale of home, 210
on rights of taxpayers, 341
on Roth IRA conversions, 298
on Roth IRA early withdrawal, 304
on short sales, 69-71
on state tuition programs, 195
on stock options, 97
on straddling, 83
on taxation of Social Security benefits,
336
on tax credits for elderly and disabled,
146
on travel, business-related, 284
on wash sales, 73
on withholding, 12
on worthless securities, 69
ISOs. See Incentive stock options
Itemized deductions. See Deductions

J
Job dismissal insurance, deductibility of, 282
Job expenses, deductibility of, 284
Job-hunting expenses, deductibility of, 281
Joint return test, for dependents, 124-125

K
Kansas state tax resources, 350
Kentucky state tax resources, 350
Keogh (HR-10) retirement plans, 332-333
Kiddie tax. See Children, tax liability of
Kiplinger TaxCut, 21
KSOPS, 332

L
Laser eye surgery, deductibility of, 239
Legal costs, deductibility of, 281, 284

The Trader's Tax Survival Guide (Tesser), 111
Trading for a Living (Elder), 112
Transportation, medically-related, deductibility of, 244-245
Travel expenses, deduction of, 223-224
　business-related, 284
　charity-related, 265
　educational, 283
　investment-related, 283
　rates, by type of travel, 266
　and Taxpayer Relief Act of 1997, 30
Trust administration fees, deductibility of, 282
Tuition, state programs for, and family income shifting, 165-166
TurboTax, 21
Two percent floor for deductions, 98, 109
Two-year rule, for capital gains tax exclusion, 207-208

Wash sales, and capital losses, 71-73
Wash sales rules, and mark-to-market traders, 110
Websites
　IRS, 348
　The Motley Fool. *See* Motley Fool website
　National Association of Investors Corp., 113
　on Roth IRAs, 320
　for state tax assistance, 348-353
　useful, 348
Weight reduction, deductibility of, 241-242
West Virginia state tax resources, 352
Wisconsin state tax resources, 352-353
Withholding, and W-4 forms, 12
Work clothes, deductibility of, 281
Wyoming state tax resources, 353

U

UGMA. *See* Uniform Gifts to Minors Act (UGMA) accounts
Unconventional medical treatments, deductibility of, 236-237
Underpayment of taxes, and Innocent Spouse rules, 34
Unforeseen circumstances, in sale of home, 209
　definition of, 210
Unified credit for gifts, 178
Uniform Gifts to Minors Act (UGMA) accounts, 173
Uniforms, deductibility of, 281
Uniform Transfers to Minors Act (UTMA) accounts, 173-175
Union dues, deductibility of, 281
Updates, on tax changes, through email, *xii, xiii,* 28
Utah state tax resources, 352
UTMA. *See* Uniform Transfers to Minors Act (UTMA) accounts

V

Vermont state tax resources, 352
Virginia state tax resources, 352

W

W-4 form
　and estimated taxes, 104
　overview of, 12
Washington state tax resources, 352

OTHER NEW OFFERINGS FROM THE MOTLEY FOOL

IN BOOKSTORES NOW

To find out about other Motley Fool products, visit us online at www.FoolMart.com or call 1-888-665-FOOL for more information

or

send in the order form below to receive your free Motley Fool Catalog.

FOOLISH INVESTING ADVICE DELIVERED TO YOU EVERY MONTH

Now you can have The Motley Fool delivered to your door every month. We've taken the best of what we do on our website and incorporated it into *The Motley Fool Monthly*, the first financial magazine that's truly fun, informative, and easy to understand. *The Motley Fool Monthly* is great for folks who don't have time to visit Fool.com every day, and is also ideal for new investors who are just getting started.

Every 32-page issue includes:

- The latest news and analysis on the market
- Personal finance advice on topics ranging from taxes to buying a home
- Topics from our Fool's School to help you become a smarter investor
- Our latest and greatest stock ideas
- Articles from The Motley Fool's co-founders, David and Tom Gardner

SUBSCRIBE NOW!

❑ Yes... start my subscription to *The Motley Fool Monthly* at the rate of $39.00 for one year (12 monthly issues)*.

Name _____

Address _____

_____

_____

E-mail (optional) _____

Payment Method: ❑ Check or Money Order ❑ VISA ❑ MC ❑ AE ❑ Discover
Credit Card Number _____
Expiration Date _____
Name as it appears on card _____
Signature _____

Send to:

FoolMart   **1-888-665-FOOL**
123 N. Pitt Street   www.foolmart.com
Alexandria, VA 22314

100% Satisfaction Guarantee

We're so sure that you're going to love *The Motley Fool Monthly* that if it fails to meet your expectations at any time, we'll gladly refund the remainder of your subscription.

First issue mails within 6–8 weeks

TX-2000